THE

BEST

OF

Gourmet

THE BEST OF Gourmet

1997

FROM THE EDITORS OF GOURMET

PHOTOGRAPHS BY ROMULO A. YANES

CONDÉ NAST BOOKS · RANDOM HOUSE, NEW YORK

LIBRARY OF CONGRESS
CATALOGING-IN-PUBLICATION DATA

The Best of Gourmet: featuring the flavors of
Greece / from the editors of Gourmet;
photographs by Romulo A. Yanes.
　　　p.　　　cm.
Includes indexes.
　　1. Cookery, Greek. I. Gourmet
TX723.5.G8B47　1997
641.59495-dc21　　　　　　　　96-39082

ISBN 0-679-45735-6
ISSN 1046-1760

Random House website address:
http://www.randomhouse.com/

Most of the recipes in this work were published previously in *Gourmet* Magazine.

Printed in the United States of America
on acid-free paper.

98765432
First Edition

New recipes in this book were developed
by: Leslie Glover Pendleton (Fresh from
the Farmers Market, pages 278-289);
Elizabeth Vought (Greek Easter Feast,
pages 251-259); Lori Walther (Summer
Dinner on Santorini, pages 261-267); and
Alexis M. Touchet (A Cocktail Party
Featuring Mezedes, pages 269-277).

Informative text in this book was written
by Diane Keitt and Caroline Schleifer.

The text of this book was set in Times
Roman by Media Projects Incorporated.
The four-color separations were done by
The Color Company, Seiple
Lithographers, and Applied Graphic
Technologies. The book was printed and
bound at R. R. Donnelley and Sons. Stock
is Citation Web Gloss, Westvaco.

For Condé Nast Books

Jill Cohen, President
Ellen Maria Bruzelius, Division Vice
　　President
Lucille Friedman, Fulfillment Manager
Tom Downing, Direct Marketing Manager
Jill Neal, Direct Marketing Manager
Jennifer Metz, Direct Marketing Associate
Paul DiNardo, Direct Marketing Assistant
Serafino J. Cambareri, Quality Control
　　Manager

For *Gourmet* Books

Diane Keitt, Director
Caroline Schleifer, Associate Editor

For *Gourmet* Magazine

Gail Zweigenthal, Editor-in-Chief

Zanne Early Stewart, Executive Food
　　Editor
Kemp Miles Minifie, Senior Food Editor
Alexis M. Touchet, Associate Food Editor
Amy Mastrangelo, Food Editor
Lori Walther, Food Editor
Elizabeth Vought, Food Editor
Katy Massam, Food Editor
Peggy Anderson, Assistant Food Editor

Romulo A. Yanes, Photographer
Marjorie H. Webb, Style Director
Nancy Purdum, Senior Style Editor

Produced in association with
Media Projects Incorporated

Carter Smith, Executive Editor
Anne B. Wright, Project Editor
John W. Kern, Production Editor
Marilyn Flaig, Indexer
Karen Salsgiver, Design Consultant

Front Jacket: "Baklava" (page 258).

Back Jacket: "Cherry Tomato, Ricotta,
and Olive Galette" (page 161).

Frontispiece: "Chilled Banana and
Pistachio Rice Pudding" (page 230);
"Melon Compote" (page 226).

ACKNOWLEDGMENTS

The editors of Gourmet Books would like to thank those who contributed to this twelfth edition of The Best of Gourmet. Special thanks goes to Zanne Early Stewart, *Gourmet*'s Executive Food Editor, who acted as consultant.

This year the Cuisines of the World section features The Flavors of Greece with menus by Liz Vought (Greek Easter Feast), Lori Walther (Summer Dinner on Santorini), and Alexis Touchet (A Cocktail Party Featuring Mezedes). Liz also created the *baklava* that appears on this year's jacket. Aglaia Kremezi, a well-known authority on Greek cuisine, kindly read through the recipes and offered invaluable suggestions. Wines for the menus were carefully chosen by Gerald Asher, *Gourmet*'s Wine Editor. Steve Jenkins gave us insight on Greek cheeses, and Maria Kourebanas shared her extensive knowledge of Greek cooking and culture with us. Jacket and menu photos by Romulo Yanes, prop styled by Jeannie Oberholtzer; photos of Greece by Helen Wisdom, Conan Owen, and Cotten Alston; and line drawings by Laura Hartman Maestro enhance these pages.

New recipes for this year's addendum—Fresh from the Farmers Market—were developed by Leslie Glover Pendleton. Joel Patraker of New York City's Greenmarket answered our many questions about seasonal produce and farmers markets; and line drawings by Meg Shields embellish the section.

The Recipe Compendium is filled with line drawings by many talented artists: Carla Borea, Jean Chandler, Beverly Charlton, Suzanne Dunaway, Vicky Harrison, Susie Howard, Tina Lang, Elisa Mambrino, Zoe Mavridis, Jeanne Meinke, Bob Palevitz, Agni Saucier, Jim Saucier, Alexis Seabrook, and Susan Hunt Yule.

Finally, thanks to Anne Wright, John Kern, and Kim Horstman of Media Projects; to Karen Salsgiver for her keen sense of design; and to Kemp Minifie, Elaine Richard, Hobby McKenney, and Kathleen Duffy Freud for their editorial contributions.

CONTENTS

INTRODUCTION

As everyone in the food magazine world knows, staying current, looking fresh, and offering informative, eye-catching articles month after month is imperative. At *Gourmet* magazine, a team of dedicated professionals manages continually to surpass my expectations. During 1996 we were joined by Felicity Keane, a talented new art director, who is adding even more vivacity to our pages. A quick glance at The Menu Collection in this edition of *The Best of Gourmet, 1997* will tell you that exciting changes are underway. Not only are there more photographs than ever before, but now many exceptional food shots by Romulo Yanes are taken outside of the studio in natural light. And locations and table settings, however sumptuous, have a contemporary look.

On the editorial side, ongoing adjustments ensure that our recipes reflect today's lifestyle. Because we know that many of our readers try to keep an eye on their waistlines, we decided to run an entire issue on spa cuisine and to make our column featuring leaner/lighter dishes, Less is More, a monthly offering. A host of favorites appear in The Recipe Compendium, with calorie and fat information included. We even gave our In Short Order column, a monthly feature filled with quick-and-easy dishes, a stylish new name—*Gourmet*'s Quick Kitchen. Since we all need plenty of speedy recipes on hand, we have chosen nearly two hundred that can be made in 45 minutes or less for this collection.

More flavor-packed, simple dishes are to be found in our Cuisines of the World section, featuring The Flavors of Greece. Included is a Santorini dinner filled with specialties from this sun-drenched isle (fabulous salads and fish), an Easter Feast of traditional favorites (including *baklava*), and an innovative cocktail party highlighting *mezedes* (Greek appetizers). More *fresh* ideas appear in the Addendum—Fresh from the Farmers Market. Here, 24 brand new seasonal recipes show you how to use less familiar ingredients—lovage, *mâche*, goat cheese, fava beans, collard greens, buttercup squash, chayote, quinces, figs—with delightful and dependable results.

Come enjoy *The Best of Gourmet, 1997*—it's fresh, often light and quick, and always delicious.

Gail Zweigenthal, Editor-in-Chief

Throughout the year, *Gourmet*'s remarkable menus mirror the best of each season. Months before publication, our food editors develop themes for new menus; then, in season, they search out the freshest ingredients—vegetables, fruits, meat, and fish—to create dishes that sparkle and perfectly balanced meals that promise to be remembered long after they are enjoyed. Indoors and out, elegant and casual, festive and relaxed, 25 of the best menus of 1996 appear in this collection. Let these pages take you on a colorful, 70-page journey of exceptional year-round entertaining.

This year, travel with *Gourmet* to New Orleans for a Celebrating Mardi Gras dinner party. A balcony overlooking the French Quarter is the ideal setting for spicy Crawfish Etouffée in Puff Pastry Shells. Then, with our Taste of India dinner, steal away to this mysterious land for exotic Tandoori Shrimp and Mango Salad. For the holidays, peek inside the luxurious home of designer Gianni Versace. With dishes such as Salt Cod, Fennel, and Potato Cannelloni, and Roasted Red Snapper with Olives, this sumptuous Italian Christmas Eve Dinner is as stylish as its surroundings.

For more casual occasions, turn to menus such as our Après-Ski Dinner. After a snowy day, warm up with Cider and Tequila Hot Toddies followed by melting-off-the-bone "Redeye"-Braised Lamb Shanks and Beans—ideal comfort food. For dessert, settle your guests around the fireplace for Apple Pie with Walnut Streusel and coffee. Naturally, there are also plenty of alfresco menus—perfect when the weather heats up. Our Picnic Afloat boasts Striped Bass Escabeche with Bell Peppers and Green Beans and a scrumptious finale, Chewy Coconut Macadamia Bars.

Gourmet's leaner/lighter menus offer a whole new way to enjoy healthful eating, and here you'll find an entire weekend of satisfying meals. From a Saturday Picnic Lunch of tender Chili-Rubbed Chicken with Rosemary and Tomato, to a tropical Poolside Dinner on Sunday featuring Grilled Citrus Salmon with Grilled Mango, you'll enjoy the art of healthy living without sacrificing taste.

Variety, flavor, and excitement are all part of entertaining with *Gourmet*'s menus. Now, all you have to do is choose a few special occasions to celebrate.

Almond-Stuffed Green Olives; Sherried Mushroom Empanadas;
Mussels in Romesco Sauce

NEW YEAR'S TAPAS PARTY

Almond-Stuffed Green Olives, p. 107

Carrot Salad with Oregano and Cumin, p. 104

Sherried Mushroom Empanadas, p. 106

Potato Saffron Omelet, p. 107

Romaine with Lemon Dressing, p. 108

Citrus-and-Clove-Marinated Shrimp, p. 108

Mussels in Romesco Sauce, p. 106

Paprika-Glazed Baby Back Ribs, p. 108

Meatballs in Tomato Garlic Sauce, p. 105

Valdespino Inocente Fino Sherry
Martin Codax Albariño Rias Baixas '94   *Viña Sol '94*

•

Manchego Cheese with Quince Paste, p. 105   *Hazelnut Cookies*, p. 208

•

Serves 8 to 10

Almond-Stuffed Green Olives;
Carrot Salad with Oregano and Cumin;
Romaine with Lemon Dressing

Manchego Cheese with Quince
Paste and Hazelnut Cookies

Paprika-Glazed Baby Back Ribs

Citrus-and-Clove-Marinated Shrimp;
Potato Saffron Omelet;
Meatballs in Tomato Garlic Sauce

Cider and Tequila Hot Toddies, Spicy Cheddar Palmiers

APRÈS-SKI DINNER

Cider and Tequila Hot Toddies, p. 231

Spicy Cheddar Palmiers, p. 90

•

"Redeye" Braised Lamb Shanks and Beans, p. 146

Sautéed Mustard Greens, p. 179

Buttermilk Biscuits, p. 111

Joseph Phelps Le Mistral '93

•

Apple Pie with Walnut Streusel, p. 214

Sour Cream Ice Cream, p. 224

•

Serves 6

"Redeye" Braised Lamb Shanks and Beans;
Sautéed Mustard Greens; Buttermilk Biscuits

A BEER TASTING PARTY

Miniature Gougères, p. 91   *Herbed Spiced Nuts, p. 97*

Pickled Onions, p. 201   *Radishes with Coarse Salt*

Pete's Wicked Ale   Belle-Vue

•

Beer-Braised Sausages and Sauerkraut, p. 142

Caraway Parsley Potatoes, p. 181

Arugula, Endive, and Radicchio Salad with Mustard Vinaigrette, p. 191

Paulaner Oktoberfest

•

Free-Form Beesting Cake, p. 204   *Honey Porter Prune Ice Cream, p. 222*

Samuel Smith's Oatmeal Stout

•

Chimay Grande Réserve

•

Serves 6

Beer-Braised Sausages and Sauerkraut;
Caraway Parsley Potatoes; Arugula, Endive,
and Radicchio Salad with Mustard Vinaigrette

Herbed Spiced Nuts; Pickled Onions; Radishes with Coarse Salt; Miniature Gougères

Free-Form Beesting Cake;
Honey Porter Prune Ice Cream

Panéed Veal with Fried Lemon Slices; Sautéed Spinach and Garlic; Confetti Vegetable Slaw

CELEBRATING MARDI GRAS

Crawfish Tomato Etouffée in Puff Pastry Shells, p. 132

Castello della Sala Orvieto Classico '93

•

Panéed Veal with Fried Lemon Slices, p. 139

Sautéed Spinach and Garlic, p. 183

Confetti Vegetable Slaw, p. 197

Castell' in Villa Chianti Classico '90

•

Frozen Chocolate Bourbon Parfaits, p. 221

Pecan Thins, p. 211

•

Serves 8

Crawfish Tomato Etouffée
in Puff Pastry Shell

Bloody Marys

BRUNCH IN THE KITCHEN

•

Serves 6

Buttermilk Waffles with Two
Toppings; Pecan Praline Bacon

Brandied Chicken Liver Pâté; Artichoke Olive Dip with Fennel Crudités

DINNER IN THE KITCHEN

Brandied Chicken Liver Pâté, p. 102

Artichoke Olive Dip with Fennel Crudités, p. 101

•

Red Wine and Mushroom Risotto, p. 172

Mixed Greens and Haricots Verts with Walnut Oil Vinaigrette, p. 193

Il Poggione Rosso di Montalcino '93

•

Apricot Soufflés with Vanilla Rum Crème Anglaise, p. 229

Robert Weil Kiedricher Gräfenberg Riesling Auslese '94

•

Serves 6

Red Wine and Mushroom Risotto

Apricot Soufflé

EASTER LUNCHEON

Carrot, Fennel, and Orange Soup, p. 119

•

Rosemary, Lemon, and Garlic Leg of Lamb with Roasted Potatoes, p. 147

Asparagus Flans, p. 175

Château Greysac Médoc '90

•

Lime Curd and Toasted Almond Tart with Fruit Compote, p. 215

•

Serves 6

Lime Curd and Toasted Almond Tart

Rosemary, Lemon, and Garlic Leg of Lamb
with Roasted Potatoes

33

Pickled Baby Carrots and Zucchini

BALLOONING PICNIC

Sorrel, Pea, and Leek Soup, p. 122

•

Asparagus, Prosciutto, and Goat Cheese Galettes, p. 162

Cherry Tomato, Ricotta, and Olive Galettes, p. 161

Pickled Baby Carrots and Zucchini, p. 202

Etude Carneros Pinot Noir '93

•

Lemon Verbena Pound Cake with Strawberries, p. 204

•

Serves 4

Sorrel, Pea, and Leek Soup; Asparagus,
Prosciutto, and Goat Cheese Galettes;
Cherry Tomato, Ricotta, and Olive Galette

Apricot Ginger Biscotti

SATURDAY PICNIC LUNCH

Chili-Rubbed Chicken with Rosemary and Tomato, p. 149

Coleslaw with Yogurt Dressing, p. 196

Potato and Green Bean Salad with Citrus Miso Dressing, p. 195

Apricot Ginger Biscotti, p. 209

Duckhorn Sauvignon Blanc '94

•

Serves 6

Each serving, not including wine, about 566 calories
and 7 grams fat (11% of calories from fat)

Minted Berry Spongecake

GRILLED STEAK DINNER

Grilled Marinated London Broil, p. 139

Yellow Pepper Orzo Gratin, p. 167

Grilled Red Onions with Balsamic Vinegar and Rosemary, p. 179

Grilled Zucchini, p. 185

Sliced Tomatoes

Romaine and Watercress Salad with Roquefort Buttermilk Dressing, p. 193

Burgess Merlot '93

•

Minted Berry Spongecakes, p. 208

•

Serves 6

Each serving, not including wine, about 725 calories
and 21 grams fat (26% of calories from fat)

White Sangría

SUNDAY BRUNCH

White Sangría, p. 231

Onion and Bell Pepper Strata with Fresh Tomato Salsa, p. 158

Cumin Black Beans with Mint, p. 188

Maple Mustard-Glazed Canadian Bacon, p. 158

•

Honeydew in Cardamom Lime Syrup with Vanilla Cream, p. 226

•

Serves 6

Each serving, not including sangría, about 764 calories
and 18 grams fat (21% of calories from fat)

Crab Jícama "Seviche" on Cucumber   Sofrito Grilled Bread

POOLSIDE DINNER

Mojitos with Basil, p. 232

Crab Jícama "Seviche" on Cucumber, p. 94

•

Grilled Citrus Salmon and Grilled Mango, p. 126

Sofrito Grilled Bread, p. 111

Bibb Lettuce with Sherry Vinaigrette, p. 192

Gunderloch Nackenheimer Rothenberg "Jean Baptiste" Riesling '94

•

Tropical Fruit Champagne Granita, p. 224

•

Serves 6

Each serving, not including mojitos and wine, about 797 calories
and 17 grams fat (19% of calories from fat)

AN ELEGANT DINNER PARTY

Domaine Chandon Etoile

•

Tatsoi and Warm Scallop Salad with Spicy Pecan Praline, p. 189

Chappellet Napa Valley Signature Chardonnay '94

•

Pork Tournedos with Blackberry Gastrique and Mango Salsa, p. 142

Buttered New Potatoes, p. 182

Wax Beans with Parsley Oil, p. 176

Estancia Alexander Valley Sangiovese '93

•

Chocolate Ganache Tartlets with Sweet Cherries, p. 219

•

Serves 6

Tatsoi and Warm Scallop Salad
with Spicy Pecan Praline

Chocolate Ganache Tartlet
with Sweet Cherries

Pork Tournedo with Blackberry Gastrique and Mango
Salsa; Buttered New Potatoes; Wax Beans with Parsley Oil

Lemon Cajun Sweet Dough Pies

LOUISIANA SEAFOOD BOIL

Spicy Boiled Crabs, Shrimp, Potatoes, Corn, and Garlic, p. 130

Horseradish Cocktail Sauce, p. 131

French Bread

Abita Amber, Abita Turbodog, Lemonade

•

Lemon Cajun Sweet Dough Pies, p. 218

Old Crustacean

•

Serves 6

Spicy Boiled Crabs, Shrimp, Potatoes, Corn,
and Garlic; Horseradish Cocktail Sauce

Brown Butter Almond Torte with Sour Cherry Sauce

DINNER ON THE FOURTH

Feta-Stuffed Eggplant Rolls with Salsa Verde, p. 178

•

Bacon and Basil-Wrapped Chicken Breasts, p. 148

Summer Vegetable Ragout, p. 187

Grilled Olive Toasts, p. 111

Cinnabar Santa Cruz Mountains Chardonnay '94

•

Brown Butter Almond Torte with Sour Cherry Sauce, p. 205

•

Serves 6

Bacon and Basil-Wrapped Chicken Breasts;
Summer Vegetable Ragout; Grilled Olive Toasts

Grilled Pizzas; Romaine, Arugula, and Avocado Salad

LUNCH ON THE DECK

Lemon Shandies, p. 231

Steamed Mussels with Orange, Fennel, and Garlic, p. 96

•

Shrimp Gazpacho with Basil Croutons, p. 120

Grilled Pizza with Fresh Corn, Bell Pepper, Pancetta, and Fontina, p. 116

Grilled Pizza with Yellow Squash, Mozzarella, and Lemon Thyme, p. 117

Romaine, Arugula, and Avocado Salad, p. 192

Fetzer California White Zinfandel '95

•

Gingered Brioche Summer Pudding with Sour Cream Mascarpone, p. 227

•

Serves 4

Steamed Mussels with Orange,
Fennel, and Garlic; Lemon Shandies

Shrimp Gazpacho with Basil Croutons

Grilled Pizza with Yellow Squash,
Mozzarella, and Lemon Thyme

PICNIC AFLOAT

Tomato Eggplant Spread and Parmesan Toasts, p. 101

Vodka and Tonics

•

Striped Bass Escabeche with Bell Peppers and Green Beans, p. 123

Goat Cheese and Thyme Potato Cake, p. 181

Chewy Coconut Macadamia Bars, p. 212

Ponzi Pinot Gris '94

•

Serves 6

Tomato Eggplant Spread
and Parmesan Toasts

Chewy Coconut Macadamia Bars

Striped Bass Escabeche with Bell Peppers and Green Beans;
Goat Cheese and Thyme Potato Cake

Pappadams

A TASTE OF INDIA

Coconut and Mint Lassi, p. 234

Coriander, Ginger, and Chili Lassi, p. 234

Pappadams, p. 97

•

Tandoori Shrimp and Mango Salad, p. 190

Fennel-Scented Spinach and Potato Samosas, p. 184

Mint Chutney, p. 202

Columbia Crest Riesling '94

•

Chilled Banana and Pistachio Rice Pudding, p. 230

Melon Compote, p. 226

•

Serves 6

Coconut and Mint Lassi;
Coriander, Ginger, and Chili Lassi

Fennel-Scented Spinach and Potato Samosas; Mint Chutney

Tandoori Shrimp and Mango Salad

Zucchini Cone Filled with Lemon Mint Pea Purée;
Herb-Baked Potato Chip with Crème Fraîche and Caviar

A SMALL COUNTRY WEDDING

Fresh Fig, Mascarpone, and Pesto Torte, p. 95

Zucchini Cones Filled with Lemon Mint Pea Purée, p. 100

Herb-Baked Potato Chips with Crème Fraîche and Caviar, p. 98

Chilled Yellow Pepper Soup with Chives, p. 121

Krug Grande Cuvée

•

Glazed Salmon Fillets with Dill Mustard Sauce, p. 124

Grilled Lemon and Garlic Leg of Lamb with Coriander Chutney, p. 145

Couscous with Dried Apricots, Currants, and Pistachios, p. 165

Roasted Onion Tarts, p. 180　　　*Grilled Vegetables, p. 185*

Vine-Ripened Tomatoes Drizzled with Balsamic Vinegar, p. 196

Breads and Rolls

Joseph Faiveley Mercurey Blanc Clos Rochette '93　　　*Château Langoa-Barton '88*

Dark Chocolate Wedding Cake
with Chocolate Orange Ganache and Orange Buttercream, p. 206

•

Strawberry and Apricot Linzertorte Hearts, p. 213

Muscat de Beaumes de Venise

•

Serves 16

Fresh Fig, Mascarpone, and Pesto Torte

Vine-Ripened Tomatoes Drizzled with Balsamic Vinegar; Grilled Lemon and Garlic Leg of
Lamb with Coriander Chutney; Roasted Onion Tarts; Grilled Vegetables; Glazed Salmon
Fillets with Dill Mustard Sauce; Couscous with Dried Apricots, Currants, and Pistachios

FEASTING ON GAME

Grilled Quail with Wilted Cabbage Slaw, p. 157

Alban Vineyard Edna Valley Viognier '94

•

Pheasant Pie, p. 152

Herbed Spätzle, p. 170

Foris Pinot Noir '94

•

Pumpkin Bread Pudding with Cranberry Caramel Sauce, p. 228

Walnuts

Cálem's 10-Year-Old Tawny Port

•

Serves 6

Pumpkin Bread Pudding with Cranberry Caramel Sauce

Pheasant Pie; Herbed Spätzle

71

THANKSGIVING DINNER

Spiced Cheese Straws, p. 92 *Dill-Pickled Vegetables*, p. 203

Lobster Lovage Stew, p. 132

Bernadus Monterey County Chardonnay '94

•

Roast Turkey with Sage and Sherried Cider Giblet Gravy, p. 154

Chestnut and Bacon Dressing, p. 155

Fresh Cranberry Orange Sauce, p. 203

Sautéed Red Swiss Chard with Garlic, p. 184 *Root Vegetable Gratin*, p. 187

Mashed Potatoes and Leeks with Thyme, p. 182

Truchard Carneros Merlot '93

•

Pear and Sour Cherry Mincemeat Pie, p. 216

Butternut and Hickory Nut Ice Cream, p. 224 *Maple Pumpkin Pie*, p. 217

Alderbrook Late-Harvest Muscat de Frontignan '94

•

Serves 8

Spiced Cheese Straws;
Dill-Pickled Vegetables;
Lobster Lovage Stew

Maple Pumpkin Pie;
Pear and Sour Cherry Mincemeat Pie

Opposite, clockwise from top left: Chestnut and Bacon Dressing;
Root Vegetable Gratin; Sautéed Red Swiss Chard with Garlic;
Mashed Potatoes and Leeks with Thyme

Tuna and Roasted Pepper Crostini; Baked Clams Oreganate

AN ITALIAN CHRISTMAS EVE

Tuna and Roasted Pepper Crostini, p. 101

Minted Fried Beets with Balsamic Vinegar Sauce, p. 104

Cauliflower Salad with Olives and Capers, p. 104

Baked Clams Oreganate, p. 102

Chilled Seafood Salad with Herbed Olive Oil and Sea Salt, p. 103

Mastroberardino Greco di Tufo '94

•

Salt Cod, Fennel, and Potato Cannelloni, p. 164

Spaghetti with Lobster and Mussels, p. 170

Roasted Red Snapper with Olives, p. 126

Steamed Broccoli Rabe, p. 177

•

Blood-Orange Crostata, p. 220

Essensia California Orange Muscat Sweet Dessert Wine '95

•

Serves 12

Blood-Orange Crostata

Roasted Red Snapper with Olives;
Steamed Broccoli Rabe; Spaghetti with Lobster
and Mussels; Salt Cod, Fennel, and Potato Cannelloni

Smoked Fish Trio

CHRISTMAS DINNER

Stilton and Quince Jam Puff Pastries, p. 93

Lillet with an orange twist

•

Smoked Fish Trio, p. 129

Chalk Hill Chardonnay '94

•

*Pan-Seared Filets Mignons with Roasted Potatoes
and Merlot Sauce, p. 135*

Mélange of Winter Vegetables, p. 186

Château Lynch-Bages Pauillac Grand Cru Classé '88

•

Ice-Cream Bombes with Brandied Dried Cranberries and Cherries, p. 222

•

Serves 6

Ice-Cream Bombe with Brandied
Dried Cranberries and Cherries

Pan-Seared Filet Mignon with
Roasted Potatoes and Merlot Sauce;
Mélange of Winter Vegetables

83

Watermelon and Raspberry Sorbet

LESS IS MORE

DINING ON THE LIGHT SIDE

Marinated Shrimp with Pickled Watermelon Rind, p. 131

Black-Eyed Pea Salad with Watercress and Peach, p. 194

Sliced Tomatoes and Cucumbers, p. 196

Cornmeal Bread, p. 110

•

Watermelon and Raspberry Sorbet, p. 225

•

Serves 4

Each serving about 494 calories
and 3 grams fat (6% of calories from fat)

Broiled Portobello Mushroom with Zucchini-Scallion Topping

LESS IS MORE

DINING ON THE LIGHT SIDE

Broiled Portobello Mushrooms with Zucchini-Scallion Topping, p. 94

•

*Turkey, Potato, and Roasted-Garlic Ravioli
with Sun-Dried Tomato Sauce*, p. 166

•

Serves 6

Each serving about 360 calories
and 7 grams fat (17% of calories from fat)

A RECIPE
COMPENDIUM

From fast supper dishes for hectic weeknights to showstopper desserts designed to impress, *Gourmet*'s recipes are ideal for any occasion. This collection of over 400 recipes includes those that make up our menus as well as hundreds of others that were developed by *Gourmet*'s food editors during 1996—dishes that were tested, tasted, and tested again, until the balance of flavors and seasonings was perfected.

Since we know how busy our readers are these days, nearly half of the recipes chosen can be made in 45 minutes or less. Recipes from *Gourmet*'s Quick Kitchen column can be enjoyed on their own, used to round out a menu, or combined to create meals. For example, Chicken with Mustard-Seed Crust and Couscous can be assembled in minutes. Add Sautéed Cucumbers with Cumin and Mint, or Avocado Radish Salad with Lime Dressing, and Strawberry Phyllo Shortcakes for a truly indulgent dinner. The Last Touch column offers quick, clever variations on a theme. If chocolate is your passion, Chocolate-Chunk Caramel Cookies and Chocolate-Dipped Orange Shortbread Hearts are sure to satisfy. When you're thirsting for hot-weather refreshers, try Orange Berry Coolers and Pineapple Mint Frozen Daiquiris. (45-minute recipes are indicated by a clock ☺ in the General Index.)

Dishes from our Less Is More column offer sensible ways to eat a little lighter and healthier without skimping on flavor. Simply toss together Fusilli with Sun-Dried Tomatoes, Zucchini, and Peas or explore more sophisticated combinations like Grilled Tuna with Warm White Bean Salad. (Leaner/lighter recipes are followed by a calorie and fat gram count and indicated by a feather ✒ in the General Index.)

Gourmet has always highlighted seasonal ingredients and specialty foods. If you've wondered how to prepare the "new" grains, now you have plenty of options—try quinoa in lamb stew, or bulgur stuffing for Cornish hens. And, for extravagant moments, you'll savor decadent treats from the Forbidden Pleasures pages like deep-fried oysters slathered in guacamole.

For every season, for any occasion, *Gourmet* recipes are sure to please. Here are the best ones of 1996 to peruse and enjoy.

APPETIZERS

Colcannon-Stuffed Brussels Sprouts

½ pound red potatoes
6 Brussels sprouts
1 tablespoon unsalted butter
½ teaspoon salt, or to taste
freshly ground black pepper to taste
3 bacon slices, cooked until crisp and crumbled

Peel potatoes. In a saucepan cover potatoes with cold water by 2 inches and simmer, covered, until very tender but not falling apart, about 20 minutes.
Preheat oven to 350° F.
While potatoes are cooking, trim Brussels sprouts: With a paring knife cut 4 firm cup-shaped leaves from stem end of each sprout and reserve. Quarter rest of each sprout and slice thin.
With a slotted spoon transfer potatoes to a colander to drain, reserving cooking water in pan, and transfer potatoes to a bowl. Add butter, salt, and pepper and with an electric mixer beat mixture until smooth.
Have ready a bowl of ice and cold water and bring reserved cooking water to a boil. Gently stir in reserved sprout leaves and blanch 5 seconds. Working quickly, with a skimmer or slotted spoon transfer leaves to bowl of ice water to stop cooking. Blanch shredded sprouts 30 seconds and drain in a sieve. Beat shredded sprouts into potato purée.
Transfer leaves to paper towels to drain upside down. Transfer purée to a pastry bag fitted with a ½-inch plain tip and pipe into upturned leaf cups. Arrange filled leaf cups in a buttered shallow baking dish. *Hors d'oeuvres may be prepared up to this point 3 hours ahead and chilled, covered.* Sprinkle tops of hors d'oeuvres with bacon and heat in middle of oven 3 minutes, or until heated through. Makes about 24 hors d'oeuvres.

Carrot Curls Stuffed with Saga Blue, Celery, and Walnuts

two 8- to 9-inch carrots
¼ cup softened Saga Blue cheese
½ cup finely chopped celery
¼ cup walnuts, toasted until pale golden,
    cooled completely, and chopped fine

Halve carrots lengthwise and, using a vegetable peeler along flat side of each half, cut about 18 long wide ribbons. Beginning with wider end, wind each ribbon around your thumb, securing ends with wooden picks. *Chill carrot curls in a bowl of ice and cold water 1 hour.*
In a small bowl cream together Saga Blue, celery, and walnuts and drop level teaspoons onto a large plate. Chill filling, covered, 45 minutes.
Drain carrot curls. Working with 1 carrot curl at a time, remove wooden pick and pat dry. Beginning with wider end, wrap each carrot curl around a teaspoon of filling and resecure ends with wooden picks. Makes about 18 hors d'oeuvres.

Spicy Cheddar Palmiers

1½ tablespoons chili powder
1½ tablespoons firmly packed light brown sugar
¾ teaspoon cayenne
¾ teaspoon salt
½ cup packed fresh parsley leaves, washed,
    spun dry, and chopped
a 17¼-ounce package frozen puff pastry sheets
    (2 pastry sheets), thawed
1½ cups shredded sharp Cheddar (about 6 ounces)

In a small bowl stir together chili powder, sugar, cayenne, and salt. On a work surface sprinkled with 2 tablespoons parsley roll out 1 puff pastry sheet into a 12-inch square. Sprinkle square evenly with half of spice mixture and ¾ cup Cheddar, pressing cheese gently onto pastry. Roll up 1 edge to middle of pastry sheet and roll up parallel edge in same manner so that the 2 rolls are touching. Repeat procedure with remaining parsley, pastry sheet, spice mixture, and Cheddar. Wrap pastry rolls in plastic wrap and chill 30 minutes. *Pastry rolls may be made 2 weeks ahead and frozen, wrapped well in plastic wrap. Thaw pastry rolls in refrigerator 2 hours before proceeding.*

Preheat oven to 375° F.

Cut pastry rolls with a sharp knife crosswise into slices just under ½ inch thick and arrange 1 inch apart on large baking sheets. Bake *palmiers* in batches in middle of oven 20 minutes, or until golden brown, and transfer with a metal spatula to racks to cool. Makes about 48 *palmiers*.

PHOTO ON PAGE 17

Beef Satés with Southeast Asian Sauce

¼ cup fresh lime juice
2 tablespoons water
4 teaspoons soy sauce
2 garlic cloves
3 slices peeled fresh gingerroot, each the size
  of a quarter
1 teaspoon sugar
¼ teaspoon dried hot red pepper flakes
3 tablespoons vegetable oil
an 8-ounce filet mignon, cut into twenty-four
  1-inch cubes
¼ cup fresh coriander sprigs, washed well,
  spun dry, and chopped fine
1 tablespoon minced fresh mint leaves
1 scallion, minced
twelve 8-inch bamboo skewers, soaked in
  water 30 minutes

In a blender or small food processor blend lime juice, water, soy sauce, garlic, gingerroot, sugar, and red pepper flakes until smooth and with motor running add 2 tablespoons oil in a stream, blending until sauce is emulsified.

In a bowl toss filet with 2 tablespoons sauce and remaining tablespoon oil and marinate 15 to 30 minutes.

Prepare grill.

In a bowl stir together coriander, mint, scallion, and remaining sauce.

Thread 2 filet cubes onto each skewer and grill on an oiled rack set 5 to 6 inches over glowing coals 3 to 4 minutes on each side for medium-rare.

Serve beef *satés* with dipping sauce at room temperature. Makes 12 *satés*.

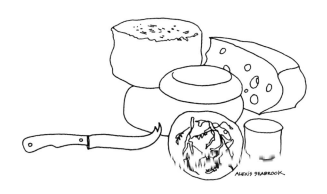

ALEXIS SEABROOK

Miniature Gougères
(Gruyère Cheese Puffs)

1 tablespoon dill seeds
1½ cups coarsely grated Gruyère
1 recipe *pâte à chou* (page 92)

Preheat oven to 375° F. Lightly grease 2 baking sheets or line with parchment paper.

In a small heavy skillet dry-roast seeds over moderate heat, shaking skillet, until fragrant and slightly darker, being careful not to burn them, 3 to 4 minutes. Transfer seeds to a small bowl and cool. With a mortar and pestle or in an electric coffee/spice grinder grind seeds coarse.

Stir Gruyère and 1 teaspoon ground seeds into *pâte à chou* and arrange level tablespoons about 1 inch apart on baking sheets. Sprinkle tops of *gougères* with remaining ground seeds and bake in upper and lower thirds of oven, switching position of sheets halfway through baking, 30 minutes, or until puffed, golden, and crisp. *Gougères keep in sealable plastic bags chilled, 2 days, or frozen, 1 week. Reheat gougères, uncovered, in a preheated 350° F, oven 10 minutes if chilled or 15 minutes if frozen.*

Serve *gougères* warm. Makes about 40 *gougères*.

PHOTO ON PAGE 20

Pâte à Chou
(Cream-Puff Pastry)

1 cup water
1 stick (½ cup) unsalted butter, cut into
  small pieces
½ teaspoon salt
1 cup all-purpose flour
4 to 5 large eggs

In a heavy saucepan bring water to a boil with butter and salt over high heat and reduce heat to moderate. Add flour all at once and beat with a wooden spoon until mixture pulls away from side of saucepan.

Transfer mixture to a bowl and with an electric mixer on high speed beat in 4 eggs, 1 at a time, beating well after each addition. Batter should be stiff enough to just hold soft peaks and fall softly from a spoon. If batter is too stiff, in a small bowl beat remaining egg lightly and add to batter, a little at a time, beating on high speed, until batter is desired consistency.

Gruyère Walnut Wafers

¼ cup coarsely grated Gruyère (about 1 ounce)
2 tablespoons coarsely chopped walnuts
1 teaspoon coarsely chopped fresh rosemary
  leaves

Preheat oven to 350° F.
On a baking sheet divide Gruyère into 8 small mounds and sprinkle walnuts and rosemary on top. Bake wafers in middle of oven until pale golden, about 4 minutes. Cool wafers on sheet 1 minute and with a spatula carefully transfer to a rack to cool completely. Makes 8 wafers.

Prosciutto and Gruyère Pinwheels

¾ cup finely grated Gruyère (about 3 ounces)
4 teaspoons chopped fresh sage leaves
1 puff pastry sheet (from one 17¼-ounce package
  frozen puff pastry sheets), thawed
1 large egg, beaten lightly
2 ounces thinly sliced prosciutto

In a bowl combine Gruyère and sage. On a lightly floured surface arrange pastry sheet with a short side facing you and cut in half crosswise. Arrange one half of sheet with a long side facing you and brush edge of far side with some egg. Arrange half of prosciutto evenly on top of pastry, avoiding egg-brushed edge, and top with half of Gruyère mixture. Starting with side nearest you, roll pastry jelly-roll fashion into a log and wrap in wax paper. Make another log in same manner. *Chill logs, seam sides down, until firm, at least 3 hours, and up to 3 days.*

Preheat oven to 400° F. and lightly grease 2 large baking sheets.

Cut logs crosswise into ½-inch-thick pinwheels and arrange, cut sides down, 1 inch apart on baking sheets. Bake pinwheels in batches in middle of oven until golden, 14 to 16 minutes. Transfer pinwheels to a rack and cool slightly. Serve pinwheels warm. Makes about 40 hors d'oeuvres.

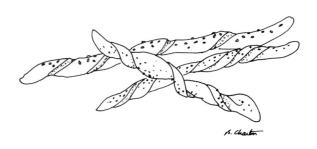

Spiced Cheese Straws

⅔ cup freshly grated Parmesan
  (about 2 ounces)
1 teaspoon ground cumin
1 teaspoon ground coriander seeds
¼ teaspoon ground cardamom
¼ teaspoon cayenne
½ teaspoon salt
1 puff pastry sheet (from one 17¼-ounce
  package frozen puff pastry sheets),
  thawed and unfolded
an egg wash made by beating 1 large egg
  with 2 tablespoons water

Preheat oven to 425° F. and butter 2 large baking sheets.

In a bowl stir together Parmesan, spices, and salt. On a lightly floured surface roll out pastry sheet into a 16- by 10-inch rectangle and brush with some egg wash. Cut pastry in half crosswise, forming two 10- by 8-inch rectangles. Sprinkle Parmesan mixture over 1 rectangle and top with other rectangle, egg-wash side down, pressing firmly to eliminate any air pockets. Roll out pastry slightly to make layers adhere (rectangle should be about 10½ by 8½ inches). Brush pastry with some egg wash and with a sharp large knife or pastry wheel cut lengthwise into ¼-inch-wide sticks.

Arrange cheese straws about 1½ inches apart on baking sheets, pressing ends onto baking sheets. Bake cheese straws in batches in middle of oven until golden, about 10 minutes. Transfer cheese straws to a rack and cool. *Cheese straws may be made 2 days ahead and kept in an airtight container. Recrisp cheese straws in a 350° F. oven until just heated through, about 5 minutes.* Makes about 36 cheese straws.

PHOTO ON PAGE 73

Stilton and Quince Jam Puff Pastries

1 puff pastry sheet (from one 17¼-ounce package
　　frozen puff pastry sheets), thawed
an egg wash made by beating 1 large egg yolk
　　with 1 teaspoon water
¼ pound chilled Stilton cheese
½ cup quince jam*

*available at specialty foods shops and by mail
　　order from Balducci's, tel. (800) BALDUCCI or
　　(212) 673-2600

Preheat oven to 425° F. and lightly butter a baking sheet.

On a lightly floured surface cut out 24 pastry rounds from pastry sheet with a 1½-inch round cutter and arrange 1 inch apart on baking sheet. Brush tops of rounds with some egg wash (be careful not to drip down sides of rounds) and bake in middle of oven until puffed and golden brown, about 12 minutes (rounds will puff unevenly). Transfer rounds with a spatula to a rack and cool slightly. Trim bottoms of rounds if necessary to create level pastries and cool

completely on rack. *Pastry rounds may be made 2 days ahead and kept in a sealable plastic bag at room temperature.*

Break Stilton into 24 small pieces (about ¼ inch) and bring to room temperature. Top each pastry round with 1 piece Stilton and ½ teaspoon jam and serve at room temperature. Makes 24 hors d'oeuvres.

Chicken Satés with Peanut Curry Sauce

1½ cups well-stirred canned unsweetened
　　coconut milk
1 tablespoon soy sauce
1½ teaspoons curry powder
¾ teaspoon ground coriander seeds
2 teaspoons cornstarch
1 whole boneless skinless chicken breast
　　(about ¾ pound)
¾ cup salted dry-roasted peanuts, ground
　　fine in a food processor
1 teaspoon fresh lime juice
⅛ teaspoon dried hot red pepper flakes, or to taste
ten 8-inch bamboo skewers, soaked in
　　water 30 minutes
1 teaspoon minced fresh coriander sprigs

In a small bowl stir together coconut milk, soy sauce, curry powder, and ground coriander until combined well. Transfer ½ cup coconut mixture to a medium bowl and stir in cornstarch, reserving remaining coconut mixture, covered and chilled.

Cut chicken lengthwise into ten ½-inch-thick strips and add to cornstarch mixture, stirring to coat. *Marinate chicken, covered and chilled, at least 1 hour and up to 24.*

Prepare grill.

In a small saucepan stir together reserved coconut mixture, peanuts, lime juice, and red pepper flakes and simmer, stirring occasionally, 10 minutes, or until thickened. Transfer dipping sauce to a small bowl and cool.

Thread 1 piece chicken onto each skewer and grill on an oiled rack set 5 to 6 inches over glowing coals until cooked through, about 3 minutes on each side.

Sprinkle dipping sauce with fresh coriander and serve at room temperature with chicken *satés*. Makes 10 *satés*.

Fennel Stuffed with Cream Cheese and Kalamata Olives

1 large fennel bulb (sometimes called anise, about 1 pound)
a 3-ounce package cream cheese, softened
⅓ cup drained Kalamata olives, pitted and chopped

Trim fennel stalks flush with bulb, reserving fronds, and cut outer 2 layers loose at base, removing them carefully and reserving rest of bulb for another use. Chop reserved fronds. In a small bowl cream together cream cheese, olives, and chopped fronds. Spread inside of larger fennel layer with cream cheese mixture and press back of other layer onto filling firmly. *Chill fennel, wrapped tightly in plastic wrap, at least 1 hour and up to 12.* Unwrap fennel and cut crosswise into ⅓-inch-thick slices. Cut slices crosswise into 1½-inch-wide sections. Makes about 14 hors d'oeuvres.

Crab Jicama "Seviche" on Cucumber

1 small *jícama**
¼ pound lump crab meat (about ¾ cup), picked over and flaked
2 tablespoons fresh lime juice
2 tablespoons chopped scallion greens
¼ teaspoon finely chopped seeded *habanero* or *jalapeño* chili (wear rubber gloves), or to taste
1 plum tomato, seeded and chopped (about ⅓ cup)
1 garlic clove, minced (about ½ teaspoon)
1 ripe avocado (preferably California, about 9 ounces)
1 seedless cucumber (about ½ pound)

*available at specialty produce markets and some supermarkets

Peel *jícama* and cut in half. Finely chop half of *jícama*, or enough to measure ½ cup, and shred remaining half, or enough to measure ⅓ cup. Reserve any remaining for another use.

In a small bowl stir together *jícama*, crab, 1½ tablespoons lime juice, scallion, chili, tomato, and

¼ teaspoon garlic. Season "*seviche*" with salt and pepper.

Halve avocado, reserving half for another use. In small bowl with a fork mash remaining avocado, remaining 1½ teaspoons lime juice, and remaining ¼ teaspoon garlic with salt to taste until smooth. *Seviche and avocado mash may be made 4 hours ahead and chilled separately, their surfaces covered with plastic wrap.*

Cut cucumber crosswise diagonally into twenty-four ¼-inch-thick slices. Top each cucumber slice with ½ teaspoon avocado mash and 1 teaspoon crab *seviche*. Makes 24 hors d'oeuvres, serving 6.

☙ Each serving about 59 calories, 2 grams fat (35% of calories from fat)

PHOTO ON PAGE 42

Broiled Portobello Mushrooms with Zucchini-Scallion Topping

1½ pounds zucchini, grated coarse
2 tablespoons salt
1 tablespoon extra-virgin olive oil
4 scallions, sliced thin
2 garlic cloves, minced
3 tablespoons water
3 tablespoons fresh basil leaves, chopped coarse
2 pounds Portobello mushrooms (about 6 large), stems discarded

Garnish: fresh basil sprigs

In a sieve set over a bowl toss zucchini with salt and drain 20 minutes. Rinse zucchini under cold water and drain well, pressing hard to extract excess liquid.

In a non-stick skillet heat 2 teaspoons oil over moderate heat until hot but not smoking and cook scallions and garlic with 2 tablespoons water, covered, stirring occasionally, until tender, about 3 minutes.

In a bowl stir together zucchini, scallion mixture, basil, and salt and pepper to taste.

Preheat broiler.

In a small bowl stir together remaining teaspoon

oil and remaining tablespoon water. Lightly brush mushroom caps with oil-water mixture and season with salt and pepper. Put mushrooms, gill sides down, on rack of a broiler pan and broil about 2 inches from heat 4 minutes. Turn mushrooms over and top with zucchini mixture, mounding it and dividing evenly. Broil filled mushrooms until zucchini is crisp-tender, about 6 minutes.

Garnish mushrooms with basil sprigs. Serves 6.

☛ Each serving about 78 calories, 3 grams fat
(35% of calories from fat)

PHOTO ON PAGE 86

*Fresh Fig, Mascarpone,
and Pesto Torte*

For crust
1 cup finely ground wheat crackers such as
    Wheat Thins
½ cup pine nuts, toasted until golden, cooled,
    and ground fine
1 tablespoon unsalted butter, melted and cooled
For filling
1¼ pounds cream cheese, softened
½ cup *mascarpone* cheese or sour cream
3 large eggs

1¼ cups homemade basil pesto (page 96)
    or store-bought basil pesto
2 pounds firm-ripe fresh figs (about 16 large),
    1 pound cut into ¼-inch-thick slices
½ cup fig preserves*
1½ tablespoons white-wine vinegar

Accompaniment: baguettes cut diagonally into
    thin slices and lightly toasted

*available at some specialty foods shops and by
    mail order from Maison Glass Delicacies,
    tel. (800) 822-5564 or (212) 755-3316

Make crust:
Preheat oven to 325° F. and butter a 10-inch springform pan.

In a small bowl with a fork stir together crust ingredients and salt and pepper to taste. Press mixture into bottom of pan and bake in middle of oven 10 minutes, or until lightly browned.
Make filling:
In a bowl with an electric mixer beat together cream cheese, *mascarpone* cheese, eggs, and salt and pepper to taste until very smooth.
Assemble torte:
Pour half of filling into crust. Drop dollops of pesto over filling and spread carefully to form an even topping. (Some filling may show through.) Top pesto layer with half of fig slices, overlapping them slightly, and pour remaining filling over fig slices, spreading evenly. Bake torte in middle of oven 1 hour and 10 minutes, or until top is golden brown and set. Cool torte in pan on a rack (filling will deflate slightly). *Chill torte, covered loosely, at least 3 hours and up to 2 days.*

In a small saucepan stir together preserves and vinegar and bring to a simmer. Remove pan from heat and cool mixture. Stir in salt to taste.

Slice remaining pound figs into ¼-inch-thick slices. Run a thin knife around edge of pan and remove side. Spread torte with preserves mixture, leaving a ¼-inch border, and top decoratively with remaining fig slices. With 2 large metal spatulas transfer torte to a serving plate.

Serve torte at room temperature to spread on toasts. Serves 16 to 32 as an hors d'oeuvre.

PHOTO ON PAGE 66

Basil Pesto

4 cups packed fresh basil leaves, washed well
½ cup pine nuts, toasted until golden, cooled,
 and chopped fine
½ cup freshly grated Parmesan (about 1½ ounces)
2 large garlic cloves, minced
¼ cup plus 3 tablespoons extra-virgin olive oil

Have ready a bowl of ice and cold water. In a saucepan of boiling salted water blanch basil, a handful at a time, 2 seconds, transferring with a slotted spoon to bowl of ice water to stop cooking. Drain basil in a sieve and pat dry.

In a food processor purée basil with remaining ingredients until smooth and season with salt and pepper. *Pesto may be made 2 days ahead and chilled, its surface covered with plastic wrap.* Makes about 1¼ cups.

Mushrooms Stuffed with Sun-Dried Tomatoes

½ ounce dried tomatoes (about 5, not
 packed in oil)
2 tablespoons olive oil
18 white mushrooms, stems pulled out
 and chopped fine and caps
 reserved
¼ cup finely chopped shallots
⅓ cup fine dry bread crumbs
1 large egg yolk, beaten lightly
¼ cup fresh parsley leaves, washed well,
 spun dry, and minced
½ teaspoon dried basil, crumbled
2 tablespoons freshly grated Parmesan

Preheat oven to 400° F. and lightly grease a shallow baking dish.

In a small bowl soak tomatoes in hot water to cover 5 minutes. Reserving 1 tablespoon soaking liquid, drain tomatoes well and chop fine. In a small skillet heat oil over moderate heat until hot but not smoking and cook chopped mushroom stems and shallots, stirring, until shallots are softened. In a bowl stir together mushroom mixture, bread crumbs, tomatoes, reserved soaking liquid, yolk, parsley, basil, and salt to taste. Mound stuffing in reserved mushroom caps and arrange caps in baking

dish. Sprinkle mushrooms with Parmesan and bake in middle of oven 15 minutes. Makes 18 stuffed mushrooms.

Steamed Mussels with Orange, Fennel, and Garlic

1 navel orange
2 large garlic cloves, minced and mashed to a
 paste with ½ teaspoon salt
2 shallots, chopped fine (about ⅓ cup)
½ cup finely chopped fennel bulb (sometimes
 called anise)
1 teaspoon fennel seeds
2 tablespoons unsalted butter
¼ cup dry white wine
½ cup chicken broth
1 pound mussels (preferably cultivated), scrubbed
 well and beards pulled off
1 tablespoon chopped fresh parsley leaves

With a vegetable peeler remove three 3- by ½-inch strips orange zest. Cut remaining peel and pith from orange with a sharp knife and discard. Cut out fruit sections from between membranes, discarding membranes, and finely chop enough fruit to measure ⅓ cup, reserving remaining fruit for another use.

In a large saucepan cook garlic paste, shallots, chopped fennel, and fennel seeds in butter over moderate heat, stirring, until chopped fennel is softened, about 5 minutes. Stir in wine and zest and boil 1 minute. Add broth and return to a boil. Add mussels and cook, covered with a tight-fitting lid, over high heat, checking them every minute, 3 to 8 minutes, transferring them as they open with a slotted spoon to a serving bowl. (Discard any mussels that are unopened after 8 minutes.)

Stir into broth chopped orange, parsley, and salt and pepper to taste and spoon over mussels. Serves 4 as an hors d'oeuvre.

PHOTO ON PAGE 53

Herbed Spiced Nuts

2 tablespoons vegetable oil
1 teaspoon dried thyme, crumbled
1 teaspoon salt
½ teaspoon cayenne
2 cups assorted nuts such as walnuts, pecans, hazelnuts, and natural almonds (with skins)

Preheat oven to 350° F.

In a bowl whisk together oil, thyme, salt, and cayenne. Add nuts and toss to coat well. Spread nuts in a shallow baking pan and roast in middle of oven 10 minutes. *Nuts may be made 3 days ahead and kept in an airtight container at room temperature.*

Serve herbed spiced nuts warm or at room temperature. Makes 2 cups.

PHOTO ON PAGE 20

Oatcakes with Goat Cheese and Fig

2 cups old-fashioned rolled oats
¼ cup plus 2 tablespoons all-purpose flour
1 teaspoon salt
¾ teaspoon baking powder
½ stick (¼ cup) cold unsalted butter, cut into bits
¼ cup plus 2 tablespoons milk
1 cup quartered dried Calimyrna figs, stems discarded
½ cup dry red wine
2 tablespoons honey
3 tablespoons tiny fresh thyme sprigs
½ cup plus 2 tablespoons soft mild goat cheese (about 5 ounces)

Preheat oven to 375° F. and butter 2 large baking sheets.

In a food processor pulse oats until chopped fine. Add flour, salt, baking powder, and butter and pulse until mixture resembles coarse meal. Add milk and pulse until a dough just forms. On a lightly floured surface roll out dough ⅛ inch thick (about a 13-inch round) and using a 1½-inch cutter cut out about 60 oatcakes. Arrange oatcakes on baking sheets 1 inch apart and bake in middle of oven 12 minutes (oatcakes will not change color). Transfer oatcakes to a rack and cool completely.

In a small saucepan combine figs, wine, honey, and 1 tablespoon thyme sprigs and simmer, stirring occasionally, until most of liquid is evaporated. Transfer fig mixture to a small bowl and cool.

Top each oatcake with about ½ teaspoon goat cheese, a fig piece, and a few thyme sprigs. Makes about 60 hors d'oeuvres.

Pappadams
(Crisp Indian Wafers)

12 sun-dried *pappadams** (Indian wafers, sometimes called *papads*) in assorted flavors such as *tandoori* and Madras-spiced
about 5 cups vegetable oil if frying

*available at East Indian markets, some specialty foods shops, and by mail order from Kalustyan's, 123 Lexington Avenue, New York, NY 10016, tel. (212) 685-3451

To fry pappadams:
In a heavy kettle heat 1½ inches oil over moderate heat until it registers 365° F. on a deep-fat thermometer and fry *pappadams* until crisp and golden, 2 or 3 seconds. With tongs transfer *pappadams* to paper towels to drain briefly.

To broil pappadams:
Preheat broiler.

Broil *pappadams* 4 to 6 inches from heat until they bubble and become opaque, about 10 seconds on each side. Serve *pappadams* within 1 hour of cooking. Makes 12 *pappadams*.

PHOTO ON PAGE 61

Herb-Baked Potato Chips with Crème Fraîche and Caviar

¼ cup olive oil
3 large russet (baking) potatoes (about
    1½ pounds total), scrubbed
1 tablespoon dried dill, crumbled
9 ounces caviar such as salmon roe
about 1 cup *crème fraîche* or sour cream

Preheat oven to 375° F. and brush 3 large baking sheets generously with some oil.

With a *mandoline* or other manual slicer cut 1 russet potato crosswise into ⅛-inch-thick slices. Immediately arrange slices in one layer on 1 baking sheet and brush with some remaining oil. Sprinkle potatoes with dill and salt and pepper to taste.

Bake slices in middle of oven until golden, 15 to 20 minutes, and with a metal spatula immediately transfer to a rack to cool completely. Repeat procedure with remaining potatoes and baking sheets in same manner. *Potato chips may be made 3 days ahead and kept in an airtight container at room temperature.*

Top potato chips with 1 teaspoon each of caviar and *crème fraîche* or sour cream, side by side. Makes about 80 hors d'oeuvres.

PHOTO ON PAGE 64

Red Bell Pepper and Coriander Pancakes with Smoked Salmon

For pancakes
⅔ cup all-purpose flour
¼ cup cornmeal
½ teaspoon dried hot red pepper flakes
⅔ cup milk
½ cup diced red bell pepper
3 tablespoons chopped fresh coriander leaves
2 large eggs, separated
1 tablespoon unsalted butter, melted

½ cup sour cream
5 ounces smoked salmon, cut into 46 strips
about 46 fresh coriander leaves, washed and dried

Make pancakes:
In a bowl stir together all pancake ingredients except egg whites and season batter with salt and pepper. In another bowl with an electric mixer beat egg whites until they just hold stiff peaks and gently fold into batter.

Heat a non-stick skillet over moderate heat and brush with some melted butter. Working in batches, drop tablespoonfuls of batter into skillet to form pancakes about 1¼ inches in diameter. Cook pancakes until bubbles appear on surface and undersides are golden, about 1 minute. Turn pancakes and cook until undersides are golden. Transfer pancakes to a rack and cool.

Spoon about ½ teaspoon sour cream onto center of each pancake and top with a twisted smoked salmon strip and a coriander leaf. Makes about 46 hors d'oeuvres.

Radishes with Chive Cream Cheese

8 medium radishes
2 tablespoons cream cheese, softened
1 teaspoon fresh lemon juice
2 tablespoons thinly sliced fresh chives

Trim root ends of radishes so radishes will stand upright and cut ¼ inch from stem ends. With a small melon-ball cutter scoop out center of each radish, leaving a ⅓-inch-thick shell.

In a small bowl whisk together cream cheese, lemon juice, chives, and salt and pepper to taste. With a small knife fill radishes with cream cheese mixture. Makes 8 hors d'oeuvres.

Shrimp Satés with Greek Garlic Sauce

7 large garlic cloves
1 pound medium shrimp (about 32),
    shelled
2 tablespoons chopped fresh rosemary leaves
½ cup plus 2 tablespoons extra-virgin olive oil
5 slices firm white sandwich bread, crusts
    removed, and bread torn into pieces
¼ cup sliced blanched almonds, ground fine
    in a food processor
6 tablespoons fresh lemon juice
sixteen 8-inch bamboo skewers, soaked in
    water 30 minutes

Chop 2 garlic cloves coarse and in a bowl stir together with shrimp, rosemary, and 2 tablespoons oil. *Marinate shrimp, covered and chilled, at least 1 hour and up to 24.*

Prepare grill.

In a small bowl soak bread in ¼ cup water 15 minutes and squeeze out excess water.

Chop remaining 5 garlic cloves fine and in a food processor purée with almonds, bread, and salt to taste until fluffy and very smooth. With motor running add remaining ½ cup oil in a slow stream, blending until sauce is emulsified, and blend in lemon juice. Transfer dipping sauce to a small bowl.

Thread 2 shrimp onto each skewer and grill on an oiled rack set 5 to 6 inches over glowing coals until just cooked through, about 2 minutes on each side.

Serve shrimp *satés* with dipping sauce at room temperature. Makes 16 *satés*.

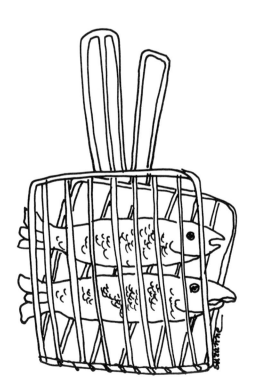

Toasted Tortillas with Herbed Goat Cheese

4 ounces soft mild goat cheese, at room
    temperature
2 teaspoons fresh thyme leaves
2 teaspoons fresh rosemary leaves, chopped fine
1 teaspoon coarsely ground black pepper
½ teaspoon coarse salt
2 teaspoons extra-virgin olive oil
four 6-inch flour tortillas

Preheat oven to 450° F.

In a bowl mash together all ingredients except tortillas. On oven rack toast tortillas in middle of oven, turning them once, until just golden and crisp, about 2 minutes on each side, and cool on a rack. Spread tortillas with goat cheese mixture and cut into serving pieces. Serves 4 as an hors d'oeuvre.

Tuna Satés with Wasabi Mayonnaise

1 cup mayonnaise
4 teaspoons soy sauce
1½ teaspoons sugar
2 teaspoons fresh lemon juice
2 teaspoons *wasabi* paste* (green horseradish
    paste), or to taste
a 12-ounce tuna steak, cut into twenty 1-inch
    cubes
ten 8-inch bamboo skewers, soaked in water
    30 minutes

*available at Japanese markets

In a bowl stir together mayonnaise, soy sauce, sugar, and lemon juice. Transfer ⅔ cup soy mayonnaise to a small bowl and stir in *wasabi* paste. Stir tuna into remaining ⅓ cup soy mayonnaise. *Chill wasabi mayonnaise, covered, at least 1 hour and up to 24. Marinate tuna, covered and chilled, at least 1 hour and up to 24.*

Prepare grill.

Thread 2 tuna cubes onto each skewer and grill tuna on an oiled rack set 5 to 6 inches over glowing coals until just cooked through, 2 to 3 minutes on each side.

Serve tuna *satés* with chilled *wasabi* mayonnaise. Makes 10 *satés*.

Zucchini Cones Filled with Lemon Mint Pea Purée

two 10-ounce packages frozen peas, thawed
1½ tablespoons unsalted butter
2 teaspoons freshly grated lemon zest
1½ tablespoons fresh lemon juice
2 teaspoons finely chopped fresh mint leaves
3 to 4 small zucchini (each about 7 inches long)

Garnish: 64 small fresh mint leaves

In a large heavy skillet cook peas in butter with salt and pepper to taste over moderate heat, stirring occasionally, 3 minutes.

In a food processor purée peas with zest until smooth. Cool purée and stir in lemon juice. *Purée may be made 2 days ahead and chilled, covered. Bring purée to room temperature before proceeding.* Stir in mint and season with salt and pepper.

Halve zucchini crosswise and trim so that each half is 3¼ inches long. With a *mandoline* or other manual slicer cut zucchini pieces lengthwise into ⅛-inch-thick slices. Transfer purée to a pastry bag fitted with a ¼-inch plain tip. Roll zucchini slices into cones and pipe some purée into each cone. Arrange cones on a tray, seam sides down. *Zucchini cones may be prepared up to this point 3 hours ahead and chilled, covered with damp paper towels and plastic wrap. Bring cones to cool room temperature before serving.*

Garnish hors d'oeuvres with mint leaves. Makes about 64 hors d'oeuvres.

PHOTO ON PAGE 64

Zucchini Stuffed with Feta and Roasted Red Peppers

two 6-ounce zucchini
⅓ cup finely chopped drained bottled roasted red peppers
⅓ cup finely chopped feta
⅛ teaspoon dried oregano, crumbled
freshly ground black pepper to taste

Cut zucchini crosswise into ¾-inch-thick sections, discarding ends, and with a melon-ball cutter scoop out center of each section, leaving ¹⁄₁₆-inch-thick shells and reserving centers for another use. In a steamer set over simmering water steam zucchini shells, covered, 4 minutes, or until barely tender but still bright green. Transfer shells to paper towels to drain upside down.

Preheat broiler and lightly oil a shallow flame-proof baking dish.

In a small bowl stir together roasted peppers, feta, oregano, and black pepper and mound in each shell. Arrange stuffed zucchini in baking dish and broil about 4 inches from heat until bubbling and beginning to turn golden, about 4 minutes. Makes about 16 hors d'oeuvres.

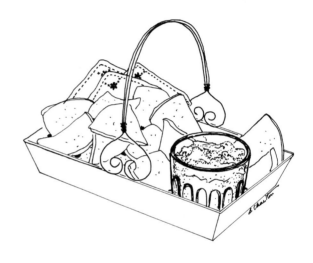

DIPS AND SPREADS

Cucumber Goat Cheese Spread

1 seedless cucumber, peeled, seeded, and chopped fine (about 1½ cups)
8 ounces soft mild goat cheese (about 1 cup), at room temperature
1½ teaspoons freshly grated lemon zest
1½ teaspoons fresh lemon juice
2 teaspoons finely chopped fresh tarragon leaves
2 tablespoons finely chopped red onion
½ teaspoon freshly ground black pepper

Accompaniment: toasted French bread slices or crackers

In a food processor purée ½ cup cucumber with goat cheese, zest, and lemon juice until almost smooth. In a bowl stir together cucumber mixture, remaining cucumber, tarragon, 1 tablespoon onion, and pepper. *Spread may be made 2 days ahead and chilled, covered. Let spread soften and stir it before serving.* Sprinkle spread with remaining tablespoon onion.

Serve spread with toasts or crackers. Makes about 1¼ cups.

Tomato Eggplant Spread and Parmesan Toasts

For Parmesan toasts
1 *baguette* (about 15 inches long), cut
    diagonally into ¼-inch-thick slices
about ¼ cup olive oil
⅓ cup freshly grated Parmesan
    (about 1 ounce)

¼ cup pine nuts
6 tablespoons olive oil
1 firm eggplant (about 1¼ pounds), cut into
    ½-inch cubes
1 onion, chopped
2 garlic cloves, 1 minced and 1 chopped and
    mashed to a paste with ½ teaspoon salt
3 vine-ripened tomatoes (about ¾ pound total),
    cut into ½-inch cubes
½ cup packed fresh basil leaves, washed well,
    spun dry, and chopped
⅓ cup packed fresh flat-leafed parsley
    leaves, washed well, spun dry, and
    chopped
3 tablespoons fresh lemon juice
½ teaspoon sugar

Make Parmesan toasts:
Preheat oven to 325° F.
On a large baking sheet arrange bread slices in one layer and lightly brush both sides of each slice with oil. Toast slices in middle of oven 15 minutes and turn over. Sprinkle slices with Parmesan and toast 15 minutes, or until golden. Transfer toasts to a rack and cool. *Parmesan toasts may be made 2 days ahead and kept in a sealable plastic bag at room temperature.*

In a large heavy skillet toast pine nuts in 3 tablespoons oil over moderate heat until golden and with a slotted spoon transfer to a small bowl. In oil remaining in skillet sauté eggplant, onion, minced garlic, and salt to taste over moderately high heat, stirring, until eggplant begins to brown. Cook mixture, covered, over moderate heat, stirring occasionally, until eggplant is tender, about 10 minutes, and transfer to a bowl. Cool mixture.

Into eggplant mixture stir garlic paste, tomatoes, basil, parsley, lemon juice, sugar, remaining 3 tablespoons oil, and salt and pepper to taste. *Spread may be made 2 days ahead and chilled, covered. Keep toasted pine nuts in a sealable plastic bag at room temperature. Bring eggplant spread to room temperature before serving.*

Just before serving, stir pine nuts into spread. Serve spread with toasts. Makes about 3 cups spread and about 45 toasts.

PHOTO ON PAGE 57

Artichoke Olive Dip with Fennel Crudités

a 14- to 16-ounce can whole artichoke hearts,
    rinsed well, drained, and patted dry
¼ cup olive oil
1 garlic clove, minced and mashed to a paste
    with ¼ teaspoon salt
½ cup brine-cured green olives such as
    picholine, pitted and chopped
3 tablespoons finely chopped parsley leaves

Garnish: fresh parsley sprigs
Accompaniment: 2 medium fennel bulbs
    (sometimes called anise), stalks trimmed flush
    with bulbs and bulbs cut lengthwise into strips
    or triangles for dipping

In a food processor purée artichoke hearts with oil until very smooth, about 2 minutes. Transfer purée to a bowl and stir in garlic paste, olives, and salt and pepper to taste. *Chill dip, covered, at least 4 hours and up to 24.* Stir chopped parsley into dip and garnish with parsley sprigs.

Serve artichoke olive dip with fennel. Makes about 1½ cups.

PHOTO ON PAGE 27

Brandied Chicken Liver Pâté

¾ cup finely chopped onion
1 large garlic clove, chopped fine
½ stick (¼ cup) unsalted butter
1 pound chicken livers, trimmed
¼ cup Cognac or other brandy
¼ teaspoon freshly grated nutmeg
a pinch ground allspice
⅓ cup dried currants

Accompaniment: toasted French bread slices
  or crackers

In a large heavy skillet cook onion and garlic in butter over moderate heat, stirring, until softened. Pat chicken livers dry and season with salt and pepper. Add livers to onion mixture and cook, stirring occasionally, until cooked through but barely pink inside, about 10 minutes. Add brandy and simmer 2 minutes. Transfer hot mixture to a food processor and add nutmeg, allspice, and salt and pepper to taste. Purée mixture until very smooth and cool pâté.

While pâté is cooling, in a bowl cover currants with boiling water and soak 5 minutes. Drain currants and pat dry between paper towels.

Transfer pâté to bowl and stir in currants. Pack pâté in a crock (or crocks). *Chill pâté, its surface covered with plastic wrap, at least 6 hours and up to 3 days. Bring pâté to room temperature before serving.*

Serve pâté with toasts or crackers. Makes about 1½ cups.

PHOTO ON PAGE 27

Baked Clams Oreganate

For crumb topping
¾ cup coarse dry bread crumbs (preferably
  from a crusty loaf of Italian bread)
1 large garlic clove, minced
2 tablespoons minced drained bottled
  roasted peppers
2 tablespoons extra-virgin olive oil
1 tablespoon minced fresh oregano leaves or
  ¾ teaspoon dried oregano, crumbled

24 small hard-shelled clams such as littlenecks,
  shucked, reserving 24 half shells
coarse sea or kosher salt for filling baking pan
  and serving platter

Preheat oven to 450° F.
Make topping:
In a small bowl stir together topping ingredients until combined well and season with salt and pepper.

Scrub reserved clam shells inside and out and dry. In a shallow baking pan spread coarse salt about ¼ inch deep and nestle shells in salt to keep them level. Return shucked clams to shells and cover generously with topping. *Clams may be prepared up to this point 1 hour ahead and chilled.*

Bake clams in middle of oven 10 minutes. Serve clams nestled in coarse salt on a platter. Makes 24 baked clams, serving 12 as part of an *antipasto* assortment.

PHOTO ON PAGE 77

Chilled Seafood Salad
with Herbed Olive Oil and Sea Salt

1 pound cleaned squid
1 pound small sea scallops
1 pound medium shrimp (about 25),
    shelled, leaving tail and connecting
    shell segment intact
For herbed olive oil
¾ cup extra-virgin olive oil
¾ cup coarsely chopped fresh flat-leafed
    parsley leaves
½ cup chopped fresh chives
1 tablespoon chopped fresh rosemary leaves
½ teaspoon table salt

2 lemons, sliced thin
fresh lemon juice to taste
coarse sea salt to taste plus additional
    for serving

Remove flaps from squid sacs if attached, reserving them, and cut sacs crosswise into ¼-inch-thick rings. Cut reserved flaps into ¼-inch-thick strips and halve tentacles lengthwise if large. Remove tough muscle from side of each scallop if necessary.

Have ready a large bowl of ice and cold water. In a large saucepan of boiling salted water cook shrimp 1 minute, or until pink and just cooked through, and transfer with a slotted spoon to ice water to stop cooking.

Add scallops to boiling water and cook at a bare simmer 2 minutes, or until just cooked through. Transfer scallops with slotted spoon to ice water to stop cooking.

Add squid to boiling water and cook 20 to 30 seconds, or until just opaque. Drain squid in a colander and transfer to ice water to stop cooking.

Drain seafood well in colander and transfer to a bowl. *Chill seafood, covered, until cold, at least 2 hours and up to 1 day.*

Make herbed oil:

In a blender blend together herbed oil ingredients on high speed 1 minute. Pour oil through a fine sieve into a bowl, pressing hard on solids, and discard solids. *Herbed oil may be made 2 days ahead and chilled, covered.*

One hour before serving, toss seafood with lemon slices and lemon juice. *Let seafood stand, covered and chilled, 1 hour to marinate.*

Divide seafood among 12 bowls and drizzle with herbed oil. Sprinkle salads with sea salt and serve additional sea salt on the side. Serves 12 as part of an *antipasto* assortment.

PHOTO ON PAGE 10

Tuna and Roasted Pepper Crostini

twenty-four ¼-inch-thick diagonal slices
    cut from a long thin loaf of Italian
    or French bread
For tuna spread
a 6-ounce can Italian tuna packed in olive
    oil such as Progresso, not drained
3 flat anchovy fillets
1 garlic clove, minced and mashed to a
    paste with a pinch salt
1 teaspoon drained capers
4 teaspoons fresh lemon juice
2 tablespoons mayonnaise

2 red bell peppers, quick-roasted and
    peeled (procedure on page 117)
    and cut into 24 strips
1 tablespoon drained capers
freshly ground black pepper

Preheat oven to 350° F.

On a large baking sheet arrange bread slices in one layer and toast in middle of oven until golden and crisp, about 10 minutes.

Make tuna spread:

In a food processor purée spread ingredients until blended well and season with salt and pepper.

Toasts, tuna spread, and roasted peppers may be prepared up to this point 3 days ahead, toasts kept in an airtight container at room temperature and tuna spread and roasted peppers chilled, covered, in separate bowls. Bring tuna spread and roasted peppers to room temperature before serving.

Top toasts with tuna spread and roasted pepper strips and sprinkle with capers and pepper to taste. Makes 24 *crostini*, serving 12 as part of an *antipasto* assortment.

PHOTO ON PAGE 77

Minted Fried Beets with Balsamic Vinegar Sauce

4 medium beets (about 1½ pounds total),
   scrubbed and trimmed, leaving about
   1 inch of stems attached
For balsamic vinegar sauce
½ cup balsamic vinegar
3 tablespoons finely chopped fresh
   mint leaves
2 tablespoons sugar
For batter
¾ cup all-purpose flour
¼ cup finely chopped fresh mint leaves
¼ teaspoon salt
¾ cup plus 1 tablespoon water

2 cups vegetable oil

In a large saucepan cover beets with salted water by 1 inch and simmer, covered, until tender, about 35 minutes. Drain beets in a colander and cool until they can be handled. Slip off and discard skins and stems. *Beets may be prepared up to this point 3 days ahead and chilled, covered.*

Make sauce:

In a very small saucepan simmer sauce ingredients, stirring occasionally, until reduced to about ¼ cup. Remove pan from heat and let sauce stand, covered, 15 minutes. Pour sauce through a fine sieve into a small bowl and cool. *Sauce may be made 3 days ahead and chilled, covered. Bring sauce to room temperature before serving.*

Make batter:

In a bowl whisk together flour, mint, and salt and add water, whisking until combined (batter will be lumpy).

Cut beets into ¼-inch-thick slices. In a deep 9-inch skillet heat oil over moderately high heat until it registers 375° F. on a deep-fat thermometer. Working in batches, dip beet slices in batter and fry, without crowding, until golden and crisp, about 1 minute on each side, making sure oil returns to 375° F. before adding next batch. Transfer beets as fried to paper towels and drain. *Beets may be made 2 hours ahead and reheated on a baking sheet in a 425° F. oven 10 minutes.*

Serve beets with sauce on the side for dipping. Serves 12 as part of an *antipasto* assortment.

Cauliflower Salad with Olives and Capers

1 head cauliflower, cut into 1-inch flowerets
   (about 6 cups)
a 3-ounce jar pimiento-stuffed olives, drained
   and chopped (about ¾ cup)
3 celery ribs, sliced thin diagonally
¼ cup chopped drained *peperoncini* (pickled
   Tuscan peppers)
2 tablespoons drained capers
½ cup drained caper berries*
For vinaigrette
3 tablespoons white-wine vinegar
3 tablespoons extra-virgin olive oil
6 flat anchovy fillets, or to taste

*available at specialty foods shops

In a large saucepan of boiling salted water cook cauliflower until just tender, about 4 minutes. In a colander drain cauliflower and rinse under cold water to stop cooking. Drain cauliflower well and in a large bowl toss with olives, celery, *peperoncini*, capers, and caper berries.

Make vinaigrette:

In a blender blend vinaigrette ingredients until combined well.

Add vinaigrette to salad, tossing well, and season with salt and pepper. *Salad will improve in flavor if kept, covered and chilled, at least 1 day and up to 3. Bring salad to room temperature before serving.* Serves 12 as part of an *antipasto* assortment.

TAPAS

Carrot Salad with Oregano and Cumin

2 tablespoons fresh oregano leaves, chopped fine
a rounded ½ teaspoon ground cumin
¼ teaspoon freshly grated lemon zest
1 tablespoon fresh lemon juice, or to taste
¼ cup extra-virgin olive oil
1 pound carrots, peeled and shredded fine

In a bowl whisk together oregano, cumin, zest, lemon juice, and salt and pepper to taste and whisk in oil in a stream until dressing is emulsified. Add carrots and toss to combine well. Serves 8 to 10 as part of a *tapas* buffet.

PHOTO ON PAGE 13

Meatballs in Tomato Garlic Sauce

For meatballs
1 large onion, chopped fine
1 large green bell pepper, chopped fine
¼ cup plus 2 tablespoons olive oil
2 pounds ground beef (not lean)
½ pound ground pork (not lean)
⅔ cup fine dry bread crumbs
2½ teaspoons salt
¼ teaspoon freshly grated nutmeg
¼ cup minced fresh parsley leaves
For sauce
4 large garlic cloves, minced
1 tablespoon olive oil
a 33½-ounce can whole tomatoes,
    including juice
¾ teaspoon dried oregano, crumbled

Make meatballs:

In a 9-inch heavy well-seasoned skillet (ideally cast-iron) cook onion and bell pepper in 2 tablespoons olive oil over moderately low heat, stirring occasionally, until softened and cool mixture. In a large bowl combine well onion mixture, ground meat, bread crumbs, salt, nutmeg, and parsley. Form level tablespoons of mixture into balls (about 90). In skillet heat 1 tablespoon oil over moderately high heat until hot but not smoking and brown meatballs in batches (about 15 at a time), shaking skillet frequently so that meatballs maintain their shape and adding remaining 3 tablespoons oil as necessary. Transfer meatballs with a slotted spoon as browned to a bowl.

Make sauce:

In a heavy kettle (at least 6 quarts) cook garlic in oil over moderately low heat, stirring, until fragrant, about 15 seconds. Add tomatoes with juice and oregano and simmer, breaking up tomatoes.

Add meatballs and simmer, covered, gently stirring occasionally, 25 minutes, or until meatballs are tender and sauce is thickened slightly. Transfer meatballs with slotted spoon to a heated serving dish. If sauce seems thin, boil gently, stirring frequently, until thickened to desired consistency. Season sauce with salt and pepper and spoon over meatballs. *Meatballs and sauce may be made 2 days ahead, cooled, uncovered, and chilled, covered. Reheat meatballs before serving.* Serves 8 to 10 as part of a *tapas* buffet.

PHOTO ON PAGE 14

Manchego Cheese with Quince Paste

1¼ pounds Manchego cheese*
a 14.1-ounce package *membrillo***
    (quince paste)

*available at some cheese shops, some specialty
    foods shops, and some supermarkets
**available at some specialty foods shops and
    some supermarkets (for stores call Goya Foods,
    tel. 201-348-4900)

Cut cheese into ¼-inch-thick wedges, discarding rind, and cut quince paste into ⅛-inch-thick rectangles. Top cheese wedges with quince paste wedges and arrange on a platter. Serves 8 to 10 as part of a *tapas* buffet.

PHOTO ON PAGE 15

Sherried Mushroom Empanadas

2 medium onions, chopped fine
¾ stick (6 tablespoons) unsalted butter
1½ pounds mushrooms, chopped fine
2 small red bell peppers, chopped fine
a 6-ounce piece *serrano* ham* or prosciutto,
    trimmed and chopped fine
⅓ cup cream Sherry
½ cup packed fresh parsley leaves, washed,
    spun dry, and minced
3 tablespoons fine dry bread crumbs
a 17¼-ounce package frozen puff pastry sheets
    (2 pastry sheets), thawed
an egg wash made by beating 1 large egg with
    1 teaspoon water

*available at specialty foods shops and by mail
    order from La Española, 25020 Doble Avenue,
    Harbor City, CA 90717, tel. (310) 539-0455

In a 12-inch heavy skillet cook onions in butter over moderately low heat, stirring occasionally, until softened. Stir in mushrooms and bell peppers and cook over moderate heat, stirring occasionally, until liquid mushrooms give off is evaporated and mixture begins to brown. Add ham and Sherry and cook, stirring, until liquid is evaporated.

In a bowl stir together mushroom mixture, parsley, bread crumbs, and salt and pepper to taste and cool, uncovered.

Preheat oven to 400° F.

On a lightly floured surface roll out 1 pastry sheet into a 14- by 10-inch rectangle. Halve rectangle lengthwise with a long sharp knife and spread about half of mushroom filling on 1 half, leaving a 1-inch border all around. Brush edges of mushroom-topped pastry with some egg wash and put remaining pastry half on top of filling. Crimp edges of dough together with fork tines and cut several slits in *empanada* with a sharp knife. Carefully transfer *empanada* with 2 spatulas to a large baking sheet, leaving room for second *empanada,* and brush with some egg wash. Make another *empanada* with remaining pastry sheet, filling, and egg wash in same manner.

Put *empanadas* in middle of oven and reduce temperature to 375° F. Bake *empanadas* until golden, about 35 minutes. *Empanadas may be made*

1 day ahead, cooled completely on a rack, and chilled, wrapped in foil. Reheat empanadas, uncovered, on a baking sheet in a preheated 375° F. oven until hot, about 6 minutes. With a serrated knife cut *empanadas* into ¾-inch slices. Serves 8 to 10 as part of a *tapas* buffet.

PHOTO ON PAGE 12

Mussels in Romesco Sauce

For sauce
2 dried mild red chilies such as New Mexico*,
    seeded and torn into large pieces (wear
    rubber gloves)
⅓ cup red-wine vinegar
¼ cup whole blanched almonds
⅔ cup olive oil
2 slices firm white sandwich bread
1 medium onion, chopped
3 large garlic cloves, chopped coarse
4 plum tomatoes (about ½ pound), peeled,
    seeded, and chopped
1 teaspoon sweet paprika

½ cup dry white wine
½ cup water
2 pounds mussels (preferably cultivated),
    scrubbed well and beards pulled off
2 tablespoons finely chopped, well-washed,
    and spun-dry fresh coriander sprigs

*available at Hispanic markets, some specialty
    foods shops, and by mail order from Chile
    Today—Hot Tamale, Inc., tel. (800) 468-7377
    or (908) 308-1151

Make sauce:

In a small bowl soak chilies, flesh sides down, in vinegar 30 minutes. Remove chilies, reserving vinegar in bowl, and scrape flesh from skins of chilies, discarding skins. Return chili flesh to reserved vinegar.

In a heavy skillet cook almonds in 2 tablespoons oil over moderately low heat, stirring, until golden and transfer with a slotted spoon to paper towels to drain. Heat oil remaining in skillet over moderate heat until hot but not smoking and fry bread, turning it, until golden. Transfer bread to a cutting board and cut into cubes.

In skillet heat remaining oil over moderate heat until hot but not smoking and cook onion, stirring, until edges are just golden. Add garlic and cook, stirring, until garlic is pale golden. Add chili mixture, almonds, bread cubes, tomatoes, and paprika and cook, stirring occasionally, 2 minutes. In a food processor purée mixture coarse and season with salt. *Sauce may be made 1 week ahead and chilled, covered.*

In a heavy kettle stir together wine, water, and 1 cup sauce, reserving remaining sauce for another use, and bring to a boil. Add mussels and boil gently, covered, 4 minutes, or until most are opened.

Transfer mussels to a serving dish, discarding any unopened ones. Simmer sauce, stirring, until reduced and slightly thickened and spoon over mussels. Sprinkle mussels with coriander. Serves 8 to 10 as part of a *tapas* buffet.

PHOTO ON PAGE 12

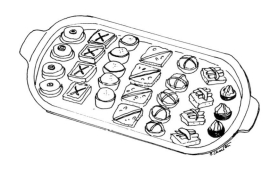

Almond-Stuffed Green Olives

two 10-ounce jars pitted large green olives (about 52), rinsed and drained
½ cup whole blanched almonds, toasted until golden and cooled
4 large garlic cloves, sliced thin
1 teaspoon dried hot red pepper flakes
1¾ cups olive oil

Stuff olives with almonds and in a glass bowl combine with remaining ingredients. *Marinate olives, covered and chilled, at least 3 days and up to 1 week.* Let olives stand at room temperature 15 minutes before serving. Makes about 4 cups.

PHOTO ON PAGE 13

Potato Saffron Omelet

2 large onions, chopped fine
5 tablespoons olive oil
3 russet (baking) potatoes (about 1½ pounds)
¼ teaspoon saffron threads
¼ cup chicken broth
6 large eggs
½ cup thinly sliced scallion greens

In a 12-inch non-stick skillet cook onions in 2 tablespoons oil over moderate heat, stirring occasionally, until golden, about 20 minutes. Transfer onions to a bowl and cool.

While onions are cooking, peel potatoes and cut into ½-inch cubes. In a saucepan of boiling salted water cook potatoes until almost tender, about 8 minutes, and drain well in a colander. Cool potatoes and add to onions. *Onion and potato mixture may be made 1 day ahead and chilled, covered.*

Crumble saffron threads into a small metal bowl. In a small saucepan heat broth until hot and pour over saffron. Let mixture stand until saffron is softened, about 5 minutes.

In a large bowl whisk together eggs, scallion greens, saffron mixture, and salt and pepper to taste and stir in onion and potato mixture. In skillet heat remaining 3 tablespoons oil over moderately high heat until hot but not smoking and add egg mixture, spreading potatoes evenly. Reduce heat to moderate and cook omelet, stirring occasionally, until eggs just begin to set, about 1 minute. Shift skillet so that one fourth of omelet is directly over center of burner and cook 1 minute. Shift skillet 3 more times, cooking remaining fourths in same manner. Center skillet and cook omelet over low heat until almost set, about 4 minutes more.

Slide omelet, bottom side down, onto a baking sheet and invert omelet back into skillet. Cook other side of omelet until golden, about 4 minutes. Slide omelet onto a platter and cool to room temperature. *Omelet may be made 1 day ahead and chilled, covered. Bring omelet to room temperature before serving.*

Cut omelet into wedges. Serves 8 to 10 as part of a *tapas* buffet.

PHOTO ON PAGE 14

Paprika-Glazed Baby Back Ribs

4 pounds baby back pork ribs, cut into
    individual ribs
6 garlic cloves, chopped fine
1½ cups dry red wine
½ cup water
2 tablespoons sweet paprika
3 tablespoons Sherry vinegar
1½ tablespoons firmly packed brown sugar
1 tablespoon salt

Divide ribs between two large heavy sealable plastic bags. In a bowl stir together remaining ingredients and pepper to taste and pour over ribs. Seal bags, pressing out excess air. *Marinate ribs, chilled, turning bags occasionally, at least 8 hours and up to 24.*

Preheat oven to 375° F.

Transfer ribs and marinade to a roasting pan large enough to hold ribs in one layer and roast ribs, turning occasionally, 2 hours, or until marinade is reduced to about 1 cup. *Ribs may be made 2 days ahead, cooled, uncovered, and chilled, covered. Reheat ribs in a preheated 375° F. oven until hot, about 12 minutes.* Serves 8 to 10 as part of a *tapas* buffet.

PHOTO ON PAGE 15

Citrus-and-Clove-Marinated Shrimp

5 cups water
1½ cups dry white wine
½ lemon, sliced
½ lime, sliced
¼ teaspoon ground cloves
1 tablespoon whole black peppercorns
1 tablespoon salt
1 bay leaf
two 2½-inch dried hot chilies*
1 large onion, quartered
3 pounds small shrimp (40 to 50 per pound),
    shelled, leaving tail and connecting shell
    segment intact
For marinade
1½ tablespoons white-wine vinegar
1 tablespoon fresh lemon juice
1 tablespoon fresh lime juice
¼ teaspoon ground cloves
½ cup extra-virgin olive oil
1 garlic clove, sliced thin

Accompaniment: lemon and lime wedges

*available at Hispanic markets, some specialty foods shops, and by mail order from Chile Today—Hot Tamale, Inc., tel. (800) 468-7377 or (908) 308-1151

In an 8-quart kettle bring water and wine to a boil with lemon, lime, cloves, peppercorns, salt, bay leaf, chilies, and onion and boil 5 minutes. Add shrimp and cook, stirring occasionally, until just cooked through, about 3 minutes. Drain shrimp in a colander and cool 5 minutes.

Make marinade:

In a bowl whisk together vinegar, lemon and lime juices, cloves, and salt and pepper to taste and whisk in oil in a stream until marinade is emulsified. Stir in garlic.

In a large glass bowl combine warm shrimp and marinade and cool shrimp completely. *Marinate shrimp, covered and chilled, stirring occasionally, at least 8 hours and up to 12.*

Serve shrimp with lemon and lime wedges. Serves 8 to 10 as part of a *tapas* buffet.

PHOTO ON PAGE 14

Romaine with Lemon Dressing

1⅓ tablespoons fresh lemon juice
2 teaspoons white-wine vinegar
⅓ cup extra-virgin olive oil
2 heads romaine, washed, spun dry, and torn
    into bite-size pieces (about 12 cups)

In a large bowl whisk together lemon juice, vinegar, and salt and pepper to taste and whisk in oil in a stream until dressing is emulsified. Add romaine and toss to combine well. Serves 8 to 10 as part of a *tapas* buffet.

PHOTO ON PAGE 13

BREADS

Classic Popovers

2 large eggs
¾ cup milk
¼ cup water
1 tablespoon unsalted butter, melted
1 cup minus 2 tablespoons all-purpose flour
½ teaspoon salt

Preheat oven to 375° F. and generously grease six ⅔-cup popover tins or nine ½-cup muffin tins.

In a bowl whisk together eggs, milk, and water and add butter in a stream, whisking. Add flour and salt and whisk mixture until combined well but still slightly lumpy. Divide batter among tins and bake in lower third of oven 45 minutes. Cut a slit about ½ inch long on top of each popover with a small sharp knife and bake 10 minutes more. Makes 6 large or 9 medium popovers.

Gruyère Caraway Popovers

½ teaspoon caraway seeds
ingredients for classic popovers (recipe precedes), eliminating butter
½ cup coarsely grated Gruyère (about 2 ounces)

With a mortar and pestle or in an electric coffee/spice grinder coarsely grind ¼ teaspoon caraway seeds. Follow recipe for classic popovers, whisking ground caraway seeds into batter. Divide half of batter among tins and sprinkle ¼ cup Gruyère over batter in tins. Divide remaining batter among tins and sprinkle remaining ¼ cup Gruyère and whole caraway seeds over popovers and bake according to recipe for classic popovers. Makes 6 large or 9 medium popovers.

Chili Cheddar Popovers

ingredients for classic popovers (recipe opposite), eliminating butter
¾ teaspoon chili powder
⅛ teaspoon cayenne, or to taste
½ cup coarsely grated extra-sharp Cheddar (about 2 ounces)

Follow recipe for classic popovers, whisking chili powder and cayenne into batter. Divide half of batter among tins. Sprinkle ¼ cup Cheddar over batter in tins and divide remaining batter among tins. Sprinkle remaining ¼ cup Cheddar over popovers and bake according to recipe for classic popovers. Makes 6 large or 9 medium popovers.

Whole-Wheat Walnut Popovers

¼ cup walnuts
½ cup all-purpose flour
⅓ cup whole-wheat flour
2 large eggs
¾ cup milk
¼ cup water
½ teaspoon salt

Preheat oven to 375° F. and generously grease six ⅔-cup popover tins or nine ½-cup muffin tins. Chop 2 tablespoons walnuts fine and coat tins with them, knocking out excess.

In a food processor blend flours and remaining 2 tablespoons walnuts until walnuts are ground fine. In a bowl whisk together eggs, milk, water, flour mixture, and salt until batter is combined well but still slightly lumpy.

Divide batter among tins and bake in lower third of oven 45 minutes. Cut a slit about ½ inch long on top of each popover with a small sharp knife and bake 8 minutes more. (Popovers will not rise as much as classic version because of walnuts.) Makes 6 large or 9 medium popovers.

Lemon, Pepper, and Thyme Popovers

ingredients for classic popovers (page 109)
1 tablespoon freshly grated lemon zest
½ teaspoon coarsely ground black pepper
2 teaspoons chopped fresh thyme leaves

Follow recipe for classic popovers, whisking zest, pepper, and 1 teaspoon thyme into batter and sprinkling remaining teaspoon thyme over popovers before baking. Makes 6 large or 9 medium popovers.

Garlic Parmesan Popovers

ingredients for classic popovers (page 109),
    eliminating butter
1 large garlic clove
½ cup freshly grated Parmesan (about 1½ ounces)

Follow recipe for classic popovers but, before adding salt, mince garlic and mash with salt. Whisk garlic paste into batter and divide half of batter among tins. Sprinkle ¼ cup Parmesan over batter in tins and divide remaining batter among tins. Sprinkle

remaining ¼ cup Parmesan over popovers and bake according to recipe for classic popovers. (Popovers will not rise as much as classic version because of Parmesan.) Makes 6 large or 9 medium popovers.

Curry Cumin Popovers

½ teaspoon cumin seeds
ingredients for classic popovers
    (page 109)
1 teaspoon curry powder

With a mortar and pestle or in an electric coffee/ spice grinder coarsely grind ¼ teaspoon cumin seeds. Follow recipe for classic popovers, whisking ground cumin seeds and curry powder into batter and sprinkling whole cumin seeds over popovers before baking. Makes 6 large or 9 medium popovers.

Cornmeal Bread

¾ cup warm water (105°–115° F.)
a ¼-ounce package (2½ teaspoons)
    fast-acting yeast
½ teaspoon sugar
1¼ cups all-purpose flour
⅓ cup yellow cornmeal
1 teaspoon salt

Lightly grease 2 loaf pans, 5½ by 3 by 2½ inches.
In a bowl stir together warm water, yeast, and sugar and let stand until foamy, about 5 minutes. In a small bowl stir together flour, cornmeal, and salt and gradually stir into yeast mixture, stirring until a soft dough is formed. On a lightly floured work surface with floured hands knead dough 5 minutes, or until smooth and elastic, and shape into a ball. Let dough rest, covered, 10 minutes.
Form dough into 2 ovals. Transfer dough to loaf pans and let rise, covered loosely with plastic wrap, in a warm place until doubled in bulk, about 30 minutes.
Preheat oven to 400° F.
Bake loaves in middle of oven 20 minutes, or until tops are golden and bread pulls away slightly from sides of pans. Cool loaves in pans on a rack. *Bread may be made 1 day ahead and kept wrapped*

in plastic wrap at room temperature or frozen, wrapped in plastic wrap, up to 2 weeks. Makes 2 loaves, each loaf serving 4.

☞ Each serving about 98 calories, 1 gram fat
(4% of calories from fat)

Grilled Olive Toasts

six ½-inch-thick slices from a loaf of olive bread
or other rustic bread
1 garlic clove if desired
extra-virgin olive oil for brushing toasts

Prepare grill or heat a well-seasoned ridged grill pan over moderately high heat until hot but not smoking.

Grill bread in batches on a rack set 5 to 6 inches over glowing coals or in hot grill pan until golden with dark grill marks, about 1 minute on each side. Lightly rub 1 side of each toast with garlic. Brush same side of each toast with oil and season with salt.

Cut toasts into serving pieces if desired. Serves 6.

PHOTO ON PAGE 50

Sofrito Grilled Bread

1 cup chopped red bell pepper (about 1 small)
½ cup chopped onion (about 1 small)
¼ cup packed fresh coriander sprigs, washed
well and spun dry
2 garlic cloves, minced
1 teaspoon dried oregano, crumbled
½ teaspoon cumin seeds
twelve ¼-inch-thick slices nonfat country-style
bread (12 ounces total)

In a blender purée all ingredients except bread until smooth. In a small heavy saucepan simmer *sofrito*, stirring, 3 minutes and season with salt and pepper. *Sofrito may be made 2 days ahead and chilled, covered.*

Prepare grill.

If desired halve bread slices. Spread some *sofrito* on 1 side of each bread slice (reserving any remaining *sofrito* for another use) and grill, *sofrito* side down, on an oiled rack set 5 to 6 inches over

glowing coals until golden brown, about 2 minutes. (Alternatively, bread may be grilled in a hot well-seasoned ridged grill pan over moderately high heat.) Transfer *sofrito* bread as grilled with tongs to a bread basket. Serves 6.

☞ Each serving about 125 calories, 1 gram fat
(5% of calories from fat)

PHOTO ON PAGE 42

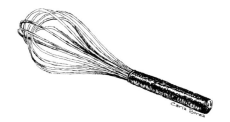

Buttermilk Biscuits

3 cups all-purpose flour
1 tablespoon baking powder
1½ teaspoons salt
½ teaspoon baking soda
¼ cup cold vegetable shortening
2 tablespoons cold unsalted butter, cut into bits
1⅓ cups well-shaken buttermilk
an egg wash made by beating 1 large egg with
1 tablespoon water

Preheat oven to 450° F.

In a large bowl whisk together flour, baking powder, salt, and baking soda until combined well. With a pastry blender or your fingertips blend in shortening and butter until mixture resembles coarse meal. Add buttermilk, stirring with a fork to form a soft dough, and with floured hands knead dough gently 4 times in bowl.

On a lightly floured surface pat dough out into a ½-inch-thick round. Cut out as many biscuits as possible with a 2-inch round cutter dipped in flour and invert ½ inch apart onto a large baking sheet. Gather scraps into a ball. Pat out dough and cut out more biscuits in same manner. Brush biscuits with egg wash and bake in middle of oven 12 minutes, or until golden. Cool biscuits on racks. *Biscuits may be made 8 hours ahead and kept, wrapped well, at room temperature. Reheat biscuits, wrapped in foil, before serving.* Makes about 18 biscuits.

PHOTO ON PAGE 16

Pumpkin Cranberry Bread

1 cup canned solid-pack pumpkin
1 cup sugar
¼ cup water
2 large eggs
¼ cup vegetable oil
2 cups all-purpose flour
2 teaspoons baking powder
½ teaspoon salt
¼ teaspoon baking soda
¼ teaspoon ground cinnamon
¼ teaspoon ground ginger
⅛ teaspoon ground cloves
1 cup picked-over fresh or frozen cranberries

Preheat oven to 350° F. and butter a loaf pan, 8½ by 4½ by 2¾ inches.

In a large bowl with an electric mixer beat together pumpkin, sugar, water, eggs, and oil. Sift in flour, baking powder, salt, baking soda, and spices and stir just until batter is smooth. Stir in cranberries and spoon batter into loaf pan, spreading evenly.

Bake bread in middle of oven 1 hour and 15 minutes, or until a tester comes out clean, and cool in pan on a rack 10 minutes. Turn bread out onto rack and cool completely. *Bread may be made 4 days ahead and chilled, covered.* Makes 1 loaf.

FOCACCIA AND PIZZAS

Leaner/Lighter Quick Focaccia

¾ cup warm water (105°–115° F.)
a ¼-ounce package (2½ teaspoons) fast-acting yeast
½ teaspoon sugar
2 cups all-purpose flour
1 teaspoon table salt
1 tablespoon freshly grated Parmesan
2 teaspoons chopped fresh rosemary leaves
coarse salt to taste

Lightly grease a baking pan, 13 by 9 by 2 inches.
In a bowl stir together water, yeast, and sugar and let stand until foamy, about 5 minutes. In a small bowl stir together flour and table salt and gradually stir into yeast mixture until mixture forms a soft dough. On a lightly floured work surface with floured hands knead dough 5 minutes, or until elastic and smooth, and shape into a ball. Invert bowl over dough and let dough rest 10 minutes.

On lightly floured surface roll out dough into a 13- by 9-inch rectangle and transfer to baking pan, pressing into corners. Let dough rise, covered loosely with plastic wrap, in a warm place 30 minutes, or until doubled in bulk.

Preheat oven to 400° F.

Sprinkle dough with Parmesan, rosemary, coarse salt, and pepper to taste. Press indentations about ¼ inch deep and 1 inch apart all over dough with lightly oiled fingertips and bake *focaccia* in middle of oven 20 minutes, or until golden. Cool *focaccia* in pan on a rack. Makes four 6- by 4-inch servings.

☙ Each serving about 242 calories, 1 gram fat
(4% of calories from fat)

Parmesan Focaccia

a ¼-ounce package (2½ teaspoons) active dry yeast
1 cup warm water (105°–115° F.)
¼ cup extra-virgin olive oil
1 cup freshly grated Parmigiano-Reggiano (about 3 ounces)
2 tablespoons finely chopped fresh sage leaves or 1 tablespoon dried sage, crumbled
¼ cup finely chopped onion
3 to 3½ cups unbleached all-purpose flour or bread flour
1 teaspoon salt

In a large bowl sprinkle yeast over water and let stand until foamy, about 5 minutes. Stir in oil, Parmigiano-Reggiano, sage, and onion. Add 3 cups flour and salt and stir until mixture forms a soft, slightly sticky dough. Knead dough on a lightly floured surface until smooth and elastic, about 10 minutes, adding some of remaining ½ cup flour if dough is too sticky.

Form dough into a ball and transfer to an oiled

bowl, turning to coat. Let dough rise, covered with a kitchen towel, in a warm draft-free place until doubled in bulk, about 1½ hours.

While dough is rising, oil a baking pan, 13 by 9 by 2 inches.

Flatten dough to eliminate air bubbles and stretch and pat out to fit bottom of pan. Let dough rise, covered loosely with towel, in a warm draft-free place about 30 minutes more, or until puffed.

While dough is rising, preheat oven to 450° F.

Bake *focaccia* in middle of oven until golden brown, about 20 minutes, and cool slightly in pan on a rack. Serve *focaccia* warm.

Radicchio, Feta, and Olive Pizzas

4 teaspoons yellow cornmeal
1 recipe leaner/lighter pizza dough (recipe follows)
¼ cup dry red wine
2 large heads *radicchio* (about 1¼ pounds), cores discarded, and *radicchio* cut into ½-inch-thick slices
1 large onion (about ¾ pound), sliced thin
16 Kalamata or other brine-cured black olives, pitted and cut into strips
2 ounces feta, crumbled (about ½ cup)
1 teaspoon cumin seeds

Preheat oven to 500° F.

On a work surface sprinkled with 1 teaspoon yellow cornmeal roll out 1 piece of pizza dough into a 12- by 6-inch oval and transfer to a baking sheet. Repeat with remaining cornmeal and dough, ending up with 2 ovals on each of 2 baking sheets.

In a large saucepan simmer wine, *radicchio*, onion, and salt to taste over moderate heat until almost all liquid is evaporated, 3 to 5 minutes.

Spoon mixture evenly over dough ovals, leaving a ½-inch border around edge of each pizza, and sprinkle with olives, feta, and cumin seeds.

Bake pizzas in lower and middle thirds of oven 15 minutes, or until crusts are crisp and pale golden. Makes 4 pizzas, serving 4.

🍂 Each serving about 400 calories, 10 grams fat
(23% of calories from fat)

Leaner/Lighter Pizza Dough

¾ cup warm water (110°–115° F.) plus additional tablespoon if necessary
a ¼-ounce package (2½ teaspoons) active dry yeast
2 cups all-purpose flour
1½ teaspoons salt

In a large bowl stir together water and yeast and let stand until foamy, about 5 minutes. Stir in flour and salt and blend until mixture forms a dough, adding additional tablespoon water if too dry. On a lightly floured surface knead dough about 10 minutes, or until smooth and elastic. (Alternatively, dough may be made in a standing electric mixer. In bowl of mixer make dough as described above. With dough hook knead dough about 5 minutes, or until smooth and elastic.)

Put dough in a very lightly oiled deep bowl and turn to coat. *Let dough rise, covered loosely, in a warm place 1½ hours, or until doubled in bulk.* Punch down dough and divide into 4 pieces. *Dough keeps, each piece put in a small sealable plastic bag and sealed, pressing out excess air, chilled overnight or frozen 2 weeks. If dough is frozen, thaw overnight in refrigerator before using.* Makes enough dough for four 12- by 6-inch oval pizzas.

🍂 Each serving about 244 calories, 1 gram fat
(2% of calories from fat)

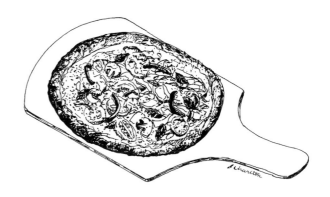

Roasted Bell Pepper, Ricotta, and Caper Pizzas

2 large red bell peppers, cut into ¼-inch strips
2 large yellow bell peppers, cut into
    ¼-inch strips
2 tablespoons balsamic vinegar
4 teaspoons yellow cornmeal
1 recipe leaner/lighter pizza dough (page 113)
½ cup reduced-fat ricotta
4 teaspoons drained capers
freshly ground black pepper to taste

Preheat oven to 450° F.

Spread bell peppers in a large shallow baking pan and season with salt. Roast peppers in middle of oven, stirring once halfway through roasting, 20 to 30 minutes, or until they begin to brown. Remove pan from oven and sprinkle peppers with vinegar, scraping up brown bits from bottom of pan. *Bell peppers may be roasted 1 day ahead and chilled, covered.*

Increase temperature to 500° F.

On a work surface sprinkled with 1 teaspoon cornmeal roll out 1 piece of dough into a 12- by 6-inch oval and transfer to a baking sheet. Repeat with remaining cornmeal and dough, ending up with 2 ovals on each of 2 baking sheets.

Spread bell peppers evenly on dough ovals, leaving a ½-inch border around edge of each pizza. Spoon half-teaspoonfuls of ricotta onto bell peppers and sprinkle pizzas with capers and black pepper.

Bake pizzas in lower and middle thirds of oven 15 minutes, or until crusts are crisp and pale golden. Makes 4 pizzas, serving 4.

🍃 Each serving about 298 calories, 2 grams fat
(5% of calories from fat)

Shiitake and Gruyère Pizzas

1 teaspoon olive oil
1 pound fresh *shiitake* mushrooms, stems
    discarded and caps cut into ½-inch-thick slices
1 pound white mushrooms, cut into ¼-inch-thick
    slices
2 large garlic cloves, minced
2 tablespoons medium-dry Sherry
1 tablespoon fresh lemon juice
4 teaspoons yellow cornmeal
1 recipe leaner/lighter pizza dough
    (page 113)
½ cup packed fresh parsley leaves, washed well,
    spun dry, and chopped
3 ounces Gruyère, grated (about ¾ cup)

Preheat oven to 500° F.

In a large heavy non-stick skillet heat oil over moderately high heat until hot but not smoking and sauté mushrooms and garlic with Sherry, lemon juice, and salt to taste 10 minutes, or until liquid is evaporated. Cool mixture slightly. *Mushroom mixture may be made 1 day ahead and chilled, covered.*

On a work surface sprinkled with 1 teaspoon cornmeal roll out 1 piece of dough into a 12- by 6-inch oval and transfer to a baking sheet. Repeat with remaining cornmeal and dough, ending up with 2 ovals on each of 2 baking sheets.

Stir parsley and Gruyère into mushroom mixture and spread evenly on dough ovals, leaving a ½-inch border around edge of each pizza.

Bake pizzas in lower and middle thirds of oven 15 minutes, or until crusts are crisp and pale golden. Makes 4 pizzas, serving 4.

🍃 Each serving about 426 calories, 10 grams fat
(21% of calories from fat)

ZOE MAVRIDIS

Butternut Squash, Parmesan, and Sage Pizzas

a 2¼-pound butternut squash, peeled, seeded,
    and cut into ½-inch cubes
1 teaspoon vegetable oil
1½ cups low-fat (1%) milk
2 tablespoons all-purpose flour
a pinch freshly grated nutmeg
4 teaspoons yellow cornmeal
1 recipe leaner/lighter pizza dough (page 113)
⅔ cup freshly grated Parmesan
    (about 2 ounces)
1 tablespoon chopped fresh sage leaves
1 large garlic clove, minced
freshly ground black pepper to taste

Garnish: fresh sage sprigs

Preheat oven to 450° F.

In a bowl toss squash with oil and salt and pepper to taste. Spread squash in one layer in a shallow baking pan and roast in middle of oven, stirring once halfway through roasting, 15 minutes, or until lightly browned. Remove pan from oven and loosen squash with a metal spatula. *Squash may be roasted 1 day ahead and chilled, covered.*

In a medium heavy saucepan stir together milk and flour and bring to a simmer over moderate heat, stirring constantly. Simmer sauce, stirring, 2 minutes and stir in nutmeg and salt to taste. *Sauce may be made 1 day ahead and chilled, covered.*

Increase temperature to 500° F.

On a work surface sprinkled with 1 teaspoon cornmeal roll out 1 piece of dough into a 12- by 6-inch oval and transfer to a baking sheet. Repeat with remaining cornmeal and dough, ending up with 2 ovals on each of 2 baking sheets.

Spread sauce on dough ovals, leaving a ½-inch border around edge of each pizza, and sprinkle with grated Parmesan, roasted squash, chopped sage, garlic, and pepper.

Bake pizzas in lower and middle thirds of oven 15 minutes, or until crusts are crisp and pale golden. Garnish pizzas with sage sprigs. Makes 4 pizzas, serving 4.

🍂 Each serving about 472 calories, 8 grams fat
(14% of calories from fat)

Roasted Tomato, Eggplant, and Smoked Mozzarella Pizzas

1 medium eggplant (about 1½ pounds), cut
    crosswise into 2 pieces
¾ pound plum tomatoes, halved
2 teaspoons red-wine vinegar
¼ teaspoon sugar
4 teaspoons yellow cornmeal
1 recipe leaner/lighter pizza dough (page 113)
½ cup fresh basil leaves, washed well, spun dry,
    and chopped coarse
¼ pound smoked mozzarella, grated coarse
    (about 1 cup)

Preheat oven to 450° F. and very lightly grease a large baking sheet.

Cut smaller eggplant piece into ¼-inch-thick slices. Spread eggplant slices in one layer on half of baking sheet and season with salt. Put remaining eggplant piece and all but 2 tomato halves on other half of baking sheet. Roast vegetables in middle of oven 15 minutes, or until eggplant slices are tender, and transfer eggplant slices to a plate. Roast remaining vegetables 15 minutes more, or until eggplant piece is very tender. Remove baking sheet from oven and cool vegetables slightly.

Scoop out flesh from eggplant piece into a food processor and purée with roasted tomatoes, unroasted tomato, vinegar, sugar, and salt to taste. *Sauce and sliced eggplant may be made 1 day ahead and kept separately, covered and chilled.*

On a work surface sprinkled with 1 teaspoon cornmeal roll out 1 piece of dough into a 12- by 6-inch oval and transfer to a baking sheet. Repeat with remaining cornmeal and dough, ending up with 2 ovals on each of 2 baking sheets.

Increase temperature to 500° F.

Spread sauce on dough ovals, leaving a ½-inch border around edge of each pizza. Arrange eggplant slices on sauce and sprinkle pizzas with basil and mozzarella.

Bake pizzas in lower and middle thirds of oven 15 minutes, or until crusts are crisp and pale golden. Makes 4 pizzas, serving 4.

🍂 Each serving about 404 calories, 8 grams fat
(18% of calories from fat)

*Grilled Pizza with Fresh Corn, Bell Pepper,
Pancetta, and Fontina*

2 rounds pizza dough for grilled pizza
    (recipe follows), rolled out
    and chilled
olive oil for brushing dough
1½ cups coarsely grated Fontina,
    preferably Italian (about
    9 ounces)
1 cup fresh corn (cut from 2 to 3 ears)
1 red bell pepper, chopped fine
2 *poblano* chilies* if desired, roasted
    (procedure on page 117)
6 slices (about 5 ounces) *pancetta* (Italian
    unsmoked cured bacon) or bacon,
    cooked until crisp
¼ cup chopped scallions
¼ cup packed fresh coriander sprigs,
    washed well and spun dry

*available at Mexican markets and some
    specialty produce markets

Prepare grill:

Open vents in lid and bottom of a kettle grill and put 25 briquets on 2 opposite sides of bottom, leaving middle clear. Oil rack and position with wider openings over briquets. Light briquets. (They will be ready for cooking as soon as they turn grayish-white, 20 to 30 minutes.)

Remove plastic wrap from 2 pieces of rolled-out pizza dough (if grill is not large, work with 1 piece at a time, keeping remaining piece chilled) and lightly brush dough with some oil. Trying not to stretch dough, carefully transfer it, oiled side down, with your hands to rack of grill. (If it's a very hot day, the dough may get too soft to transfer easily; if so, freeze it until firm again, about 15 minutes.) Lightly brush top with some oil. When grilling pizzas, rotate them if one side of grill is hotter than the other. Grill crusts, covered, until undersides are golden brown, about 4 minutes. Flip crusts over with 2 metal spatulas and top each crust with half of Fontina, corn, bell pepper, *poblanos*, *pancetta* or bacon, and scallions. Grill pizzas, covered, about 5 minutes more, or until undersides are golden brown and cheese is melted.

Top pizzas with coriander and cut into wedges. Makes 2 pizzas, serving 2.

PHOTO ON PAGE 52

Pizza Dough for Grilled Pizza

⅔ cup lukewarm water (105°–115° F.)
a ¼-ounce package (2½ teaspoons) active
    dry yeast
½ teaspoon sugar
2 tablespoons olive oil
1¾ to 2 cups unbleached all-purpose flour
¼ cup finely ground yellow cornmeal
2 teaspoons coarse salt

In a large bowl stir together ⅓ cup water, yeast, and sugar and let stand until foamy, about 10 minutes. Stir in remaining ⅓ cup water, oil, 1¾ cups flour, cornmeal, and salt and blend until mixture forms a dough. Knead dough on a floured surface, incorporating as much of remaining ¼ cup flour as necessary to prevent dough from sticking, until smooth and elastic, 5 to 10 minutes.

Alternatively, dough may be made in a food processor. Proof yeast as described above. In food processor process yeast mixture with 1¾ cups flour, cornmeal, and salt until mixture forms a ball, adding more water, 1 teaspoon at a time, if too dry or more flour, 1 tablespoon at a time, if too wet, and knead dough by processing 15 seconds more.

Put dough, prepared by either method, in an oiled deep bowl and turn to coat with oil. *Let dough rise, covered with plastic wrap, in a warm place 1 hour, or until doubled in bulk.* Punch down dough and form into 4 balls.

Lightly brush a baking sheet with olive oil.

On a lightly floured surface roll out 1 ball of dough ⅛ inch thick (about 10 inches in diameter). Brushing off excess flour, transfer dough with your hands to baking sheet and cover surface completely with plastic wrap. Repeat procedure with remaining dough balls and plastic wrap in same manner, stacking rolled-out pieces on top of one another on baking sheet. Wrap baking sheet with more plastic wrap to ensure that dough is completely covered. *Chill dough at least until firm, about 1 hour, and up to 4.* Makes four 10-inch pizza rounds.

To Roast Bell Peppers or Chilies

Note: Wear rubber gloves when handling chilies.

Gas stove method:

Lay peppers on their sides on racks of burners (preferably 1 to a burner) and turn flame on high. Char peppers, turning them with tongs, until skins are blackened, 6 to 8 minutes. (If peppers are small, as are chilies, spear through stem end with a long-handled fork and rest on burner rack.)

Transfer peppers to a bowl and let stand, covered, until cool enough to handle. Peel peppers. Cut off tops and discard seeds and ribs.

Broiler method:

Preheat broiler.

Broil peppers on rack of a broiler pan under broiler about 2 inches from heat, turning them every 5 minutes, until skins are blistered and charred, 15 to 20 minutes.

Transfer peppers to a bowl and let stand, covered, until cool enough to handle. Peel peppers. Cut off tops and discard seeds and ribs.

Quick broiler method:

Quarter peppers lengthwise, discarding stems, seeds, and ribs. Put peppers, skin sides up, on rack of a broiler pan and broil about 2 inches from heat until skins are blistered and charred, 8 to 12 minutes.

Transfer peppers to a bowl and let stand, covered, until cool enough to handle. Peel peppers.

Grilled Pizza with Yellow Squash, Mozzarella, and Lemon Thyme

1 garlic clove, chopped
3 tablespoons extra-virgin olive oil
1 medium yellow squash
2 rounds pizza dough for grilled pizza, rolled out and chilled (page 116)
¾ cup coarsely grated fresh mozzarella (about 3 ounces)
¾ cup freshly grated Parmesan (about 2¼ ounces)
4 teaspoons chopped fresh thyme leaves (preferably lemon thyme)

Garnish: fresh thyme sprigs

In a small bowl stir together garlic and oil and let stand 15 minutes.

With a *mandoline* or other manual slicer, slice yellow squash crosswise into 1/16-inch-thick rounds, transferring to a plate.

Prepare grill:

Open vents in lid and bottom of a kettle grill and put 25 briquets on 2 opposite sides of bottom, leaving middle clear. Oil rack and position with wider openings over briquets. Light briquets. (They will be ready for cooking as soon as they turn grayish-white, 20 to 30 minutes.)

Remove plastic wrap from 2 pieces of rolled-out pizza dough (if grill is not large, work with 1 piece at a time, keeping remaining piece chilled) and lightly brush dough with some garlic oil. Trying not to stretch dough, carefully transfer it, oiled side down, with your hands to rack of grill. (If it's a very hot day, the dough may get too soft to transfer easily; if so, freeze it until firm again, about 15 minutes.) Lightly brush top with some garlic oil. When grilling pizzas, rotate them if one side of grill is hotter than the other. Grill crusts, covered, until undersides are golden brown on bottom, about 4 minutes. Flip crusts over with 2 metal spatulas and top each crust with half of cheeses, squash, and thyme. Lightly brush pizzas with some garlic oil and grill, covered, about 5 minutes, or until undersides are golden brown and cheeses are melted.

Garnish pizzas with thyme sprigs and cut into wedges. Makes 2 pizzas, serving 2.

PHOTO ON PAGE 55

SOUPS

Chilled White Bean Salsa Soup

1 cup dried white beans such as *cannellini*
    or Great Northern, picked over
1 yellow onion, halved
1 bay leaf
1 fresh thyme sprig
2¼ pounds vine-ripened tomatoes, cored
    and quartered
1 medium red bell pepper, chopped fine
1 medium yellow bell pepper, chopped fine
1 medium red onion, chopped fine
1 small fresh *jalapeño* chili, minced (wear
    rubber gloves)
3 tablespoons red-wine vinegar
1 tablespoon extra-virgin olive oil
¼ cup packed fresh coriander sprigs, washed
    well, spun dry, and chopped fine

In a 4-quart saucepan simmer beans, yellow onion, bay leaf, and thyme in water to cover by 3 inches, partially covered with lid, until beans are tender, about 50 minutes. Season beans with salt and cool completely in cooking liquid. Drain beans in a colander and discard yellow onion, bay leaf, and thyme. *White beans may be cooked 1 day ahead and chilled, covered.*

Finely chop enough of tomatoes to measure 1½ cups and reserve. In a blender purée remaining tomatoes, half of bell peppers, and half of red onion until smooth and in a bowl stir together purée, beans, reserved tomatoes, remaining bell peppers and red onion, *jalapeño*, vinegar, oil, and salt to taste. *Chill soup, covered, at least until cold, about 6 hours, and up to 1 day.* Before serving, stir in coriander and season with salt and pepper if necessary. Makes about 8 cups, serving 4 as a main course.

🍃 Each serving about 258 calories, 5 grams fat
(17% of calories from fat)

Chilled Corn Soup with Herbed Chicken

1 pound boneless skinless chicken breast
1½ cups chicken broth
1 tablespoon fresh dill sprigs, chopped fine
1 tablespoon finely chopped fresh chives
½ pound boiling potatoes (about 2 medium)
5 cups water
4 cups corn (cut from about 6 large ears),
    reserving 3 cobs
½ teaspoon ground cumin
½ teaspoon cayenne
½ to ¾ cup ice water for thinning soup

In a deep skillet or saucepan simmer chicken in broth, covered, turning it once, 10 minutes and remove skillet or pan from heat. Let chicken stand in broth, covered, 20 minutes, or until just cooked through, and cool, uncovered. *Chill mixture, covered, at least until cold, about 6 hours, and up to 1 day.* Drain chicken and shred into a bowl. Add dill, chives, and salt and pepper to taste and toss to combine well.

Peel potatoes and cut into ½-inch pieces. In a 4-quart saucepan simmer water, potatoes, corn, reserved cobs, and cumin, partially covered, until potatoes are very tender, about 15 minutes, and cool. Discard cobs and in a blender purée half of corn mixture in batches until smooth, transferring to a bowl. Stir in remaining corn mixture, cayenne, and salt to taste. *Chill soup, covered, at least until cold, about 6 hours, and up to 1 day.* Before serving, thin soup with ice water if desired and season with salt and pepper if necessary.

Divide soup among 4 bowls and mound chicken in center. Makes about 9 cups of soup and chicken, serving 4 as a main course.

🍃 Each serving about 293 calories, 4 grams fat
(11% of calories from fat)

Curried Cauliflower Apple Soup

1 small onion, chopped fine
1 small garlic clove, minced
½ teaspoon curry powder
1½ tablespoons unsalted butter
1 large Granny Smith apple
4 cups cauliflower flowerets (about
   1 small head)
1½ cups chicken broth
1 cup water
¼ cup heavy cream

In a 3½- to 4-quart saucepan cook onion, garlic, and curry powder in butter over moderately low heat, stirring, until onion is softened. Peel and core apple. Chop apple coarse and add to curry mixture. Add cauliflower, broth, and water and simmer, covered, until cauliflower is very tender, 15 to 20 minutes.

In a blender or food processor purée soup in batches until very smooth, transferring as puréed to another saucepan. Stir in cream and salt and pepper to taste and heat over moderate heat until hot. Makes about 4 cups.

Chilled Cream of Celery Soup

3 cups water
3½ cups chopped celery
1 cup chopped onion
½ teaspoon caraway seeds
1 cup well-shaken low-fat (1½%)
   buttermilk

In a 2½- to 3-quart heavy saucepan simmer water, celery, onion, and caraway seeds until celery is very tender, about 30 minutes. Cool mixture slightly and in a blender purée in batches until smooth, transferring to a bowl. Stir in buttermilk and salt and pepper to taste. *Chill soup, covered, at least until cold, about 6 hours, and up to 1 day.* Before serving, season with salt and pepper if necessary. Makes about 4 cups, serving 4 as a first course.

🍃 Each serving about 63 calories, 1 gram fat
(18% of calories from fat)

Carrot, Fennel, and Orange Soup

1 medium fennel bulb (sometimes called anise),
   stalks trimmed flush with bulb and bulb
   sliced thin crosswise
2 tablespoons unsalted butter
1½ pounds carrots, sliced thin (about 4 cups)
1 garlic clove, sliced thin
6 cups water
1 teaspoon salt, or to taste
⅓ cup fresh orange juice
¼ cup sour cream

Garnish: fresh chervil leaves or
   fennel fronds

In a 3-quart heavy saucepan cook fennel bulb in butter over moderate heat, stirring, until softened and beginning to turn golden. Add carrots and garlic and cook, stirring, 1 minute. Add water and salt and simmer, covered, 20 minutes, or until carrots are very tender.

In a blender purée vegetable mixture in batches with orange juice, sour cream, and salt and pepper to taste until smooth, transferring to another heavy saucepan. Heat soup, stirring, just until heated through (do not boil).

Serve soup garnished with chervil leaves or fennel fronds. Makes about 8 cups.

PHOTO ON PAGE 30

Sherried Mushroom Soup

2 tablespoons unsalted butter
1 tablespoon olive oil
3 large shallots, chopped fine (about ½ cup)
¾ pound mushrooms, half sliced and remainder
    chopped fine
3 tablespoons cream Sherry
2 cups low-salt chicken broth
¼ cup chopped fresh chives or scallion greens

In a saucepan melt butter with oil over moderate heat until foam subsides and sauté shallots and mushrooms over moderately high heat, stirring, until liquid mushrooms give off is evaporated and mushrooms begin to brown. Add Sherry and boil until evaporated. Stir in broth and simmer 15 minutes, or until mixture is reduced to about 2½ cups. Stir in chives or scallion greens and season soup with salt and pepper. Serves 2.

Shrimp Gazpacho with Basil Croutons

2 pounds vine-ripened large tomatoes (about 5),
    chopped
1 red bell pepper, chopped (about 1 cup)
½ cup peeled, seeded, and finely chopped
    cucumber
¼ cup finely chopped red onion
2 garlic cloves, minced and mashed to a paste
    with ½ teaspoon salt
½ teaspoon ground cumin
1 fresh *jalapeño* chili, chopped fine (wear
    rubber gloves)
½ pound vine-ripened cherry tomatoes, quartered
2 tablespoons red-wine vinegar, or to taste
½ pound small to medium shrimp, shelled and,
    if desired, deveined
¼ to ½ cup ice water for thinning gazpacho

Accompaniment: basil croutons (recipe follows)
Garnish: finely diced cucumber and red bell
    pepper and chopped fresh basil leaves

In a blender or food processor purée half of large tomatoes, ½ cup bell pepper, ¼ cup cucumber, 2 tablespoons onion, garlic paste, cumin, and *jalapeño.* Transfer purée to a bowl and stir in cherry tomatoes

with remaining chopped large tomatoes, bell pepper, cucumber, and onion. Stir in vinegar and salt and pepper to taste. *Chill gazpacho, covered, at least 3 hours and up to 1 day.*

In a saucepan of generously salted boiling water boil shrimp 30 seconds, or until just cooked through. Transfer shrimp with a slotted spoon to a bowl and cool. *Shrimp may be cooked 1 day ahead and chilled, covered.* Chop shrimp and stir into gazpacho.

Before serving, thin gazpacho with ice water and top with croutons and garnish. Makes about 6 cups, serving 4 as a first course.

PHOTO ON PAGE 54

Basil Croutons

¾ cup packed fresh basil leaves, washed well
    and spun dry
3 tablespoons extra-virgin olive oil
4 slices firm white sandwich bread, cut into
    ½-inch cubes (about 3 cups)

In a blender or small food processor purée basil with oil and season with salt and pepper to taste.
Preheat oven to 350° F.
On a baking sheet toss bread with basil oil and bake in middle of oven, shaking baking sheet occasionally, 10 to 15 minutes, or until croutons are golden brown and crisp. Season croutons with salt and pepper. *Croutons may be made 3 days ahead and kept in a sealable plastic bag in a cool dry place.* Makes about 2 cups.

Chilled Yellow Pepper Soup with Chives

5 medium onions, sliced (about 6½ cups)
½ stick (¼ cup) unsalted butter
6 large garlic cloves, minced and mashed
    to a paste with ¼ teaspoon salt
    (about 2½ tablespoons)
½ cup dry white wine
9 pounds yellow bell peppers, cut into 1-inch
    pieces (about 17½ cups)
4 cups chicken broth or water
1 cup sour cream

Garnish: ½ cup chopped fresh chives

In a 6- to 8-quart kettle cook onions in butter over moderate heat, stirring occasionally, 5 minutes. Stir in garlic paste and cook, stirring, 1 minute. Add wine and boil until liquid is reduced to about 1 tablespoon. Stir in bell peppers and broth and simmer, covered, until peppers are tender, 20 to 25 minutes.

In a blender or food processor purée mixture in batches (use caution when blending hot liquids) until smooth and transfer to a large bowl. Season purée with salt and pepper and cool completely. *Chill soup, covered, until cold, at least 4 hours, and up to 2 days.* Whisk in sour cream and season with salt and pepper.

Garnish soup with chives. Makes about 17 cups, serving 16 as a first course.

Cheddar Vegetable Chowder

1 tablespoon vegetable oil
1 medium onion, chopped
1 medium carrot, halved lengthwise and
    sliced thin
1 celery rib, sliced thin
½ red bell pepper, cut into ¼-inch dice
1 medium boiling potato, cut into ¼-inch dice
2 tablespoons all-purpose flour
1 cup chicken broth
¾ cup water
¾ teaspoon ground cumin
a pinch cayenne
⅔ cup coarsely grated Cheddar (about 2 ounces)
2 teaspoons minced fresh coriander

In a 2-quart saucepan heat oil over moderate heat until hot but not smoking and cook vegetables, stirring, until onion is softened. Add flour and cook over moderately low heat, stirring, 3 minutes. Stir in broth, water, cumin, cayenne, and salt and pepper to taste and simmer until potato is tender, about 10 minutes. Remove pan from heat and stir in Cheddar, a little at a time, and coriander, stirring until cheese is melted. Serves 2.

Cold Cucumber Soup with Mint

1 hard-boiled large egg yolk
1 tablespoon rice vinegar
½ cup chilled sour cream
1 chilled seedless cucumber (about 1 pound),
    peeled, halved lengthwise, cored, and cut
    into ½-inch pieces
¼ cup fresh mint leaves, washed and
    spun dry
½ cup chilled well-shaken buttermilk

In a bowl with a fork mash together yolk and vinegar to form a smooth paste and stir in sour cream until smooth.

In a blender purée cucumber and mint with buttermilk and salt to taste until smooth. Add purée to sour cream mixture in a stream, whisking.

Divide soup between 2 chilled bowls. Serves 2.

African Peanut Soup

1 tablespoon vegetable oil
1 garlic clove, chopped
⅓ cup tomato paste
⅔ cup creamy peanut butter
⅛ teaspoon cayenne
4 cups low-salt chicken broth

In a saucepan heat oil over moderate heat until hot but not smoking and cook garlic, stirring, until golden, about 1 minute. Add tomato paste, peanut butter, cayenne, and ¼ cup broth and stir until smooth. Stir in remaining 3¾ cups broth and simmer, covered, stirring occasionally, 10 minutes. Simmer soup, uncovered, 10 minutes, or until oil floats to the surface, and skim oil. Makes about 4 cups.

Chick-Pea and Coriander Soup

2 cups chopped onion (about 2 medium)
1 tablespoon olive oil
4 cups water
a 19-ounce can chick-peas, rinsed and drained
2 large garlic cloves, chopped
½ teaspoon salt, or to taste
½ cup packed fresh coriander sprigs, washed well and spun dry
2 teaspoons fresh lemon juice, or to taste

Accompaniment: cumin pita crouton-crisps (recipe follows)

In a 3-quart heavy saucepan cook onion in oil over moderate heat, stirring, until softened and golden brown. Add water, chick-peas, garlic, and salt and simmer, uncovered, 15 minutes. In a blender purée chick-pea mixture and coriander with lemon juice until smooth.

Serve soup topped with pita crouton-crisps. Makes about 3⅔ cups, serving 2.

Cumin Pita Crouton-Crisps

3 mini pita loaves, halved crosswise
4 teaspoons extra-virgin olive oil
1 teaspoon ground cumin
½ teaspoon salt

Preheat oven to 400° F.

Cut pita halves into ⅓-inch-wide strips and in a small bowl toss with oil until coated evenly. Add cumin and salt and toss until they adhere.

In a baking pan spread strips in one layer and bake in middle of oven 3 minutes, or until crisp. *Crouton-crisps keep in an airtight container 2 weeks.*

Serve crouton-crisps in soups or salads or as a snack. Makes about 2 cups.

Sorrel, Pea, and Leek Soup

white and pale green parts of 3 leeks (about ¾ pound), chopped, washed well, and drained
1½ tablespoons olive oil
1 small boiling potato (about ¼ pound)
1½ cups chicken broth
1½ cups cold water plus additional for thinning soup
½ cup peas, thawed if frozen
¼ pound sorrel*, stems discarded and leaves washed, spun dry, and cut crosswise into thin strips (about 3 cups loosely packed)
⅓ cup sour cream
1 teaspoon fresh lemon juice, or to taste

Garnish: chopped hard-boiled egg and thin strips of sorrel

*available seasonally at specialty produce markets and some supermarkets

In a large saucepan cook leeks in oil with salt and pepper to taste over moderately low heat, stirring, until softened. Peel potato and cut into 1-inch cubes. Add potato, broth, and 1 cup water to leeks and simmer, covered, about 10 minutes, or until potato is tender. Stir in peas and simmer, uncovered, about 5 minutes, or until peas are tender.

In a blender purée potato mixture with sorrel in 2 batches until very smooth, transferring to a bowl. Whisk in sour cream and ½ cup water, adding additional water to thin soup to desired consistency. *Chill soup, covered, at least 2 hours and up to 24.*

Just before serving, stir in lemon juice and salt and pepper to taste. Serve soup garnished with egg and sorrel. Makes about 4½ cups.

PHOTO ON PAGE 34

FISH AND SHELLFISH

FISH

Striped Bass Escabeche with Bell Peppers and Green Beans

For marinade
½ cup dry white wine
¼ cup white-wine vinegar
¼ cup Sherry vinegar
¼ cup fresh orange juice
2 tablespoons firmly packed brown sugar
2 tablespoons fresh lemon juice
2 tablespoons extra-virgin olive oil
1 tablespoon pickling spices
1 teaspoon salt
½ teaspoon dried hot red pepper flakes

½ cup drained brine-cured green olives such as
    picholines, pitted and halved
3 small red bell peppers, cut into very thin rings
3 small yellow bell peppers, cut into very
    thin rings
1 red onion, cut into very thin rings
6 striped bass or snapper fillets with skin (about
    2¼ pounds total), halved lengthwise
⅓ cup all-purpose flour
4 tablespoons olive oil
¾ pound green beans, trimmed

Make marinade:
In a bowl combine marinade ingredients, stirring until brown sugar is dissolved.

To marinade add olives, bell peppers, and onion. Season fish with salt and pepper and in a bowl toss with flour to coat, shaking off excess. Line a shallow baking pan with paper towels. In a large heavy skillet heat 3 tablespoons oil over moderately high heat until hot but not smoking and sauté fish, 6 pieces at a time, turning once and adding remaining tablespoon oil to skillet as necessary, until golden on both sides and just cooked through, about 6 minutes. Transfer fish as sautéed to paper-towel-lined pan to drain.

Transfer fish to a 13- by 9-inch shallow baking dish and pour marinade mixture over fish, spreading vegetables in one layer. Marinate fish, covered and chilled, at least 1 day and up to 3.

In a large saucepan of boiling salted water cook beans 3 minutes, or until crisp-tender, and drain in a colander. Refresh beans under cold water and drain. Beans may be cooked 2 days ahead and chilled in a sealable plastic bag.

Remove fish from marinade mixture and add beans to dish, tossing to coat. Transfer mixture to a large deep platter and arrange fish on top. Serves 6.

PHOTO ON PAGE 58

Pan-Seared Swordfish Steaks with Shallot, Caper, and Balsamic Sauce

two 1-inch-thick swordfish steaks, each
    about 6 ounces
1 tablespoon unsalted butter
½ tablespoon olive oil
3 shallots, sliced thin
¼ cup dry white wine
2 tablespoons balsamic vinegar
1 tablespoon drained capers, chopped
1 tablespoon water
1 tablespoon chopped fresh parsley leaves

Pat swordfish dry and season with salt and pepper. In a heavy skillet heat butter and oil over moderately high heat until foam subsides and sauté shallots with salt to taste, stirring, 1 minute. Push shallots to side of skillet. Add swordfish and sauté until golden, about 3 minutes. Turn fish over and add wine, vinegar, capers, and water. Simmer mixture 3 minutes, or until fish is just cooked through.

Transfer fish to 2 plates and stir parsley into sauce. Spoon sauce over fish. Serves 2.

Sautéed Sea Bass on Bruschetta

two 28-ounce cans whole tomatoes, drained,
    seeded, and cut into ¼-inch dice
¾ cup loosely packed fresh coriander sprigs,
    washed well, spun dry, and chopped
3 tablespoons minced shallots
½ teaspoon freshly grated orange zest
2 tablespoons fresh lemon juice
2 tablespoons red-wine vinegar
4 diagonal ¼-inch-thick slices fat-free French
    or Italian bread (about 4 ounces total),
    lightly toasted
four 4-ounce sea bass, flounder, or sole fillets
2 tablespoons all-purpose flour
1 tablespoon unsalted butter
2 tablespoons fresh orange juice

In a large bowl stir together tomatoes, coriander, shallots, zest, lemon juice, vinegar, and salt and pepper to taste. Drain mixture in a sieve set over a bowl 10 minutes, reserving liquid, and divide among toasts, spreading to cover.

Season fish with salt and pepper and dredge in flour to coat, shaking off excess. In a large non-stick skillet heat butter over moderately high heat until foam subsides and cook fish 3 minutes on each side, or until just cooked through. Arrange 1 fillet over each *bruschetta* and keep warm. Add reserved tomato liquid and orange juice to skillet and boil until reduced to about ¼ cup. Pour sauce over fish. Serves 4.

✍ Each serving about 280 calories, 7 grams fat
(21% of calories from fat)

Sautéed Cod Steaks and Tomatoes with Green Sauce

⅓ cup watercress leaves, washed well and
    spun dry
½ cup arugula leaves, washed well and spun dry
2 tablespoons mayonnaise
1 teaspoon fresh lemon juice, or to taste
two 6-ounce cod steaks (each about 1 inch thick)
1 tablespoon olive oil
2 plum tomatoes, seeded and chopped
1 teaspoon balsamic vinegar

In a food processor blend watercress, arugula, mayonnaise, and juice until leaves are chopped fine and sauce is smooth, adding 1 to 2 teaspoons water if necessary to thin sauce to consistency of thin mayonnaise. Transfer sauce to a small bowl.

Season cod with salt and pepper. In a heavy non-stick skillet heat oil over moderately high heat until hot but not smoking and sauté fish 3 minutes, or until crisp and golden. Turn fish over and sauté 2 minutes more. Move fish to one side of skillet and to other side add tomatoes, vinegar, and salt and pepper to taste. Sauté tomatoes and fish 1 minute, or until tomatoes are just wilted and fish is just cooked through and barely flakes with a fork.

Transfer fish with a spatula to each of 2 plates and spoon tomato mixture on top. Pour some green sauce over fish and serve remaining on the side. Serves 2.

Glazed Salmon Fillets with Dill Mustard Sauce

For glaze and sauce
⅔ cup white-wine vinegar
1 cup Dijon mustard
½ cup firmly packed light brown sugar
2 cups vegetable oil
freshly ground black pepper to taste
3 tablespoons soy sauce
¼ cup chopped fresh dill sprigs

two 2½- to 3-pound whole salmon fillets with
    skin, any small bones removed with tweezers

Make glaze and sauce:
In a bowl whisk together vinegar, mustard, and brown sugar. Whisk in oil in a stream until emulsified and season with pepper and salt. *Mixture may*

be made 3 days ahead and chilled, covered. Bring mixture to room temperature and whisk before proceeding. Transfer ¾ cup mixture to a small bowl and stir in soy sauce to make glaze. Whisk dill into remaining mixture to make sauce.

Preheat broiler and grease a broiler pan or jelly-roll pan.

Rinse salmon fillets and pat dry. Arrange fillets, skin sides down, in pan. (Cook 1 at a time if broiler is small.) Brush salmon with glaze and season with pepper and salt. Broil salmon 3 to 4 inches from heat about 8 minutes, or until just cooked through.

Serve salmon warm or at room temperature with sauce. Serves 16 as part of a buffet.

PHOTO ON PAGE 67

Roasted Monkfish with Chanterelles, Leeks, and Ginger

4 medium leeks (about 1 pound, white and
    pale green parts only), cut crosswise
    into ¼-inch-thick slices
3 small boiling potatoes (about ¾ pound total)
1 large garlic clove
a 1-inch piece peeled fresh gingerroot
a 1¾-pound piece monkfish fillet cut in half
    crosswise or two smaller fillets (1¾ pounds
    total), any membrane and any dark meat
    cut away
½ pound fresh chanterelle mushrooms*, cleaned
    with a dampened kitchen towel, stem ends
    trimmed and large mushrooms halved
3 tablespoons warm clarified butter
    (procedure follows)
freshly ground white pepper
2 tablespoons Tawny Port
1 tablespoon soy sauce

Garnish: fresh chives, cut into 1-inch pieces

*available at specialty produce shops and by
    mail order from Aux Delices des Bois,
    tel. (800) 666-1232 or (212) 334-1230

Preheat oven to 475° F.

In a large bowl of water soak leeks 10 minutes, agitating occasionally to dislodge any sand and letting sand sink to bottom of bowl. Lift leeks out of water with a slotted spoon and drain on paper towels.

Peel potatoes and trim if necessary to match diameter of leeks. Cut potatoes crosswise into ¼-inch-thick slices. In a saucepan of boiling water blanch potatoes 5 minutes and drain.

Cut half of garlic clove into several slivers and finely chop remaining half. Cut half of gingerroot into several slivers and finely chop remaining half. With a paring knife make several shallow slits in monkfish and insert a sliver of garlic and gingerroot into each.

Heat a flameproof roasting pan, 13 by 9 by 2 inches, in oven 10 minutes. In heated pan toss together leeks, potatoes, mushrooms, chopped garlic and ginger, salt and pepper to taste, and 2 tablespoons clarified butter. Roast vegetables in middle of oven 15 minutes.

Heat a 12-inch non-stick skillet over moderately high heat. Pat fish dry and season with white pepper and salt. Add remaining tablespoon butter to skillet and brown fish about 2 minutes on each side. With a slotted spatula transfer fish to a plate.

To skillet add Port and soy sauce and on top of stove deglaze over moderately high heat, scraping up any brown bits, 30 seconds. Pour liquid over roasted vegetables, tossing to coat, and arrange fish on top. Roast fish and vegetables in middle of oven 15 to 18 minutes, or until fish is just cooked through (fish will be firm rather than flaky).

Garnish fish with chives. Cut fish crosswise into slices and serve with vegetables. Serves 4.

To Clarify Butter

unsalted butter, cut into 1-inch pieces

In a heavy saucepan melt butter over low heat. Remove saucepan from heat and let butter stand 3 minutes. Skim froth and pour melted butter through a sieve lined with a double thickness of rinsed and squeezed cheesecloth into a bowl, leaving milky solids in bottom of pan. Pour clarified butter into a jar or crock. *Butter keeps, covered and chilled, indefinitely.* When clarified, butter loses about one fourth of its original volume.

Roasted Red Snapper with Olives

For sauce
⅓ cup dry white wine
3 garlic cloves, sliced thin
¼ cup fresh lemon juice
⅓ cup extra-virgin olive oil
1½ tablespoons chopped fresh thyme leaves
1½ cups mixed green and black brine-cured
 olives (preferably unpitted)

six 6- to 7-ounce red snapper fillets with skin
6 tablespoons extra-virgin olive oil

Preheat oven to 425° F.
Make sauce:
In a small skillet boil wine with garlic until re-duced to about 2 tablespoons. Add remaining sauce ingredients and salt and pepper to taste and bring to a simmer. *Sauce may be made 1 day ahead and chilled, covered. Reheat sauce to warm before proceeding.*

Pat snapper fillets dry and season with salt and pepper. Divide oil between 2 shallow baking pans large enough to hold fillets in one layer without touching and spread oil evenly. Heat baking pans in upper and lower thirds of oven 7 minutes. Working quickly, put fillets, skin sides down, in hot baking pans and roast in upper and lower thirds of oven 7 to 10 minutes, or until fish is just cooked through.

Transfer fillets with a metal spatula to a large platter, turning them skin sides up, and top with sauce. Serves 12 as part of a buffet.

PHOTO ON PAGE 78

Grilled Citrus Salmon and Grilled Mango

⅓ cup fresh orange juice
⅓ cup fresh lemon juice
⅓ cup fresh lime juice
¼ cup lime marmalade
½ teaspoon sugar
½ cup chopped onion
2 tablespoons chopped peeled fresh gingerroot
six 6-ounce center-cut pieces salmon fillets
 with skin
½ cup fresh coriander sprigs, washed well,
 spun dry, and chopped

Accompaniment: grilled mango (recipe follows)

In a blender blend citrus juices and marmalade until combined well. Pour ½ cup juice mixture into a bowl and stir in sugar until sugar is dissolved. Reserve juice mixture in bowl.

Add onion and gingerroot to juice mixture in blender and purée until smooth. Transfer mixture to a shallow baking dish just large enough to hold salmon in one layer and stir in coriander. Arrange salmon, skin side up, in baking dish. *Marinate salmon, covered and chilled, 1 hour.*

Prepare grill.

Remove salmon from marinade and discard marinade. Pat salmon dry. Season salmon with salt and pepper and grill, skin side down, on an oiled rack set 5 to 6 inches over glowing coals 4 minutes. Put lid on grill and grill salmon until just cooked through, 3 to 4 minutes more. (Alternatively, salmon may be grilled in a hot well-seasoned ridged grill pan with a lid over moderate heat.) Carefully transfer salmon with a metal spatula to a warm platter and remove skin.

Pour reserved juice mixture over salmon and serve with grilled mango. Serves 6.

🍂 Each serving with accompaniment
about 369 calories, 11 grams fat
(27% of calories from fat)

PHOTO ON PAGE 43

Grilled Mango

3 firm-ripe mangoes (2¼ pounds total)

Standing mango upright, cut two lengthwise slices, each about ½ inch thick, from a broad side of mango pit (see drawing A). Cut remaining broad side and remaining mangoes in same manner. (There should be a total of 12 slices, 6 of them end pieces.) Discard pits and reserve any remaining mango for another use.

Prepare grill.

Working with end pieces only, score flesh in a cross-hatch pattern (see drawing B), being careful not to cut through skin, and grill, cut side down, on a well-oiled rack set 5 to 6 inches over glowing coals until golden brown, about 2 minutes. (Alternatively, mango may be grilled in a hot well-seasoned ridged grill pan over moderately high heat in same manner.) Transfer mango as grilled to a platter. When end pieces of mango are cool enough to handle, push from skin side to turn inside out (see drawing C). Grill remaining mango slices about 2 minutes on each side. Serves 6.

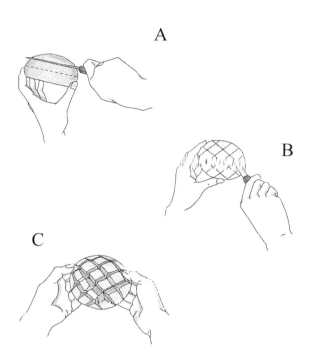

A

B

C

Grilled Tuna with Warm White Bean Salad

½ pound dried Great Northern beans (1¼ cups)
4 cups salted water
2 garlic cloves, 1 crushed and 1 chopped and mashed to a paste with ½ teaspoon salt
2 cups packed arugula leaves, washed well and spun dry
1 small red onion, sliced thin
2 tablespoons chopped fresh flat-leafed parsley leaves
3 tablespoons fresh lemon juice
four 4-ounce skinless tuna steaks (each about ½ inch thick)
1 teaspoon fennel seeds, crushed
freshly ground black pepper

Accompaniment: lemon wedges

In a large saucepan simmer beans in salted water with crushed garlic until tender, about 1 hour, and drain, reserving ¼ cup cooking liquid. In a small bowl mash ½ cup beans with a fork and return mashed and whole beans to pan with reserved liquid. Chop 1 cup arugula and stir into beans (off heat) with garlic paste, onion, parsley, 2 tablespoons lemon juice, and salt and pepper to taste. Keep bean salad warm, covered, over very low heat while cooking tuna.

Prepare grill while beans are cooking.

Rinse tuna and pat dry. On a plate combine tuna steaks with remaining tablespoon lemon juice, turning to coat, and sprinkle both sides with fennel seeds, pepper, and salt to taste. Grill fish on an oiled rack set 5 to 6 inches over glowing coals about 3 minutes on each side, or until just cooked through. (Alternatively, fish may be cooked in a heated well-seasoned ridged grill pan in same manner.)

Arrange bean salad and remaining cup arugula on 4 plates and top with fish. Squeeze lemon over fish. Serves 4.

🖤 Each serving about 339 calories, 6 grams fat (17% of calories from fat)

Smoked Trout and Roasted Pepper Toasts

¾ teaspoon caraway seeds, crushed
1½ tablespoons fresh lemon juice
1 teaspoon Dijon mustard
1 teaspoon minced shallot
1 smoked trout (about ½ pound), head, tail, skin, and bones discarded
a 7-ounce jar roasted red peppers, drained and chopped
2 tablespoons chopped fresh parsley leaves
fourteen ¼-inch-thick French bread slices (about 2 ounces of 1 *baguette*), toasted and rubbed with ½ garlic clove

In a bowl stir together caraway seeds, lemon juice, mustard, and shallot and add trout, mashing with a fork until finely flaked. Gently stir in roasted peppers and parsley and season with salt and pepper. Top toasts with trout mixture. Serves 2 generously as a light main course.

🖤 Each serving about 178 calories, 5 grams fat (26% of calories from fat)

Seared Tuna Kebabs

½ fennel bulb (sometimes called anise, about
    ½ pound), stalks trimmed flush with bulb
⅓ cup extra-virgin olive oil
2 garlic cloves, minced
a 2-inch piece of fresh gingerroot, peeled
    and grated fine
⅓ cup fresh lime juice (from about 2 limes)
2 teaspoons fresh thyme leaves
a 4-inch piece of seedless cucumber,
    halved lengthwise, seeded, and cut into
    1-inch chunks
½ pound tuna steak, cut into 1-inch cubes

Prepare grill.

Cut fennel into 1-inch-thick wedges and halve crosswise into 1-inch pieces. In a medium saucepan of boiling salted water blanch fennel 2½ minutes. In a colander drain fennel and refresh under cold water.

In a bowl stir together oil, garlic, gingerroot, lime juice, and thyme. Add fennel, cucumber, and tuna, tossing to coat, and let stand, covered, at room temperature 15 minutes.

Thread fennel, cucumber, and tuna cubes onto two 10-inch metal skewers and grill kebabs on an oiled rack set 5 to 6 inches over glowing coals, turning them, until tuna is cooked through, about 12 minutes. Serves 2.

Oven-Steamed Whole Snapper with Black Bean Sauce

two 1½-pound red snappers, cleaned, leaving
    heads and tails intact
1 tablespoon minced peeled fresh gingerroot
2 garlic cloves, minced
¼ cup medium-dry Sherry
3 tablespoons soy sauce
½ pound fresh *shiitake* mushrooms, stems
    discarded and caps sliced thin
4 medium carrots (about ½ pound), cut into
    julienne strips
6 scallions, cut into julienne strips
2 tablespoons fermented black beans*,
    rinsed lightly
2 tablespoons water
2 teaspoons cornstarch

Accompaniment: 1 cup long-grain white rice,
    cooked according to package instructions
    without butter or margarine

*available at Asian markets and some specialty
    foods shops

Preheat oven to 450° F.

Rinse fish and pat dry with paper towels. Cut 3 slashes about ½ inch deep on each side of fish and rub gingerroot, garlic, and salt to taste into slashes. Arrange fish in one layer in a 13- by 9-inch baking dish and drizzle on both sides with Sherry and soy sauce. Sprinkle *shiitake* mushrooms, carrots, scallions, and black beans over fish and cover dish tightly with foil.

Bake fish in middle of oven 40 minutes, or until just cooked through. Gently push black bean mixture off fish. Transfer fish to a platter with large metal spatulas and keep warm.

Transfer black bean mixture and pan juices to a saucepan. In a small bowl stir together water and cornstarch and stir into black bean mixture. Simmer sauce 1 minute, or until thickened slightly, and pour over fish.

Serve fish with rice. Serves 4.

🐟 Each serving with accompaniment
about 437 calories, 3 grams fat
(7% of calories from fat)

Smoked Fish Trio

For pink-peppercorn sour cream sauce
¼ cup sour cream
1 teaspoon pink peppercorns*, crushed
For lemon-chive vinaigrette
½ cup coarsely chopped fresh chives
3 tablespoons extra-virgin olive oil
⅛ teaspoon coarse salt
1 tablespoon plus ½ teaspoon fresh lemon
    juice, or to taste

1 cup loosely packed *mesclun* (mixed baby
    greens), rinsed and dried
4 ounces peppered smoked mackerel**,
    cut into twelve 2-inch pieces
4 ounces thinly sliced smoked salmon
6 lemon wedges
6 wedges smoked trout mousse (recipe follows)
about 18 anchovy toasts (page 130)

*available at specialty foods shops and some
    supermarkets
**available at fish markets, deli counter at many
    supermarkets, and by mail order from Ducktrap
    River Fish Farm, tel. (800) 828-3825

Make sauce:
In a small bowl whisk together sour cream and
peppercorns. *Sauce may be made 1 day ahead and
chilled, covered.*
Make vinaigrette:
In a blender purée chives with oil and salt until
smooth. Pour purée through a fine sieve into a bowl,
pressing on solids, and discard solids. *Chive oil may
be made 1 day ahead and chilled, covered. Bring
chive oil to room temperature before proceeding.*
Whisk lemon juice into chive oil and season with
pepper.

In a bowl toss *mesclun* with just enough vinaigrette to coat and season with salt and pepper. On
each of 6 chilled plates decoratively layer *mesclun*
and mackerel in small mounds and drizzle with some
remaining vinaigrette. On each plate decoratively
arrange salmon with a dollop of sauce and 1 lemon
wedge, and a wedge of mousse and some toasts.
Serves 6.

PHOTO ON PAGE 80

Smoked Trout Mousse

2 smoked trout fillets* (about 8 ounces total),
    skin and bones discarded and fish broken
    into small pieces (about 1 cup packed)
¾ cup well-chilled heavy cream
1 tablespoon unsalted butter, softened
2 tablespoons fresh lemon juice
½ teaspoon coarse salt
1 teaspoon unflavored gelatin
2 tablespoons water
3 tablespoons salmon roe
¼ cup fresh dill sprigs, chopped coarse
3 tablespoons black sesame seeds**

*available at fish markets, deli counter of many
    supermarkets, and by mail order from Ducktrap
    River Fish Farm, tel. (800) 828-3825
**available at Asian markets and some specialty
    foods shops and supermarkets

Lightly oil a straight-sided 2-cup mold or soufflé
dish.

In a food processor purée trout with ¼ cup cream,
butter, lemon juice, and salt until smooth and transfer
to a bowl. In a very small saucepan sprinkle gelatin
over water and let soften 1 minute. Heat mixture
over moderately low heat, stirring, just until gelatin
is dissolved (do not boil) and cool to room temperature. In a bowl with an electric mixer beat remaining
½ cup cream until it just holds stiff peaks and fold
into trout purée with gelatin mixture and salt to taste
until combined well.

Spoon half of mousse into mold or soufflé dish
and smooth top. Spoon roe evenly over mousse (roe
will not cover mousse completely) and sprinkle
evenly with dill. Spoon remaining mousse over dill,
spreading mousse evenly (being careful not to
disturb roe and dill), and gently smooth surface.
*Chill mousse, covered, at least 12 hours and up
to 2 days.*

To unmold mousse, run a thin knife around edge
of mold or soufflé dish and dip bottom into a bowl
of hot water 5 seconds. Invert mousse onto a plate
and cut into 8 wedges (reserve 2 wedges for another
use). Put sesame seeds in a shallow bowl and carefully dip outside edge of each wedge in seeds to
coat. Makes 8 small wedges.

Anchovy Toasts

2 teaspoons anchovy paste
¼ cup extra-virgin olive oil
1 *baguette* (preferably day-old, about
    18 by 2 inches), cut diagonally into
    ⅛-inch-thick slices

Preheat oven to 400° F.

In a small bowl whisk together anchovy paste and oil. Brush both sides of *baguette* slices lightly with anchovy oil and arrange in one layer on baking sheets. Toast slices in middle and lower thirds of oven 5 minutes, or until golden brown. Cool toasts on a rack. *Toasts may be made 4 days ahead and kept in an airtight container at room temperature.* Makes about 18 toasts.

Grilled Swordfish and Green Olive Relish

For relish
¼ cup drained bottled pimiento-stuffed
    green olives
1 small garlic clove, minced and
    mashed to a paste with a
    pinch salt
2 tablespoons finely chopped fresh
    parsley leaves
2 tablespoons extra-virgin olive oil
2 teaspoons fresh lemon juice

two 6-ounce swordfish steaks (each about
    1 inch thick)
olive oil for brushing swordfish

Prepare grill.
Make relish:
In a food processor pulse olives until chopped fine. Add remaining relish ingredients and pulse until olives are minced.

Brush both sides of swordfish with oil and season with salt and pepper. Grill fish on a rack set 5 to 6 inches over glowing coals 4 minutes on each side, or until just cooked through. (Alternatively, fish may be grilled in a hot well-seasoned ridged grill pan over moderate heat.)

Serve swordfish topped with relish. Serves 2.

SHELLFISH

Use caution when handling live crabs—their claws can pinch hard enough to cause injury.

Spicy Boiled Crabs, Shrimp, Potatoes, Corn, and Garlic

24 live blue crabs
two 3-ounce packets Zatarain's crab boil* or
    5 tablespoons Old Bay seasoning*
1 tablespoon cayenne
½ cup table salt
3 lemons, quartered
2 onions, halved
1½ pounds small potatoes (about 2 inches in
    diameter)
2 heads garlic (not separated into cloves)
6 ears corn, shucked
2 tablespoons Old Bay seasoning*, or to taste,
    for sprinkling over boiled seafood
2 pounds large shrimp (about 30, preferably
    with heads)

Accompaniments
horseradish cocktail sauce (recipe follows)
French bread

*available at seafood markets, specialty foods
    shops, and some supermarkets

In a 7- to 8-gallon kettle bring 5 gallons water to a boil.

While water is coming to a boil, in a deep sink rinse crabs in 2 or 3 changes of water. (Do not fill sink too full or crabs may crawl out.)

Add Zatarain's crab boil or 5 tablespoons Old Bay seasoning, cayenne, salt, lemons, and onions to boiling water and boil 5 minutes. Add potatoes and garlic and boil until tender, about 15 minutes. Transfer potatoes and garlic with a large sieve to a large platter and keep warm, covered with foil. Add corn to boiling water and cook until tender, about 5 minutes. Transfer corn with tongs to platter and keep warm, covered with foil.

Return water to a boil. Transfer about 6 crabs

carefully with long tongs to sieve, holding them down in sieve with tongs, and turn crabs out into boiling water. Add remaining crabs in same manner. Return water to a boil and cook crabs until just cooked through, about 10 minutes. (To determine doneness, remove a claw and crack it with the handle of a dinner knife. Use knife to extract meat from claw.) Transfer crabs with sieve to another large platter and sprinkle with 1 tablespoon Old Bay seasoning.

Return water to a boil and cook shrimp until just cooked through, about 2 minutes. Transfer shrimp with sieve to large platter with crabs and sprinkle with remaining tablespoon Old Bay seasoning.

Serve crabs, shrimp, and vegetables with horseradish cocktail sauce and French bread. Serves 6.

PHOTO ON PAGE 49

How to Eat a Crab

Hold cooked crab (top side up) in palm of one hand, holding down one of the back fins with your thumb.

With other hand, grasp one of the pointed sides of shell. Pop shell open, using heel of that hand for leverage, and pull off.

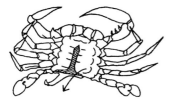

Flip crab over, and pull off "apron flap." Scoop out and discard innards

Split crab in half to get at the meat.

Horseradish Cocktail Sauce

1 cup ketchup
⅔ cup mayonnaise
2 tablespoons drained bottled horseradish, or to taste
Tabasco to taste

In a bowl whisk together all ingredients with salt to taste. *Cocktail sauce may be made 1 day ahead and chilled, its surface covered with plastic wrap.* Makes about 1⅔ cups.

Marinated Shrimp with Pickled Watermelon Rind

a 10-ounce jar pickled watermelon rind*
  (½ cup rind and ½ cup pickling liquid)
3 tablespoons cider vinegar
1 teaspoon coriander seeds, crushed
1 teaspoon mixed peppercorns, crushed
½ large sweet onion, such as Vidalia or Walla Walla, sliced thin
1¼ pounds large shrimp (about 26), shelled (leaving tails intact) and deveined
½ lemon
2 teaspoons salt

*available at specialty foods shops and some supermarkets

In a sieve set over a bowl drain pickled watermelon, reserving liquid and rind. Cut rind into ¼-inch-thick slices and toss in a large bowl with reserved liquid, vinegar, coriander seeds, peppercorns, and onion.

In a large saucepan of boiling water cook shrimp with lemon and salt until just cooked through, about 3 minutes and drain in a colander. Toss shrimp with rind and marinade and season with salt. *Chill shrimp mixture, covered, at least 2 hours and up to 8, tossing occasionally.* Serves 4.

Each serving about 171 calories, 1 gram fat (5% of calories from fat)

PHOTO ON PAGE 85

Lobster Lovage Stew

2 cups dry white wine
three 1¼-pound live lobsters
4 large carrots
2 onions, quartered
1 cup packed fresh lovage leaves or celery leaves
2 bay leaves
¾ teaspoon dried thyme, crumbled
½ cup packed fresh parsley sprigs,
    washed and spun dry
¼ teaspoon whole black peppercorns
1 cup finely chopped shallot
½ stick (¼ cup) unsalted butter
1 tablespoon all-purpose flour
a 28- to 32-ounce can tomatoes, drained
    and chopped
1 cup heavy cream

In a 10- to 12-quart kettle bring 8 quarts water and 1½ cups wine to a boil. Plunge lobsters into liquid headfirst and return liquid to a boil. Simmer lobsters, covered, 12 minutes. Have ready a bowl of ice and cold water. With tongs plunge lobsters immediately into bowl of ice water to stop cooking and reserve cooking liquid.

Working over a bowl to catch juices, twist off tails and claws and reserve juices. Discard head sacs. Reserve tomalley and any roe if desired and remove meat from tails and claws, reserving shells. Cut meat into bite-size pieces and chill, covered, in a bowl.

Chop 2 carrots and add to reserved cooking liquid with reserved lobster juices, reserved tomalley and roe if using, reserved shells, onions, ½ cup lovage or celery leaves, bay leaves, thyme, parsley, and peppercorns. Simmer stock gently, uncovered, skimming froth occasionally, 1¼ hours.

Pour stock through a large sieve into a large bowl and transfer to cleaned kettle. Boil stock until reduced to about 7 cups and return to bowl.

Finely chop remaining 2 carrots and in a 5- to 6-quart kettle cook with shallot in butter over moderately low heat, stirring occasionally, until crisp-tender. Sprinkle flour over mixture and cook, stirring, 3 minutes, but do not brown vegetables. Add remaining ½ cup wine and boil, stirring, until most of wine is evaporated. Add tomatoes and stock and simmer, covered, 10 minutes. Stir in cream and

salt and pepper to taste and cook stew, stirring occasionally, until heated through. *Stew and lobster meat may be prepared 2 days ahead and chilled, covered. Reheat stew before proceeding.*

Finely chop remaining ½ cup lovage or celery leaves and stir into stew with lobster meat. Cook stew, stirring, until just heated through. Makes about 12 cups.

PHOTO ON PAGE 73

Crawfish Tomato Etouffée in Puff Pastry Shells

1 onion, chopped fine
1 green bell pepper, chopped fine
½ stick (¼ cup) unsalted butter
1 tablespoon all-purpose flour
a 16-ounce can whole tomatoes in purée,
    drained, reserving 2 tablespoons purée,
    and chopped fine
½ cup water
¼ teaspoon cayenne, or to taste
a 1-pound bag frozen crawfish tail meat*
    (preferably Louisiana), thawed
½ cup thinly sliced scallion greens
4 teaspoons white-wine vinegar
⅓ cup olive oil
8 cups *mesclun* (mixed baby greens, about
    ¾ pound), washed well and spun dry
8 puff pastry shells (recipe follows)

*available from January through June at some
    seafood shops and by mail order from
    Louisiana Premium Seafood, P.O. Box 68,
    Palmetto, LA 71358, tel. (318) 989-0062

In a heavy skillet cook onion and bell pepper in butter, covered, over moderately low heat, stirring occasionally, until softened but not browned. Sprinkle flour over onion and bell pepper and cook, stirring, 3 minutes. Stir in tomatoes and reserved purée, water, and cayenne and simmer, stirring, until thickened slightly, about 1 minute. Stir in crawfish and heat mixture over moderate heat until just hot. *Etouffée may be prepared up to this point 2 days ahead, cooled completely, uncovered, and chilled, covered. Reheat etouffée before proceeding.* Stir in scallions and salt to taste.

In a large bowl whisk together vinegar and salt and pepper to taste and whisk in oil in a stream until emulsified. Add *mesclun* and toss well.

Spoon *etouffée* into warm pastry shells and arrange *mesclun* around shells. Serves 8 as a first course.

PHOTO ON PAGE 22

Puff Pastry Shells

3 puff pastry sheets (from two 17¼-ounce
    packages frozen puff pastry sheets), thawed
an egg wash made by beating 1 large egg with
    1 teaspoon water

Preheat oven to 400° F.

On a lightly floured surface roll out 1 pastry sheet ⅛ inch thick (about 15 by 11 inches) and with a 4-inch round cutter cut out 6 rounds. Roll out second pastry sheet and cut out 6 more rounds in same manner. Roll out remaining pastry sheet and cut out 4 more rounds in same manner. (There will be a total of 16 rounds.) Transfer 8 rounds to a large baking sheet. With a 2½-inch round cutter cut out and discard centers from remaining 8 rounds to make rings. Prick rounds on baking sheet with a fork and brush lightly with some egg wash, being careful not to let wash run over edges. Center pastry rings on rounds, pressing together lightly to adhere. Brush tops of rings lightly with some egg wash, being careful not to let wash run over edges.

Bake pastry shells in middle of oven until golden, about 9 minutes, and transfer to a rack. With a paring knife carefully cut out and remove pastry centers to form cavities. *Pastry shells may be made 2 days ahead and kept in airtight containers at room temperature. Reheat pastry shells in middle of a 400° F. oven until warm before serving.* Makes 8 shells.

Crab Burger Po' Boys

For mustard mayonnaise
⅓ cup mayonnaise
3 tablespoons finely chopped sweet pickle
1 tablespoon drained capers, chopped fine
1 tablespoon Creole or Dijon mustard
For crab burgers
¼ cup minced onion
¼ cup minced green bell pepper
2 tablespoons unsalted butter
½ pound lump crab meat, picked over
¼ cup thinly sliced scallion greens
3 tablespoons mayonnaise
2 tablespoons lightly beaten egg
½ cup plus 1 tablespoon fine dry bread crumbs
½ teaspoon Worcestershire sauce
cayenne to taste
vegetable oil for frying

two 5-inch lengths soft-crumb French bread,
    split and lightly toasted
2 iceberg lettuce leaves, sliced thin

Make mustard mayonnaise:
In a bowl whisk together mayonnaise ingredients and reserve.

Make crab burgers:
In a small heavy skillet cook onion and bell pepper in butter over moderately low heat, stirring occasionally, until softened. In a bowl stir together onion mixture, crab meat, scallions, mayonnaise, egg, 1 tablespoon bread crumbs, Worcestershire sauce, cayenne, and salt to taste.

Put remaining ½ cup bread crumbs in a small bowl and put a piece of plastic wrap on a work surface. Form one fourth crab mixture into a 3-inch patty (it will be soft) and coat with bread crumbs, transferring to plastic wrap. Make 3 more patties in same manner with remaining crab and crumbs.

In a 10-inch heavy deep skillet heat ¼ inch oil over moderately high heat until hot but not smoking and fry patties until golden and cooked through, about 2½ minutes on each side, transferring to paper towels to drain.

Spread bread with reserved mustard mayonnaise and sandwich crab burgers and lettuce between bread. Makes 2 sandwiches.

Oyster Loaf with Guacamole

2½ tablespoons mayonnaise
½ teaspoon Tabasco
3½ teaspoons fresh lemon juice, or to taste
2 ripe avocados (preferably California)
2 tablespoons minced scallion
a 15½- by 3½-inch loaf soft-crusted French or
    Italian bread
2 tablespoons unsalted butter, melted
18 shucked oysters, drained but not rinsed or
    patted dry
vegetable oil for deep frying
½ cup finely shredded iceberg lettuce

Preheat oven to 375° F.

In a bowl stir together mayonnaise, Tabasco, and ½ teaspoon lemon juice.

Halve and pit avocados. With a fork mash avocado flesh in skins and scoop flesh into a bowl. Stir in scallion, remaining lemon juice, and salt to taste. Chill *guacamole,* its surface covered with plastic wrap.

Cut off top third of bread loaf, reserving top, and pull out soft crumb from bottom, leaving a ½-inch shell and reserving crumb. Brush inside of shell and of reserved top with butter and arrange in a shallow baking pan with reserved crumb alongside. Bake bread in middle of oven until pale golden and just crisp, 7 to 10 minutes. Keep shell and top, loosely wrapped in foil, in the middle of a 275° F. oven and in a food processor or blender grind crumb coarse.

In a shallow dish coat oysters with crumbs. In a heavy kettle heat 1½ inches oil to 375° F. on a deep-fat thermometer and in 2 batches fry oysters until golden and just cooked through, about 1 minute.

With a slotted spoon transfer oysters as cooked to paper towels to drain.

Fill bread shell with *guacamole* and top with lettuce. Arrange oysters on lettuce and top with mayonnaise. Replace top of loaf. Serves 2.

Minted Lobster Salad in Pitas

four 6-inch pita pockets
2 tablespoons low-fat mayonnaise
1 tablespoon fresh lemon juice
¾ teaspoon freshly grated orange zest
½ teaspoon anise seeds, crushed
⅛ teaspoon cayenne
1 medium fennel bulb (sometimes called anise,
    about 1 pound), stalks trimmed flush with bulb
    and bulb cut into very thin slices
¾ pound cooked lobster meat, chopped
2 cups shredded romaine
¼ cup packed fresh mint leaves, washed well,
    spun dry, and chopped coarse

Preheat oven to 350° F.

Cut off one fourth of each pita pocket and reserve larger portions of pitas wrapped in plastic wrap. Chop smaller portions of pitas into ½-inch pieces and in a shallow baking pan toast in middle of oven until golden, about 7 minutes.

In a bowl stir together mayonnaise, lemon juice, zest, anise seeds, and cayenne until smooth. Add fennel, lobster, romaine, mint, and pita croutons and toss to coat. Fill reserved pitas with lobster salad. Makes 4 sandwiches.

🌿 Each serving about 282 calories, 5 grams fat
(16% of calories from fat)

MEAT

BEEF

Pan-Seared Filet Mignon with Roasted Potatoes and Merlot Sauce

For garnish
12 assorted red and yellow pearl onions,
    unpeeled
2 cups vegetable oil for frying onions

4 large russet (baking) potatoes (about
    2 pounds total)
about ¼ cup vegetable oil
six 1¼-inch-thick filets mignons (about
    3 pounds total)

Accompaniment: about 2 cups Merlot sauce
    (recipe follows)

Make garnish:

In a medium saucepan of salted boiling water blanch onions 3 minutes, or until barely tender, and drain in a colander. Peel skin away from each onion, keeping it attached at root end, and pat onion dry. In a heavy saucepan heat 2 cups oil until a deep-fat thermometer registers 375° F. and fry onions in 2 batches until crisp and brown, about 1 minute. Transfer onions as fried with a slotted spoon to paper towels and drain. Season onions with salt and pepper and cool. *Onions may be made 8 hours ahead and kept, covered, at room temperature.*

Preheat oven to 425° F. and oil 2 baking sheets.

Cut potatoes lengthwise into ½-inch-thick slices and arrange in one layer on baking sheets. Lightly brush slices with some oil and season with salt and pepper. Roast potatoes in middle and lower thirds of oven until golden brown and tender, about 35 minutes, and keep warm.

Pat filets mignons dry and season with salt and pepper. In a large heavy skillet heat 2 tablespoons oil over moderately high heat until hot but not smoking and brown filets on both sides, without crowding, about 5 minutes total. Transfer filets to a shallow baking pan and roast in middle of oven about 10 minutes for medium-rare.

On each of 6 plates fan 3 potato slices and top with a filet. Drizzle filets with some Merlot sauce and garnish with onions. Serve remaining sauce on the side. Serves 6.

PHOTO ON PAGE 82

Merlot Sauce

¼ cup water
¼ cup sugar
3 tablespoons red-wine vinegar
1 cup finely chopped onion (about 1 medium)
3 tablespoons unsalted butter
2 cups Merlot or other dry red wine
2 cups rich veal stock* or *demiglace**

*available at specialty foods shops, some
    supermarkets, and by mail order from
    D'Artagnan, tel. (800) 327-8246

In a small heavy saucepan bring water with sugar to a boil, stirring until sugar is dissolved. Boil syrup, without stirring, until a golden caramel. Remove pan from heat and carefully add vinegar down side of pan (caramel will steam and harden). Cook caramel over moderate heat, stirring, until dissolved, about 3 minutes, and remove pan from heat.

In a heavy saucepan cook onion in butter over moderate heat, stirring, until golden, about 5 minutes. Stir in wine and boil until mixture is reduced to about 1 cup, about 15 minutes. Stir in stock or *demiglace* and boil until mixture is reduced to about 2 cups, about 10 minutes. Remove pan from heat and stir in caramel. Pour sauce through a sieve into a bowl. *Sauce may be made 2 days ahead, cooled completely, and chilled, covered. Reheat sauce before serving.*

*Standing Rib Roast with Potatoes and
Portobello Mushrooms*

For seasoning mixture
1 tablespoon chopped fresh rosemary leaves
1 tablespoon chopped fresh thyme leaves
2 garlic cloves, chopped
1½ teaspoons coarse kosher salt
1 teaspoon freshly ground black pepper

a 3-rib standing beef rib roast (about
    8½ pounds), all but ¼-inch layer of
    fat removed
1 tablespoon vegetable oil
5 pounds russet (baking) potatoes (about 10)
1½ pounds Portobello mushrooms, wiped clean
1¾ cups beef broth (a 15½-ounce can)
1 cup water
a *beurre manié* made by kneading together
    1 tablespoon softened unsalted butter and
    1 tablespoon all-purpose flour

Garnish: chopped fresh flat-leafed parsley leaves

Preheat oven to 475° F.
Make seasoning mixture:
In a small bowl stir together seasoning mixture ingredients.

Put roast, ribs side down, in center of a flameproof roasting pan, 18 by 12 by 2 inches, and rub oil on top and sides of beef so herbs will adhere. Reserve 1 tablespoon seasoning mixture and rub remainder on top and sides of beef. Roast beef in lower third of oven 20 minutes.

Peel potatoes and halve crosswise. Remove pan from oven and skim all but about ½ cup fat from pan with a bulb baster or spoon. Arrange potatoes around beef and turn with tongs to coat with fat. Season potatoes with salt and pepper. Reduce heat to 350° F. and roast beef and potatoes, turning potatoes occasionally to brown evenly, 1½ hours, or until a meat thermometer inserted in fleshy part of beef registers 130° F. for medium-rare.

While beef and potatoes are roasting, separate mushroom stems and caps. Slice caps ⅓-inch thick. In a food processor pulse stems until chopped coarse and in a small saucepan combine with broth and water. Simmer mixture 10 minutes. Pour mixture

through a sieve into a bowl, pressing hard on solids, and discard solids.

Transfer beef to a platter and let rest, covered loosely with foil, 20 to 30 minutes. Transfer potatoes to another platter and keep warm.

With bulb baster or spoon skim all but about ¼ cup fat from pan. In pan on top of stove sauté mushroom caps over moderately high heat, stirring, 2 minutes. Add reserved tablespoon seasoning mixture, mushroom liquid, and any juices from beef and boil 5 minutes. Stir in *beurre manié* and boil, stirring, about 3 minutes, or until thickened slightly.

Serve beef with sauce and sprinkle potatoes with parsley. Serves 8.

Shiitake Beef Stroganov

two 5- to 6-ounce filets mignons, cut crosswise
    into ¼-inch-thick pieces
2 tablespoons all-purpose flour seasoned with
    salt and pepper
2 tablespoons olive oil
⅓ cup finely chopped shallots (about 2 large)
½ cup finely chopped onion
½ cup dry red wine
¼ pound fresh *shiitake* mushrooms, stems
    discarded and caps sliced (about 2 cups)
¼ pound white mushrooms, trimmed and sliced
¾ cup beef broth
¼ cup sour cream
1½ teaspoons Worcestershire sauce, or to taste
2 tablespoons finely chopped fresh parsley leaves

Accompaniment: turnip potato purée (page 185)
    or buttered egg noodles

In a bowl toss beef with flour until coated well. In a 10- to 12-inch heavy skillet heat 1 tablespoon oil over moderately high heat and brown beef in batches, transferring beef to a plate with a slotted spoon.

Add remaining tablespoon oil to skillet and cook shallots and onion with salt and pepper to taste over moderate heat, stirring, until softened. Add red wine and boil until cooking liquid is almost evaporated. Add mushrooms and cook, stirring, until tender and liquid they give off is evaporated. Add broth and simmer 1 minute. Stir in sour cream and Worcestershire sauce. Return beef to skillet and gently simmer, covered, stirring occasionally, 3 to 5 minutes, or until sauce is thickened. Stir in parsley and salt and pepper to taste.

Serve Stroganov with turnip potato purée or egg noodles. Serves 2.

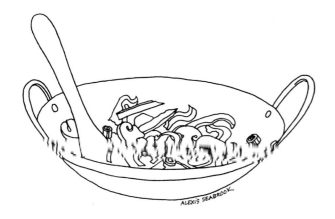

ALEXIS SEABROOK

Stir-Fried Sesame Beef

2 tablespoons dark soy sauce
3 tablespoons vegetable oil
1 teaspoon honey
½ teaspoon Dijon mustard
a ½-pound piece boneless sirloin steak, cut
    into ⅓-inch-thick slices
1 garlic clove, minced
¼ cup sliced red onion
1 red bell pepper, cut into ½-inch strips
1 yellow bell pepper, cut into ½-inch strips
2 celery ribs, cut diagonally into ¼-inch slices
4 scallions, cut diagonally into ¼-inch slices
    (about ½ cup)
3 tablespoons sesame seeds, toasted

In a bowl whisk together soy sauce, 2 tablespoons oil, honey, and mustard. Add steak, tossing to coat, and let marinate, covered, at room temperature 15 minutes.

In a 10-inch heavy skillet heat remaining tablespoon oil over moderately high heat until hot but not smoking and sauté garlic, red onion, and bell peppers, stirring, until crisp-tender, about 5 minutes.

Add celery and sauté, stirring, 2 minutes. Transfer mixture with a slotted spoon to another bowl.

Heat oil remaining in skillet over high heat until hot but not smoking and sauté steak, stirring, until medium-rare, about 2 minutes. Stir in sautéed vegetables, scallions, sesame seeds, and salt and pepper to taste and heat until just heated through. Serves 2.

Stir-Fried Beef and Broccoli Rabe

1 tablespoon soy sauce
2 teaspoons minced peeled fresh gingerroot
a scant ⅛ teaspoon dried hot red pepper flakes
3 teaspoons cornstarch
1½ teaspoons sugar
½ pound sirloin tip, cut into ⅓- by ½- by 1½-inch
    pieces
1 tablespoon Worcestershire sauce
¾ cup beef broth
½ teaspoon salt
1 tablespoon vegetable oil
1 garlic clove, sliced thin
½ bunch broccoli rabe (about ½ pound),
    hollow or coarse stems discarded
    and remainder washed, drained well,
    and cut into 2-inch pieces
⅓ cup water

In a bowl stir together soy sauce, gingerroot, red pepper flakes, 1 teaspoon cornstarch, and ½ teaspoon sugar and add sirloin, stirring to coat well. In a small bowl stir together remaining 2 teaspoons cornstarch, remaining teaspoon sugar, Worcestershire sauce, broth, and salt.

In a 12-inch non-stick skillet heat oil over high heat until it just begins to smoke and stir-fry sirloin until browned but still pink inside, about 2 minutes. With a slotted spoon transfer sirloin to another bowl.

In fat remaining in skillet stir-fry garlic over moderate heat just until golden. Add broccoli rabe and stir-fry until wilted. Add water and cook mixture, stirring, just until water is evaporated. Stir broth mixture and stir into broccoli rabe. Simmer mixture until liquid is thickened, about 1 minute. Stir in beef and simmer just until heated through, about 30 seconds. Serves 2.

Grilled Spiced Garlic Skirt Steak

a ¾- to 1-pound skirt steak
2 large garlic cloves, minced and mashed to a
    paste with ½ teaspoon salt
1½ teaspoons fresh lime juice
1 teaspoon olive oil
½ teaspoon ground coriander seeds
½ teaspoon ground cumin
¼ teaspoon cinnamon

Accompaniment if desired: sweet-onion
    quesadillas (page 163)

Prepare grill.

Cut skirt steak into large pieces if necessary to fit on grill.

In a small bowl stir together remaining ingredients. On a sheet of wax paper arrange steak and spread spice paste evenly on both sides of steak. Marinate steak at room temperature 15 minutes.

Grill steak on an oiled rack set 5 to 6 inches over glowing coals 3 to 5 minutes on each side, or until just springy to the touch, for medium-rare meat. (Alternatively, steak may be grilled in a hot well-seasoned ridged grill pan over moderately high heat.)

On a cutting board let steak stand 5 minutes and cut diagonally across grain into thin slices. Serve steak with *quesadillas.* Serves 2 generously.

Grilled Flank Steak and Red Onion with Orange Gremolata

a ¾-pound piece flank steak
four ⅓-inch-thick slices red onion, secured
    with wooden picks
1½ tablespoons balsamic vinegar
¼ cup olive oil
For gremolata
1 small garlic clove, minced
2 tablespoons fresh parsley leaves,
    minced
½ teaspoon freshly grated orange zest

Prepare grill.

In a shallow baking dish large enough to hold steak and onion slices in one layer whisk together vinegar, oil, and salt and pepper to taste. Add steak and onions and turn to coat with marinade. Marinate steak and onions, covered, 15 minutes.

Make gremolata:

In a small bowl toss together garlic, parsley, and orange zest.

Drain steak and grill on an oiled rack set 5 to 6 inches over glowing coals 5 minutes on each side for medium-rare. Transfer steak to a cutting board and let stand 10 minutes.

While steak is standing, drain onions, discarding marinade, and grill 5 minutes on each side, or until tender. (Alternatively, steak and onions may be cooked in a hot well-seasoned ridged grill pan.)

Slice steak thin across grain. Serve steak and onions sprinkled with *gremolata.* Serves 2.

Spicy Beef Shanks with Julienne Carrots

4 meaty cross-cut sections beef shanks (about
    4¼ pounds total)
4 teaspoons Worcestershire sauce
1 pound carrots, cut into 2-inch julienne strips
2 tablespoons unsalted butter
1 tablespoon bottled horseradish, drained, or
    grated fresh horseradish to taste
2 teaspoons minced fresh parsley leaves

Preheat oven to 275° F.

In a heavy ovenproof kettle large enough to hold beef shanks in one layer arrange shanks and season with salt and pepper. Roast meat, covered tightly, in middle of oven 2½ hours, or until tender. (Meat will give off juices as it cooks.)

Stir Worcestershire sauce into pan juices and cool meat, covered partially, basting it as it cools. Transfer meat with a slotted spoon to a platter and discard bones and gristle. Skim fat from pan juices. Return meat to pan juices and heat, covered partially, over moderate heat until just heated through.

In a steamer set over simmering water steam carrots, covered, 3 minutes, or until crisp-tender, and transfer to a bowl. Toss carrots with butter, horseradish, parsley, and salt and pepper to taste.

Divide carrots among 4 plates, mounding slightly, and arrange meat over them. Drizzle meat with pan juices. Serves 4.

Grilled Marinated London Broil

For marinade
5 large garlic cloves
1 teaspoon salt
¼ cup dry red wine
¼ cup balsamic vinegar
1 tablespoon soy sauce
1 teaspoon honey

a 1½-pound top-round London broil
(about 1¼ inches thick)

Accompaniment: sliced vine-ripened tomatoes

Make marinade:
Mince and mash garlic to a paste with salt and in a blender blend with remaining marinade ingredients.

In a heavy-duty sealable plastic bag combine London broil with marinade. Seal bag, pressing out excess air, and put in a shallow baking dish. *Marinate steak, chilled, turning occasionally, at least 4 hours and up to 24.*

Prepare grill.

Bring steak to room temperature (which should take about 1 hour) before grilling. Remove steak from marinade, letting excess drip off, and grill on an oiled rack set 5 to 6 inches over glowing coals 7 to 9 minutes on each side for medium-rare. Transfer steak to a cutting board and let stand 10 minutes.

Holding a knife at a 45° angle, cut steak across grain into thin slices and serve with sliced tomatoes. Serves 6.

Each serving about 146 calories, 4 grams fat
(24% of calories from fat)

PHOTO ON PAGE 38

Panéed Veal with Fried Lemon Slices

2 large eggs
½ cup water
1½ cups fine dry bread crumbs
1½ teaspoons freshly grated lemon zest
1¼ teaspoons dried thyme, crumbled
eight ¼-pound veal cutlets, pounded ⅛ inch thick
vegetable oil for deep-frying
sixteen ⅛-inch-thick lemon slices
¾ cup all-purpose flour seasoned with salt and
pepper for dredging

In a shallow baking dish whisk together eggs and water and in a large, shallow baking dish stir together bread crumbs, zest, thyme, and salt and pepper to taste. Dip cutlets, 1 at a time, into egg mixture, letting excess drip off, and dredge in bread crumb mixture, pressing lightly until mixture adheres. Transfer cutlets as coated to a large rack and let dry at room temperature at least 15 minutes and up to 30 minutes. *Veal may be prepared up to this point 1 hour ahead and chilled, uncovered.*

Preheat oven to 225° F.

In a deep heavy skillet (preferably cast-iron) heat 1 inch oil over moderately high heat until hot but not smoking. While oil is heating, dredge 4 lemon slices in flour, knocking off excess. Fry lemon slices, turning them occasionally, until golden, about 45 seconds. Transfer slices as fried with tongs to paper towels to drain briefly and arrange in one layer on another large rack set on a baking sheet. Coat and fry remaining 12 lemon slices in batches in same manner. (Carefully remove skillet from heat if necessary while coating slices to prevent oil from overheating.) Keep lemon slices, arranged in one layer, warm on baking sheet in oven.

With a slotted spoon remove any food particles in oil remaining in skillet and discard. Heat oil if necessary until hot but not smoking and fry cutlets, 1 at a time, turning them once, until golden and just cooked through, about 45 seconds, transferring with tongs to paper towels to drain briefly. Transfer veal to cleaned rack set on another baking sheet and keep warm in oven. Serves 8.

PHOTO ON PAGE 23

Veal Shanks, Artichoke Hearts, and Chick Peas with Preserved Lemon

six to eight 2-inch-thick veal shanks (5 pounds total), each tied securely with kitchen string to keep meat attached to bone
1½ cup dried chick-peas, picked over
1 tablespoon olive oil
1 large onion, chopped
two 10-ounce packages frozen artichoke hearts, thawed, halved lengthwise if large
¼ cup packed fresh coriander sprigs, washed well, spun dry, and minced
3 tablespoons four-day preserved lemon zest (recipe follows), slivered, or preserved lemon*, slivered

*available by mail order from The Gardener, 1836 Fourth St., Berkeley, CA 94710, tel. (510) 548-4545

Preheat oven to 275° F.

In a heavy kettle large enough to hold veal shanks in one layer without crowding arrange shanks and season with salt and pepper. Roast shanks in middle of oven, covered tightly, 3 hours, or until tender. (Meat will give off juices as it cooks.)

While shanks are roasting, in a large saucepan combine chick-peas with enough water to cover by 4 inches and simmer, covered partially, 1½ to 2 hours, or until tender but not falling apart. Drain chick-peas in a colander. *Chick-peas may be cooked 2 days ahead, cooled, uncovered, and chilled, covered.*

Transfer shanks to a deep platter and keep warm, reserving pan juices.

In a large heavy skillet heat oil over moderate heat until hot but not smoking and cook onion, stirring, until softened. Add artichoke hearts, chick-peas, and reserved pan juices and simmer, covered, until artichoke hearts are just tender, about 3 minutes. Transfer about ½ cup chick-peas with a slotted spoon and about 1 cup pan juices from skillet to a blender and purée. Stir purée into artichoke and chick-pea mixture to thicken and stir in coriander and salt and pepper to taste.

Spoon artichoke and chick-pea mixture over roasted shanks and sprinkle with preserved lemon. Serves 6.

Four-Day Preserved Lemon Zest

3 large lemons
2 teaspoons coarse kosher salt
⅔ cup fresh lemon juice

Scrub lemons and with a vegetable peeler remove zest in strips. In a saucepan of boiling water blanch zest 1 minute and drain in a sieve. Transfer zest to a glass jar (about 1-cup capacity). Add salt and lemon juice, pressing zest down to keep it covered by juice, and cover jar with a tight-fitting glass lid or plastic-coated lid. Let zest stand at room temperature 4 days, shaking jar each day. *Preserved lemon zest keeps, covered and chilled, 6 months.* Makes ½ cup.

Osso Buco with Mushroom Sauce

six to eight 2-inch-thick veal shanks (5 pounds total), each tied securely with kitchen string to keep meat attached to bone
3 tablespoons olive oil
3 tablespoons unsalted butter
1½ pounds onion, sliced thin
2 celery ribs, sliced thin
½ pound fresh *cremini* or white mushrooms, tough stem ends trimmed
½ pound fresh *shiitake* mushrooms, stems discarded
½ pound fresh Portobello mushrooms, stems discarded
¾ teaspoon dried thyme, crumbled
½ cup dry vermouth or dry white wine
1 tablespoon fresh lemon juice
½ to ¾ cup water
1 to 2 tablespoons balsamic vinegar, or to taste
¼ cup fresh parsley leaves, washed well, spun dry, and minced

Accompaniment: cooked couscous

Preheat oven to 275° F.

In a heavy ovenproof kettle large enough to hold veal shanks in one layer heat 1 tablespoon each of oil and butter over moderately high heat until foam begins to subside. Sauté onion and celery until vegetables begin to turn golden.

Pat shanks dry between paper towels and season

with salt and pepper. Arrange shanks on onion mixture and roast, covered tightly, in middle of oven 3 hours. (Meat will give off juices as it cooks.) *Shanks may be prepared up to this point 1 day ahead and cooled, uncovered, before chilling, covered. Reheat shanks before proceeding.*

Cut mushrooms into ¼-inch-thick slices. In a large skillet heat remaining 2 tablespoons each of oil and butter over moderately high heat until foam begins to subside and sauté mushrooms with thyme and salt and pepper to taste, stirring, until mushrooms begin to give off their liquid. Stir in vermouth or wine and lemon juice and cook, stirring, until all but about ⅓ cup of liquid is evaporated. *Mushrooms may be made 1 day ahead and cooled completely before chilling, covered.*

Transfer shanks to a platter and keep warm. Transfer onions, celery, and pan juices to a blender with ½ cup water and purée until smooth, adding more water if necessary to thin sauce to desired consistency. Pour sauce into a saucepan and stir in mushroom mixture, vinegar, and salt and pepper to taste. Heat sauce over moderate heat until heated through and stir in parsley.

Arrange shanks on couscous and spoon sauce over them. Serves 6.

Veal Scallops with Peperoncini and Scallions

¾ pound veal scallops, pounded thin between
    sheets of plastic wrap
½ cup all-purpose flour
2 tablespoons olive oil
½ cup dry vermouth or dry white wine
2 tablespoons minced *peperoncini*
    (Tuscan peppers)
2 scallions, minced
1 tablespoon unsalted butter, cut into bits

Pat veal scallops dry and season with salt and pepper. Dredge veal in flour, shaking off excess, and arrange in one layer on a sheet of wax paper.

In a large heavy skillet heat oil over moderately high heat until hot but not smoking and sauté veal in batches, without crowding, 30 seconds on each side, or until pale golden, transferring with tongs to a platter.

Add vermouth or wine to skillet and deglaze over high heat, stirring and scraping up brown bits. Add *peperoncini* and scallions and boil mixture 1 minute. Add butter and salt and pepper to taste and cook sauce, swirling skillet, until butter is just melted. Return veal to skillet with any juices accumulated on platter and coat with sauce. Serves 2.

PORK

Pork Chops in Mustard Mushroom Sauce

1 large shallot, minced
1 tablespoon plus 1 teaspoon vegetable oil
4 white mushrooms, sliced thin
½ cup dry white wine or dry vermouth
¼ cup heavy cream
⅛ teaspoon fresh thyme leaves or a pinch
     dried thyme, crumbled
1 teaspoon coarse-grained mustard
four ½-inch-thick loin or rib pork chops

In a small saucepan cook shallot in 1 tablespoon oil over moderate heat, stirring, until softened. Add mushrooms and sauté over moderately high heat, stirring, until liquid mushrooms give off is evaporated. Add wine or vermouth and boil until liquid is reduced to about 2 tablespoons. Stir in cream, thyme, and salt and pepper to taste and simmer just until sauce is thickened. Stir in mustard and keep sauce warm over very low heat.

Pat pork chops dry with paper towels and season with salt and pepper. Heat remaining teaspoon oil in a 10-inch non-stick skillet until hot but not smoking and sauté chops until golden and just cooked through, 2 to 3 minutes on each side.

Divide chops between 2 plates and spoon sauce over them. Serves 2.

Pork Tournedos with Blackberry Gastrique and Mango Salsa

For salsa
1 firm-ripe mango, pitted, peeled, and cut into
     ¼-inch dice
2 tablespoons finely chopped red onion
¼ teaspoon freshly grated lime zest
1 tablespoon fresh lime juice
2 tablespoons fresh mint leaves,
     chopped
For gastrique
¾ cup red-wine vinegar
3 tablespoons seedless blackberry preserves
¼ teaspoon salt

six 1½-inch-thick center-cut boneless pork
     loin chops (about 6 ounces each)
freshly ground black pepper
2 tablespoons unsalted butter

Make salsa:
In a bowl stir together salsa ingredients with salt to taste and let stand, covered, at room temperature. *Salsa may be made 2 hours ahead and kept at room temperature, covered.*
Make gastrique:
In a small saucepan simmer vinegar until reduced to about 2 tablespoons, about 3 minutes. Whisk in preserves and salt, whisking until smooth, and keep warm, covered.

Season pork with pepper and salt. In a 12-inch heavy skillet melt butter over moderately high heat until foam subsides and sauté pork until golden, about 3 minutes on each side. Cook pork, covered, over moderate heat until just cooked through, about 5 minutes more.

Divide *gastrique* among 6 plates and top with pork and salsa. Serves 6.

PHOTO ON PAGE 46

Beer-Braised Sausages and Sauerkraut

9 cups drained sauerkraut (from 5 to 6 pounds
     packaged, not canned, sauerkraut)
¼ pound smoked bacon (preferably slab)*, cut
     crosswise into ¼-inch pieces
2 onions, sliced thin
4 carrots, cut crosswise into ¼-inch-thick slices
5½ cups Oktoberfest lager (44 ounces)
     such as Paulaner
1 cup chicken broth
3 bay leaves
1 teaspoon salt
½ teaspoon whole black peppercorns
1 tablespoon vegetable oil if desired
1¾ pounds assorted smoked and precooked
     fresh sausages* (we used smoked *kielbasa* cut
     into thick slices, frankfurters, and *baernwurst*;
     and precooked fresh bratwurst, *weisswurst*,
     and *chipolata*)
a 1-pound piece smoked boneless pork loin
     (Canadian bacon)*, cut into 4 slices

*available at some specialty butcher shops and some supermarkets and by mail order from Schaller and Weber, tel. (800) 847-4115

Accompaniment: coarse-grained mustard

Preheat oven to 325° F.

In a large bowl soak sauerkraut in cold water to cover 20 minutes, changing water once halfway through soaking.

While sauerkraut is soaking, in a heavy skillet cook bacon pieces over moderate heat, stirring, until golden. Pour off all but about 2 tablespoons drippings and add onions to bacon. Cook mixture, stirring, until onions are softened.

Drain sauerkraut well in a colander, pressing out excess liquid, and in a large flameproof roasting pan combine with bacon mixture, carrots, beer, broth, bay leaves, salt, and peppercorns. Bring sauerkraut mixture to a boil on top of stove and boil 1 minute. Cover pan tightly with foil and braise in middle of oven 4 hours. *Sauerkraut may be prepared up to this point 1 day ahead, cooled, uncovered, and chilled, covered with plastic wrap. Reheat sauerkraut before proceeding.*

If desired, in a heavy skillet heat oil over moderate heat until hot but not smoking and in batches brown sausages. Add sausages and pork loin to sauerkraut, partially submerging them. Braise sausages and sauerkraut, covered tightly with foil, in middle of oven 30 minutes and transfer with a slotted spoon to a heated platter, discarding bay leaves if desired. (Do not eat bay leaves if leaving as garnish.)

Serve beer-braised sausages with sauerkraut and mustard. Serves 6.

PHOTO ON PAGE 19

Grilled Sausages, Peppers, and Onions on Rolls

1 tablespoon olive oil
1 red bell pepper, cut into
    ¼-inch rings
1 yellow bell pepper, cut into
    ¼-inch rings
1 onion, cut into ¼-inch slices
1 tablespoon Worcestershire sauce
1 teaspoon balsamic vinegar

4 sweet or hot Italian sausages (about
    12 ounces total)
2 hero, hoagie, or grinder rolls (each about
    7 inches long by 3 inches wide)

Prepare grill.

In a small bowl drizzle 2 teaspoons oil over bell pepper rings, tossing to coat well. Secure each slice of onion horizontally with a wooden pick (to prevent separation into rings) and brush with remaining teaspoon oil.

Grill bell peppers and onions on an oiled rack set 5 to 6 inches over glowing coals 3 minutes on each side, or until tender. (Alternatively, bell peppers and onions may be grilled in batches in a hot well-seasoned ridged grill pan over moderately high heat.)

Transfer bell peppers and onions to a bowl, discarding wooden picks, and toss with Worcestershire sauce and vinegar.

Prick sausages with a fork and grill, turning them, until golden and just cooked through (about 160° F. on an instant-read thermometer), 10 to 15 minutes.

Halve sausages lengthwise and rolls horizontally and grill, cut sides down, 1 minute, or until sausages are cooked through but still juicy and rolls are lightly toasted.

Divide bell peppers and onions between rolls and top with sausages. Serves 2.

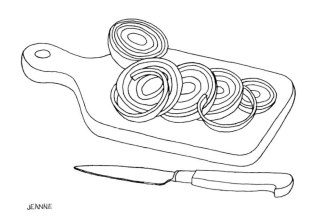

JEANNE

Roast Pork Loin in Horseradish Crust

1 cup fresh bread crumbs (about 2 slices)
2 tablespoons olive oil
2 tablespoons drained bottled horseradish,
    or to taste
a 1-pound piece boneless pork loin
1½ tablespoons Dijon mustard

Accompaniment if desired: balsamic-braised
    red cabbage and onions (page 177)

Preheat oven to 425° F.

In a heavy skillet cook bread crumbs in 1 table-spoon oil with salt and pepper to taste over moderate heat, stirring, until golden brown. Transfer bread crumbs to a bowl and toss well with horseradish.

Pat pork dry and season with salt and pepper. In skillet heat remaining tablespoon oil over moderately high heat until hot but not smoking and brown pork on all sides, about 5 minutes. Transfer pork to a shallow baking pan and coat top and sides evenly with mustard. Press bread crumb mixture evenly onto mustard and roast pork in middle of oven until a meat thermometer inserted in center registers 155° F. for slightly pink meat (if bread crumbs begin to brown too quickly arrange a sheet of foil loosely over pork), 25 to 30 minutes. Transfer pork to a cutting board and let stand 5 minutes.

Cut pork into ¼-inch-thick slices and serve with cabbage and onions. Serves 2.

LAMB

Lamb Quinoa Stew

1½ pounds plum tomatoes, quartered lengthwise
1 pound firm eggplant (about 1 small), cut
    into 1-inch cubes
¼ cup olive oil
2 red bell peppers, cut into 1-inch pieces
2 yellow onions, cut into 1-inch pieces
1 red onion, cut into 1-inch pieces
3 large carrots, cut crosswise into ½-inch pieces
2 pounds boneless lamb shoulder, trimmed
    and cut into 1-inch cubes
a 1-pound piece butternut squash, peeled
    and cut into 1-inch cubes
    (about 2 cups)
5 large garlic cloves, minced
2 cinnamon sticks, halved
½ teaspoon ground cumin
¼ teaspoon ground ginger
¼ teaspoon ground allspice
6 cups chicken broth
¾ cup quinoa*, rinsed well in a
    fine sieve

Garnish: blanched whole almonds, toasted
    with salt and oil, if desired

*available at natural foods stores

Preheat oven to 450° F. and set oven racks in middle and lower thirds of oven.

In a large bowl toss tomatoes and eggplant with 1 tablespoon oil and salt and pepper to taste. In a large shallow baking pan arrange tomatoes and eggplant in one layer. In bowl toss bell peppers, onions, and carrots with 1 tablespoon oil and salt and pepper to taste. In another large shallow baking pan arrange bell pepper mixture in one layer.

Roast vegetables in middle and lower thirds of oven, stirring occasionally and switching pans halfway through roasting, until golden brown and tender, about 20 minutes. If desired, peel tomatoes.

Pat lamb dry and season with salt and pepper. While vegetables are roasting, in a large heavy kettle (about 8-quart capacity) heat 1 tablespoon oil over moderately high heat until hot but not smoking and brown lamb in 2 batches, transferring with a slotted spoon to a bowl.

Add remaining tablespoon oil to kettle and cook squash, garlic, and spices over moderate heat, stirring, 2 minutes. Return lamb to kettle and add roasted vegetables and broth. Bring stew to a boil and simmer, covered, 1 hour.

Stir in quinoa and simmer, uncovered, stirring occasionally, 30 minutes, or until quinoa is tender. Discard cinnamon sticks and add water to thin stew if desired.

Serve stew garnished with almonds. Makes about 12 cups, serving 6 to 8.

*Grilled Lemon and Garlic Leg of Lamb
with Coriander Chutney*

two 7- to 8-pound legs of lamb, trimmed of
    excess fat, boned, and butterflied by butcher
    (each 4 to 4¾ pounds boneless)
1 cup fresh lemon juice
12 garlic cloves, chopped fine
¼ cup chopped fresh thyme leaves
¼ cup chopped fresh oregano leaves
½ cup chopped fresh rosemary leaves
3 tablespoons coarse salt
1 cup olive oil
freshly ground black pepper to taste

Garnish: fresh herb sprigs
Accompaniment: coriander chutney (recipe
    follows)

Put each leg of lamb into a large sealable plastic
bag, folding meat if necessary.

In a bowl whisk together remaining ingredients
and divide between bags. Seal bags, pressing out
excess air, and stack in a shallow baking pan.
*Marinate lamb, chilled, turning it once or twice, at
least 8 hours and up to 1 day.*

Prepare grill.

Remove lamb from bags, discarding marinade,
and grill on an oiled rack set 5 to 6 inches over
glowing coals 8 to 12 minutes on each side (thin

parts of meat will be medium-rare; thicker parts will
be rare). (Alternatively, lamb may be broiled 3 to 4
inches from heat.) Cool lamb to room temperature.
*Lamb may be cooked 1 day ahead and chilled,
wrapped well.* Slice lamb thin and arrange on a
platter. Bring lamb to cool room temperature, its
surface covered with plastic wrap.

Garnish lamb with herb sprigs and serve with
chutney. Serves 16 as part of a buffet.

PHOTO ON PAGE 67

Coriander Chutney

8 cups firmly packed fresh coriander sprigs,
    washed well and spun dry
8 scallion greens, chopped coarse (about 1 cup)
2⅔ cups sweetened flaked coconut (about
    1 package), lightly toasted and cooled
4 fresh *jalapeño* chilies, seeded and chopped
    (wear rubber gloves)
6 tablespoons white-wine vinegar
¼ cup grated peeled fresh gingerroot
½ cup vegetable oil

In a food processor coarsely purée chutney
ingredients in 2 batches. *Chutney may be made 2
days ahead and chilled, covered. Bring chutney to
cool room temperature before serving.* Makes about
3 cups.

"Redeye" Braised Lamb Shanks and Beans

6 lamb shanks (about 1 pound each)
3 tablespoons vegetable oil
1 pound dried kidney beans (about 2¼ cups),
    picked over
1 large onion, chopped fine
1 red bell pepper, chopped fine
1 large carrot, cut into ¼-inch dice
4 garlic cloves, chopped
2 slices bacon, chopped
4 cups water plus 2 cups additional if not
    using coffee
2 cups brewed coffee if desired
a *bouquet garni* composed of 5 fresh parsley
    sprigs, 3 fresh thyme sprigs, and 2 fresh
    rosemary sprigs, tied
2 bay leaves
½ teaspoon dried hot red pepper flakes

Preheat oven to 300° F.

Pat lamb shanks dry and season with salt. In a heavy ovenproof kettle large enough to hold shanks tightly in one layer heat oil over moderate heat until hot but not smoking and brown shanks in 2 batches, transferring to a plate. Add beans to kettle and top with shanks. Add remaining ingredients and bring to a boil over high heat, without stirring. Braise shank mixture, covered, in middle of oven 3 hours, or until lamb and beans are very tender.

Alternatively, brown shanks in a large heavy skillet in same manner, transferring to a 17- by 11-inch roasting pan. Put beans around shanks and scatter mixture with vegetables and bacon. In a saucepan bring 4 cups water and coffee to a boil. Deglaze skillet with about 1 cup coffee mixture, scraping up brown bits, and add to shank mixture with remaining coffee mixture and remaining ingredients. Cover pan with foil and braise in same manner.

Shank mixture may be prepared up to this point 2 days ahead, cooled, uncovered, and chilled, covered. Reheat shank mixture in middle of a preheated 350° F. oven, covered, 30 minutes, or until heated through, before proceeding.

Transfer shanks and beans with a slotted spoon to a heated platter, discarding *bouquet garni* and bay leaves, and bring braising liquid to a boil. (If using roasting pan, pour braising liquid into a large saucepan and bring to a boil.) Boil braising liquid until thickened slightly, about 5 minutes, and pour over shanks and beans. Serves 6 generously.

PHOTO ON PAGE 16

Lamb Shank Stifado with Sautéed Potatoes

¼ cup sugar
½ cup red-wine vinegar
a 28- to 32-ounce can whole tomatoes
    including juice, chopped
1 cup dry red wine
2 teaspoons dried rosemary, crumbled
1 cinnamon stick
1 bay leaf
6 lamb shanks (about 6 pounds total)
1 pound pearl onions (about 3 cups)
2 pounds small red potatoes
3 large garlic cloves, sliced thin
1 tablespoon olive oil

Preheat oven to 350° F.

In a 9-quart heavy ovenproof kettle cook sugar on top of stove over moderate heat, without stirring, until it begins to melt. Continue to cook sugar, stirring with a fork, until melted and cook without stirring, swirling kettle, until a deep golden caramel. Add vinegar and stir until caramel is dissolved. Stir in tomatoes with juice, wine, rosemary, cinnamon, and bay leaf and bring to a boil. Add lamb shanks and braise, covered, in middle of oven until tender, about 2 hours. *Braised shanks improve in flavor if made 1 day ahead. Cool mixture, uncovered, and chill, covered. Skim and discard fat from mixture and reheat on top of stove before proceeding.*

In a saucepan of boiling water blanch onions 10 minutes, or until just tender, and drain. Cool onions and peel.

Quarter potatoes and in a steamer set over simmering water steam potatoes, covered, 8 to 10 minutes, or until just tender. In a large non-stick skillet cook garlic in oil over moderate heat, stirring, until pale golden. Add potatoes with salt and pepper to taste and sauté mixture over moderately high heat 5 minutes, or until potatoes are golden.

Transfer meat with a slotted spoon to a platter.

Discard cinnamon stick and bay leaf. Add onions to sauce and boil until sauce is thickened slightly. Spoon sauce and onions over meat and surround with potatoes. Serves 4.

Rosemary, Lemon, and Garlic Leg of Lamb with Roasted Potatoes

2 large lemons, zest of 1 removed in strips
   with a vegetable peeler
¼ cup fresh rosemary leaves
3 large garlic cloves
2 tablespoons olive oil
2 teaspoons fresh lemon juice
½ teaspoon salt
a 7-pound leg of lamb (ask butcher to remove
   pelvic bone and tie lamb for easier carving)
2½ pounds small red potatoes
3 tablespoons minced fresh chives

Garnish: fresh rosemary sprigs and lemon wedges

Preheat oven to 350° F.

Cut off and discard pith from zested lemon and cut off and discard zest and pith from other lemon. In a saucepan of boiling water blanch zest 1 minute and drain in a colander. Cut each lemon crosswise into 6 slices.

In a small food processor blend rosemary, garlic, zest, 1 tablespoon olive oil, lemon juice, and salt until mixture is chopped fine.

With tip of a small sharp knife cut small slits all over lamb and rub rosemary mixture over lamb, rubbing into slits. Arrange lemon slices in middle of a large roasting pan and arrange lamb on them. Roast lamb in middle of oven 45 minutes.

Quarter small red potatoes and in a saucepan cover with salted cold water by 1 inch. Bring water to a boil and cook potatoes, covered, 5 minutes. Drain potatoes in colander and in a large bowl toss with remaining tablespoon olive oil. Arrange potatoes around lamb and sprinkle with salt and pepper to taste.

Roast lamb and potatoes, stirring potatoes occasionally, 55 minutes, or until a meat thermometer registers 140° F. for medium-rare. Transfer lamb to a cutting board and let stand 15 minutes. Increase temperature to 500° F. and roast potatoes and lemons in one layer 5 to 10 minutes more, or until golden. Transfer potatoes and lemons with a slotted spoon to bowl and toss with chives. Transfer potato mixture to a platter.

Serve leg of lamb, sliced thin across grain, with potatoes, garnished with rosemary sprigs and lemon wedges. Serves 6.

PHOTO ON PAGE 32

POULTRY

The following recipe uses whole chicken breasts with the "tenders" (fillet strips) still attached. If you use chicken without the tenders, simply stuff the chicken breasts with basil and wrap with bacon.

Bacon and Basil-Wrapped Chicken Breasts

21 large fresh basil leaves, washed well and
    spun dry
3 whole boneless skinless chicken breasts
    (about 2 pounds total)
about 15 bacon slices (about ¾ pound)
1 teaspoon whole black peppercorns,
    crushed coarse

Preheat oven to 400° F.

In a small saucepan of boiling water blanch basil 2 seconds and drain in a sieve. Rinse basil under cold water to stop cooking and pat dry on paper towels.

Put 1 whole chicken breast, skinned side down, on a work surface and remove "tender" (fillet strip located on either side of where breast bone was) from each breast half, keeping rest of chicken breast intact. (There should be 2 tenders from each whole breast.)

Put 2 tenders side by side and wrap 7 basil leaves around them to enclose. Season remainder of whole breast with salt and pepper and put basil-wrapped tenders lengthwise down middle of 1 breast half. Fold other breast half over to enclose tenders.

Beginning on underside at 1 end of breast, wrap bacon slices snugly but without stretching, 1 at a time, around breast in a continuous overlapping spiral from 1 end to the other. (You will need about 4 to 5 bacon slices for each breast.)

Remove tenders from remaining 2 chicken breasts and stuff and wrap breasts in same manner. Sprinkle crushed peppercorns evenly over bacon wrappings.

Heat a 9- to 10-inch cast-iron skillet over moderately high heat until hot. Sliding a metal spatula under wrapped chicken breasts to keep bacon intact, transfer 2 breasts, undersides down, to skillet. Cook chicken, turning it only after bacon on underside is golden, until bacon is golden and crisp on all sides, about 4 minutes total. Transfer chicken as browned to a plate and cook remaining breast in same manner.

Pour off fat from skillet and return all 3 chicken breasts to skillet. Roast chicken breasts in middle of oven 15 minutes, or until firm to the touch and just cooked through. Transfer chicken with tongs to a cutting board and let stand 10 minutes before slicing. Serves 6.

PHOTO ON PAGE 50

Chicken and Gravy

1 garlic clove, minced and mashed to a paste
    with ½ teaspoon salt
½ teaspoon dried thyme, crumbled
4 teaspoons fresh lemon juice
1 whole chicken breast (about ¾ pound),
    halved
½ tablespoon vegetable oil
½ tablespoon unsalted butter
1½ tablespoons all-purpose flour
¾ cup low-salt chicken broth
1 teaspoon minced fresh parsley leaves

Accompaniment: cooked rice

In a shallow bowl stir together garlic paste, thyme, and 3 teaspoons lemon juice. Add chicken breast halves, turning to coat, and marinate, covered, 15 minutes. Pat chicken dry.

In a 9-inch heavy skillet heat oil and butter over moderately high heat until foam subsides and sauté chicken halves, skin side down, until golden, about 2 minutes on each side. Transfer chicken with tongs to a plate. Add flour to skillet and cook *roux* over moderately low heat, whisking, 3 minutes. Whisk in broth and remaining teaspoon lemon juice in a stream, whisking until gravy is smooth. Return chicken to skillet with any juices accumulated on plate and simmer, covered, 15 minutes, or until springy to the touch and just cooked through.

Stir in parsley and serve over rice. Serves 2.

Chili Rubbed Chicken with Rosemary and Tomato

3 whole boneless skinless chicken breasts
   (about 2 pounds), halved
3 tablespoons tomato paste
2 tablespoons chili powder
3 tablespoons water
1 tablespoon seasoned rice vinegar
2 garlic cloves, minced and mashed to a
   paste with ½ teaspoon salt
2 firm vine-ripened tomatoes (each about
   3 inches in diameter)
6 fresh rosemary sprigs
six 10-inch wooden skewers, soaked in
   water 1 hour

Arrange chicken breasts, skinned side down, on a cutting board. Remove fillet strip from each breast and reserve for another use.

In a small bowl whisk together tomato paste, chili powder, water, rice vinegar, and garlic paste. In a shallow baking dish large enough to hold chicken in one layer coat chicken with chili paste. *Marinate chicken, covered and chilled, at least 1 hour and up to 24.*

Prepare grill.

With a serrated knife cut off stem end of tomatoes and cut each tomato into three ¼-inch-thick slices. Arrange 1 tomato slice and 1 rosemary sprig on wide end of skinned side of 1 chicken breast and fold narrow end over to sandwich tomato and rosemary.

Thread a skewer through ends of chicken breast and then through folded side, letting pointed end of skewer extend about 1½ inches beyond chicken breast. Stuff remaining chicken with remaining tomatoes and rosemary and thread with remaining skewers in same manner.

Grill chicken on an oiled rack set 5 to 6 inches over glowing coals until cooked through, about 8 minutes on each side.

Serve grilled chicken warm or at room temperature. Serves 6.

   👁 Each serving about 152 calories, 2 grams fat
(13% of calories from fat)

PHOTO ON PAGE 37

Garlic Soy Chicken

¼ cup soy sauce
¼ cup medium-dry Sherry
2 tablespoons firmly packed brown sugar
2 large garlic cloves, minced
1 tablespoon grated peeled fresh gingerroot
1 whole boneless skinless chicken breast
   (about ¾ pound), halved
1 tablespoon vegetable oil

Accompaniment if desired: sesame vegetables
   (page 187)

In a small bowl combine soy sauce, Sherry, brown sugar, garlic, gingerroot, and salt and pepper to taste and stir until sugar is dissolved. Gently pound chicken between 2 sheets of plastic wrap until about ¼ inch thick. In a large sealable plastic bag marinate chicken in soy sauce mixture, turning occasionally, 25 minutes.

In a heavy skillet heat oil over moderate heat until hot but not smoking. Remove chicken from marinade, letting excess drip off and reserving marinade, and cook until browned and cooked through, 3 to 4 minutes on each side. Transfer chicken to a plate and keep warm. Pour reserved marinade through a sieve into skillet and boil until reduced to about 2 tablespoons.

Drizzle chicken with sauce and serve with sesame vegetables. Serves 2.

Shiitake-Crusted Chicken with Creamed Mushrooms

For coating

2 teaspoons olive oil

6 ounces fresh *shiitake* mushrooms, stems
  discarded and caps chopped coarse

⅓ cup fine dry bread crumbs

⅓ cup all-purpose flour, seasoned with salt
  and pepper

1 large egg, beaten lightly

2 whole boneless skinless chicken breasts
  (about 1½ pounds), halved

2 tablespoons olive oil

For creamed mushrooms

1 large shallot, minced (about ¼ cup)

1 tablespoon unsalted butter

½ pound fresh *shiitake* mushrooms, stems
  discarded and caps chopped coarse

½ cup dry white wine

1 tablespoon white-wine vinegar

1 teaspoon chopped fresh rosemary leaves or a
  rounded ¼ teaspoon dried rosemary, crumbled

½ cup heavy cream

Prepare coating:

Preheat oven to 450° F.

In a shallow baking pan drizzle oil over *shiitakes*
and toss to coat. Roast mushrooms, stirring once or
twice, 12 to 15 minutes, or until golden. Keep oven
at 450° F.

Mince roasted *shiitakes* and in a shallow bowl stir
together with bread crumbs and salt and pepper to
taste. Have ready in separate shallow bowls seasoned flour and egg.

Working with 1 chicken breast at a time, dredge
in flour, shaking off excess, and dip in egg, letting
excess drip off. Coat chicken with mushroom mixture, gently knocking off excess, and transfer to a
plate. *Chicken may be prepared up to this point 2
hours ahead and chilled, uncovered, on a rack.*

In a 12-inch non-stick skillet heat oil over moderately high heat until hot but not smoking and sauté
chicken until golden, about 1 minute on each side.
Transfer chicken with tongs to baking pan and roast
in middle of oven 10 minutes, or until just cooked
through.

*Make creamed mushrooms while chicken is
roasting:*

Wipe out skillet and cook shallot in butter over
moderately low heat, stirring, until softened. Add
shiitakes and salt and pepper to taste and sauté over
moderately high heat, stirring, until mushrooms are
softened and browned lightly. Stir in wine, vinegar,
and rosemary and boil until all liquid is evaporated.
Add cream and simmer, stirring, until thickened
slightly, about 1 minute. Season mixture with salt
and pepper.

Serve *shiitake*-crusted chicken with creamed
mushrooms. Serves 4.

*Sesame Chicken with Napa Cabbage and
Spinach Slaw on Baguette*

1½ tablespoons all-purpose flour

2 tablespoons sesame seeds

1 large egg white

1 teaspoon water

2 small whole boneless skinless chicken breasts
  (about 1 pound total), halved and flattened
  slightly

2 teaspoons Asian sesame oil

1 tablespoon fresh lemon juice

20 inches (about 10 ounces) of *baguette*, cut
  crosswise into 4 pieces

4 cups shredded Napa cabbage

2 cups packed trimmed spinach leaves, washed
  well, spun dry, and shredded

1 carrot, shredded

Put flour and sesame seeds on separate sheets of wax paper and in a shallow bowl beat together egg white and water.

Season chicken breasts with salt and dip them, 1 at a time, in flour, shaking off excess. Dip chicken in egg white, letting excess drip off, and coat with sesame seeds on 1 side, shaking off excess. Transfer chicken breasts as coated to a plate.

In a large non-stick skillet heat 1 teaspoon oil over moderate heat until hot but not smoking and cook chicken, sesame-seed sides down, until golden, about 4 minutes. Turn chicken and cook 4 minutes more, or until just cooked through. Add lemon juice to skillet. Turn chicken to coat with juice and cook until juice is almost evaporated, about 1 minute. Transfer sesame chicken to a cutting board and halve lengthwise.

Make a horizontal cut through center of each *baguette* piece with a serrated knife, cutting almost but not all the way through, and spread open. In a bowl toss together cabbage, spinach, carrot, remaining teaspoon oil, and salt to taste.

Make sandwiches with slaw, chicken, and bread, pressing together gently. Makes 4 sandwiches.

🍂 Each sandwich about 381 calories, 7 grams fat
(17% of calories from fat)

Cold Poached Chicken with Ginger Scallion Oil

For poached chicken
2 cups water
four ¼-inch-thick slices fresh gingerroot
¼ cup Scotch or medium-dry Sherry
1 whole boneless skinless chicken breast
  (about ¾ pound)
For ginger scallion oil
2 tablespoons vegetable oil
2 teaspoons finely grated peeled fresh gingerroot
2 teaspoons minced scallion
1 teaspoon Asian sesame oil

Accompaniment if desired: cold sesame spinach
  (page 183)

Poach chicken:
In a 1½-quart saucepan bring water to a boil with gingerroot, Scotch or Sherry, and salt to taste. Add chicken and simmer, covered, 12 minutes, or until just cooked through. Transfer chicken with tongs to a bowl and chill, covered, 20 minutes.
Make ginger scallion oil while chicken is cooling:
In a small bowl stir together ginger scallion oil ingredients.

Halve chicken lengthwise and cut across grain into thin slices. Stir ginger scallion oil and spoon over chicken. Serves 2.

Chicken with Mustard-Seed Crust and Couscous

1 small whole boneless skinless chicken breast
  (½ pound), halved
1 tablespoon mustard seeds
1 tablespoon chopped fresh parsley leaves
¾ cup plus 1 tablespoon water
¼ teaspoon salt
½ cup couscous
2 teaspoons unsalted butter
1 tablespoon fresh lemon juice

Accompaniment if desired: carrot, snow pea,
  and red bell pepper julienne in honey
  vinaigrette (page 194)

Season chicken with salt and pepper to taste. On a plate combine mustard seeds and parsley and press chicken into seed mixture, coating both sides.

In a small saucepan bring ¾ cup water and salt to a boil. Stir in couscous and let stand, covered, off heat 5 minutes.

In a non-stick skillet heat butter over moderate heat until foam subsides and cook chicken on 1 side until golden, about 5 minutes. Turn chicken and cook, covered, over moderately low heat until just cooked through, about 5 minutes.

Fluff couscous with a fork and divide between 2 plates. Top couscous with chicken. To skillet add lemon juice and remaining tablespoon water and simmer, scraping up brown bits, 1 minute. Pour sauce over chicken and serve with carrot, snow pea, and red bell pepper julienne. Serves 2.

🍂 Each serving without accompaniment
about 365 calories, 8 grams fat
(20% of calories from fat)

Pheasant Pie

three 2- to 2½-pound pheasants* (preferably
    hens, which come with feet attached)
For spice rub
1 tablespoon whole juniper berries
1 teaspoon salt
1 teaspoon freshly ground black pepper
½ teaspoon dried thyme

1 ounce dried *porcini* mushrooms**
1 cup hot water
1 tablespoon olive oil
3 large shallots, chopped fine
3 garlic cloves, minced
½ pound fresh *shiitake* mushrooms, stems
    discarded and caps quartered
½ pound white mushrooms, sliced
¾ cup gin
¾ cup dry white wine
about 6 cups pheasant stock (page 154)
3 celery ribs, cut diagonally into ½-inch-thick
    slices
¾ pound turnips (about 4 medium), peeled
    and cut lengthwise into ½-inch-thick
    wedges
¾ pound parsnips (about 4 medium), peeled
    and cut diagonally into ½-inch-thick
    slices
10 ounces pearl onions, blanched in boiling
    water 3 minutes and peeled
¾ pound baby carrots (about 3 cups)
4 tablespoons cornstarch stirred together with
    ¼ cup cold water
2 puff pastry sheets (from one 17¼-ounce package
    frozen puff pastry sheets), thawed, unfolded,
    and chilled in one layer on a tray
an egg wash made by beating 1 large egg with
    1 tablespoon water

*available at some butcher shops and by mail
    order from D'Artagnan, tel. (800) 327-8246
    or (201) 792-0748
**available at specialty foods shops and some
    supermarkets

With a sharp knife cut off legs, including thigh portion, of 1 pheasant and cut legs into drumstick and thigh portions. Reserve drumsticks and feet if attached for stock (page 154). Cut off wings and reserve for stock. Cut breast meat from pheasant carcass, keeping breast halves intact, and remove skin. Reserve carcass and skin for stock. Cut up and reserve parts of remaining 2 pheasants in same manner.

Trim any excess fat from thighs and pat thighs and breasts dry. Arrange thighs and breasts in a flat-bottomed dish just large enough to hold them in one layer.

Make spice rub:

In a small heavy skillet dry-roast juniper berries over moderately high heat, stirring, until fragrant and shiny and in an electric coffee/spice grinder grind to a powder with salt, pepper, and thyme. Rub pheasant evenly with spice powder. *Marinate pheasant, covered and chilled, at least 1 day and up to 2.*

Make pheasant stock (page 154) while pheasant is marinating.

In a small bowl soak *porcini* in hot water 20 minutes, or until softened. Remove *porcini*, squeezing out excess liquid, and reserve liquid. Wash *porcini* under cold water to remove any grit and chop them.

Preheat oven to 350° F.

Pat thighs dry, keeping breasts covered and chilled, and season with salt and pepper. In a 12-inch heavy skillet heat oil over moderately high heat until hot but not smoking and brown thighs on all sides, skin sides down first, transferring with tongs to a large flameproof casserole (preferably shallow).

Pour off all but about 2 tablespoons fat from skillet and in fat remaining in skillet cook shallots and garlic over moderate heat, stirring, until softened. Add *porcini*, *shiitake*, white mushrooms, and salt and pepper to taste and sauté over moderately high heat, stirring, until liquid mushrooms give off is evaporated. Slowly add all but about 1 tablespoon reserved *porcini* liquid, discarding last tablespoon (which contains sediment), and boil until liquid is evaporated. Add gin and wine and bring to a boil. Remove skillet from heat and ignite liquid carefully. When flames die out return skillet to heat and boil until liquid is evaporated. Add 2 cups pheasant stock and bring to a boil.

Pour mushroom mixture over thighs in casserole

and braise thighs, covered, in middle of oven 1½ hours, or until tender. Transfer thighs with tongs to a bowl and cool. Add breasts to mushroom mixture in skillet and cook on top of stove at a bare simmer, uncovered, turning once, 8 minutes, or until just cooked through. Transfer breasts with tongs to bowl and cool.

Pour cooking liquid through a large fine sieve into a large measuring cup, reserving mushrooms, and add enough remaining pheasant stock to measure 4 cups liquid total.

In a steamer set over boiling water steam vegetables separately, transferring all vegetables to a large bowl. Allow about 5 minutes cooking time for just-tender celery; 8 minutes for just-tender turnips, parsnips, and pearl onions; and 10 minutes for just-tender baby carrots.

Cut pheasant breasts into 1½-inch chunks and cut thighs into chunks, discarding skin and bones. In a 3-quart oval gratin dish (about 15 by 10½ by 2½ inches) or other shallow baking dish toss together vegetables and pheasant chunks.

In a large saucepan combine stock mixture and reserved mushrooms and bring to a boil. Stir cornstarch mixture and add to stock mixture, stirring. Simmer sauce 2 minutes and season with salt and pepper. Pour sauce over pheasant mixture. *Filling may be made 2 days ahead and chilled, covered. Bring filling to room temperature before proceeding.*

On a lightly floured surface roll out 1 pastry sheet into a 14-inch square, keeping remaining pastry sheet chilled. Cut three ¼-inch-wide pastry strips and braid together for pastry braid around rim of baking dish. Continue to cut and braid more strips from pastry to fit around rim of baking dish, transferring braids to a tray. From remaining rolled-out pastry cut out 2 long feathers for decoration, transferring to tray. Chill braids and feathers.

Preheat oven to 375° F.

On lightly floured surface roll out remaining pastry sheet into a rectangle at least 2 inches larger than baking dish and brush evenly with some egg wash. Drape pastry, egg-wash side down, over baking dish. Trim corners of overhang and press overhang along rim and side of baking dish to seal.

Brush crust evenly with some egg wash. Arrange pastry feathers on crust and braids around rim, pressing gently to make them adhere. Brush pastry decorations with some egg wash and if desired with a small sharp knife score pastry feathers decoratively.

Bake pie in middle of oven 35 to 40 minutes, or until pastry is golden brown and puffed slightly. *Pie may be baked 1 day ahead, cooled completely, and chilled, covered loosely. Reheat pie, uncovered, in a 375° F. oven 35 minutes, or until heated through (pastry will darken slightly).* Serves 6 generously.

PHOTO ON PAGE 70

Pheasant Stock

carcasses, drumsticks, feet if attached, wings,
and skin reserved from pheasants for pie
(page 152)
1 large onion, sliced thick
2 large carrots, chopped coarse
1 large celery rib, chopped coarse
12½ cups water
1 teaspoon salt
6 long fresh parsley sprigs
½ teaspoon dried thyme, crumbled
1 bay leaf
½ teaspoon whole black peppercorns

Preheat oven to 450° F.

With poultry or kitchen shears cut backbone away from breastbone of each pheasant carcass and break each backbone into 2 pieces. In a flameproof roasting pan arrange carcasses, drumsticks, feet, wings, and skin in one layer and roast in middle of oven, stirring once or twice, 30 minutes. Stir in vegetables and roast until bones and vegetables are browned well, 30 to 45 minutes.

With a slotted spoon transfer mixture to a stockpot or kettle (at least 6-quart capacity) and pour off any fat from roasting pan. Add 2 cups water to roasting pan and deglaze pan over high heat, scraping up brown bits. Transfer deglazing liquid to stockpot or kettle and add 10 cups water. Bring mixture to a boil, skimming froth. Add remaining ½ cup water and bring to a simmer, skimming froth.

Add salt, herbs, and peppercorns and simmer, uncovered, 3 hours. Pour stock through a large fine sieve into a large bowl, discarding solids. Measure stock and if necessary boil in cleaned stockpot or kettle until reduced to about 6 cups. Cool stock, uncovered. *Chill stock, covered, at least 8 hours and up to 2 days.* Discard fat. Makes about 6 cups.

Roast Turkey with Sage and Sherried Cider Giblet Gravy

a 12- to 14-pound turkey, neck and giblets
(excluding liver) reserved for making stock
½ lemon, cut into 2 wedges
7 large fresh sage sprigs
2 slices firm whole-wheat sandwich bread
½ Granny Smith apple, quartered lengthwise
½ onion, quartered lengthwise
1 stick (½ cup) unsalted butter, softened
1 cup water
For gravy
1 cup dry Sherry
1 cup apple cider (preferably sparkling)
6 tablespoons all-purpose flour
2 cups turkey giblet stock (recipe follows) or
chicken broth plus additional stock or broth
for thinning gravy

Garnish: assorted fresh sage sprigs
Accompaniment if desired: chestnut and bacon
dressing (page 155)

Preheat oven to 425° F.

Rinse turkey and pat dry inside and out. Season turkey inside and out with salt and pepper and pack neck cavity with 1 lemon wedge, 1 sage sprig, and 1 bread slice. Fold neck skin under body and fasten with a skewer. Fill body cavity with apple, onion, 3 sage sprigs, and remaining lemon wedge and bread slice and truss turkey.

Rub turkey with remaining 3 sage sprigs and arrange sprigs on a rack set in a roasting pan. Spread turkey with butter and arrange on rack in roasting pan. Roast turkey in middle of oven 30 minutes.

Reduce temperature to 325° F. and baste turkey with pan juices. Add water to roasting pan and roast turkey, basting every 20 minutes, 2½ to 3 hours more, or until a meat thermometer inserted in fleshy part of a thigh registers 180° F. and juices run clear when thigh is pierced. Transfer turkey to a heated platter, reserving juices in roasting pan, and discard string. Keep turkey warm, covered loosely with foil.

Make gravy:

Skim fat from pan juices, reserving ¼ cup fat, and on top of stove deglaze pan with Sherry over moderately high heat, scraping up brown bits. Stir in cider. Bring Sherry mixture to a boil and remove pan from heat.

In a heavy saucepan whisk together reserved fat and flour and cook *roux* over moderately low heat, whisking, 3 minutes. Add Sherry mixture and 2 cups stock or broth in a stream, whisking to prevent lumping, and simmer, whisking occasionally, 10 minutes. Whisk in additional stock or broth to thin gravy if desired. Season gravy with salt and pepper and transfer to a heated gravy boat.

Garnish turkey with sage. Serves 8.

PHOTO ON PAGE 72

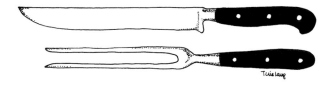

Turkey Giblet Stock

neck and giblets (excluding liver) from
   a 12- to 14-pound turkey
5 cups chicken broth
6 cups water
1 celery rib, chopped
1 carrot, chopped
1 onion, quartered
1 bay leaf
2 fresh flat-leafed parsley sprigs
½ teaspoon dried thyme, crumbled
1 teaspoon whole black peppercorns

In a large deep saucepan bring neck, giblets, broth, water, celery, carrot, and onion to a boil, skimming froth. Add remaining ingredients and cook, uncovered, at a bare simmer 2 hours, or until liquid is reduced to about 6 cups. Pour stock through a fine sieve into a bowl. *Stock may be made 2 days ahead. Cool stock completely, uncovered, and keep chilled or frozen in an airtight container.* Makes about 6 cups.

Chestnut and Bacon Dressing

6 cups torn bite-size pieces crusty country-style
   bread (about ½ pound)
6 bacon slices, chopped
½ stick (¼ cup) unsalted butter

2 onions, chopped
4 celery ribs, chopped
1 tablespoon fresh rosemary leaves,
   minced
1 pound fresh chestnuts*, shelled and peeled
   (procedure follows) and chopped coarse or
   ¾ pound vacuum-packed whole chestnuts*,
   chopped coarse (about 2 cups)
½ cup packed fresh flat-leafed parsley leaves,
   washed, spun dry, and minced
2 cups turkey giblet stock (recipe precedes) or
   chicken broth

*available at specialty foods shops and some
   supermarkets

Preheat oven to 325° F. and butter a 4-quart baking dish.

In a shallow baking pan arrange bread pieces in one layer and bake in middle of oven, stirring occasionally, until pale golden, about 20 minutes. Transfer bread to a large bowl.

In a large skillet cook bacon over moderate heat, stirring occasionally, until crisp and transfer with a slotted spoon to bread. To fat in skillet add butter, onions, celery, and rosemary and cook over moderately low heat, stirring occasionally, until vegetables are softened. Add chestnuts and cook, stirring, 1 minute. Add mixture to bread, tossing well, and stir in parsley and salt and pepper to taste. Transfer dressing to baking dish. *Dressing may be made 1 day ahead and chilled, covered.*

Drizzle dressing with stock or broth and bake, covered, in oven 1 hour. Uncover dressing and bake 30 minutes more. (Dressing may be baked with turkey.) Serves 8.

PHOTO ON PAGE 75

To Shell and Peel Chestnuts

Preheat oven to 450° F.

Cut an X on round side of each chestnut with a sharp knife and in a shallow baking pan spread chestnuts in one layer. Add ¼ cup water and bake chestnuts in middle of oven 10 minutes, or until shells open. Cool chestnuts just until they can be handled. Shell and peel chestnuts.

ALEXIS SEABROOK

Cornish Hens with Dried Apricot, Bacon, and Jalapeño Bulgur Stuffing

1 cup coarse bulgur*
2½ cups water
2½ teaspoons salt
¼ pound bacon, cooked until crisp, bacon fat
    reserved and bacon chopped fine
2 onions, chopped (about 1½ cups)
2 to 3 fresh *jalapeño* chilies, seeded and chopped
    fine (wear rubber gloves)
½ cup dried apricots, chopped
2 tablespoons chopped fresh tarragon leaves
freshly ground black pepper to taste
½ stick (¼ cup) unsalted butter
6 Cornish hens (about 1½ pounds each)

*available at natural foods stores and many
    supermarkets

In a large dry heavy skillet toast bulgur over moderately high heat, stirring occasionally, 5 to 10 minutes, or until it makes popping sounds and is browned lightly. Transfer bulgur to a bowl and cool slightly.

In a saucepan bring water with 1 teaspoon salt to a boil and stir in toasted bulgur. Reduce heat and simmer bulgur, covered, about 20 minutes, or until tender but not mushy (drain bulgur in a sieve if any liquid remains). Spread bulgur in a shallow baking pan and cool completely.

Preheat oven to 450° F.

While bulgur is cooling, in skillet heat 2 teaspoons reserved bacon fat over moderate heat until hot but not smoking and cook onions and *jalapeños,* stirring, until softened. Transfer onion mixture to a bowl. Add apricots, tarragon, bacon, bulgur, and pepper and salt to taste and toss to combine. Cool stuffing completely.

In a small saucepan melt butter with pepper and remaining 1½ teaspoons salt, stirring.

Rinse hens and pat dry inside and out. Pack each cavity with about ¾ cup stuffing and arrange hens, breast sides up, on rack of a broiler pan. Brush hens all over with melted butter and roast in middle of oven 30 to 40 minutes, or until juices run clear when fleshy part of a thigh is pierced (or until a meat thermometer inserted in fleshy part of thigh registers 175° F.). Serves 6.

Roasted Quail with Red Grapes and Pearl Onions

1 cup balsamic vinegar
2 tablespoons honey
10 fresh thyme sprigs plus 1 teaspoon chopped
    fresh thyme leaves
3 tablespoons warm clarified butter (procedure
    on page 125)
1 pound small pearl onions
8 whole quail* (5 to 6 ounces each), cleaned
    and necks and feet removed if necessary
1 pound red seedless grapes (about 3 cups)

Garnish: fresh thyme leaves
Accompaniment: baked wild rice amandine
    (page 174)

*available at some butcher shops and by mail
    order from D'Artagnan, tel. (800) 327-8246 or
    (201) 792-0748

Preheat oven to 475° F.

In a small saucepan boil vinegar, honey, and thyme sprigs over moderate heat, stirring occasionally, until reduced to about ½ cup, about 5 minutes. Pour glaze through a fine sieve into a small bowl, discarding thyme, and reserve. In another small bowl stir together 2 tablespoons reserved glaze and 2 tablespoons clarified butter.

In a saucepan of boiling salted water blanch onions 3 minutes. Drain onions and peel.

Heat a flameproof roasting pan, 15 by 10 by 2 inches, in oven 10 minutes. In heated pan toss onions with remaining tablespoon clarified butter, chopped thyme, and salt and pepper to taste and roast in upper third of oven, stirring occasionally, about 15 minutes.

While onions are roasting, prepare quail. Rinse quail and pat dry. Season quail inside and out with salt and pepper. Brush quail inside and out with about one third glaze-butter mixture and tie legs together with kitchen string.

Add grapes to pan and toss with onions. Arrange quail, breast sides down, over onions and grapes and roast 15 minutes. Turn quail over and baste with about half of remaining glaze-butter mixture. Roast quail, basting with remaining glaze-butter mixture, 10 minutes more, or until juices run clear when fleshy part of a thigh is pierced.

Discard string from quail and transfer to a platter. Arrange grapes and onions around quail using a slotted spoon and keep warm.

To pan add reserved glaze and on stovetop boil over high heat 5 minutes, or until thickened and reduced to about ½ cup. Season sauce with salt and pepper and drizzle over quail.

Garnish quail with thyme and serve with baked wild rice amandine. Serves 4.

Grilled Quail with Wilted Cabbage Slaw

For marinade
¼ cup cider vinegar
¼ cup molasses
¼ cup olive oil
1 teaspoon ground allspice
1 teaspoon salt
1 teaspoon freshly ground black pepper

6 semi-boneless quail*
For slaw
3 tablespoons cider vinegar
2 teaspoons honey

4 bacon slices, chopped coarse
1 teaspoon caraway seeds, crushed lightly
3 cups very thinly sliced red cabbage
2 medium carrots, shredded fine
3 cups very thinly sliced Napa cabbage
4 scallions, sliced thin

*available at some butcher shops and by mail order from D'Artagnan, tel. (800) 327-8246 or (201) 792-0748

Make marinade:
In a small bowl whisk together all marinade ingredients.

Rinse quail and pat dry. Arrange quail in a flat-bottomed dish large enough to hold them in one layer and add marinade, turning quail to coat well. *Marinate quail, covered and chilled, turning them once or twice, at least 1 day and up to 2.*

Prepare grill and bring quail to room temperature (about 30 minutes).

Remove quail from marinade, discarding marinade, and pat dry with paper towels. Season quail with salt and pepper and grill on an oiled rack set about 5 to 6 inches over glowing coals 3 to 4 minutes on each side, or until just cooked through. Meat should still be pink. (Alternatively, grill quail in batches without crowding in a hot oiled well-seasoned ridged grill pan.) Transfer quail as cooked to a plate and keep warm, covered.

Make slaw:
In a cup stir together vinegar and honey. In a 12-inch heavy skillet cook bacon over moderate heat, stirring, until crisp. Transfer bacon with a slotted spoon to a small bowl and pour off all but about 2 tablespoons bacon fat from skillet.

Heat bacon fat remaining in skillet over moderately high heat until hot but not smoking and cook caraway seeds, stirring, until fragrant, about 30 seconds. Add vinegar mixture, red cabbage, carrots, and salt and pepper to taste and sauté, stirring, until cabbage is just wilted, about 1 minute.

Remove skillet from heat and add Napa cabbage and scallions, tossing until cabbage is wilted slightly.

Divide slaw among 6 plates. Cut each quail into 4 serving pieces and arrange decoratively over slaw. Top salads with bacon. Serves 6 as a first course.

PHOTO ON PAGE 68

BREAKFAST, BRUNCH, AND CHEESE DISHES

BREAKFAST AND BRUNCH DISHES

Pecan Praline Bacon

1 pound thick-cut bacon (about 12 slices)
3 tablespoons sugar
1½ tablespoons chili powder
¼ cup pecans, chopped fine

Preheat oven to 425° F.

On rack of a large broiling pan arrange bacon in one layer and cook in middle of oven 10 minutes, or until it just begins to turn golden. In a small bowl stir together sugar and chili powder. Remove pan from oven and sprinkle bacon with sugar mixture and pecans. Return pan to oven and cook until bacon is crisp and browned, about 5 minutes. Transfer bacon, praline-sides up, to paper towels to drain. Serves 6.

PHOTO ON PAGE 25

Maple Mustard-Glazed Canadian Bacon

1½ tablespoons Dijon mustard
2 teaspoons pure maple syrup
cayenne to taste
¾ pound thinly sliced Canadian bacon
(about 18 slices)

Preheat broiler.

In a small bowl stir together mustard, syrup, and cayenne. Arrange bacon slices in one layer on rack of a broiler pan or in a jelly-roll pan and brush 1 side of each bacon slice generously with glaze. Broil bacon about 4 inches from heat 3 minutes. Turn bacon and broil just until golden around edges, 3 to 4 minutes. Serves 6.

☛ Each serving about 100 calories, 4 grams fat
(39% of calories from fat)

PHOTO ON PAGE 40

Onion and Bell Pepper Strata with Fresh Tomato Salsa

vegetable-oil cooking spray
1 onion, sliced thin (about 3 cups)
1½ tablespoons minced garlic (about 2 large cloves)
1½ teaspoons olive oil
1 large green bell pepper, sliced thin
1 large yellow bell pepper, sliced thin
12 very thin slices firm white sandwich bread,
    cut into ¾-inch squares (about 5 cups)
½ cup freshly grated Parmesan (about 1½ ounces)
4 large whole eggs
4 large egg whites
2½ cups skim milk
½ cup packed fresh parsley leaves, washed well,
    spun dry, and chopped fine

Accompaniment: fresh tomato salsa (recipe follows)

Lightly spray a 2½-quart baking dish, 13 by 9 by 2 inches, with cooking spray.

In a large non-stick skillet cook onion and 1 tablespoon garlic in oil over moderate heat, stirring, until onion is pale golden. Stir in bell peppers and salt and black pepper to taste and cook, covered, over moderately low heat 5 minutes, or until bell peppers are just tender. Uncover skillet and cook vegetables, stirring, until any excess liquid is evaporated, 2 to 3 minutes.

Spread half of bread evenly in baking dish and top with half of vegetables. Sprinkle ¼ cup Parmesan evenly over vegetables and top with remaining bread and vegetables.

In a bowl whisk together whole eggs, whites, milk, parsley, remaining 1½ teaspoons garlic, and salt and pepper to taste and pour evenly over bread and vegetables. *Chill strata, covered, at least 3 hours and up to 12.*

Preheat oven to 375° F. and let *strata* stand at room temperature 20 minutes.

Sprinkle remaining ¼ cup Parmesan over *strata* and bake in middle of oven 45 to 55 minutes, or until puffed and golden brown around edges.

Serve *strata* topped with fresh tomato salsa. Serves 6.

Each serving with accompaniment
about 283 calories, 8 grams fat
(25% of calories from fat)

PHOTO ON PAGE 40

Fresh Tomato Salsa

1½ pounds vine-ripened tomatoes (about 5 medium), seeded and chopped coarse
⅓ cup finely chopped onion
2 scallions, chopped fine (about ¼ cup)
½ cup fresh coriander sprigs, washed well, spun dry, and chopped fine
1 tablespoon fresh lemon or lime juice
Tabasco to taste if desired

In a bowl stir together salsa ingredients. *Salsa may be made 2 hours ahead and chilled, covered.* Makes about 3 cups.

Salmon Roe Omelets with Scallion Potatoes

½ cup plain low-fat yogurt
2 scallions, minced
1 pound red potatoes
1 tablespoon salmon roe
2 large egg whites
1 large whole egg
1 large egg yolk
3 tablespoons all-purpose flour
2 tablespoons water
1 teaspoon unsalted butter

In a small bowl stir together yogurt and scallions. Cut potatoes into ¼-inch-thick slices and in a large saucepan of boiling salted water cook until just tender, about 5 minutes. Drain potatoes and return to pan. Stir in all but 2 tablespoons yogurt mixture with salt and pepper to taste and keep warm, covered. Stir salmon roe into remaining yogurt mixture.

In a bowl with an electric mixer beat whites with a pinch salt until they just hold soft peaks. In another bowl whisk whole egg, yolk, flour, water, and salt to taste until frothy. Gently fold in whites.

In a 10-inch non-stick skillet heat half of butter over moderately high heat, tilting skillet to coat bottom, and pour in half of egg mixture, tilting skillet to spread evenly over bottom.

Spoon half of roe mixture down center of omelet and cook, covered, over moderately low heat until eggs are just set, about 2 minutes. Gently loosen omelet with a rubber spatula and, tilting skillet, slide omelet onto a plate. Fold omelet into thirds over filling and keep warm while making 1 more omelet in same manner.

Serve omelets with potatoes. Serves 2.

Each serving about 335 calories, 14 grams fat
(27% of calories from fat)

Broiled Grapefruit with Vanilla Ginger Sugar

⅔ cup sugar
3 tablespoons chopped crystallized ginger
¾ teaspoon vanilla
6 large pink grapefruits

Preheat broiler.

In an electric coffee/spice grinder combine sugar, ginger, and vanilla and grind fine.

Halve each grapefruit crosswise and run a knife around each section to loosen it from membranes. Arrange grapefruits, cut sides up, in a flameproof baking dish just large enough to hold them in one layer and sprinkle with sugar mixture. Broil grapefruits about 1½ inches from heat until sugar melts and tops begin to brown, 10 to 15 minutes.

Serve grapefruits at room temperature. Serves 6.

Buttermilk Waffles with Two Toppings

3 cups all-purpose flour
1 tablespoon baking powder
¾ teaspoon baking soda
1 teaspoon salt
3¼ cups well-shaken buttermilk
1½ sticks (¾ cup) unsalted butter, melted
  and cooled
3 large eggs, beaten lightly
For toppings
tarragon Brie sauce with hard-boiled eggs
  (recipe follows)
apple and dried-fruit compote (page 161)

Preheat a well-seasoned or non-stick Belgian or standard waffle iron. Preheat oven to 200° F.

In a large bowl whisk together flour, baking powder, baking soda, and salt and stir in buttermilk, butter, and eggs, stirring until smooth (batter will be thick).

Spoon batter into waffle iron, using ½ cup batter for a 4-inch-square Belgian waffle or ¼ cup batter for a 4-inch-square standard waffle. Spread batter evenly and cook according to manufacturer's instructions. Transfer waffle to a baking sheet and keep warm, uncovered, in middle of oven. Make more waffles with remaining batter in same manner.

Serve waffles with Brie sauce and hard-boiled eggs or compote. Makes about twelve 4-inch Belgian waffles or about twenty-four 4-inch standard waffles, serving 6 generously.

PHOTO ON PAGE 25

Tarragon Brie Sauce with Hard-Boiled Eggs

2 tablespoons all-purpose flour
¼ teaspoon dry mustard
3 tablespoons unsalted butter
1½ cups whole milk
1 tablespoon dry white wine
¾ pound Brie, rind discarded, cut into
  1-inch pieces
1 tablespoon fresh lemon juice
1 teaspoon minced fresh tarragon leaves
1 teaspoon minced fresh flat-leafed parsley
  leaves
freshly ground white pepper to taste

Accompaniment: 6 hard-boiled eggs, shelled
  and kept warm in a saucepan of hot water

In a small bowl stir together flour and mustard. In a heavy saucepan melt butter over moderately low heat and whisk in flour mixture until smooth. Cook *roux*, whisking, 3 minutes. Whisk in milk in a stream and simmer mixture, whisking occasionally, 2 minutes, or until thickened. Add white wine and simmer, whisking occasionally, 1 minute.

Remove pan from heat and stir in Brie. Cook sauce over low heat, stirring constantly, until cheese is melted and sauce is smooth (do not boil). Pour sauce through a sieve into another heavy saucepan. *Sauce may be made up to this point 1 day ahead, cooled, uncovered, and chilled, its surface covered with plastic wrap. Reheat sauce over low heat, stirring, before proceeding (do not boil).* Stir into sauce lemon juice, tarragon, parsley, pepper, and salt to taste.

Cut eggs into wedges. Arrange eggs on waffles and top with sauce. Makes about 2½ cups sauce.

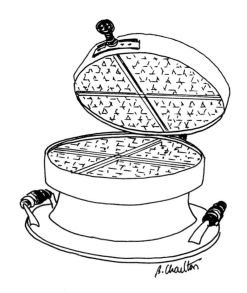

B. Charlton

Apple and Dried-Fruit Compote

3 medium Golden Delicious apples (about
   1½ pounds)
1 cup sugar
½ cup dried sour cherries
   (about 4 ounces)
¼ cup golden raisins
¼ cup dried currants
1½ cups cranberry-raspberry juice
4 teaspoons arrowroot
1 tablespoon fresh lemon juice

Peel and core apples and cut into ¾-inch-thick
wedges. In a large saucepan combine apples, sugar,
dried fruit, and 1¼ cups cranberry-raspberry juice
and bring to a boil. Simmer mixture over moderate
heat 1 minute, or until apples are just tender, and
remove pan from heat.

In a small bowl stir together remaining ¼ cup
cranberry-raspberry juice and arrowroot and stir into
compote. Cook compote over moderately low heat,
stirring gently, until liquid is thickened and clear (do
not boil). *Compote may be made up to this point 1
day ahead, cooled, uncovered, and chilled, covered.
Reheat compote over low heat, stirring gently,
before proceeding (do not boil).* Stir lemon juice into
compote and serve warm over waffles. Makes about
5 cups compote.

Banana Waffles with Pecan Maple Syrup

½ cup pure maple syrup
¼ cup pecans, lightly toasted and
   chopped coarse
2 teaspoons orange juice or
   fresh lemon juice
⅓ cup all-purpose flour
⅓ cup yellow cornmeal
1 tablespoon sugar
2 teaspoons baking powder
¼ teaspoon salt
1 ripe medium banana
⅓ cup water
2 large eggs
2 tablespoons unsalted butter, melted
   and cooled
vegetable oil for brushing waffle iron

Preheat oven to 200° F.
In a small saucepan bring maple syrup and pecans
to a boil and stir in juice. Remove syrup from heat
and keep warm, covered.

In a bowl whisk together flour, cornmeal, sugar,
baking powder, and salt.

Quarter banana and in a blender purée with water.
Transfer purée to another bowl and whisk in eggs
and melted butter. Add flour mixture and stir until
combined well.

Heat a well-seasoned or non-stick waffle iron until
hot and brush lightly with oil. Pour half of batter into
iron and cook waffle according to manufacturer's
instructions. Transfer waffle to a baking sheet and
keep warm, uncovered, in oven. Make another waffle with remaining batter in same manner.

Serve waffles with syrup. Serves 2.

CHEESE DISHES

Cherry Tomato, Ricotta, and Olive Galettes

3 tablespoons *olivada* or other bottled
   black-olive paste
½ cup loosely packed fresh basil leaves,
   washed, spun dry, and cut crosswise into
   thin strips
¼ cup ricotta
¼ cup freshly grated Parmesan
   (about ¾ ounce)
2 *galette* rounds (page 162), baked
1 pint small vine-ripened red cherry tomatoes,
   larger tomatoes halved

Preheat oven to 400° F.
In a bowl stir together olive paste and basil. In
another bowl stir together ricotta, Parmesan, and salt
and pepper to taste. Spread olive mixture evenly
onto *galette* rounds and spread cheese mixture over
it. Cover cheese mixture with tomatoes and season
with salt and pepper. Bake *galettes* on a baking sheet
in middle of oven 15 minutes. Transfer *galettes* to a
rack and cool.

Serve *galettes,* cut into wedges, at room temperature. Makes 2 *galettes,* serving 2.

PHOTO ON PAGE 34

Galette Rounds

¼ cup milk
¾ stick (6 tablespoons) unsalted butter,
  melted and cooled
3 large egg yolks
1 large whole egg
2 cups all-purpose flour
1¾ teaspoons salt
3 tablespoons chopped fresh chives

In a bowl whisk together milk, butter, yolks, and whole egg. In another bowl whisk together flour, salt, and chives and stir into milk mixture until just combined.

On a lightly floured surface with floured hands knead dough about 8 times, or until just smooth. *Chill dough, wrapped in plastic wrap, 1 hour.*

Preheat oven to 450° F.

Divide dough into 4 pieces. On a lightly floured surface with a floured rolling pin roll out each piece into an 8-inch round. Transfer rounds to 2 baking sheets and crimp edges decoratively. Chill dough 10 minutes and bake in middle and lower thirds of oven about 5 minutes, or until golden brown. Transfer *galettes* to racks and cool completely. *Galettes may be made 1 day ahead and kept in a sealable plastic bag at room temperature.* Makes 4 *galette* rounds.

Asparagus, Prosciutto, and Goat Cheese Galettes

2 medium onions, chopped
1 tablespoon olive oil
1 tablespoon unsalted butter
½ pound thin asparagus, trimmed
2 *galette* rounds (recipe precedes), baked
¼ pound thinly sliced prosciutto, cut crosswise
  into thin strips
⅓ cup soft mild goat cheese (about 4 ounces) at
  room temperature

In a skillet cook onions in oil and butter with salt and pepper to taste over moderately low heat 15 minutes, or until golden. Transfer onions to a bowl to cool.

Have ready a large bowl of ice and cold water. Cut asparagus crosswise into ½-inch pieces and cook in a large saucepan of boiling salted water 3 to 5

minutes, or until just tender. Drain asparagus in a colander and transfer to bowl of ice water to stop cooking. Lift asparagus out of water and pat dry.

Preheat oven to 400° F.

Spread onions evenly onto *galette* rounds and top with prosciutto, asparagus, and goat cheese. Bake *galettes* on a baking sheet in middle of oven about 15 minutes, or until tops are lightly browned. Transfer *galettes* to a rack and cool.

Serve *galettes*, cut into wedges, at room temperature. Makes 2 *galettes*, serving 2.

PHOTO ON PAGE 34

*Mozzarella, Arugula, and
Marinated Tomatoes on Focaccia*

3 large vine-ripened tomatoes (about 1½ pounds
  total), cut into ¼-inch-thick slices
1 red onion, sliced thin
3 tablespoons red-wine vinegar
freshly ground black pepper
4 cups packed trimmed arugula, washed well,
  spun dry, and chopped coarse
leaner/lighter quick *focaccia* (page 112), halved
  horizontally with a serrated knife
½ pound fresh mozzarella, sliced thin

In a large bowl or baking dish combine tomatoes, onion, and vinegar and season with pepper and salt. Marinate mixture, covered, tossing occasionally with a rubber spatula, 30 minutes.

Transfer tomatoes and onion to a plate with a slotted spoon and add arugula to marinade remaining in bowl or baking dish. Season arugula with pepper and salt and toss. Arrange arugula on bottom half of *focaccia* and top with mozzarella, tomatoes, onion, and remaining *focaccia* half, pressing together gently. Cut *focaccia* sandwich into 4 pieces. Makes 4 sandwiches.

Each serving about 470 calories, 14 grams fat
(27% of calories from fat)

PHOTO ON PAGE 7

Sweet-Onion Quesadillas

1 medium-large sweet onion such as Vidalia or
  Walla Walla
olive oil for brushing onion and tortillas
four 6- to 7-inch flour tortillas
¾ cup grated Monterey Jack cheese with hot
  peppers (about 3 ounces)
¼ cup packed fresh coriander sprigs, washed well,
  spun dry, and chopped coarse

Prepare grill.

Cut onion crosswise into ¼-inch-thick slices and
arrange slices on a tray, keeping them intact. Brush
both sides of slices lightly with oil and season with
salt and pepper. Grill onion on a lightly oiled rack
set 5 to 6 inches over glowing coals 4 minutes on
each side, or until lightly charred and softened.
Transfer onion slices as grilled to a bowl, separating rings.

Brush 2 tortillas lightly with oil on one side and
put, oiled side down, on a platter. Divide onion,
Monterey Jack, and coriander between tortillas and
cover with remaining 2 tortillas. Brush tops of
quesadillas lightly with oil.

With a metal spatula transfer quesadillas to a rack
set 5 to 6 inches over glowing coals and grill until
undersides are golden brown, about 1 minute. Sandwiching each quesadilla between 2 metal spatulas,
flip quesadillas over and grill until undersides are
golden brown, about 1 minute.

Transfer quesadillas to a cutting board and cut
into wedges. Serves 2 as a light luncheon main
course or side dish.

Turkey Hash Quesadillas

1 medium boiling potato
3 bacon slices, chopped
1 medium onion, chopped
2½ tablespoons olive oil
1 cup chopped cooked turkey
½ cup coarsely grated Gruyère or
  Swiss cheese
1 tablespoon chopped fresh parsley leaves
four 6- to 7-inch flour tortillas
¼ cup canned whole-berry cranberry sauce
8 fresh parsley leaves

Preheat oven to 500° F.

Cut potato into ¼-inch dice. In a saucepan of
boiling salted water simmer potato 5 minutes, or
until barely tender, and drain in a colander. In a
heavy skillet cook bacon and onion in ½ tablespoon
oil over moderate heat, stirring occasionally, until
onion is softened, about 5 minutes. Add potato and
cook, stirring occasionally, 5 minutes, or until
golden and tender. Cool mixture slightly and stir
in turkey, cheese, and parsley.

Put 2 tortillas on a baking sheet and brush with
some remaining oil. Turn tortillas over and top each
with half of turkey hash, spreading evenly. Cover
with remaining 2 tortillas and brush tops of
quesadillas with remaining oil.

Bake quesadillas in middle of oven until golden,
8 to 10 minutes. Transfer quesadillas to a cutting
board and cut into wedges.

Top wedges with cranberry sauce and parsley
leaves. Serves 2 as a light main course.

PASTA AND GRAINS

Salt Cod, Fennel, and Potato Cannelloni

For filling
½ pound skinless boneless salt cod (preferably
    center cut), rinsed well and cut into 1-inch
    pieces
1 pound large red potatoes
1 large egg
¼ cup milk
1 fennel bulb (sometimes called anise), stalks
    trimmed flush with bulb, reserving any fennel
    fronds, and bulb cut into ¼-inch dice
1 teaspoon fennel seeds, ground fine in
    an electric coffee/spice grinder
3 tablespoons olive oil
¼ cup water
¼ cup chopped reserved fennel fronds
    if desired

ten 7- by 3½-inch sheets dried no-boil lasagne
For sauce
3 cups milk
½ stick (¼ cup) unsalted butter
4 tablespoons all-purpose flour

Make filling:
In a large bowl cover salt cod with cold water by 2 inches. *Soak cod, covered and chilled, changing water several times, at least 1 day and up to 2.*

In a colander drain salt cod and in a saucepan simmer in water to cover by 1 inch until cod just flakes, about 3 minutes. Drain cod in colander and cool. Flake cod.

Peel potatoes and cut into 1½-inch cubes. In a saucepan simmer potatoes in salted water to cover by 1 inch until tender, about 15 minutes. Drain potatoes in colander and force through a ricer or food mill fitted with medium disk into a bowl. In a small bowl whisk together egg and milk and add to potatoes, stirring until combined well.

In a 9-inch skillet cook fennel bulb, fennel seeds, and salt to taste in oil over moderate heat, stirring, until fennel is pale golden. Cover skillet and cook fennel, stirring occasionally, until tender, about 5 minutes more. Add cod and sauté over moderately high heat, stirring, 2 minutes. Add ¼ cup water and deglaze skillet, scraping up brown bits.

Stir cod mixture and reserved fennel fronds into potato mixture until combined well and season with salt and pepper. *Filling may be made 1 day ahead and chilled, covered.*

In a large flat-bottomed dish soak lasagne sheets in very hot water to cover until soft and pliable, about 15 minutes.

Remove 1 lasagne sheet from water and halve crosswise to form 2 squares. Spread a scant ¼ cup filling lengthwise along 1 edge of each square and roll each square to enclose filling, leaving ends open. Arrange both cannelloni, seam sides down, in a buttered 3-quart gratin dish, 15 by 10 by 2 inches, or other shallow baking dish. Make 18 more cannelloni with remaining 9 lasagne sheets (halved crosswise) and filling in same manner.

Preheat oven to 400° F.

Make sauce:
In a small heavy saucepan bring milk just to a simmer over moderately low heat. Remove pan from heat and keep warm, covered. In a heavy saucepan melt butter over moderately low heat and whisk in flour. Cook *roux*, whisking, 3 minutes and whisk in warm milk. Bring sauce to a boil, whisking, and simmer, whisking, 3 minutes. Season sauce with salt and pepper and pour evenly over cannelloni. *Cannelloni may be prepared up to this point 1 day ahead and chilled, covered.*

Bake cannelloni in upper third of oven 30 minutes, or until bubbling and lightly browned. Serves 12 as part of a buffet.

PHOTO ON PAGE 78

Couscous with Dried Apricots, Currants, and Pistachios

4½ cups water
¼ cup extra-virgin olive oil
3 cinnamon sticks, halved
1½ teaspoons ground cumin
2½ teaspoons coarse salt
1 cup chopped dried apricots
two 10-ounce boxes couscous
    (about 3¼ cups)
¾ cup dried currants
1 cup shelled natural pistachios, lightly
    toasted, cooled, and chopped coarse
3 tablespoons chopped fresh mint leaves

In each of two 3-quart saucepans bring half of water, oil, cinnamon, cumin, salt, and apricots to a boil. Stir 1 box couscous into each pan and let stand, covered, off heat 5 minutes. Fluff couscous with a fork and transfer to 2 shallow baking pans to cool as quickly as possible. Cool couscous completely and with your fingers break up any large lumps. *Couscous may be made 1 day ahead and chilled, covered. Bring couscous to room temperature before proceeding.*

Fluff couscous with fork again and stir in currants, pistachios, mint, and salt and pepper to taste. Serves 16 as part of a buffet.

PHOTO ON PAGE 67

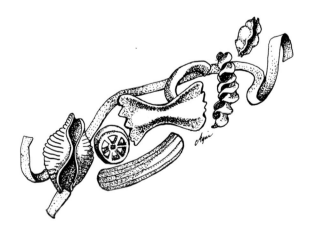

Farfalle with Peas and Prosciutto

1 cup shelled fresh or frozen peas
½ pound *farfalle* (bow-tie pasta)
2 tablespoons chopped fresh mint leaves
½ teaspoon freshly grated lemon zest
2 ounces thinly sliced prosciutto, chopped fine
    (a generous ⅓ cup)
2 tablespoons freshly grated Parmesan
    plus additional for serving

Fill a 5-quart kettle to within 1 inch of top with salted water and bring to a boil for peas and pasta. Into kettle fit a large sieve so that its bottom is submerged in several inches of boiling water. Add peas to sieve and boil until just tender, 3 to 5 minutes. Remove sieve, keeping water at a boil, and rinse peas under cold water. Drain peas and transfer to a small bowl.

In a blender purée ⅔ cup peas with mint, zest, ½ cup hot cooking water from kettle, and salt and pepper to taste.

Cook pasta in boiling salted water until *al dente*. Ladle out ¼ cup cooking water, reserving it, and drain pasta in a colander. Return pasta to kettle with pea purée, prosciutto, 2 tablespoons Parmesan, and remaining ⅓ cup peas and heat over moderate heat, stirring and thinning mixture to desired consistency with reserved cooking water, until heated through. Season pasta with salt and pepper.

Serve pasta with additional Parmesan on the side. Serves 2.

Sesame Scallion Pasta Stars

¾ cup tiny pasta stars *(stellette)* or other
    very small pasta
¼ cup minced scallions
2 tablespoons sesame seeds, lightly
    toasted
1 tablespoon unsalted butter
¼ teaspoon Asian sesame oil

Bring a 1½-quart saucepan of salted water to a boil for pasta stars. Add pasta and cook until *al dente*, about 7 minutes. Drain pasta in a large fine sieve and in a bowl toss with remaining ingredients and salt and pepper to taste. Serves 2 as a side dish.

Fusilli with Sun-Dried Tomatoes, Zucchini, and Peas

6 ounces *fusilli* or other spiral-shaped pasta
1½ cups water
¾ cup dried tomatoes (not packed in oil)
¼ cup Kalamata or other brine-cured black
    olives, pitted and chopped
½ cup fresh parsley leaves, washed well, spun
    dry, and chopped
1 cup shelled fresh or frozen peas
1 zucchini (about 6 ounces), cut into
    ½-inch cubes

In a 5-quart kettle bring 4 quarts salted water to a boil for pasta.

In a small saucepan bring 1½ cups water and tomatoes to a boil. Remove pan from heat and let tomatoes stand until softened, about 15 minutes. Drain tomatoes, reserving ½ cup soaking liquid, and chop. In a large bowl stir together tomatoes, reserved soaking liquid, olives, and parsley.

Cook pasta in boiling water until *al dente*, adding peas and zucchini during last minute of cooking. Drain pasta mixture well in a colander and add to tomato mixture with salt and pepper to taste, tossing until most of liquid is absorbed. Serves 2.

☙ Each serving about 450 calories, 4 grams fat
(8% of calories from fat)

Turkey, Potato, and Roasted-Garlic Ravioli with
Sun-Dried Tomato Sauce

½ cup low-fat plain yogurt
For sauce
4½ cups non-fat chicken broth
3 ounces dried tomatoes, cut into ¼-inch dice
    (about ½ cup)
1½ cups finely diced roasted peeled red bell
    peppers (about 3 roasted bell peppers;
    procedure on page 117)
10 fresh plum tomatoes (about 2 pounds), peeled,
    seeded, and cut into ¼-inch dice
1 tablespoon minced fresh thyme leaves
½ teaspoon sugar

1 medium russet (baking) potato (about ¼ pound)
1 tablespoon extra-virgin olive oil

1 large red onion, minced
10 ounces skinless boneless roasted turkey breast
    (left over or purchased), torn into small shreds
    (about 3 cups)
2 tablespoons roasted-garlic purée (procedure
    follows)
a pinch freshly grated nutmeg
30 won ton wrappers*, thawed if frozen
30 fresh chervil or flat-lcafed parsley sprigs,
    washed well and spun dry

*available at Asian markets and many specialty
    foods shops and supermarkets

In a colander lined with paper towels and set over a bowl drain yogurt 1 hour.

Make sauce while yogurt is draining:

In a saucepan bring broth to a boil. Remove pan from heat and add dried tomatoes. Let mixture stand, covered, 20 to 30 minutes, or until tomatoes are softened. Add roasted peppers and fresh tomatoes and simmer over moderate heat 5 minutes. Stir in thyme, sugar, and salt and pepper to taste. *Sauce may be made 4 days ahead and chilled, covered. Reheat sauce before serving.*

Peel and quarter potato and put into a small saucepan with enough salted cold water to cover by 2 inches. Simmer potato 12 to 15 minutes, or until very tender, and drain in a colander. Force hot potato through a ricer or food mill fitted with medium disk into a bowl.

In a medium non-stick skillet heat oil over moderately high heat until hot but not smoking and sauté onion, stirring, until softened, about 5 minutes. To potato mixture add drained yogurt, onion, turkey, garlic purée, nutmeg, and salt and pepper to taste. *Filling may be made 1 day ahead and chilled, covered.*

Bring a kettle of salted water to a boil for ravioli.

Put 1 won ton wrapper on a lightly floured surface and mound 1 tablespoon filling in center. Top filling with 1 chervil or parsley sprig. Lightly brush edges of wrapper with water and put a second wrapper over first, pressing down around filling to force out air and sealing edges well. If desired, trim excess dough with a round cutter or a sharp knife and transfer ravioli to a dry kitchen towel. Make more ravioli with remaining wrappers, filling, and chervil or parsley in same manner, transferring as formed to kitchen towel. *Ravioli may be made 3 hours ahead, spread in one layer on a baking sheet, and chilled, covered with plastic wrap.*

Cook ravioli in gently boiling water in batches 2 minutes, or until they rise to surface and are tender. (Do not boil water vigorously once ravioli have been added.) Transfer ravioli as cooked with a slotted spoon to a clean dry kitchen towel to drain.

Divide sauce among 6 soup plates and top with ravioli. Serves 6.

Each serving about 282 calories, 4 grams fat
(12% of calories from fat)

PHOTO ON PAGE 87

Roasted-Garlic Purée

1 large garlic head

Preheat oven to 400° F.

Separate garlic head into cloves, discarding loose papery outer skin but keeping skin intact on cloves, and wrap in foil, crimping seams to seal tightly. Roast garlic in middle of oven 30 minutes, or until soft. Unwrap garlic and cool slightly. Peel skins from each clove and on a plate with a fork mash garlic pulp until smooth. Makes about 2 tablespoons.

Yellow Bell Pepper Orzo Gratin

½ pound *orzo* (rice-shaped pasta, about 1⅛ cups)
1 pound yellow bell peppers, chopped (about 3)
½ cup dry white wine
½ cup low-salt chicken broth
¼ teaspoon salt
1 large egg
¼ teaspoon olive oil for oiling baking pan
2 scallions, minced
2 tablespoons chopped fresh chives
2 tablespoons freshly grated Parmesan

In a 4-quart saucepan bring 3 quarts salted water to a boil for *orzo*.

In a heavy saucepan simmer bell peppers in wine and broth with salt, covered, until tender, about 15 minutes. Remove lid and simmer until liquid is

evaporated. Cool bell pepper mixture and in a food processor or blender purée with egg. Transfer bell pepper mixture to a large bowl.

Preheat oven to 350° F. and lightly oil an 8-inch square baking pan with the oil.

Cook *orzo* in boiling salted water until *al dente* and drain in a colander. Rinse *orzo* under cold water and drain well. Stir *orzo* into bell pepper mixture with scallions, chives, 1 tablespoon Parmesan, and salt and pepper to taste. Spread *orzo* in baking pan, smoothing top, and sprinkle with remaining tablespoon Parmesan. *Gratin may be prepared up to this point 8 hours ahead and chilled, covered.*

Bake gratin in middle of oven 25 minutes, or until set and top is pale golden. Serves 6 as a side dish.

Each serving about 197 calories, 3 grams fat
(17% of calories from fat)

PHOTO ON PAGE 30

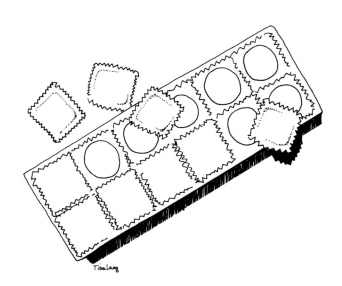

Parsnip Parmesan Ravioli with Mushroom Ragout

For mushroom ragout
2 tablespoons unsalted butter
2 tablespoons olive oil
1 onion, sliced thin
1 pound Portobello mushrooms, caps (halved if large) and stems sliced thin
¾ pound white mushrooms, sliced thin
2 garlic cloves, minced
1 teaspoon chopped fresh sage leaves
a 28- to 32-ounce can whole tomatoes, drained, reserving juice, and chopped coarse

For ravioli filling
2 pounds parsnips, peeled and cut into 1-inch pieces
½ cup freshly grated Parmesan (about 2 ounces)
1½ teaspoons chopped fresh sage leaves
30 won ton wrappers*, thawed if frozen

*available at Asian markets and many specialty foods shops and supermarkets

Make mushroom ragout:

In a large heavy kettle heat butter and oil over moderate heat until butter is melted and cook onion, stirring, about 5 minutes, or until softened. Stir in all mushrooms, garlic, sage, and salt and pepper to taste and cook, stirring, about 15 minutes, or until liquid mushrooms give off is evaporated. Stir in tomatoes with reserved juice and cook, uncovered, stirring occasionally, 30 minutes, or until sauce is thickened. *Ragout may be made 2 days ahead, cooled completely, and chilled, covered.*

Make ravioli filling:

In a saucepan boil parsnips in salted water to cover by 2 inches, uncovered, until very tender, about 15 minutes. Drain parsnips well. In a food processor purée parsnips with Parmesan, sage, and salt and pepper to taste until smooth, and cool. *Filling may be made 1 day ahead and chilled, covered.*

Bring a kettle of salted water to a gentle boil for ravioli.

Put 1 wrapper on a lightly floured surface and mound 1 level tablespoon filling in center. Brush edges of wrapper with water and fold wrapper in half to form a triangle, pressing around filling to force out air. Transfer ravioli to a dry kitchen towel to drain. Make more ravioli with remaining wrappers and filling in same manner, transferring to towel and turning occasionally to dry slightly.

In a saucepan heat ragout over low heat, stirring occasionally, until hot. Cook ravioli in gently boiling water in 3 batches 6 to 8 minutes, or until they rise to surface and are tender. (Do not boil water vigorously once ravioli have been added.) With a spoon transfer ravioli as cooked to shallow baking pans, arranging them in one layer with about ½ inch cooking water. Keep ravioli warm, covered.

Transfer ravioli with a slotted spoon to 6 plates and top with ragout. Serves 6.

Mexican Pasta with Black Beans

¾ pound *fusilli* or other spiral-shaped pasta
⅓ cup finely chopped onion
1 garlic clove, minced
1 tablespoon vegetable oil
a 15-ounce can black beans, rinsed and
    drained (about 1⅓ cups)
a 10-ounce can mild enchilada sauce
a 3-inch pickled *jalapeño* chili if desired,
    chopped fine (wear rubber gloves)
¼ cup sour cream
freshly grated Monterey Jack or sharp Cheddar
    to taste
2 scallions, sliced thin

In a 6-quart kettle bring 5 quarts salted water to
a boil for pasta. Cook pasta until tender, about 12
minutes.

While pasta is cooking, in a 2- to 3-quart heavy
saucepan cook onion and garlic in oil over moderately low heat, stirring occasionally, until softened.
Add beans, enchilada sauce, and *jalapeño* and
simmer gently, stirring occasionally, until thickened,
about 6 minutes. Remove pan from heat and stir sour
cream and salt to taste into sauce.

In a colander drain pasta well and in a large bowl
toss with sauce.

Serve pasta sprinkled with cheese and scallions.
Serves 2 generously.

Penne with Citrus Cream Sauce

½ pound *penne* or other tubular pasta
1 pink grapefruit
2 navel oranges
2 tablespoons unsalted butter
½ cup heavy cream
1 tablespoon freshly grated Parmesan
1 tablespoon minced fresh parsley
    leaves

In a 3-quart saucepan bring 2 quarts salted water
to a boil for pasta.

With a small sharp knife cut peel and pith from
grapefruit and oranges. Working over a bowl cut
grapefruit and orange sections free from membranes,
transferring sections to a plate, and halve them.

Squeeze excess juice from membranes into juice in
bowl and reserve ¼ cup juice.

In a 12-inch skillet combine reserved juice, butter,
and cream and heat sauce over moderate heat until
butter is just melted. Keep cream sauce warm over
very low heat.

Add pasta to boiling water and cook until *al
dente*. Drain pasta well in a colander. Add pasta,
fruit, Parmesan, and parsley to sauce and toss with
salt to taste until most of sauce is absorbed. Serves 2.

Penne with Mushroom Pesto

For pesto
4 tablespoons extra-virgin olive oil
a 10-ounce package fresh white mushrooms,
    chopped fine (preferably in a food processor)
1 tablespoon Worcestershire sauce
1 tablespoon medium-dry Sherry if desired
1 garlic clove, minced and mashed to a paste
    with ¼ teaspoon salt
¼ cup pine nuts
¼ cup freshly grated Parmesan
½ cup packed fresh parsley leaves

1 pound *penne rigate* (ridged *penne*)

In a 6-quart kettle bring 5 quarts salted water to a
boil for pasta.

Make pesto:
In a 10-inch non-stick skillet heat 1 tablespoon oil
over moderately high heat until hot but not smoking
and sauté mushrooms with Worcestershire sauce,
Sherry, and salt and pepper to taste, stirring, until
liquid mushrooms give off is evaporated and mushrooms begin to brown, about 10 minutes.

In a food processor purée mushroom mixture
with garlic, pine nuts, Parmesan, and remaining 3
tablespoons oil. Add parsley and blend until parsley
is chopped fine. *Pesto keeps, its surface covered with
plastic wrap, chilled, 1 week.*

Cook pasta in boiling water until *al dente*. Reserve 1 cup cooking water and drain pasta.

In a large bowl whisk together *pesto* and ⅔ cup
reserved hot cooking water. Add pasta and toss well,
thinning *pesto*, if necessary, with remaining reserved
cooking water. Serves 6.

Spaghetti with Broccoli, Brie, and Walnuts

½ pound spaghetti
1½ tablespoons olive oil
1 bunch broccoli (about 1¼ pounds), cut into
    ½-inch flowerets, reserving stems for
    another use
1 garlic clove, minced
8 ounces Brie, rind discarded, cut into
    1-inch pieces
½ cup walnuts, toasted and chopped coarse

In a 6-quart kettle bring 5 quarts salted water to a boil. Add spaghetti and cook until *al dente*. Reserve ⅓ cup cooking liquid and drain pasta in a colander. Return pasta to kettle with reserved liquid.

While pasta is cooking, in a large heavy skillet heat oil over moderate heat until hot but not smoking and cook broccoli with salt to taste, stirring occasionally, until crisp-tender, about 5 minutes. Add garlic and cook, stirring, until golden, about 30 seconds.

To pasta add broccoli mixture, Brie, and walnuts, tossing until cheese is just melted, and season with salt and pepper. Serves 2 as a main course.

Spaghetti with Lobster and Mussels

1 cup dry white wine
1 cup water
two 1½-pound live lobsters
1 pound spaghetti
4 cups spicy tomato sauce
    (page 200)
1 pound mussels (preferably cultivated),
    scrubbed well and beards pulled off
2 tablespoons minced fresh parsley leaves

In a large kettle bring wine and water to a boil. Add lobsters and cook, covered, 3 minutes. (They will be partially cooked.) Transfer lobsters with tongs to a large bowl and boil cooking liquid until reduced to about ⅓ cup.

Twist off claws and with flat side of a heavy knife crack claws on one side. Cut off tails and cut each tail crosswise into 4 pieces, cutting through shell and discarding dark intestinal vein. Halve body sections and discard head sacs. Reserve tomalley and any roe

if desired. *Lobsters may be prepared up to this point 4 hours ahead and chilled, covered.*

In a 6-quart kettle bring 5 quarts salted water to a boil for pasta.

In a 5-quart heavy kettle bring tomato sauce, lobster cooking liquid, and reserved tomalley and roe if using to a simmer, whisking. Add claws and bodies and simmer, covered, 5 minutes, or until claw meat is just cooked through. Transfer claws with tongs to a bowl and keep warm, covered.

Add tail pieces to sauce and simmer, covered, 3 to 4 minutes, or until just cooked through. Transfer tail pieces with tongs to bowl and keep warm, covered. Remove and discard lobster bodies.

Add mussels to sauce and simmer, covered, 3 to 8 minutes, checking mussels every minute or so and transferring as opened with tongs to bowl. Keep mussels warm, covered. (Discard any mussels that are unopened after 8 minutes.) Season sauce with salt and pepper and keep warm, covered.

While seafood is cooking, cook spaghetti in boiling water until *al dente* and drain in a colander. Add spaghetti, lobster, and mussels to sauce and heat over moderate heat until heated through, stirring and tossing until spaghetti is coated well with sauce.

Transfer spaghetti and seafood to a platter and sprinkle with parsley. Serves 12 as part of a buffet.

PHOTO ON PAGE 78

Spätzle are small German dumplings made by forcing a soft batterlike dough through holes in a Spätzle-maker into boiling water. To order a Spätzle-maker contact Schaller and Weber, 1654 Second Avenue, New York, NY 10028, tel. (212) 879-3047.

Herbed Spätzle

2½ cups all-purpose flour
1¼ teaspoons salt
2 cups packed fresh parsley leaves (preferably
    flat-leafed), washed and spun dry
¾ cup milk
3 large eggs
½ cup water
1 teaspoon finely chopped fresh rosemary leaves
½ stick (¼ cup) unsalted butter

In a 6-quart kettle bring 5 quarts salted water to a boil for *Spätzle*. In a large bowl whisk together flour and salt. Put parsley in a blender.

In a heavy saucepan bring milk just to a simmer. With blender motor running add milk to parsley and blend until milk is very green. In a bowl whisk together eggs and water and add green milk in a slow stream, whisking constantly.

Add milk mixture to flour mixture, whisking until mixture forms a soft, smooth batterlike dough. Force dough through a *Spätzle*-maker into kettle of boiling water.

Preheat oven to 375° F.

Stir *Spätzle* gently to separate and boil 5 minutes, or until just tender. In a large colander drain *Spätzle* and rinse well under cold water. Drain *Spätzle* well and transfer to a large baking dish.

In a small heavy saucepan cook rosemary with salt and pepper to taste in butter over moderate heat, stirring, 2 minutes and drizzle over *Spätzle*, tossing well. Season *Spätzle* with salt and pepper. *Spätzle may be prepared up to this point 1 day ahead and chilled, covered.*

Bake *Spätzle*, covered with foil, in oven 20 minutes, or until heated through. Serves 6.

PHOTO ON PAGE 70

GRAINS

Gingered Beet Risotto

2 pounds beets with greens, beets scrubbed
    and trimmed, leaving about 1 inch of
    stems attached and reserving greens
3 cups water
1 small onion, chopped
    (about ½ cup)
1 tablespoon minced peeled fresh
    gingerroot
3 large garlic cloves, minced
3 tablespoons unsalted butter
1 cup Arborio or long-grain rice
½ cup dry white wine
¼ cup freshly grated Parmesan (about 2
    ounces), or to taste

Preheat oven to 450° F.

Wrap beets tightly in foil and roast in middle of oven until tender, about 1½ hours. Unwrap beets carefully and let stand until cool enough to handle. Discard stems and peel beets. In a blender purée half of beets with 1 cup of water and transfer to a saucepan, whisking in remaining 2 cups water to make beet broth.

Wash beet greens well and drain. Remove and discard stems from leaves. Chop enough leaves to measure 2½ cups and chop remaining beets.

Bring beet broth to a simmer and keep warm.

In a large heavy saucepan cook onion, gingerroot, and garlic in butter over moderate heat, stirring, until onion is softened. Stir in rice and cook, stirring constantly, about 1 minute. Add wine and cook, stirring, until absorbed. Stir in ½ cup beet broth and cook, simmering throughout and stirring constantly, until absorbed. Continue simmering and adding beet broth, about ½ cup at a time, stirring constantly and letting each addition be absorbed before adding next, until about half of broth has been added. Stir in chopped beets and beet leaves and continue simmering and adding broth in same manner until rice is tender but still *al dente*, about 18 minutes. Stir in ¼ cup Parmesan and salt and pepper to taste.

Serve risotto sprinkled with remaining Parmesan. Serves 4.

Red Wine and Mushroom Risotto

1 ounce dried *porcini* mushrooms*
2 cups boiling water
1½ pounds fresh *cremini* or white mushrooms
¾ stick (6 tablespoons) unsalted butter
5 to 6 cups low-salt chicken broth
6 ounces ¼-inch-thick slices *pancetta* (Italian
    unsmoked cured bacon)*, chopped
1 cup finely chopped onion
1 tablespoon finely chopped fresh rosemary
    leaves or 1 teaspoon dried rosemary, crumbled
1 tablespoon finely chopped fresh sage leaves
    or 1 teaspoon dried sage, crumbled
3 cups Arborio rice
2 cups dry red wine such as Rosso di Montalcino
3 tablespoons finely chopped fresh parsley leaves
1 cup freshly grated Parmesan

Garnish: curls shaved with a vegetable peeler
    from a ¼-pound piece of Parmesan, fresh
    rosemary sprigs

*available at specialty foods shops and some
    supermarkets

In a small bowl soak *porcini* in boiling water 30 minutes. Pour soaking liquid through a fine sieve lined with a dampened paper towel or coffee filter into a small bowl and reserve. Wash *porcini* under cold water to remove any grit and pat dry. Chop *porcini* fine.

Chop fine ¼ pound *cremini* or white mushrooms (about 1½ cups) and reserve. Depending on size, halve and/or quarter remaining 1¼ pounds *cremini* or white mushrooms and in a large heavy skillet cook in 4 tablespoons butter with salt and pepper to taste over moderate heat, stirring, until tender, 5 to 10 minutes. Remove skillet from heat and reserve mushrooms in skillet. (They will be reheated just before serving.)

In a large saucepan heat broth and keep at a bare simmer.

In a 5- to 6-quart saucepan cook *pancetta* over moderate heat, stirring, 5 minutes. Add reserved finely chopped *cremini* or white mushrooms, remaining 2 tablespoons butter, onion, rosemary, sage, and salt and pepper to taste and cook, stirring, until onion is softened. Stir in rice and cook, stirring, until well coated with fat, about 1 minute. Add 1 cup wine and cook, stirring constantly, until absorbed. Add remaining cup wine and cook, stirring constantly, until absorbed.

Add 1 cup simmering broth and cook, stirring constantly, until absorbed. Continue cooking and adding broth, ½ cup at a time, stirring constantly and letting each addition be absorbed before adding next, until rice is tender and creamy-looking but still *al dente*, 20 to 25 minutes.

About halfway through cooking, add reserved *porcini* soaking liquid and chopped *porcini*, stirring constantly until liquid is absorbed, and continue cooking and adding broth in same manner.

During last few minutes of cooking, reheat reserved *cremini* or white mushrooms in skillet over moderate heat, stirring, until hot, and stir in parsley and salt and pepper to taste. Stir grated Parmesan and salt and pepper to taste into risotto.

Serve risotto immediately, topped with *cremini* or white mushrooms and garnished with Parmesan curls and rosemary. Serves 6.

PHOTO ON PAGE 28

Kasha Varnishkes with Dilled Sour Cream
(Buckwheat Groats and Pasta)

½ cup sour cream
¼ cup chopped fresh dill
freshly ground black pepper to taste
2½ tablespoons unsalted butter
1 tablespoon olive oil
6 cups chopped onions (about 6 medium)
2 cups chopped yellow bell peppers (about 2
    large)
2 cups chopped zucchini (about 1 large)
½ pound *farfalle* (bow-tie pasta)
1 large egg, beaten lightly
1 cup medium kasha* (toasted buckwheat groats)
2 teaspoons salt
2 cups boiling water

*available at natural foods stores and some
    supermarkets

In a bowl whisk sour cream with 2 tablespoons

dill and pepper and salt to taste. Chill mixture, covered.

In a large heavy skillet melt butter with oil over moderately high heat until foam subsides and sauté onions, stirring, until golden brown, about 10 minutes. Stir in bell peppers and zucchini and sauté, stirring, until vegetables are tender, about 10 minutes.

Bring a kettle of salted water to a boil for pasta.

While vegetables are cooking, in a saucepan whisk together egg and kasha until kasha is coated well. Stir in salt and cook kasha over moderate heat, stirring, 3 to 5 minutes, or until grains are separated and dry. Stir in boiling water and simmer kasha, covered, about 15 minutes, or until tender but not mushy (drain kasha in a sieve if any liquid remains). Season kasha with salt and pepper and keep warm, covered.

While kasha is cooking, cook pasta in boiling salted water until *al dente* and drain in a colander. Return pasta to kettle and toss with vegetables, kasha, remaining 2 tablespoons dill, and pepper and salt to taste.

Serve *kasha varnishkes* hot with dilled sour cream. Serves 6 as a main course or 8 as a side dish.

Sweet Potato, Swiss Chard, and Quinoa Gratin

1½ pounds sweet potatoes (about 3)
1 cup quinoa (small disk-shaped seeds)*
4 tablespoons olive oil
2 cups coarse fresh bread crumbs
2½ pounds Swiss chard, washed well and stems
    trimmed, removed, and reserved
3 tablespoons minced garlic (about 6 cloves),
    or to taste

*available at natural foods stores and specialty
    foods shops

Preheat oven to 450° F. and butter a 2-quart shallow baking dish.

Prick each potato with a fork 3 times and bake on a baking sheet in middle of oven about 1 hour, or until very tender.

While potatoes are baking, in a bowl wash quinoa in at least 5 changes cold water, rubbing grains and letting them settle before pouring off most of water, until water runs clear and drain in a fine sieve.

In a saucepan combine quinoa with 2 cups salted water and bring to a boil. Simmer quinoa, covered, until all liquid is absorbed, about 15 minutes, and remove lid.

In a skillet heat 1 tablespoon oil over moderate heat and cook bread crumbs until golden brown. Season crumbs with salt and pepper.

While quinoa is cooking, finely chop reserved Swiss chard stems and coarsely chop leaves, keeping both separate. In a deep heavy 12-inch kettle heat remaining 3 tablespoons oil over moderate heat and cook stems until tender, about 5 minutes. Stir in leaves, a handful at a time, and stir in garlic, tossing. Cook leaves until just wilted, about 4 minutes. Remove kettle from heat and stir in quinoa until combined well. Season mixture with salt and pepper.

Reduce oven temperature to 350° F.

When potatoes are cool enough to handle, peel and mash with a fork. Season potatoes with salt and pepper.

With a large spoon drop mounds of potatoes and Swiss chard mixture in baking dish, alternating them to cover bottom decoratively, and smooth surface. Top gratin with bread crumbs.

Bake gratin in middle of oven about 30 minutes, or until hot. Cool gratin 5 minutes before serving. Serves 6.

Baked Wild Rice Amandine

⅓ cup sliced almonds
2 tablespoons unsalted butter, cut into pieces
    and softened
1 cup wild rice (about 6 ounces), rinsed well in
    several changes of cold water and drained
2¼ cups chicken broth, heated
¼ teaspoon salt

Preheat oven to 475° F.

In a 10-inch round baking dish toast almonds in oven until golden, about 5 minutes. Add butter and rice and toss to coat. Stir in broth and salt.

Bake rice, covered with foil, in lower third of oven 1 hour and 15 minutes, or until rice is tender. If all of broth has not been absorbed, bake rice, uncovered, 5 minutes more. *Rice may be made 1 day ahead and reheated before serving.* Serves 4.

Italian Sausage and Bell Pepper Paella

2 links hot and/or sweet Italian sausage (about
    6 ounces total)
½ red bell pepper, cut into ½-inch-wide strips
½ green bell pepper, cut into ½-inch-wide strips
1 small onion, cut into ½-inch wedges
½ tablespoon olive oil
¾ cup Arborio or other medium-grain rice or
    converted rice
½ cup dry white wine
1 cup drained canned tomatoes, chopped coarse
1½ cups water

Preheat oven to 400° F.

Squeeze sausage meat from casings into a 10-inch heavy ovenproof skillet and add bell pepper strips, onion, and oil. Sauté mixture over moderately high heat, breaking up sausage with a fork and stirring occasionally, 5 minutes, or until vegetables begin to brown. Add rice and sauté, stirring, 1 minute. Stir in wine, tomatoes, and water and bring to a boil, stirring to loosen brown bits. Transfer skillet to oven and bake, uncovered, 25 minutes, or until most liquid is absorbed. Season paella with salt and pepper. Serves 2.

Walnut Tarragon Bulgur

1 large shallot, chopped fine
½ teaspoon salt
1 tablespoon tarragon white-wine vinegar
½ cup bulgur*
¾ cup water
2 teaspoons chopped fresh tarragon leaves
1 tablespoon olive oil
¼ cup walnuts, lightly toasted and
    chopped

* available in natural foods stores or use packaged
    Near East *tabbouleh* mix (without
    accompanying seasoning pouch)

In a small bowl stir together shallot, ¼ teaspoon salt, and vinegar and let mixture stand while cooking bulgur.

In a small heavy saucepan bring water with remaining ¼ teaspoon salt to a boil. Stir in bulgur and cook, covered, over low heat 10 to 12 minutes, or until water is absorbed. Transfer bulgur to a large bowl and cool completely, stirring occasionally with a fork to break up lumps. Stir in shallot mixture, tarragon, oil, walnuts, and salt and pepper to taste. Serves 2 as a side dish.

VEGETABLES AND BEANS

Artichoke and Cherry Tomato Tarts

1 large egg yolk, beaten lightly
¼ cup sour cream
1 sheet (½ pound) frozen puff pastry, thawed
    and cut into two 4-inch squares, reserving
    the rest for another use
1 cup quartered drained marinated artichoke
    hearts
10 vine-ripened cherry tomatoes, halved
1 teaspoon fresh thyme leaves

Preheat oven to 400° F. and lightly flour a baking
sheet.

In a bowl whisk together yolk, sour cream, and
salt and pepper to taste. Arrange pastry squares on
baking sheet and spoon one fourth of mixture onto
center of each. Top mixture with artichokes and
tomatoes. Spoon remaining sour cream mixture over
vegetables and sprinkle with thyme.

Bake tarts in middle of oven until pastry is
golden, about 15 minutes. Serves 2 as a light main
course.

Asparagus Flans

2 pounds asparagus
2 tablespoons heavy cream
½ teaspoon dried tarragon, crumbled
½ stick (¼ cup) unsalted butter, softened
¼ cup freshly grated Parmesan (about ¾ ounce)
½ teaspoon salt
3 large eggs

Preheat oven to 350° F. and butter six ¾-cup
soufflé dishes or custard cups. Line bottoms of
dishes or cups with rounds of wax paper and butter
paper. Line a baking pan large enough to hold dishes
or cups with a double layer of kitchen towels.

Trim asparagus and cut off tips. Halve asparagus
tips lengthwise and cut stalks crosswise into 1-inch
pieces. In a steamer rack set over boiling water
steam asparagus tips, covered, until crisp-tender,
about 1 minute. Transfer asparagus tips with a
slotted spoon to a colander and rinse under cold
water to stop cooking. Drain tips well and pat dry.

Steam asparagus stalks, covered, until tender but
still bright green, about 8 minutes. Transfer stalks
with slotted spoon to paper towels and pat dry well.
In a blender purée stalks, cream, tarragon, 3 tablespoons butter, Parmesan, and salt until smooth. In a
bowl whisk eggs until combined and add asparagus
purée in a stream, whisking until smooth.

Divide mixture among dishes or cups and put
on towels in pan. Add enough hot water to pan to
reach halfway up sides of dishes or cups and bake
flans in lower third of oven 35 to 40 minutes, or until a thin knife inserted in center comes out clean.
Remove dishes or cups from pan and cool on a rack
5 minutes.

In a small saucepan heat asparagus tips in
remaining tablespoon butter until heated through.
Run knife around edges of dishes or cups and invert
flans onto 6 plates. Top flans with asparagus tips.
Serves 6.

Roasted Asparagus with Anise Seeds

½ teaspoon anise seeds
1 pound asparagus, trimmed
1 tablespoon olive oil

Preheat oven to 450° F.

In an electric coffee/spice grinder or with a mortar
and pestle grind anise seeds fine. Cut asparagus
diagonally into 2-inch pieces and in a shallow baking pan large enough to hold asparagus in one layer
toss with anise, oil, and salt and pepper to taste.
Roast asparagus in middle of oven, shaking pan
occasionally, until crisp-tender and golden, 5 to 8
minutes. Serves 2.

Green Beans with Bacon Vinaigrette

1 pound green beans, trimmed
¼ pound sliced bacon (about 4 slices)
1 tablespoon red-wine vinegar

In a kettle of boiling salted water cook beans until *al dente*, about 3 minutes. Drain beans in a colander and plunge into a bowl of ice and cold water to stop cooking. Drain beans well.

In a large heavy skillet cook bacon over moderate heat until crisp and transfer to paper towels to drain. Crumble bacon.

Pour off all but about 1 tablespoon fat from skillet and cook beans with vinegar and half of bacon over moderate heat, tossing, until tender. Season beans with salt and pepper and serve topped with remaining bacon. Serves 2.

Wax Beans with Parsley Oil

2 tablespoons olive oil
1 tablespoon unsalted butter
¼ cup packed parsley leaves, washed well
  and spun dry
1¼ pounds wax beans, trimmed

In a small skillet heat oil and butter until hot and butter is melted and transfer to a blender. Add parsley and blend mixture until smooth, scraping down side of blender occasionally. Return mixture to skillet.

Cook beans in a large saucepan of boiling salted water until crisp-tender, about 3 minutes. Drain beans well and return to pan. Add parsley oil, tossing to coat. Season beans with salt and pepper and serve warm. Serves 6.

PHOTO ON PAGE 46

Green Beans with Lemon and Cloves

½ cup water
¾ pound green beans, trimmed
1 tablespoon olive oil
¾ teaspoon finely grated fresh lemon zest
scant ⅛ teaspoon ground cloves

In a 10-inch heavy skillet bring water with green beans to a boil and cook, covered, 5 minutes, or until beans are crisp-tender. Using lid to hold back beans, drain liquid from skillet. Add oil, zest, cloves, and salt and pepper to taste and cook over moderate heat, stirring, 2 minutes to blend flavors. Serves 2.

Steamed Broccoli with Hummus

a 19-ounce can chick-peas, rinsed and drained
  (about 2 cups)
3 tablespoons well-stirred *tahini* (sesame seed
  paste)*
3 tablespoons fresh lemon juice
1 tablespoon extra-virgin olive oil
1 garlic clove, minced and mashed to a paste
  with 1 teaspoon salt
3 to 6 tablespoons water
¼ cup fresh parsley leaves, washed well, spun
  dry, and minced
1 pound broccoli, tough ends of stems discarded

*available at specialty foods shops and most
  supermarkets

In a food processor purée chick-peas, *tahini*, lemon juice, oil, and garlic paste. If a smoother texture is desired, force through a fine sieve into a bowl. Whisk in enough water to reach a pourable but thick consistency and stir in parsley and salt to taste.

Cut broccoli stems into spears about 5 inches long with flowerets 1½ inches wide. On a steamer rack set over boiling water steam broccoli, covered, until crisp-tender, about 4 minutes.

Serve broccoli topped with *hummus*. Serves 2 generously.

Steamed Broccoli Rabe

4 bunches broccoli rabe (about 4 pounds),
  coarse and hollow stems discarded and
  remainder washed and drained
¼ cup extra-virgin olive oil
¼ teaspoon dried hot red pepper flakes

In a large steamer set over boiling water steam broccoli rabe, covered, until tender, about 5 minutes, and transfer to a platter. In a small skillet heat oil with red pepper flakes over moderate heat until hot but not smoking and drizzle over broccoli rabe. Gently toss broccoli rabe and season with salt. Serve broccoli rabe warm or at room temperature. Serves 12 as part of a buffet.

PHOTO ON PAGE 78

Balsamic-Braised Red Cabbage and Onions

2 tablespoons vegetable oil
¾ pound red cabbage, sliced thin
  (about 6 cups)
1 medium red onion, sliced thin
¼ cup water
½ cup balsamic vinegar
1 tablespoon sugar

In a large heavy skillet heat oil over moderate heat until hot but not smoking and cook cabbage and onion, stirring, 10 minutes, or until just tender. Stir in water, vinegar, sugar, and salt and pepper to taste and simmer, stirring occasionally, until almost all liquid is evaporated and vegetables are tender, about 15 minutes. Serves 2.

Shredded Brussels Sprouts and Scallions

a 10-ounce container Brussels sprouts
  (about 26), trimmed
2 tablespoons unsalted butter
3 scallions, sliced thin diagonally
1 teaspoon fresh lime juice, or to taste

Cut sprouts in half and slice thin lengthwise. In a heavy skillet melt butter over moderately high heat until foam subsides and sauté sprouts and scallions, stirring, until tender and lightly browned, about 8 minutes. In a bowl toss vegetables with lime juice and salt and pepper to taste. Serves 2.

Stir-Fried Carrots and Garlic

4 medium carrots, halved crosswise
2 teaspoons olive oil
1 garlic clove, sliced thin lengthwise
⅓ cup water
2 teaspoons unsalted butter
fresh lemon juice to taste

Halve carrot pieces lengthwise and cut crosswise into ⅛-inch-thick slices. In a heavy medium skillet heat oil over moderately high heat until hot but not smoking and stir-fry carrots until they begin to turn golden. Add garlic and stir-fry 30 seconds. Add water and butter and simmer, covered, until carrots are just tender, about 3 minutes. Boil carrots, uncovered, until most of liquid is evaporated. Stir in lemon juice and salt and pepper to taste. Serves 2.

Zested Carrot Zucchini Julienne

1 large carrot
1 large zucchini
½ tablespoon unsalted butter
1 teaspoon freshly grated orange zest
½ teaspoon freshly grated lemon zest
2 tablespoons slivered almonds,
  toasted

Using a *mandoline* or other hand-held slicer, cut carrot and zucchini lengthwise into ⅛-inch ribbons. Lay ribbons flat and cut lengthwise into ⅛-inch julienne. In a non-stick skillet heat butter over moderately high heat until foam subsides and sauté carrot, zucchini, and zests, stirring, until vegetables are tender, about 3 minutes. Stir in almonds and season with salt and pepper. Serves 2.

Cauliflower with Toasted Bread Crumbs

2 tablespoons fine dry bread crumbs
1½ tablespoons vegetable oil
1 large onion, halved lengthwise and sliced
    thin lengthwise
2 teaspoons balsamic vinegar
½ small head cauliflower, cut into
    1-inch flowerets
⅓ cup water

In a small non-stick skillet sauté bread crumbs in ½ tablespoon oil over moderately high heat, stirring, until fragrant and transfer to a small bowl.

In skillet heat remaining tablespoon oil over moderate heat until hot but not smoking and cook onion, stirring, until golden. Add vinegar and cauliflower and sauté over moderately high heat, stirring, until cauliflower begins to turn golden. Add water and salt to taste and simmer, covered, 10 minutes, or until tender. Sprinkle cauliflower mixture with bread crumbs. Serves 2.

Feta-Stuffed Eggplant Rolls with Salsa Verde

a 1-pound firm eggplant
olive oil for brushing eggplant
3 ounces feta, crumbled (about ½ cup)
⅓ cup whole-milk ricotta
¼ cup fresh mint leaves, washed well,
    spun dry, and chopped fine
3 red bell peppers, roasted (procedure on
    page 117), or two 7-ounce jars roasted
    peppers, rinsed, drained, and patted dry
1 bunch arugula or small bunch spinach,
    coarse stems discarded and leaves washed
    well and spun dry

Accompaniment: salsa verde (recipe follows)

Preheat broiler and oil a baking sheet.

Cut eggplant lengthwise into ¼-inch-thick slices and arrange 6 center slices on baking sheet in one layer, reserving remaining eggplant for another use. Brush eggplant with oil and season with salt.

Broil eggplant about 3 inches from heat until golden, about 5 minutes. Carefully turn eggplant over with a metal spatula and broil until golden,

about 4 minutes more. Transfer eggplant to a platter large enough to hold slices in one layer and cool. *Eggplant may be prepared up to this point 3 hours ahead and kept, covered loosely with foil, at room temperature.*

In a small bowl with a fork mash together feta, ricotta, mint, and salt and pepper to taste. Cut peppers lengthwise into pieces about same width as eggplant slices.

Assemble rolls:

Top eggplant slices with roasted pepper pieces, arranging them in one layer. Put 1 tablespoon cheese mixture near narrow end of each slice and into it gently press 4 or 5 arugula or spinach leaves so that they stick out on both sides. Beginning with cheese end, roll up each slice to enclose cheese mixture and leaves. *Rolls may be made 2 hours ahead and kept, covered loosely, at room temperature.*

Serve rolls drizzled with *salsa verde*. Serves 6 as a first course.

Salsa Verde

1 cup packed fresh parsley leaves (preferably
    flat-leafed), washed well and spun dry
1 small garlic clove
⅓ cup extra-virgin olive oil
1 tablespoon red-wine vinegar
½ teaspoon anchovy paste

In a blender blend salsa ingredients until smooth. *Salsa verde may be made 1 day ahead and chilled, covered. Bring salsa to room temperature before serving.* Makes about 1 cup.

Eggplant and Arugula Sandwiches with Chick-Pea Spread

a ¾-pound firm eggplant, cut into ½-inch-thick
    slices
1 cup canned chick-peas, rinsed and drained
¼ cup fresh parsley leaves, washed well and
    spun dry
1 small garlic clove, chopped and mashed to
    a paste with ½ teaspoon salt
2 tablespoons water
1½ tablespoons fresh lemon juice

2 cups arugula, washed well and spun dry
1 teaspoon olive oil
1 teaspoon red-wine vinegar
4 large slices fat-free country-style white bread
  (about 1 ounce each), lightly toasted

Preheat broiler.

On rack of a broiler pan arrange eggplant slices in one layer, seasoning both sides with salt and pepper. Broil eggplant about 4 inches from heat, turning once, until golden, 3 to 5 minutes on each side.

In a food processor purée chick-peas, parsley, garlic paste, water, lemon juice, and salt and pepper to taste until smooth. In a bowl toss arugula with oil, vinegar, and salt and pepper to taste.

Spread chick pea purée evenly on 2 bread slices and top each slice with half of eggplant slices, half of arugula mixture, and remaining 2 bread slices. Makes 2 sandwiches, serving 2.

🍃 Each serving about 338 calories, 5 grams fat
(13% of calories from fat)

Sautéed Cucumbers with Cumin and Mint

a ¾- to 1-pound seedless cucumber
2 teaspoons olive oil
½ teaspoon ground cumin
¼ cup water
2 tablespoons chopped fresh mint leaves

Peel cucumber and quarter lengthwise. Cut out and discard core. Cut each quarter crosswise into 4 pieces. Cut each piece lengthwise into 4 strips.

In an 8- to 9-inch non-stick skillet heat oil over moderately high heat until hot but not smoking and sauté cucumber with salt to taste, stirring, 3 minutes. Stir in cumin and water. Boil mixture, stirring, until liquid is evaporated and stir in mint and salt and pepper to taste. Serves 2.

Sautéed Mustard Greens

2 tablespoons olive oil
2 large bunches mustard greens (about 2
  pounds), washed well, spun dry, coarse
  stems discarded, and leaves cut
  into 3-inch pieces

In a large heavy skillet heat oil over high heat until hot but not smoking and add greens. Turn greens with tongs until wilted. Sauté greens, turning occasionally, about 5 minutes, or until any liquid is evaporated, and season with salt. Serves 6.

PHOTO ON PAGE 16

Grilled Red Onions with Balsamic Vinegar and Rosemary

1½ teaspoons chopped fresh rosemary leaves
2 tablespoons balsamic vinegar
1 tablespoon olive oil
2 pounds red onions, cut crosswise into
  ½-inch-thick slices
½ cup fresh parsley leaves, washed well, spun
  dry, and chopped fine

Prepare grill.

In a very small saucepan heat rosemary and vinegar over low heat until hot (do not boil). Remove pan from heat and let mixture stand, covered, 20 minutes.

In a metal measure heat oil over low heat until warm. (Heating thins oil, making it easier to thinly coat onions.) Arrange onion slices in one layer on trays, keeping slices intact, and brush both sides of each slice lightly with oil. Season onions with salt and pepper and grill in batches on a lightly oiled rack set 5 to 6 inches over glowing coals 4 to 6 minutes on each side, or until lightly charred and softened. Transfer onions as grilled to a large bowl, separating rings, and toss with vinegar mixture, parsley, and salt and pepper to taste.

Serve grilled onions warm or at room temperature. Serves 6.

🍃 Each serving about 74 calories, 2 grams fat
(29% of calories from fat)

PHOTO ON PAGE 38

Roasted Fennel and Red Onions

2 large fennel bulbs (sometimes called anise,
    about 2 pounds), stalks trimmed flush with
    bulb and any tough outer layers discarded
2 small red onions, quartered
1 tablespoon unsalted butter, melted
1 tablespoon olive oil
1 tablespoon balsamic vinegar

Preheat oven to 400° F.

Cut each fennel bulb lengthwise into 8 wedges and in a roasting pan toss fennel and onions with butter, oil, and salt and pepper to taste. Roast vegetables, stirring once halfway through roasting, 25 minutes, or until tender. Add vinegar and toss to coat. Serves 2 generously.

Roasted Onion Tarts

14 red onions (about 3 inches in diameter)
14 yellow onions (about 3 inches in diameter)
3 tablespoons olive oil plus additional if desired
3 tablespoons heavy cream
two 17¼-ounce packages frozen puff pastry
    (4 sheets total), thawed and unfolded

Preheat oven to 425° F. and lightly grease 2 large baking sheets.

Slice enough of red and yellow onions to measure 5 cups each and in a large skillet cook in 3 tablespoons oil with salt and pepper to taste, covered, over moderate heat, stirring occasionally, until golden and tender, about 15 minutes. Stir in cream and cool.

Trim remaining onions and cut lengthwise into sixths, keeping wedges intact, and arrange, narrow sides up, ½ inch apart on baking sheets. Sprinkle onion wedges with salt and pepper to taste and roast in middle and lower thirds of oven 20 minutes, or until tender. Cool onion wedges.

On a lightly floured surface with a lightly floured rolling pin roll out 1 pastry sheet into a 13-inch square. Using an inverted 6-inch plate as a guide, cut out four 6-inch rounds, discarding scraps. Cut out 12 more rounds from remaining 3 pastry sheets in same manner to make a total of 16 rounds.

Fold in edge of each pastry round to form a ¼-inch-wide border. (If pastry becomes too soft to work with, chill until firm.) Transfer rounds to 2 large baking sheets and chill until firm, about 10 minutes. Top each round evenly with a scant ¼ cup sliced onion mixture. Arrange roasted onions on their sides decoratively (alternating yellow and red) on top of tarts and season with salt and pepper. Bake tarts in middle and lower thirds of oven, switching positions of pans halfway through baking, 20 to 25 minutes, or until bottoms are golden brown and roasted onions are very tender. Transfer tarts to racks to cool. *Tarts may be made 1 day ahead and chilled, covered loosely with plastic wrap. Bring tarts to room temperature before serving or heat in a preheated 350° F. oven until heated through.*

Brush tarts with additional oil and serve whole or halved. Makes 16 tarts.

PHOTO ON PAGE 67

Parsnip Chips

two 9-inch-long parsnips, scrubbed
vegetable oil for frying

With a *mandoline* or other manual slicer cut parsnips crosswise into paper-thin slices. In a large deep saucepan heat 2 inches oil until a deep-fat thermometer registers 375° F. and fry parsnips in 4 batches until crisp and golden, about 2 minutes, making sure oil returns to 375° F. before adding next batch. Transfer chips as fried with a slotted spoon to paper towels and drain. Sprinkle chips with salt. Makes about 3 cups, serving 2.

Glazed Parsnips

1½ tablespoons unsalted butter
1 tablespoon firmly packed brown sugar
¼ teaspoon salt
½ cup water
½ pound parsnips, peeled and cut into
    3- by ¼-inch sticks
½ teaspoon fresh lemon juice, or to taste

In a 9- to 10-inch heavy skillet combine butter, brown sugar, salt, and water and simmer, stirring, until butter is melted and sugar is dissolved. Add parsnips and simmer, covered, until tender, 4 to 5 minutes. Transfer parsnips with a slotted spoon to a bowl and boil cooking liquid until reduced to a glaze. Return parsnips to skillet. Cook parsnips over low heat, stirring, until heated through and coated with glaze. Stir in lemon juice and salt and pepper to taste. Serves 2.

Goat Cheese and Thyme Potato Cake

1½ pounds small red potatoes
¾ stick (6 tablespoons) unsalted butter, softened
½ cup sour cream
4 ounces goat cheese (preferably aged, about ½ cup), grated if aged or forced through a grater if soft
2 large eggs
1 teaspoon fresh thyme leaves

Generously oil or butter a 9-inch square baking pan and line with a 14- by 8-inch piece parchment paper, allowing ends of paper to overhang 2 opposite edges of pan. Press on paper to coat underside with oil or butter and turn over, keeping ends of paper overhanging.

Preheat oven to 375° F.

Cut potatoes into ¼-inch-thick slices and in a kettle of boiling salted water cook until tender but not falling apart, about 8 minutes. Drain potatoes in a colander and cool 15 minutes.

In a large bowl whisk together butter and sour cream until smooth and whisk in goat cheese and eggs until combined well. Add potatoes, tossing gently, and transfer mixture to baking pan. Smooth top with a spatula, spreading potatoes evenly, and sprinkle with thyme. Bake potato cake in middle of oven 35 minutes, or until top is golden, and cool in pan on a rack. *Potato cake may be made 2 days ahead and chilled, covered.*

Using parchment paper, lift potato cake from pan and transfer to a cutting board. Cut cake into squares, discarding parchment, and serve at room temperature. Serves 6 generously.

PHOTO ON PAGE 58

Caraway Parsley Potatoes

2½ pounds small red potatoes
    (about twenty-four, 1½ inches
    in diameter)
1 tablespoon caraway seeds
1½ tablespoons unsalted butter
2 tablespoons minced fresh parsley leaves

Peel potatoes and in a 3- to 4-quart saucepan cover with salted cold water by 2 inches. Simmer potatoes until just tender, 12 to 15 minutes, and drain in a colander.

While potatoes are cooking, in a small heavy skillet dry-roast seeds over moderate heat, shaking skillet, until fragrant and slightly darker, being careful not to burn them, 3 to 4 minutes. Transfer seeds to a small bowl and cool. With a mortar and pestle or in an electric coffee/spice grinder grind seeds coarse.

In a large heavy skillet melt butter over moderately low heat and add potatoes, stirring and shaking skillet to coat. Sprinkle potatoes with ground caraway seeds, parsley, and salt and pepper to taste and stir, shaking skillet occasionally, to coat. Serves 6.

PHOTO ON PAGE 19

181

Buttered New Potatoes

1¼ pounds small new potatoes (about 1½ inches
    in diameter)
1½ tablespoons unsalted butter

In a saucepan combine potatoes and water to
cover by 1 inch and bring water to a boil. Simmer
potatoes 10 minutes, or until tender, and drain well.
Return potatoes to pan and toss with butter and salt
and pepper to taste. Serve potatoes warm. Serves 6.

PHOTO ON PAGE 46

Roasted Potatoes with Lime and Basil

¾ pound small potatoes (about 1½ inches in
    diameter), halved
1½ tablespoons extra-virgin olive oil
¼ cup packed fresh basil leaves, washed well,
    spun dry, and chopped fine
1½ teaspoons fresh lime juice

Preheat oven to 450° F.
In a baking dish large enough to hold potatoes in
one layer toss them with oil and salt and pepper to
taste. Roast potatoes in middle of oven until tender,
about 15 minutes. In a bowl toss potatoes with basil
and lime juice. Serves 2.

Mashed Potatoes and Leeks with Thyme

3 pounds russet (baking) potatoes (about 6)
6 leeks (white and pale green parts only),
    chopped, washed well, and drained
¾ stick (6 tablespoons) unsalted butter
1 tablespoon fresh thyme leaves, minced
1 cup milk
½ cup heavy cream

In an 8-quart kettle combine potatoes with cold
water to cover by 2 inches. Bring water to a boil and
simmer potatoes until tender, 35 to 45 minutes.
While potatoes are cooking, in a heavy skillet cook
leeks in 4 tablespoons butter over moderately low
heat, stirring occasionally, until softened. Stir in
thyme and salt and pepper to taste.
Drain potatoes in a colander and return to kettle.

Dry potatoes over low heat, shaking kettle, 1 minute.
Cool potatoes just until they can be handled and
peel. While potatoes are still warm, force through a
ricer into a large bowl. In a small saucepan heat milk
and cream until mixture just comes to a boil. Stir
leeks and milk mixture into potatoes and season with
salt and pepper. Spread potato mixture in a buttered
4-quart shallow baking dish. *Chill potato mixture,
covered, 1 day.*
Preheat oven to 350° F.
Dot potato mixture with remaining 2 tablespoons
butter and bake, covered with foil, in middle of oven
until heated through and butter is melted, about 15
minutes. Serves 8.

PHOTO ON PAGE 75

Potato Casserole with Prosciutto

2 pounds russet (baking) potatoes (about
    6 medium)
3 tablespoons fine dry bread crumbs
1 cup whole-milk ricotta
1 cup milk
1 cup plus 2 tablespoons freshly grated
    Parmigiano-Reggiano (about 3 ounces)
¼ pound thinly sliced prosciutto, cut into
    narrow strips
½ pound mozzarella, cut into ½-inch cubes
2 large eggs, beaten lightly
¼ teaspoon freshly grated nutmeg
freshly ground black pepper to taste

In a 6-quart kettle cover potatoes with cold water
by 2 inches and simmer until tender, about 40 minutes. Drain potatoes in a colander and cool slightly.
Preheat oven to 375° F. Butter an oval baking
dish, 12 by 9 by 2 inches (2½ quarts), and sprinkle
evenly with 1 tablespoon bread crumbs.
Peel potatoes and force through a ricer or food
mill into a large bowl. Stir in ricotta, milk, 1 cup
Parmigiano-Reggiano, prosciutto, mozzarella, eggs,
nutmeg, pepper, and salt to taste and transfer to
baking dish. Sprinkle potato mixture evenly with
remaining 2 tablespoons Parmigiano-Reggiano and
2 tablespoons bread crumbs and bake in middle of
oven until golden, 40 to 45 minutes. Serves 8 to 10
as a side dish.

Shredded Sweet Potato and White Potato Cake

6 ounces boiling potato (about 1 medium)
6 ounces sweet potato (about 1 small)
1 tablespoon olive oil
1 tablespoon unsalted butter

In a food processor fitted with coarse shredding disk shred boiling potato and transfer to a bowl of cold water, swishing it around to remove excess starch. Drain potato in a colander and pat dry with paper towels. Peel sweet potato and shred in food processor.

In a bowl toss together shredded potatoes. In a 10-inch non-stick skillet heat ½ tablespoon oil and ½ tablespoon butter over moderate heat until foam subsides. Spread potatoes evenly in skillet and season with salt and pepper. Cook potato cake, tamping down firmly with a spatula, until underside is golden, about 5 minutes. Reduce heat to moderately low and cook 5 minutes more.

Slide cake onto a large plate. Invert another large plate over cake and invert cake onto it. Heat remaining oil and butter over moderate heat until foam subsides and slide cake back into skillet. Season cake with salt and pepper and cook until underside is golden and cake is cooked through, about 5 minutes.

Cut cake into 4 wedges. Serves 2.

Cold Sesame Spinach

a 10-ounce bag fresh spinach or 2 small
    bunches (about 1¼ pounds total)
1 cup water
½ teaspoon Asian sesame oil
½ teaspoon soy sauce
2 teaspoons sesame seeds
½ teaspoon rice vinegar
    (preferably seasoned)

Wash spinach well, discarding any coarse stems, and drain leaves in a colander. In a 3- to 4-quart saucepan bring water to a boil. Add spinach and steam, covered, 2 minutes. Drain spinach in colander, gently pressing out most of liquid. In a bowl toss spinach with oil, soy sauce, and salt and pepper to taste. Chill spinach, uncovered, 25 minutes.

While spinach is chilling, in a dry small heavy skillet (not non-stick) toast sesame seeds over moderate heat, stirring, until golden, 3 to 5 minutes.

Toss spinach with sesame seeds and vinegar. Serves 2.

Sautéed Spinach and Garlic

1 tablespoon olive oil
3 large garlic cloves, sliced thin lengthwise
3 pounds spinach (about 3 large bunches),
    coarse stems discarded and leaves washed
    well and drained in a colander

In an 8-quart heavy kettle heat oil over high heat until hot but not smoking and add garlic and spinach with water clinging to leaves. Sauté garlic and spinach, turning with tongs, until spinach is wilted but still bright green, about 2 minutes, and season with salt and pepper. *Spinach and garlic may be made 6 hours ahead and chilled, covered.* Serves 8.

PHOTO ON PAGE 23

Sautéed Spinach with Peanuts

1 tablespoon vegetable oil
1 pound fresh spinach, coarse stems discarded
    and leaves washed well and spun dry
¼ cup unsalted dry-roasted peanuts, chopped
a pinch dried hot red pepper flakes
2 teaspoons *tamari* or other soy sauce, or to taste

In a large non-stick skillet heat oil over moderately high heat until hot but not smoking and sauté spinach with peanuts, red pepper flakes, and soy sauce, stirring, until tender, about 1 minute. Season spinach with salt and pepper. Serves 2.

Sautéed Red Swiss Chard with Garlic

3½ pounds Swiss chard (preferably red;
    about 4 bunches), washed
¼ cup olive oil
4 garlic cloves, minced
½ cup water

Cut stems and center ribs away from Swiss chard leaves. Thinly slice stems and center ribs. Chop leaves coarse and reserve separately.

In a 10- to 12-quart heavy kettle heat oil over moderately high heat until hot but not smoking and sauté stems and ribs, stirring, until crisp-tender. Add garlic and sauté, stirring, until garlic is fragrant. Add reserved leaves with water clinging to them and cook, turning with tongs, until wilted. Add ½ cup water and cook, covered, over moderate heat until leaves are tender, about 4 minutes. Season chard with salt and pepper. *Swiss chard may be made 1 day ahead and chilled, covered.* Serves 8.

PHOTO ON PAGE 75

184

Fennel-Scented Spinach and Potato Samosas
(Savory Stuffed Pastries)

½ pound red potatoes (about 5, each about
    2 inches in diameter)
1 tablespoon fennel seeds
1 tablespoon ground cumin
½ teaspoon turmeric
¼ cup vegetable oil
1 onion, chopped
3 small *serrano* or *jalapeño* chilies, chopped
    fine (wear rubber gloves)
a 2-inch piece fresh gingerroot, peeled and
    grated fine
3 garlic cloves, minced
1 pound fresh spinach, coarse stems discarded
    and leaves washed well and drained
    (about 3 cups packed)
ten 17- by 12-inch *phyllo* sheets, thawed if
    frozen, stacked between 2 sheets wax
    paper and covered with a kitchen towel
1 stick (½ cup) unsalted butter, melted

Garnish: fresh mint sprigs
Accompaniment: mint chutney (page 202)

In a saucepan simmer potatoes in salted water to cover until barely tender, about 12 minutes, and drain in a colander. Cut potatoes into ¼-inch dice. In a heavy skillet dry-roast fennel seeds, cumin, and turmeric over moderate heat, stirring occasionally, until fragrant and several shades darker, about 2 minutes, being careful not to burn them. Add oil, onion, chilies, gingerroot, and garlic and cook, stirring, until onion is softened. Add potatoes and spinach and sauté over moderately high heat, stirring, until spinach is wilted but still bright green, about 2 minutes. Season filling with salt and pepper and cool. *Filling may be made 1 day ahead and chilled, covered.*

Preheat oven to 400° F. and lightly grease a baking sheet.

On a work surface arrange 1 *phyllo* sheet with a long side facing you and brush lightly with some butter. Top with a second *phyllo* sheet and brush lightly with butter. Cut stacked *phyllo* crosswise into 5 strips, each 12 by about 3½ inches. Put 2 teaspoons filling near one corner of each strip and fold corner of *phyllo* over to enclose filling and form a triangle. Continue folding strip, maintaining triangle shape. Put *samosa,* seam side down, on baking sheet and cover with plastic wrap. Make 24 more *samosas* with remaining *phyllo* and filling in same manner. *Samosas may be prepared up to this point 6 hours ahead and chilled, covered.* Bake *samosas* in middle of oven until golden brown, about 10 minutes.

Garnish *samosas* with mint and serve warm with chutney. Makes 25 *samosas,* serving 6 as a side dish.

PHOTO ON PAGE 62

Turnip Potato Purée

½ pound white turnips
a ½-pound russet (baking) potato
1½ tablespoons unsalted butter, softened

Peel turnips and potato and cut into 1-inch pieces. In a 3- to 4-quart saucepan cover turnips and potato with cold water by 1 inch and simmer, covered, until very tender, 15 to 20 minutes. Drain turnips and potatoes in a colander and in batches force through a ricer or food mill fitted with medium disk into pan. Stir in butter and salt and pepper to taste. Serves 2.

Baked Zucchini with Parmesan and Prosciutto

1 tablespoon unsalted butter, softened
3 small zucchini (about 1 pound)
¼ pound thinly sliced prosciutto
¼ cup freshly grated Parmigiano-Reggiano
   (about 1 ounce)
freshly ground black pepper to taste

Preheat oven to 400° F. and spread butter in a baking pan, 13 by 9 by 2 inches.

In a large saucepan of boiling water cook zucchini until crisp-tender, about 5 minutes. Drain zucchini and cool until they can be handled.

Trim ends of zucchini and quarter lengthwise to form spears. Wrap each zucchini spear in a slice of prosciutto and arrange side by side in pan. (Zucchini will be touching.) Sprinkle zucchini with Parmigiano-Reggiano and pepper and bake until lightly browned, 10 to 15 minutes. Serve zucchini warm. Serves 4 to 6 as a first course or side dish.

Grilled Zucchini

2 teaspoons olive oil
1½ pounds zucchini (about 4 medium), cut
   diagonally into ¼-inch-thick slices

Prepare grill.

In a metal measure heat oil over low heat until warm. (Heating thins oil, making it easier to thinly coat zucchini.) In a bowl drizzle oil over zucchini, tossing to coat, and season with salt and pepper. Grill zucchini, in batches if necessary, on a lightly oiled rack set 5 to 6 inches over glowing coals 2 to 4 minutes on each side, or until lightly charred and just tender.

Serve zucchini warm or at room temperature. Serves 6.

Each serving about 29 calories, 2 grams fat
(53% of calories from fat)

PHOTO ON PAGE 38

Grilled Vegetables

8 red bell peppers, cut vertically into
   6 pieces and seeds discarded
12 small yellow squash (about 4 inches
   long), halved lengthwise
12 small eggplants (about 4 inches long),
   halved lengthwise
¼ cup olive oil plus additional
   if desired
freshly ground black pepper to taste

Prepare grill.

In a large bowl toss vegetables with ¼ cup oil, pepper, and salt to taste. Grill vegetables in batches on a rack set 5 to 6 inches over glowing coals, turning them, 5 to 10 minutes for just-tender bell peppers and 10 to 15 minutes for just-tender squash and eggplant. Transfer vegetables to a platter to cool completely. *Vegetables may be grilled 1 day ahead and chilled, covered. Bring vegetables to room temperature before serving or heat on a baking sheet in a preheated 350° F. oven until just heated through.* Brush vegetables with additional oil. Serves 16 as part of a buffet.

PHOTO ON PAGE 67

Mélange of Winter Vegetables

8 medium beets, scrubbed and trimmed, leaving
  about 1 inch of stems attached
9 baby turnips with tops, peeled and tops trimmed
  to ¼ inch, or 3 medium turnips, peeled and cut
  into 6 wedges
18 baby carrots with tops, peeled and tops
  trimmed to ¼ inch, or 3 large carrots, peeled
  and cut into 3- by ½-inch sticks
¾ pound assorted red and yellow pearl onions
  (about 2½ cups)
3 tablespoons unsalted butter
1 tablespoon olive oil
¼ cup loosely packed fresh flat-leafed parsley
  leaves, washed well, dried, and chopped
freshly ground black pepper

Preheat oven to 425° F.

Wrap beets tightly in foil and roast in middle of oven 1 to 1½ hours, or until tender. Unwrap beets carefully and cool until they can be handled. Slip off and discard skins and stems. Cut each beet into 6 wedges. *Beets may be prepared up to this point 1 day ahead and chilled, covered.*

Have ready a large bowl of ice and cold water. In a large saucepan of salted boiling water blanch turnips 3 to 6 minutes (depending on size), or until barely tender, and transfer with a slotted spoon to ice water. Return water in pan to a boil and blanch carrots 5 minutes, or until barely tender. Transfer carrots with a slotted spoon to ice water and drain turnips and carrots in a colander. If using baby turnips, cut each in half.

Return water in pan to a boil and blanch onions 3 minutes, or until barely tender. Drain onions in another colander until cool enough to handle and peel. *Vegetables may be prepared up to this point 1 day ahead, patted dry, and chilled, covered. Bring vegetables to room temperature before proceeding.*

In a large non-stick skillet heat butter over moderately high heat until foam subsides and sauté turnips and carrots with pepper and salt to taste, stirring, until tender and golden, about 4 minutes. Transfer turnips and carrots with slotted spoon to a bowl and keep warm, covered. Add oil to skillet and heat over moderately high heat until hot but not smoking. Sauté onions with pepper and salt to taste, stirring, until tender and golden brown, about 4 minutes, and with slotted spoon transfer to turnip mixture. Stir parsley into vegetable mixture.

In oil remaining in skillet cook beets with pepper and salt to taste over moderate heat, stirring, until heated through.

Serve beets with other vegetables (but do not toss together). Serves 6.

PHOTO ON PAGE 82

Sesame Vegetables

1 tablespoon vegetable oil
1 medium red bell pepper, cut into
  thin strips
¼ pound white mushrooms, trimmed and
  quartered
4 scallions, root ends and dark green
  parts discarded, cut crosswise into
  1½-inch pieces
a pinch dried hot red pepper flakes,
  or to taste
1 teaspoon Asian sesame oil, or to taste

In a small heavy skillet heat vegetable oil over moderate heat until hot but not smoking and cook bell pepper, mushrooms, scallions, and red pepper flakes, stirring, until vegetables are golden and cooked through, about 5 minutes. Toss vegetables with sesame oil and salt and pepper to taste. Serves 2.

Root Vegetable Gratin

1½ pounds rutabaga (about 1 small)
1 pound white turnips (about 5 medium)
¾ pound parsnips (about 5 medium)
2 tablespoons all-purpose flour
1¼ cups grated Gruyère (about
  5 ounces)
1 cup heavy cream
1 cup milk

With a sharp knife peel rutabaga and cut into ⅛-inch-thick wedges. In a large saucepan of boiling salted water cook rutabaga until crisp-tender, 6 to 8 minutes, and transfer with a slotted spoon to a colander. Drain rutabaga and pat dry between paper towels.

Peel turnips and cut into ⅛-inch-thick wedges. Cook turnips in boiling salted water until crisp-tender, 3 to 4 minutes, and transfer with slotted spoon to colander. Drain turnips and pat dry between paper towels.

Peel parsnips and cut diagonally into ⅛-inch-thick slices. Cook parsnips in boiling salted water until crisp-tender, 3 to 4 minutes, and transfer with slotted spoon to colander. Drain parsnips and pat dry between paper towels.

In a bowl toss together vegetables. *Vegetables may be cooked 1 day ahead and chilled, covered.*

Preheat oven to 350° F. and butter a 2-quart gratin dish, about 12 by 9 by 2 inches.

In gratin dish arrange one third vegetables and sprinkle with 1 tablespoon flour, ¼ cup Gruyère, and salt and pepper to taste. Top cheese with half of remaining vegetables, remaining tablespoon flour, ¼ cup cheese, and salt and pepper to taste. Arrange remaining vegetables over cheese and pour cream and milk over vegetables.

Sprinkle remaining ¾ cup cheese over vegetables and bake in middle of oven, covered, 30 minutes. Uncover gratin and bake until bubbling and golden, about 40 minutes more. Serves 8.

PHOTO ON PAGE 75

Summer Vegetable Ragout

3 garlic cloves, minced
3 tablespoons olive oil
white and pale green parts of 12 scallions,
  cut crosswise into 1½-inch-long pieces
½ pound baby zucchini (about 22), halved
  lengthwise
½ pound baby yellow pattypan squash
  (about 22), halved lengthwise
1½ cups fresh corn (cut from about 3 ears)
1 cup chicken broth
3 cups vine-ripened small cherry tomatoes,
  halved
2 teaspoons chopped fresh tarragon
  leaves

In a 12-inch heavy skillet sauté garlic in oil over moderately high heat, stirring just until fragrant. Add scallions, zucchini, pattypan squash, corn, and salt and pepper to taste and sauté, stirring occasionally, until zucchini and squash are golden in spots, about 4 minutes.

Add broth and simmer ragout, covered, 3 minutes, or until squash is just tender. Add tomatoes and tarragon and simmer, covered, 1 minute, or until tomatoes are softened.

Season ragout with salt and pepper and serve warm or at room temperature. Serves 6.

PHOTO ON PAGE 50

BEANS

Chick-Pea Tomato Stew with Moroccan Flavors

1 pound dried chick-peas (about 2⅓ cups),
    picked over
2 cinnamon sticks, broken in half
1 teaspoon cumin seeds
¼ cup olive oil
3 large onions, sliced thin (about 7 cups)
two 28- to 32-ounce cans whole tomatoes,
    drained, reserving juice, and chopped
1 cup raisins
⅓ cup four-day preserved lemon zest (page 140),
    chopped, or chopped peel of preserved lemons*
¾ teaspoon ground cumin
½ teaspoon ground coriander
1½ pounds fresh spinach, stems trimmed
    and leaves washed well and drained
    (about 10 cups packed)

Accompaniments
couscous
crusty bread

*available by mail order from The Gardener,
    1836 Fourth Street, Berkeley, CA 94710,
    tel. (510) 548-4545

In a bowl soak chick-peas in water to cover by 2 inches overnight or quick-soak (procedure follows) and drain.

In a 3-quart saucepan combine chick-peas, cinnamon, cumin seeds, and water to cover by 2 inches and simmer, covered partially, adding more water if necessary, 1 to 1¼ hours, or until chick-peas are just tender. Discard cinnamon. *Chick-peas may be made 1 day ahead, cooled completely, and chilled in their cooking liquid, covered.*

In a large heavy kettle heat oil over moderate heat and cook onions, stirring occasionally, until deep golden brown, about 15 minutes. Stir in chick-peas with cooking liquid, tomatoes with reserved juice, raisins, preserved lemon peel, ground cumin, and coriander and bring to a simmer. Cook stew about 45 minutes, or until chick-peas are tender and liquid is thickened slightly. Stir in spinach, a heaping handful at a time, and cook until wilted and just tender.

Season stew with salt and pepper and serve with couscous and bread. Serves 8 as a main course.

To Quick-Soak Dried Beans

In a large saucepan combine dried beans, picked over, with triple their volume of cold water. Bring water to a boil and cook beans, uncovered, over moderate heat 2 minutes. Remove pan from heat and soak beans 1 hour.

Cumin Black Beans with Mint

1 cup finely chopped onion
1½ tablespoons minced garlic (about 2 large
    cloves)
1¼ teaspoons cumin seeds
1 tablespoon olive oil
two 14- to 16-ounce cans black beans, rinsed
    and drained well
¼ cup fresh orange juice
1 cup packed fresh mint leaves, washed well,
    spun dry, and chopped

In a small heavy saucepan cook onion, garlic, and cumin seeds with salt and pepper to taste in oil over moderate heat, stirring, until onion is pale golden, about 5 minutes. Remove pan from heat and cool onion completely.

In a bowl toss onion with beans, orange juice, and salt and pepper to taste. Add mint and toss gently. Serves 6.

🍃 Each serving about 168 calories, 4 grams fat
(19% of calories from fat)

PHOTO ON PAGE 40

SALADS

PHOTO ON PAGE 44

MAIN COURSE SALADS

*Tatsoi and Warm Scallop Salad
with Spicy Pecan Praline*

For praline
⅓ cup pecans, chopped fine
½ teaspoon salt
⅛ teaspoon cayenne, or to taste
3 tablespoons sugar

¾ pound sea scallops
1 tablespoon all-purpose flour
¾ teaspoon salt
¾ teaspoon ground cumin
⅛ teaspoon cayenne
½ tablespoon unsalted butter
1 tablespoon olive oil
3 tablespoons fresh lemon juice
3 tablespoons extra-virgin olive oil
¾ teaspoon Dijon mustard
1 large firm-ripe avocado (preferably California)
7 cups *tatsoi* (thick, spoon-shaped Asian greens)*
   or baby spinach leaves, washed well and
   spun dry

*available at specialty produce markets

Make praline:
In a bowl stir together pecans, salt, and cayenne. In a dry small heavy skillet or saucepan cook sugar over moderate heat, stirring with a fork, until melted and cook, without stirring, swirling skillet or pan, until a golden caramel. Add pecan mixture and stir to coat nuts with caramel. Spoon praline onto a sheet of foil and cool. Transfer praline to a cutting board and chop fine. *Praline can be made 3 days ahead and kept in an airtight container.*

Remove tough muscle from side of each scallop if necessary and halve any large scallops. On a sheet of wax paper combine flour, salt, cumin, and cayenne and dip flat sides of each scallop into mixture to coat, knocking off excess. In a skillet heat butter and olive oil over moderately high heat until foam subsides and sauté scallops, flat sides down, until golden and just cooked through, about 2 minutes on each flat side. Remove skillet from heat and cool scallops slightly.

In a large bowl whisk together lemon juice, extra-virgin olive oil, mustard, and salt and pepper to taste until emulsified. Peel and pit avocado and cut into ½-inch-thick wedges. Cut wedges in half crosswise and add to dressing. Add scallops with any liquid remaining in skillet, *tatsoi* or spinach, and praline and gently toss to coat. Serves 6.

PHOTO ON PAGE 44

Spinach Salad with Smoked Trout and Tart Apple

½ tart apple such as Granny Smith
1½ tablespoons extra-virgin olive oil
1 tablespoon fresh lemon juice
¼ teaspoon Dijon mustard
4 cups packed spinach (about 6 ounces),
   washed well, spun dry, and coarse
   stems discarded
1 smoked trout* (about 8 ounces), skin and bones
   discarded and fish broken into bite-size pieces
3 tablespoons sliced almonds, toasted until golden
3 tablespoons dried currants

*available at deli counter of many supermarkets

Into a large bowl cut apple into 1-inch wedges and core. Cut wedges crosswise into ¼-inch-thick slices. In a large bowl whisk together oil, lemon juice, and mustard and add apple, tossing to coat. Add remaining ingredients, tossing to combine, and season with salt and pepper. Serves 2 as a light main course.

189

Tandoori Shrimp and Mango Salad

For dressing
½ cup bottled Major Grey's chutney
⅔ cup fresh lime juice
½ cup vegetable oil
1 teaspoon cayenne
For tandoori marinade
1 tablespoon paprika
2 teaspoons ground cumin
2 teaspoons ground coriander seeds
4 garlic cloves, crushed
a 1-inch piece fresh gingerroot, peeled and
    chopped
2 fresh *serrano* or *jalapeño* chilies, seeded
    and chopped (wear rubber gloves)
¾ cup plain yogurt
1 teaspoon freshly grated lime zest (about 1 lime)

2 pounds medium shrimp (about 50), shelled
    and deveined
¼ cup vegetable oil for frying
6 cups packed tender watercress sprigs,
    washed well and spun dry
1 cup fresh coriander sprigs, washed well
    and spun dry
3 red bell peppers, cut into julienne strips
2 firm-ripe mangoes, peeled and cut into
    julienne strips

Make dressing:
Force chutney through a sieve into a small bowl and whisk in lime juice, oil, cayenne, and salt to taste. *Dressing may be made 1 day ahead and chilled, covered. Bring dressing to room temperature before using.*

Make marinade:
In a large non-stick skillet dry-roast paprika, cumin, and coriander seeds over moderate heat, stirring occasionally, until fragrant and several shades darker, about 2 minutes, being careful not to burn them, and transfer to a bowl. Cool spices and stir in remaining marinade ingredients and salt and pepper to taste.

Pat shrimp dry and add to marinade, stirring to coat well. Marinate shrimp at room temperature 15 minutes. *Alternatively, shrimp may be marinated, covered and chilled, up to 1 day.*

In large non-stick skillet heat oil over moderately high heat until hot but not smoking and sauté shrimp in batches, turning once, until golden and cooked through, 3 to 4 minutes. Transfer shrimp as sautéed with tongs to paper towels to drain and cool slightly.

In a large bowl gently toss together shrimp, watercress, coriander sprigs, bell peppers, mangoes, and dressing. Serves 6.

PHOTO ON PAGE 63

Citrus Shrimp, Rice, and Black Bean Salad

1 cup water
½ teaspoon salt
a 2- by 1-inch strip orange zest, removed with
    a vegetable peeler
a 2- by ½-inch strip lime zest, removed with a
    vegetable peeler
¾ pound large shrimp (about 16), shelled and
    deveined
½ cup long-grain white rice
¼ cup fresh orange juice
2 tablespoons fresh lime juice
2 tablespoons white-wine vinegar
½ teaspoon ground cumin
⅛ teaspoon dried hot red pepper flakes
1 cup canned black beans, rinsed and drained
1 red bell pepper, cut into ¼-inch dice
½ cup fresh coriander sprigs, washed well,
    spun dry, and chopped
1 cup shredded romaine

In a small saucepan bring water and salt to a boil and simmer zests 1 minute. With a slotted spoon transfer zests to a cutting board. Add shrimp to cooking water and simmer, covered, 2 minutes, or until just cooked through. With slotted spoon transfer shrimp to a colander to drain. Stir rice into cooking water and cook, covered, over moderately low heat until liquid is absorbed, about 20 minutes.

While rice is cooking, cut zests into julienne strips and in a large bowl stir together with orange and lime juices, vinegar, cumin, and red pepper flakes. Halve shrimp lengthwise and add to zest mixture, tossing to coat. Chill mixture, covered, 15 minutes. Add rice, beans, bell pepper, and coriander, tossing to combine, and cool slightly.

Just before serving, add romaine and salt and pepper to taste and toss salad. Serves 2.

☛ Each serving about 464 calories, 5 grams fat
(10% of calories from fat)

ZOE MAVRIDIS

SALADS WITH GREENS

Endive, Orange, Avocado, and Bacon Salad

1 tablespoon white-wine vinegar
¼ teaspoon Dijon mustard
2½ tablespoons extra-virgin olive oil
1 large navel orange
1 small firm-ripe avocado (preferably
 California)
2 Belgian endives
3 slices bacon, cooked until crisp and
 crumbled fine

In a small bowl whisk together vinegar, mustard, and salt and pepper to taste and whisk in oil in a stream until emulsified.

With a sharp knife cut peel and pith from orange and cut sections free from membranes. Cut sections into ½-inch pieces and transfer to a bowl. Peel and pit avocado. Cut avocado into ½-inch pieces and add to orange. Trim endives and slice thin crosswise.

Add endives and dressing and toss salad lightly. Sprinkle salad with bacon. Serves 2.

Artichoke, Walnut, and Mesclun Salad

a ½-inch-thick slice whole-wheat bread
2½ tablespoons extra-virgin olive oil
2 teaspoons white-wine vinegar
¼ cup walnuts, chopped coarse, toasted
 until golden, and cooled
a 6-ounce jar marinated artichoke hearts,
 drained and chopped
6 cups loosely packed *mesclun* (mixed baby
 greens, about ¼ pound), rinsed and
 spun dry

Preheat oven to 375° F.

Brush bread with 1 tablespoon oil and cut into ½-inch cubes. On a baking sheet toast cubes in middle of oven until golden, about 5 minutes, and cool.

In a bowl whisk together vinegar, remaining 1½ tablespoons oil, and salt and pepper to taste until emulsified. Add croutons, walnuts, artichokes, and *mesclun* and toss until combined. Serves 2.

Arugula, Endive, and Radicchio Salad
with Mustard Vinaigrette

1½ bunches arugula, trimmed and leaves halved
 crosswise if large (about 6 cups)
2 medium heads *radicchio*, torn into bite-size
 pieces
3 Belgian endives, cut crosswise into thirds and
 leaves separated
1½ tablespoons malt vinegar or Sherry vinegar
2 teaspoons Dijon mustard
5 tablespoons extra-virgin olive oil
freshly ground black pepper to taste

In a large bowl wash arugula, *radicchio*, and endives in several changes of cold water and spin dry. In a serving bowl whisk together vinegar, mustard, and salt to taste and whisk in oil in a stream until emulsified. Add greens and toss to coat with vinaigrette. Season salad with pepper and toss again. Serves 6.

PHOTO ON PAGE 19

Bibb Lettuce with Sherry Vinaigrette

For vinaigrette
3 tablespoons Sherry vinegar
2 tablespoons plus 1 teaspoon Dijon mustard
1 tablespoon plus 1 teaspoon honey
2 tablespoons water
1 tablespoon olive oil
freshly ground black pepper to taste

6 large radishes with tops (about ½ pound), tops
    trimmed, leaving 1 inch stem, and radishes
    halved lengthwise
1 pound Bibb lettuce (about 8 small heads),
    washed well and spun dry (about 8 cups)
½ cup sliced red onion (about 1 small)

Make vinaigrette:
In a small bowl whisk together all vinaigrette
ingredients and salt to taste. *Vinaigrette may be
made 2 days ahead and chilled, covered.*

With a small melon-ball cutter scoop white flesh
from center of each radish half, discarding flesh and
leaving a ¼-inch-thick shell. Fill shells with vinaigrette. In a bowl toss together lettuce and onion.

Serve salad with radish shells. Serves 6.

    Each serving about 64 calories, 3 grams fat
        (45% of calories from fat)

PHOTO ON PAGE 43

Romaine, Arugula, and Avocado Salad

1 tablespoon cider vinegar
3 tablespoons extra-virgin olive oil
1 firm-ripe avocado (preferably California)
3 cups coarsely chopped romaine, washed
    well and spun dry
3 cups packed arugula, washed well, spun
    dry, and torn into bite-size pieces
¼ cup thinly sliced red onion

In a large bowl whisk together vinegar and salt
and pepper to taste and whisk in oil until emulsified.
Peel, pit, and chop avocado. Add avocado, romaine,
arugula, and onion to vinaigrette and toss to coat.
Serves 4.

PHOTO ON PAGE 52

Chopped Salad with Feta, Olives, and Pita Croutons

1½ tablespoons olive oil
one 6-inch pita loaf, cut into ½-inch pieces
1 small head romaine, washed well, spun dry,
    and cut into ½-inch pieces
    (about 4 cups)
½ red bell pepper, cut into ½-inch pieces
½ yellow bell pepper, cut into ½-inch pieces
½ red onion, cut into ½-inch pieces
⅓ cup crumbled feta (about 1½ ounces)
¼ cup Kalamata or other brine-cured black olives,
    pitted and chopped coarse
2 tablespoons extra-virgin olive oil
1½ tablespoons red-wine vinegar

In a skillet heat olive oil over moderate heat until
hot but not smoking and cook pita pieces, stirring
occasionally, until golden. Season croutons with salt
and pepper and transfer to paper towels to drain.

In a large bowl combine romaine, bell peppers,
onion, feta, and olives and drizzle with extra-virgin
olive oil and vinegar. Add croutons and salt and pepper to taste and toss until combined. Serves 2.

Romaine with Garlic Lemon Anchovy Dressing

1 garlic clove, minced
2 flat anchovy fillets, rinsed and patted dry
2 teaspoons fresh lemon juice
¼ cup extra-virgin olive oil
1 small head romaine, leaves separated
    and cut crosswise into ½-inch-wide
    pieces, washed well, and spun dry
    (about 6 cups)
⅓ cup Parmesan curls, shaved with a
    vegetable peeler from at least a
    ¼-pound piece of Parmesan at room
    temperature

In a blender purée garlic and anchovies with
lemon juice. With motor running add oil in a stream
until dressing is emulsified and season with salt and
pepper.

In a bowl toss romaine with dressing, ¼ cup
Parmesan curls, and salt and pepper to taste. Divide
salad between 2 plates and sprinkle with remaining
Parmesan curls. Serves 2.

Romaine and Watercress Salad with Roquefort Buttermilk Dressing

For dressing
⅓ cup well-shaken low-fat (1½%) buttermilk
½ teaspoon Worcestershire sauce
1 teaspoon red-wine vinegar
1½ teaspoons Dijon mustard
1 ounce (about 2 tablespoons) crumbled
    Roquefort or other blue cheese

8 cups baby romaine leaves or bite-size pieces
    hearts of romaine, washed well and spun dry
1 bunch watercress, coarse stems discarded and
    sprigs washed well and spun dry
½ cup thinly sliced radishes

Make dressing:
In a blender blend all dressing ingredients until smooth and season with salt and pepper. *Dressing may be made 3 days ahead and chilled, covered.*
Transfer dressing to a sauceboat. In a large bowl toss together romaine, watercress, and radishes.
Serve salad with dressing on the side. Serves 6.

🍃 Each serving about 40 calories, 2 grams fat
(43% of calories from fat)

PHOTO ON PAGE 38

Mushroom Spinach Salad with Tarragon Egg Dressing

For dressing
2 hard-boiled large eggs, yolks mashed and whites
    chopped fine
3 tablespoons tarragon white-wine vinegar
1 tablespoon Dijon mustard
6 tablespoons extra-virgin olive oil
3 tablespoons minced shallots (about 2)
2 tablespoons finely chopped fresh tarragon
    leaves
½ pound fresh spinach, coarse stems discarded
    and leaves washed well and spun dry
10 ounces fresh white mushrooms

Make dressing:
In a small bowl whisk together yolks, vinegar, and mustard and add oil in a stream, whisking constantly

until salad dressing is emulsified. Stir in egg whites, shallots, tarragon, and salt and pepper to taste.

Thinly slice spinach leaves and arrange on a platter. Cut mushrooms into very thin slices and mound on spinach. Spoon tarragon egg dressing over salad. Serves 6.

ALEXIS SEABROOK

Mixed Greens and Haricots Verts with Walnut Oil Vinaigrette

2 tablespoons white-wine vinegar
⅓ cup walnut oil* or extra-virgin olive oil
½ pound *haricots verts* (thin French green
    beans)*, trimmed
½ pound baby lettuce, washed and spun dry
½ pound *frisée* (French or Italian curly endive)*,
    washed and spun dry
2 tablespoons minced red onion

*available at specialty foods shops or produce
    markets, and some supermarkets

In a small jar with a tight-fitting lid combine vinegar, oil, and salt and pepper to taste and shake jar until vinaigrette is emulsified. *Vinaigrette may be made 1 day ahead and chilled. Bring vinaigrette to room temperature and shake before using.*
In a saucepan of boiling salted water boil *haricots verts* until crisp-tender, 3 to 4 minutes, and transfer to a bowl of ice water to stop cooking. Drain beans in a colander and pat dry between paper towels. *Beans may be made 1 day ahead and chilled, wrapped in a paper towel in a sealable plastic bag.*
Divide greens among 6 salad plates and top with beans. Sprinkle salads with onion and drizzle with vinaigrette. Serves 6.

VEGETABLE SALADS AND SLAWS

Avocado with Sesame Soy Dressing

1 tablespoon soy sauce
2 teaspoons fresh lemon juice
1 teaspoon Asian sesame oil
⅛ teaspoon sugar
1 chilled firm-ripe avocado (preferably California)
4 to 6 leaves soft-leafed lettuce, washed and
    spun dry
1 teaspoon sesame seeds, lightly toasted

In a small bowl whisk together soy sauce, juice, oil, sugar, and pinch salt until sugar is dissolved.

Quarter, pit, and peel avocado and cut crosswise into ½-inch slices. Add avocado to dressing and turn gently with a rubber spatula to coat.

Line 2 plates with lettuce and divide avocado and dressing between them. Sprinkle sesame seeds over avocado. Serves 2.

Carrot, Snow Pea, and Red Bell Pepper Julienne in Honey Vinaigrette

3 medium carrots, cut into julienne strips
¼ pound snow peas, trimmed and cut into
    julienne strips
3 tablespoons seasoned rice vinegar
1 teaspoon Dijon mustard
½ teaspoon honey
1 small red bell pepper, cut into
    julienne strips

In a large saucepan of boiling salted water blanch carrots 1 minute. Add snow peas and cook mixture 10 seconds more. In a colander drain carrots and snow peas and rinse under cold water. Drain carrots and snow peas well.

In a bowl stir together rice vinegar, mustard, and honey and add carrots, snow peas, and bell pepper, tossing to coat. Season salad with salt and pepper. Serves 2.

☙ Each serving about 104 calories, 1 gram fat
(9% of calories from fat)

Cucumber, Smoked Trout, and Pickled Beet Salad

a 16-ounce jar sliced pickled beets
¼ cup sour cream
freshly ground black pepper
1 smoked trout fillet, skin and bones
    discarded and fish broken into ½-inch pieces
    (about ½ cup)
¼ cup fresh small dill sprigs
1 cucumber, quartered lengthwise and cut
    crosswise into ¼-inch-thick slices
    (about 2 cups)
1 small onion, sliced thin (about ½ cup)

In a sieve set over a bowl drain beets, reserving ¼ cup juice, and halve beet slices. In a bowl whisk together reserved beet juice and sour cream and season with pepper and salt.

Stir in half of trout, half of dill, beets, cucumber, and onion and season with pepper and salt. Top salad with remaining trout and dill. Chill salad, covered, until cold, about 30 minutes. Serves 4 to 6 as a side dish.

Black-Eyed Pea Salad with Watercress and Peach

8 cups salted water
⅔ cup dried black-eyed peas
1 bunch watercress, tough stems discarded, the
    rest washed well, spun dry, and chopped
1 large firm-ripe peach, peeled and cut into
    ½-inch pieces
2 scallions, chopped
1 celery rib, chopped fine
4 teaspoons fresh lemon juice
½ teaspoon ground cumin

In a saucepan bring water and peas to a boil and simmer 20 minutes, or until tender. Drain peas in a colander and rinse under cold water to cool. Drain peas well and in a bowl toss with remaining ingredients and salt and pepper to taste. *Salad may be made 2 hours ahead and chilled, covered.* Serves 4.

☙ Each serving about 115 calories, 1 gram fat
(8% of calories from fat)

PHOTO ON PAGE 85

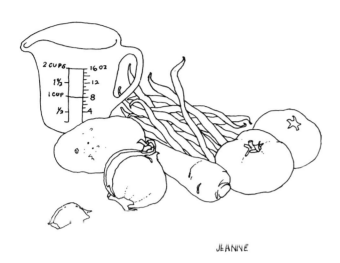

JEANNE

Avocado Radish Salad with Lime Dressing

2 teaspoons fresh lime juice, or to taste
1½ tablespoons extra-virgin olive oil
1 firm-ripe avocado (preferably California),
    peeled and cut into ½-inch cubes
3 cups shredded romaine, washed well and
    spun dry
3 radishes, chopped fine

In a bowl whisk together lime juice, oil, and salt and pepper to taste. Add avocado and toss gently with a rubber spatula to coat.

Divide romaine between 2 salad plates, making a nest on each, and put avocado mixture in centers. Sprinkle salads with radishes. Serves 2.

*Potato and Green Bean Salad
with Citrus Miso Dressing*

1½ pounds red potatoes
1½ pounds green beans or a combination of
    green and wax beans, trimmed and cut
    diagonally into 1½-inch pieces
2 tablespoons yellow *miso* (fermented soybean
    paste)*
2 tablespoons fresh lemon juice

2 tablespoons fresh orange juice
1 tablespoon vegetable oil
1 teaspoon Sherry vinegar or *umeboshi* vinegar*
½ cup fresh parsley leaves, washed well, spun
    dry, and chopped
2 tablespoons minced drained bottled *peperoncini*
    (pickled Tuscan peppers)

*available at natural foods stores and some
    specialty foods shops

Cut red potatoes into ¾-inch wedges. On a large steamer rack set over boiling water steam potatoes, covered, until just tender, about 10 minutes, and transfer to a bowl. Steam beans on rack over boiling water, covered, until just tender, about 6 minutes, and transfer to bowl. *Vegetables may be steamed 1 day ahead and chilled, covered. Bring vegetables to room temperature before proceeding.*

In a large bowl whisk together *miso,* citrus juices, oil, and vinegar and add steamed vegetables, parsley, and *peperoncini,* tossing to combine well. Season salad with salt if necessary. Serves 6.

PHOTO ON PAGE 37

Each serving about 139 calories, 3 grams fat
(18% of calories from fat)

Potato, Cucumber, and Fresh Dill Salad

¾ pound boiling potatoes
½ cup plain low-fat yogurt
1 tablespoon chopped fresh dill
½ teaspoon ground coriander seeds
1 tablespoon fresh lemon juice
1 large cucumber, seeded and cut into
    ½-inch cubes

Peel potatoes and cut into ½-inch cubes. In a large saucepan of boiling salted water cook potatoes until just tender, about 5 minutes. In a colander drain potatoes and rinse under cold water. Drain potatoes.

In a bowl stir together yogurt, dill, coriander, and lemon juice. Add potatoes, cucumber, and salt and pepper to taste and toss to coat. Serves 2.

Each serving about 121 calories, 2 grams fat
(14% of calories from fat)

Butternut Squash, Red Cabbage, and Feta Salad

3 bacon slices, cut into ½-inch pieces
a ¼-pound wedge red cabbage, cut into ½-inch
    pieces (about 2 cups)
3 tablespoons balsamic vinegar plus additional
    if desired
a ¾-pound piece butternut squash, peeled,
    seeded, and cut into ½-inch cubes
    (about 2 cups)
3 ounces feta, cut into ½-inch cubes
    (about ½ cup)
⅓ cup fresh flat-leafed parsley leaves,
    washed and spun dry

In a large non-stick skillet cook bacon over moderate heat, stirring, until crisp. Transfer bacon with a slotted spatula to paper towels and drain.

Pour off bacon fat into a small bowl and return ½ tablespoon to skillet. Add cabbage with salt and pepper to taste and sauté over moderately high heat, stirring occasionally, until wilted. Stir in 3 tablespoons vinegar and sauté, stirring occasionally, until cabbage is crisp-tender, about 3 minutes. With slotted spatula transfer cabbage to another bowl.

In skillet heat remaining bacon fat over moderately high heat until hot but not smoking and add squash and salt and pepper to taste. Sauté squash, stirring, until tender and golden, about 5 minutes, and add to cabbage. Stir in feta, parsley, bacon, and additional vinegar. Serve salad warm or at room temperature. Serves 2.

Vine-Ripened Tomatoes Drizzled with Balsamic Vinegar

12 large vine-ripened tomatoes (about 6 pounds),
    sliced
freshly ground black pepper
    to taste
½ cup balsamic vinegar

On a large platter overlap tomatoes slightly and sprinkle with pepper and salt to taste.

Drizzle tomatoes with vinegar and serve at room temperature. Serves 16 as part of a buffet.

PHOTO ON PAGE 67

Sliced Tomatoes and Cucumbers

4 small vine-ripened tomatoes (about 1 pound),
    sliced
1 large cucumber, peeled and sliced
freshly ground black pepper

Arrange vegetables on plates and season with salt and pepper. Serves 4.

    Each serving about 36 calories,
        0 grams fat

PHOTO ON PAGE 85

JEANNE

Coleslaw with Yogurt Dressing

½ cup plain low-fat yogurt
2 tablespoons Dijon mustard
1 tablespoon water
2 teaspoons low-fat mayonnaise
2 teaspoons fresh lemon juice
6 cups thinly sliced cabbage
    (about 1 large)
4 medium carrots, shredded
1 cup thinly sliced red onion
    (about 1 large)
½ teaspoon dill seeds

In a large bowl whisk together yogurt, mustard, water, low-fat mayonnaise, and lemon juice and add remaining ingredients, tossing to combine well. Season coleslaw with salt and pepper. *Coleslaw may be made 1 day ahead and chilled, covered.* Serves 6.

☛ Each serving about 68 calories, 1 gram fat
(15% of calories from fat)

PHOTO ON PAGE 37

Confetti Vegetable Slaw

4 teaspoons white-wine vinegar
⅓ cup olive oil
1 large red bell pepper, cut into 2-inch-long
 thin strips
1 large yellow bell pepper, cut into 2-inch-long
 thin strips
1 medium carrot, shredded fine
2 celery ribs, cut into 2-inch-long thin strips

In a bowl whisk together vinegar and salt and pepper to taste and whisk in oil in a stream until emulsified. Add vegetables and toss until combined well. *Slaw may be made 6 hours ahead and chilled, covered.* Serves 8 as a side dish.

PHOTO ON PAGE 23

PASTA AND GRAIN SALADS

Couscous Salad with Corn and Red Bell Pepper

2 tablespoons olive oil
¾ cup fresh corn (cut from about 2 ears)
⅓ cup finely chopped red onion
⅓ cup finely chopped red bell pepper
1 garlic clove, minced
¼ teaspoon ground cumin
1¼ cups water
⅔ cup couscous
2 teaspoons red-wine vinegar
¼ cup fresh coriander sprigs, washed well,
 spun dry, and chopped fine
cayenne to taste

In a heavy skillet heat 1 tablespoon oil over moderately high heat until hot but not smoking and sauté

corn, stirring, until golden. Add onion, bell pepper, garlic, cumin, and ¼ cup water and cook over moderately low heat, stirring occasionally, until bell pepper is crisp-tender.

While vegetables are cooking, in a small heavy saucepan bring remaining cup water to a boil and stir in couscous and salt to taste. Cover pan and remove from heat. Let couscous stand 5 minutes and fluff with a fork.

In a large bowl whisk together vinegar, remaining tablespoon oil, and salt to taste until emulsified. Add vegetable mixture, couscous, coriander, and cayenne and toss to combine well. Serves 2 as a side dish.

Gingered Soba Noodles

6 ounces soba (buckwheat) noodles*
For dressing
1 tablespoon grated fresh gingerroot
2 tablespoons rice vinegar
2 teaspoons Asian sesame oil
1 teaspoon soy sauce
¼ to ½ teaspoon sugar
 if desired

*available at Asian markets, natural foods stores,
 and by mail order from Uwajimaya,
 tel. (800) 889-1928

In a 4-quart kettle bring 3½ quarts salted water to a boil for noodles. Have ready a large bowl of ice and cold water.
Make dressing:
In a sieve set over a bowl press gingerroot to extract juice. In a bowl stir together 1 teaspoon ginger juice and remaining dressing ingredients with salt to taste.

Add soba noodles to boiling water and cook 2 to 4 minutes, or until *al dente*. Drain noodles in a colander and immediately transfer to ice water. Swish noodles until cold and drain well. Add noodles to dressing and toss well. *Noodles may be made 1 hour ahead and chilled, covered. Toss noodles before serving.* Serves 4

☛ Each serving about 189 calories, 3 grams fat
(15% of calories from fat)

Brown Rice and Green Bean Salad

2 cups water
¾ cup long-grain brown rice
1 cup green beans, cut diagonally into
    1-inch pieces
2 teaspoons chopped fresh tarragon leaves
2 tablespoons extra-virgin olive oil

In a 2-quart heavy saucepan bring 2 cups salted water to a boil and stir in rice. Cook rice, covered, over moderately low heat until water is absorbed, about 40 minutes. Refresh rice in a colander under cold water and drain.

While rice is cooking, in a small saucepan of boiling salted water blanch beans 2 minutes and drain in colander. Rinse beans under cold water and drain.

In a bowl toss together rice, beans, tarragon, oil, and salt and pepper to taste. Serves 2.

SALAD DRESSINGS

Low-Fat Bacon Mustard Dressing

1 teaspoon finely chopped uncooked bacon
    (about ¼ slice)
6 tablespoons fresh orange juice
½ cup nonfat sour cream
1½ tablespoons fresh lemon juice
1 tablespoon Dijon mustard
3 tablespoons chopped white part of scallions
    (about 3)
1 large garlic clove, minced
1 teaspoon firmly packed brown sugar

In a small heavy skillet cook bacon over moderate heat, stirring, until crisp and remove skillet from heat. Add orange juice to skillet and scrape up brown bits. In a blender blend bacon mixture, remaining ingredients, and salt and pepper to taste until smooth. *Dressing keeps, covered and chilled, 1 week.* Serve dressing with crisp lettuce, sliced tomatoes, or potato salad. Makes about 1 cup.

🍃 Each tablespoon about 14 calories,
0 grams fat

Cucumber Feta Salad Dressing

1 cucumber, peeled and seeded
¼ cup feta (about 4 ounces) at room temperature
½ cup plain yogurt
1 small garlic clove, chopped and mashed to a
    paste with ¼ teaspoon salt
freshly ground black pepper to taste

Chop enough of cucumber to measure 1 cup and in a blender purée with feta, yogurt, and garlic until smooth. Transfer dressing to a bowl and season with pepper and salt. Chill dressing, covered, until cold, about 30 minutes. *Dressing may be made 1 day ahead and chilled, covered.* Makes about 1 cup.

Low-Fat Chipotle Chutney Dressing

¼ cup bottled Major Grey's chutney
¼ cup fresh orange juice
1 tablespoon fresh lime juice
2 tablespoons water
1 teaspoon minced canned *chipotle* chili
    in *adobo* sauce*
1 teaspoon ground cumin
1 garlic clove, minced

*available at Hispanic markets, some specialty
    foods shops, and by mail order from Adriana's
    Caravan, tel. (800) 316-0820

In a blender blend all ingredients and salt to taste until smooth. *Dressing keeps, covered and chilled, 1 week.* Serve dressing with soft lettuce, potato salad, or fresh fruit such as honeydew melon, apples, or oranges. Makes about 1 cup.

🍃 Each tablespoon about 16 calories,
0 grams fat

Low-Fat Herbed Ranch Dressing

¾ cup well-shaken low-fat (1½%) buttermilk
2 tablespoons low-fat mayonnaise
2 tablespoons nonfat sour cream
1 tablespoon packed fresh basil leaves,
    minced

1 tablespoon finely chopped fresh chives
2 teaspoons cider vinegar
1 teaspoon dry mustard
1 teaspoon fresh thyme leaves
1 garlic clove, minced
½ teaspoon sugar

In a blender or food processor blend all ingredients and salt and pepper to taste until smooth. *Dressing keeps, covered and chilled, 1 week.* Serve dressing with soft lettuce, shellfish salad, or salmon salad. Makes about 1 cup.

Each tablespoon about 12 calories,
0 grams fat

Low-Fat Thousand Island Dressing

⅓ cup low-fat mayonnaise
2 tablespoons ketchup
2 tablespoons fresh lemon juice
2 tablespoons minced red bell pepper
1 tablespoon minced onion
1 tablespoon minced fresh parsley
   leaves
1 tablespoon sweet pickle relish
a pinch of cayenne
¼ cup water

In a blender or food processor blend all ingredients and salt to taste until smooth, adding up to 2 tablespoons additional water if necessary to thin to desired consistency. *Dressing keeps, covered and chilled, 1 week.* Serve dressing with lettuce, sliced tomatoes, or seafood salad. Makes about 1 cup.

Each tablespoon about 12 calories,
0 grams fat

Low-Fat Roasted Tomato Dressing

4 plum tomatoes, halved lengthwise
1 tablespoon red-wine or Sherry vinegar
1½ teaspoons honey, or to taste
1 teaspoon freshly grated lemon zest
½ cup water

Preheat oven to 450° F.
In a shallow baking pan arrange tomatoes in one layer, cut sides up, and season with salt and pepper. Roast tomatoes in middle of oven about 35 minutes, or until very soft and skin is dark brown, and cool to room temperature.
In a blender purée tomatoes with vinegar, honey, zest, water, and salt and pepper to taste. *Dressing keeps, covered and chilled, 1 week.* Serve dressing with crisp lettuce or steamed vegetables. Makes about 1 cup.

Each tablespoon about 6 calories,
0 grams fat

Low-Fat Yogurt Honey Mint Dressing

¾ cup plain low-fat (1½%) yogurt
1 tablespoon honey
1 tablespoon canned unsweetened
   pineapple juice
2 tablespoons packed fresh mint leaves,
   washed well, spun dry, and chopped fine

In a bowl whisk together all ingredients until honey is dissolved. *Dressing keeps, covered and chilled, 1 week.* Serve dressing tossed with fruit salad. Makes about 1 cup.

Each tablespoon about 11 calories,
0 grams fat

SAUCES

Spicy Peanut Sauce

2 tablespoons vegetable oil
3 scallions, chopped fine
1 garlic clove, chopped fine
1 tablespoon finely grated peeled fresh
   gingerroot
1 cup water
½ cup creamy or chunky peanut butter
¼ cup soy sauce
¼ cup distilled white vinegar
3 tablespoons firmly packed brown sugar
¼ teaspoon dried hot red pepper flakes

In a saucepan heat oil over moderate heat until hot but not smoking and cook scallions, garlic, and gingerroot, stirring, until fragrant, about 1 minute. Stir in remaining ingredients and bring to a simmer, stirring. Simmer sauce, stirring, until smooth and cool to room temperature. *Sauce may be made up to 3 days ahead and chilled, covered. If sauce is too thick after chilling, stir in 1 to 2 tablespoons hot water until sauce reaches desired consistency.*

Serve sauce with grilled poultry or meat, on noodles, or as a dressing for spinach salad. Makes about 2 cups.

Spicy Tomato Sauce

3 garlic cloves, minced
3 tablespoons olive oil
1 large onion, chopped fine
½ teaspoon dried hot red pepper flakes
two 28- to 32-ounce cans tomatoes
   including juice, puréed coarse in
   a blender in 2 batches
½ teaspoon dried thyme, crumbled

In a heavy 5-quart saucepan cook garlic in oil over moderate heat, stirring, until golden and add onion and red pepper flakes. Cook mixture, stirring, until onion is softened and add tomato purée, thyme, and salt and pepper to taste. Simmer sauce, stirring occasionally, 35 minutes, or until thickened slightly. *Sauce may be made 3 days ahead and chilled, covered.* Makes about 6 cups.

Mushroom Gravy

1 pound mixed fresh white and exotic
   mushrooms such as *cremini,* oyster, or
   shiitake (discard *shiitake* stems)
4 large garlic cloves, minced
2 tablespoons unsalted butter
1 onion, chopped fine
1 tablespoon soy sauce
½ cup dry red wine
1 tablespoon balsamic vinegar
1 tablespoon cornstarch dissolved in 1½ cups
   cold water
½ teaspoon sugar
2 tablespoons finely chopped fresh parsley
   leaves

Slice mushrooms. In a 10-inch heavy non-stick skillet cook garlic in butter over moderately low heat, stirring, until pale golden. Add onion and cook, stirring, until softened. Add mushrooms and soy sauce and sauté mixture over moderately high heat, stirring, until liquid mushrooms give off is evaporated and mushrooms begin to brown.

Add wine and vinegar and boil until liquid is evaporated. Stir cornstarch mixture and add to skillet with sugar. Bring mixture to a boil, stirring, and simmer 2 minutes. Stir in parsley and season gravy with salt and pepper. *Gravy may be made 1 day ahead and chilled, covered. When reheating gravy, add water if necessary to thin to desired consistency.*

Serve mushroom gravy spooned over baked or mashed potatoes and/or steak or chicken. Makes about 2½ cups.

DESSERT SAUCES

Peanut Butter Caramel Sauce

½ cup sugar
1 cup heavy cream
⅓ cup creamy peanut butter

In a dry heavy saucepan cook sugar over moderate heat, without stirring, until it begins to melt. Continue cooking sugar, stirring with a fork, until melted and cook, without stirring, swirling pan, until a deep golden caramel. Remove pan from heat and add cream (caramel will bubble and steam). Return pan to heat and simmer, stirring, until caramel is dissolved. Add peanut butter and simmer, stirring, until smooth. *Sauce may be made up to 1 week ahead and kept in an airtight container, chilled. Warm sauce before serving.* Serve sauce over ice cream. Makes about 1¼ cups.

Easy Dark Chocolate Sauce

½ cup unsweetened Dutch-process cocoa powder
½ cup sugar
½ cup water
1 teaspoon vanilla

In a small bowl stir together cocoa powder, sugar, and a pinch salt. In a small saucepan bring water to a boil and add cocoa mixture, a little at a time, stirring until smooth. Simmer sauce, stirring occasionally, 5 minutes. Remove pan from heat and stir in vanilla. Cool sauce. *Sauce keeps, covered and chilled, 2 to 3 weeks.* Makes about ½ cup.

CONDIMENTS

Pickled Onions

a 10-ounce package white pearl onions, unpeeled
1 cup water
2 tablespoons table salt
⅞ cup cider vinegar
1 tablespoon sugar
1 tablespoon pickling spices

In a 3-quart saucepan bring 2 quarts water to a boil and boil onions 2 minutes. Remove pan from heat and cool onions in cooking liquid until they can be handled. Carefully trim root ends and peel.

In a small bowl stir together water and salt until salt is dissolved and add onions. *Let onions stand, covered, at room temperature 24 hours.*

In a sieve drain onions and rinse well. Drain onions again and transfer to a sterilized 1-pint Mason-type jar (procedure on page 202).

In a small saucepan bring vinegar, sugar, and pickling spices to a boil, stirring until sugar is dissolved. Pour mixture over onions and seal jar with lid. *Marinate onions, covered and chilled, at least 4 days to develop flavors. Onions keep, covered and chilled, about 1 month, if they are removed with a clean fork or spoon.*

Serve onions slightly chilled or at room temperature. Makes 1 pint.

PHOTO ON PAGE 20

To Sterilize Jars for Pickling and Preserving

Wash jars in hot suds and rinse in scalding water. Put jars in a kettle and cover with hot water. Bring water to a boil, covered, and boil jars 15 minutes from time that steam emerges from kettle. Turn off heat and let jars stand in hot water. Just before they are filled, invert jars onto a kitchen towel to dry. (Jars should be filled while they are still hot.) Sterilize jar lids 5 minutes, or according to manufacturer's instructions.

Pickled Baby Carrots and Zucchini

35 to 40 baby carrots with tops* (about
    1 pound), stems trimmed to about ¾ inch
    and carrots peeled
16 to 20 baby zucchini* (about ½ pound),
    washed, trimmed, and halved
    lengthwise
¾ cup white-wine vinegar
1¼ cups water
⅓ cup sugar
five ¼-inch-thick slices fresh gingerroot
2 large garlic cloves, halved
1 teaspoon yellow mustard seeds
1 teaspoon salt
¾ teaspoon dried hot red pepper
    flakes
6 fresh tarragon sprigs

*available at specialty produce markets and some
    supermarkets

In a sterilized 1-quart Mason-type jar (procedure precedes) arrange carrots and zucchini standing up decoratively.

In a saucepan bring remaining ingredients except tarragon sprigs to a boil and simmer, stirring occasionally, 3 minutes, or until sugar is dissolved. Pour hot pickling mixture over vegetables and arrange tarragon sprigs on top. Cool pickled vegetables completely. Wipe rim of jar with a dampened cloth and seal jar with lid. *Chill pickled vegetables at least overnight to develop flavor. Pickled vegetables keep, covered and chilled, 1 month.* Makes about 1 quart.

PHOTO ON PAGE 35

Mint Chutney

2 tablespoons vegetable oil
3 fresh *serrano* or *jalapeño* chilies, seeded and
    chopped coarse (wear rubber gloves)
1 tablespoon fennel seeds
1 teaspoon cumin seeds
1 teaspoon coriander seeds
⅓ cup unsweetened shredded coconut*
3 cups packed fresh mint leaves, washed well
    and spun dry
½ cup packed fresh coriander sprigs, washed
    well and spun dry
¾ cup plain yogurt
¼ cup blanched slivered almonds,
    lightly toasted
2 tablespoons white-wine vinegar
¼ cup fresh lemon juice
1 teaspoon sugar

*available at natural foods stores

In a small heavy skillet heat oil over moderate heat until hot but not smoking and cook chilies, spices, and coconut, stirring, until coconut is golden, about 5 minutes, being careful not to burn. In a blender blend spice mixture with remaining ingredients until smooth. *Chill chutney, covered, until cold, at least 2 hours and up to 2 days.* Makes about 1½ cups.

PHOTO ON PAGE 62

Dill-Pickled Vegetables

¾ pound red, white, and/or yellow pearl onions
    (about 2 cups)
1 pound baby carrots with tops* (about 40),
    peeled and trimmed
1½ cups white-wine vinegar
2½ cups water
⅔ cup sugar
2 teaspoons dill seeds
2 teaspoons salt
4 large celery ribs, cut into 4- by ½-inch sticks

*available at specialty produce markets and some
    supermarkets

In a large saucepan of boiling water blanch onions
3 minutes and drain in a colander. Cool onions just
until they can be handled and peel. Arrange onions
and carrots in two 1-quart Mason-type jars.

In pan bring vinegar, water, sugar, dill seeds, and
salt to a boil and simmer 3 minutes. Pour hot mixture
over onions and carrots and cool completely. Add
celery. *Chill vegetables, covered, at least 12 hours to
develop flavors. Pickled vegetables may be made up
to 3 weeks ahead but do not add celery until 1 day
before serving.* Makes about 2 quarts.

PHOTO ON PAGE 72

Fresh Cranberry Orange Sauce

2 large navel oranges
a 12-ounce bag fresh or unthawed
    frozen cranberries, picked over
    (about 3½ cups)
¾ cup honey

With a vegetable peeler remove three 3-inch-long
strips zest from 1 orange. In a saucepan of boiling
water blanch zest 1 minute and drain in a colander.
Chop zest fine and transfer to a large bowl.

Cut away peel and pith from oranges with a sharp
knife and discard them. Quarter oranges. In a food
processor pulse oranges and cranberries until chopped coarse and add to zest. Stir in honey. *Chill
sauce, covered, at least 1 day and up to 3.* Makes
about 4 cups.

DESSERTS

CAKES

Lemon Verbena Pound Cake with Strawberries

For cake
1 cup cake flour (not self-rising)
½ teaspoon baking powder
¼ teaspoon salt
3 tablespoons finely chopped fresh lemon
   verbena leaves or 1 tablespoon freshly
   grated lemon zest
1 tablespoon freshly grated lemon zest
1 stick (½ cup) unsalted butter, softened
1 cup granulated sugar
3 large eggs
¾ teaspoon vanilla
2 tablespoons milk
2 tablespoons fresh lemon juice
For glaze
½ cup plus 1 tablespoon confectioners' sugar
1 tablespoon fresh lemon juice

Accompaniment: strawberries

Make cake:
Preheat oven to 325° F and butter and flour a
1-quart *kugelhopf* pan, knocking out excess flour.

In a bowl whisk together flour, baking powder,
salt, verbena (or zest), and zest. In another bowl with
an electric mixer beat butter and sugar until light and
fluffy. Beat in eggs, 1 at a time, beating well after
each addition, and beat in vanilla. Beat in half of
flour mixture. Beat in milk and lemon juice and beat
in remaining flour mixture until just combined.

Spoon batter into pan, smoothing top, and bake in
middle of oven 45 to 55 minutes, or until golden
brown on top and a tester comes out clean. Cool
cake in pan on a rack 15 minutes and invert onto
rack to cool completely.

Make glaze while cake is cooling:

In a small bowl whisk confectioners' sugar, a
little at a time, into juice until smooth and thick.

When cake is completely cooled, drizzle glaze
over cake and let it drip down sides. *Cake may be
made 1 day ahead and chilled, covered.*

Serve cake at room temperature with strawberries.

Free-Form Beesting Cake

⅔ cup warm milk (105°–115° F.)
a ¼-ounce package active dry yeast
   (2½ teaspoons)
⅓ cup sugar
½ teaspoon salt
1 large egg yolk
about 2¾ cups all-purpose flour
1 stick (½ cup) unsalted butter, cut into 8 pieces
   and softened
For topping
½ stick (¼ cup) unsalted butter
⅓ cup sugar
2 tablespoons milk
½ teaspoon cinnamon
¼ teaspoon salt
¾ cup sliced almonds

Accompaniment: honey porter prune ice cream
   (page 222)

In a large bowl whisk together milk, yeast, and
1 teaspoon sugar and let stand until foamy, about
5 minutes. With an electric mixer on medium speed
beat in remaining sugar, salt, yolk, and 1 cup flour
until combined well and beat in butter, 1 piece at a
time, adding each new piece just as previous one is
incorporated. With a wooden spoon stir in 1½ cups
flour, adding some of remaining ¼ cup if necessary,
until mixture forms a soft dough. On a lightly
floured surface knead dough 6 minutes, or until
smooth and elastic. (Alternatively, dough may be

made in bowl of a standing electric mixer, attaching dough hook to knead 4 minutes.)

Transfer dough to a lightly oiled bowl. *Let dough rise, covered tightly with plastic wrap, in a warm place until doubled in bulk, 1 to 1½ hours.* Punch down dough. *Dough may be prepared up to this point 1 day ahead: Put dough in a sealable plastic bag, pressing out excess air, and chill. Bring dough to room temperature before proceeding.*

Make topping:

In a small saucepan melt butter over moderate heat and stir in remaining ingredients. Simmer mixture 1 minute and cool to warm.

Preheat oven to 375° F. Line a baking sheet with parchment paper or lightly grease it.

Stretch and press dough onto baking sheet to form a 12-inch round. Spread topping evenly over dough and let rise, uncovered, in a warm place 30 minutes. Press indentations all over cake with your fingertips and bake in middle of oven 18 to 20 minutes, or until puffed and golden. Cool cake on baking sheet 10 minutes and transfer to a rack. *Cake keeps, wrapped well in foil and chilled, 1 day, or frozen, 1 week. Reheat cake in middle of a preheated 350° F. oven 15 minutes if chilled or 20 minutes if frozen.*

Serve cake warm with ice cream. Serves 6.

PHOTO ON PAGE 21

Brown Butter Almond Torte with Sour Cherry Sauce

1 stick (½ cup) unsalted butter
1 teaspoon vanilla
1 cup blanched whole almonds
½ cup all-purpose flour
1 cup sugar
¾ teaspoon salt
6 large egg whites
⅓ cup sliced almonds

Accompaniment: sour cherry sauce
  (recipe follows)

In a small saucepan melt butter over moderately low heat and continue to heat until golden brown with a nutlike fragrance. (Bottom of pan will be covered with brown specks.) Cool butter to warm and stir in vanilla.

Preheat oven to 375° F. Butter and flour a 9-inch round cake pan, knocking out excess flour.

In a food processor finely grind whole almonds with flour, ⅔ cup sugar, and ½ teaspoon salt.

In a large bowl with an electric mixer beat whites with remaining ¼ teaspoon salt until they hold soft peaks. Add remaining ⅓ cup sugar gradually, beating until meringue just holds stiff peaks. Fold in nut mixture gently but thoroughly. Fold in butter gently but thoroughly (batter will deflate) and spread in cake pan.

Sprinkle top of batter evenly with sliced almonds and bake in middle of oven 35 to 40 minutes, or until it begins to pull away from side of pan and a tester comes out clean.

Cool torte in pan on a rack 15 minutes and invert onto rack. Turn torte right side up and cool completely. *Torte may be made 1 day ahead and kept in an airtight container at room temperature.*

Serve torte with sauce.

PHOTO ON PAGE 51

Sour Cherry Sauce

3 cups sour cherries (about 1½ pounds)
½ cup sugar
½ cup water
1 teaspoon cornstarch mixed with
  1 tablespoon water

Working over a heavy saucepan pit cherries. In pan bring cherries, sugar, and water to a boil. Stir cornstarch mixture and add to sauce, stirring. Simmer sauce 2 minutes and cool to room temperature. *Sauce may be made 2 days ahead and chilled, covered. Bring sauce to room temperature before serving.* Makes about 3 cups.

Dark Chocolate Wedding Cake with Chocolate Orange Ganache and Orange Buttercream

For cake layers

1¾ cups unsweetened cocoa powder
 (not Dutch-process)
1¾ cups boiling water
4 ounces fine-quality bittersweet chocolate
 (not unsweetened), chopped
one 8-ounce container sour cream
1 tablespoon plus 1 teaspoon vanilla
3 cups all-purpose flour
2½ teaspoons baking soda
1 teaspoon salt
3¾ sticks (1¾ cups plus 2 tablespoons)
 unsalted butter, softened
1¾ cups granulated sugar
¾ cup firmly packed light brown sugar
5 large eggs

For ganache

1 cup heavy cream
8 ounces fine-quality bittersweet chocolate
 (not unsweetened), chopped
2 tablespoons unsalted butter,
 softened
2 teaspoons freshly grated orange zest
1 tablespoon Cointreau or other
 orange-flavored liqueur

For assembly

one 8-inch cardboard round*
one 6-inch cardboard round*
orange buttercream (recipe follows)
three 8-inch plastic straws

NOTE: *A cake-decorating turntable* is extremely helpful for assembling and decorating a wedding cake.*

Decoration: fraises des bois (wild strawberries)**
 and small roses with some leaves attached
 (both fruit and flowers must be nontoxic
 and pesticide-free)

*available at specialty cookware shops and by
 mail order from The Chocolate Gallery,
 34 West 22nd Street, New York, NY 10010,
 tel. (212) 675-CAKE

**available by mail order from Chefs' Produce
 Team, 1400 East Olympic Boulevard, Suite C,
 Los Angeles, CA 90021, tel. (213) 624-8909

Make cake layers:

Preheat oven to 350° F. and line 2 buttered 7- by 2-inch round cake pans and 2 buttered 9- by 2-inch round cake pans with rounds of wax paper. Butter paper and dust pans with flour, knocking out excess.

Put cocoa powder in a bowl and whisk in boiling water in a stream until smooth. Stir in chopped chocolate and let stand 5 minutes. Stir mixture until smooth and cool mixture. Whisk in sour cream and vanilla.

Into another bowl sift together flour, baking soda, and salt. In large bowl of a standing electric mixer beat together butter and sugars until light and fluffy and add eggs, 1 at a time, beating well after each addition and scraping down side of bowl. With mixer on low speed, add flour mixture and chocolate mixture alternately in batches, beginning and ending with flour mixture and beating until batter is combined well.

Pour 2 cups batter into each 7-inch pan and smooth tops. Divide remaining batter between 9-inch pans (about 3¾ cups each) and smooth tops. In middle and lower thirds of oven arrange one 9-inch layer and one 7-inch layer on each rack, putting 7-inch layers in front part of oven. Bake 7-inch layers 25 to 30 minutes and 9-inch layers 35 to 40 minutes, or until a tester comes out with crumbs adhering. Run a thin knife around edges of pans and invert cakes onto racks. Peel off paper and cool cakes completely. *Cake layers may be made 2 days ahead and kept at cool room temperature, wrapped well in plastic wrap, or 2 weeks ahead and frozen, wrapped well in plastic wrap and foil. Defrost cake layers (without unwrapping) at room temperature.*

Make ganache:

In a small saucepan bring cream just to a boil. Remove pan from heat and add chocolate, butter, zest, and liqueur. Let *ganache* stand 3 minutes and whisk until chocolate is melted. Chill *ganache* just until cool, about 40 minutes.

In a bowl with an electric mixer beat *ganache* just until light and fluffy before using (do not overbeat).

Assemble cake:

Put one 9-inch cake layer on 8-inch cardboard

round and spread evenly with 2 cups *ganache.* Top with remaining 9-inch cake layer and gently press layers together to form an even tier. Put one 7-inch cake layer on 6-inch cardboard round and top with remaining *ganache* and remaining 7-inch cake layer in same manner.

Frost top and sides of 9-inch tier with some buttercream and chill while frosting 7-inch tier. Chill both tiers until buttercream is firm.

Cut straws in half and insert 1 straw piece all the way into center of 9-inch tier. Trim straw flush with top of tier and insert remaining 5 straw pieces in same manner in a circle about 1½ inches from center straw. Center 7-inch tier (still on cardboard) on top of 9-inch tier. Fill in any gaps between tiers with buttercream and transfer cake to a cake stand or platter. *Chill cake at least 6 hours and up to 1 day.*

Arrange *fraises des bois* and roses decoratively on top and around sides of cake. *Let cake stand at cool room temperature (buttercream is sensitive to warm temperatures) 2 to 4 hours before serving.* Serves about 30 (including top tier).

PHOTO ON PAGE 65

Orange Buttercream

For orange curd
5 large egg yolks
¼ cup sugar
½ cup fresh orange juice
½ stick (¼ cup) unsalted butter, softened
1½ teaspoons fresh lemon juice
For buttercream
1¼ cups sugar
½ cup water
5 large egg whites
½ teaspoon cream of tartar
6½ sticks (3¼ cups) unsalted butter, cut
    into pieces and softened to cool
    room temperature
½ teaspoon salt
2 tablespoons freshly grated orange zest

Make orange curd:
In a small heavy saucepan whisk together yolks and sugar and whisk in orange juice, butter, and a pinch salt. Cook mixture over moderately low heat,

whisking, until it just reaches boiling point, 5 to 7 minutes (do not boil), and pour through a fine sieve into a bowl. Whisk in lemon juice and cool curd, its surface covered with plastic wrap. *Chill orange curd, covered, until cold, at least 4 hours and up to 2 days.*

Make buttercream:
In a heavy saucepan bring sugar and water to a boil, stirring until sugar is dissolved. Boil syrup, undisturbed, until it registers 248° F. on a candy thermometer. While syrup is boiling, in large bowl of a standing electric mixer beat whites with a pinch salt until foamy and beat in cream of tartar. Beat whites until they just hold stiff peaks and beat in hot syrup in a stream (try to avoid side of bowl and beaters). Beat mixture at medium speed until *completely* cool, 15 to 20 minutes. Beat in butter, 1 piece at a time, and beat until thickened and smooth. (Buttercream will at first appear very thin and at some point look like it is breaking, but, as more butter is beaten in, it will thicken and become glossy and smooth.) Beat in orange curd, salt, and zest until smooth. *Buttercream may be made 4 days ahead and chilled in an airtight container or 2 weeks ahead and frozen in an airtight container. Bring buttercream completely to room temperature (this may take several hours if frozen) and beat before using. (If buttercream is too cold when beaten it will not be glossy and smooth.)* Makes about 8 cups.

Minted Berry Spongecakes

½ cup water
⅔ cup sugar
½ cup packed fresh mint leaves, washed well
    and spun dry
1½ tablespoons fresh lemon juice
1 pint strawberries, hulled and, depending
    on size, halved or quartered
½ pint blackberries or black or red raspberries,
    picked over
6 individual spongecakes (recipe follows)
6 tablespoons sour cream

Garnish: fresh mint sprigs

In a small saucepan bring water and sugar to a boil, stirring until sugar is dissolved. Add mint and simmer 1 minute. Remove pan from heat and with a wooden spoon crush mint against bottom and side of pan. Let syrup stand, covered, 20 minutes. Pour syrup through a fine sieve into a bowl, pressing hard on mint and add lemon juice and berries. *Let berry mixture stand at least 30 minutes and up to 2 hours to blend flavors.*

Peel off paper liners from spongecakes and halve horizontally. Put spongecake bottoms on 6 plates and spoon berry mixture over them. Divide sour cream among spongecakes and arrange spongecake tops on desserts.

Garnish desserts with mint. Serves 6.

Each serving about 239 calories, 8 grams fat
    (29% of calories from fat)

PHOTO ON PAGE 39

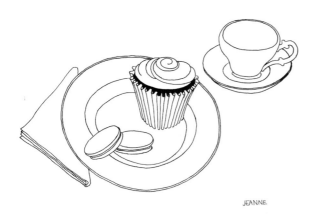

JEANNE

Individual Spongecakes

2 large eggs
⅓ cup sugar
⅓ cup all-purpose flour
1 tablespoon cornstarch
3 tablespoons unsalted butter, melted and
    cooled to warm

Preheat oven to 350° F. and line nine ½-cup muffin tins with paper liners.

In a double boiler or a metal bowl set over a saucepan of barely simmering water whisk together eggs and sugar just until sugar is dissolved, 1 to 2 minutes. Remove top of double boiler or bowl from heat and with a hand-held electric mixer beat mixture at moderately high speed until doubled in volume, about 3 minutes.

Sift flour, cornstarch, and a pinch salt over egg mixture and fold in gently but thoroughly. Drizzle butter over batter and fold in gently but thoroughly.

Divide batter among muffin tins and bake in middle of oven 12 to 15 minutes, or until pale golden. Cool spongecakes in tins on a rack 10 minutes. Remove spongecakes from tins and cool completely on rack. *Spongecakes may be made 1 day ahead and kept in an airtight container at room temperature.* Makes 9 spongecakes.

COOKIES AND BARS

Hazelnut Cookies

1 stick (½ cup) unsalted butter, softened
½ cup superfine sugar
1 teaspoon vanilla
½ teaspoon freshly grated orange zest
1 cup all-purpose flour
½ teaspoon salt
¼ teaspoon baking powder
¾ cup hazelnuts, chopped fine, toasted
    until golden, and cooled

Preheat oven to 325° F. Lightly butter 2 baking sheets.

In a bowl with an electric mixer beat together

butter and sugar until light and fluffy and beat in vanilla and zest. Into another bowl sift together flour, salt, and baking powder and beat into butter mixture until just combined. Stir in nuts.

Roll level teaspoons of cookie dough into balls and arrange about 2 inches apart on baking sheets. (Alternatively, drop teaspoons of dough about 2 inches apart onto baking sheets.) Bake cookies in batches in middle of oven until pale golden, about 18 minutes. Cool cookies on baking sheets 2 minutes and carefully transfer with a metal spatula to racks to cool completely. *Cookies keep 3 days in airtight containers.* Makes about 60 cookies.

PHOTO ON PAGE 15

Apricot Ginger Biscotti

⅓ cup dried apricots (about 2 ounces)
2 large eggs
1 teaspoon water
1⅓ cups all-purpose flour
½ cup sugar
¼ teaspoon baking soda
¼ teaspoon baking powder
¼ teaspoon salt
½ teaspoon vanilla
2 tablespoons chopped candied ginger*
  (about 1 ounce)

*available at specialty foods shops and some
  supermarkets

Preheat oven to 325° F. Lightly butter a baking sheet and dust with flour, knocking out excess.

In a bowl soak apricots in boiling-hot water to cover 5 minutes. Drain apricots well and pat dry with paper towels. Chop apricots fine. In another bowl lightly whisk together eggs. Transfer 1 teaspoon egg to a small bowl and whisk in 1 teaspoon water. Reserve egg wash.

In a large bowl with an electric mixer blend flour, sugar, baking soda, baking powder, and salt. Add remaining egg and vanilla and beat until a dough forms (dough will be sticky). Stir in apricots and ginger.

On a floured surface knead dough 6 times. Working on baking sheet, with floured hands form dough into a 6½- by 4½-inch rectangle. Brush rectangle with some reserved egg wash and bake in middle of oven 30 minutes. Cool rectangle on baking sheet on a rack 10 minutes. Loosen rectangle from baking sheet with a metal spatula and carefully transfer to a cutting board.

Cut rectangle crosswise into ½-inch-thick slices. Arrange *biscotti,* cut sides down, on baking sheet and bake 10 minutes on each side, or until pale golden. Transfer *biscotti* to rack and cool. *Biscotti keep in an airtight container at room temperature, 3 days, or frozen, 1 month.* Makes about 12 *biscotti.*

Each biscotti about 104 calories, 1 gram fat
(8% of calories from fat)

PHOTO ON PAGE 36

Chocolate-Chunk Caramel Cookies

2½ cups all-purpose flour
1 teaspoon baking soda
½ teaspoon baking powder
1 teaspoon salt
2 sticks (1 cup) unsalted butter
1 cup granulated sugar
½ cup firmly packed brown sugar
2 large eggs
6 ounces fine-quality bittersweet (not
  unsweetened) or semisweet chocolate,
  chopped coarse
18 caramels such as Kraft, chopped coarse
  (about 1 cup)
1 cup coarsely chopped pecans

Preheat oven to 375° F.

In a bowl whisk together flour, baking soda, baking powder, and salt. In another bowl with an electric mixer cream butter and sugars until light and fluffy. Beat in eggs, 1 at a time, beating well after each addition, and beat in flour mixture.

Stir chocolate, caramels, and pecans into dough and drop rounded tablespoons about 2 inches apart onto baking sheets. Bake cookies in batches in middle of oven 12 to 15 minutes, or until golden. Cool cookies on baking sheets on racks until firm. *Cookies keep in airtight containers 5 days.* Makes about 50 cookies.

Mexican Chocolate Brownies

¾ stick (6 tablespoons) unsalted butter, cut into
   pieces
3 ounces fine-quality bittersweet chocolate
   (not unsweetened), chopped
2 ounces unsweetened chocolate, chopped
1 cup sugar
½ cup whole blanched almonds, toasted until
   golden and cooled
2 large eggs
½ cup all-purpose flour
½ teaspoon salt
½ teaspoon cinnamon

Preheat oven to 350° F. and butter and flour a
9-inch square baking pan, knocking out excess flour.

In a heavy 1½-quart saucepan melt butter and
both chocolates over low heat, stirring, until smooth
and remove pan from heat. Cool chocolate mixture
10 minutes.

In a food processor process sugar and almonds
until ground fine. Stir almond mixture into chocolate
mixture and add eggs, 1 at a time, beating well with
a wooden spoon until mixture is glossy and smooth.
Stir in flour, salt, and cinnamon until just combined.

Spread batter evenly in pan and bake in middle
of oven 25 to 30 minutes, or until a tester comes
out with some crumbs adhering to it. Cool brownies
completely in pan on a rack before cutting into 16
squares. *Brownies keep, layered between sheets of
wax paper in an airtight container at cool room
temperature, 5 days.*

Chocolate-Dipped Orange Shortbread Hearts

1 cup all-purpose flour
1 tablespoon freshly grated orange zest
   (from about 2 navel oranges)
¾ teaspoon salt
1 stick (½ cup) unsalted butter, softened
1 teaspoon fresh orange juice
¾ cup plus 2 tablespoons confectioners' sugar
6 ounces fine-quality bittersweet chocolate
   (not unsweetened), chopped

Preheat oven to 325° F.
In a bowl whisk together flour, zest, and salt. In
another bowl with an electric mixer beat butter,
orange juice, and confectioners' sugar until light and
fluffy and beat in flour mixture until a dough forms.
Pat dough into a disk and chill, wrapped in plastic
wrap, 30 minutes, or until firm.

On a lightly floured surface with a floured rolling
pin roll out dough into a 13- by 12-inch rectangle
(about ⅓ inch thick). Cut out cookies with a 3½- to
4-inch heart-shaped cutter dipped in flour and
arrange 1 inch apart on baking sheets. Using dough
scraps, roll and cut out more cookies in same manner. Bake shortbread in batches in middle of oven
10 to 15 minutes, or until pale golden, and cool completely on baking sheets on racks.

Line a tray with wax paper.

In a double boiler or in a metal bowl set over a
saucepan of barely simmering water melt chocolate,
stirring until smooth. Pour warm chocolate onto a
plate and dip in half of top side of each cookie,
transferring cookies, chocolate sides up, to tray.
Chill cookies until chocolate is hardened. *Cookies
keep, chilled, in an airtight container 4 days.* Makes
about 12 cookies.

210

Rich Chocolate Rum Cookies

1¼ cups all-purpose flour
1½ teaspoons baking powder
½ teaspoon salt
½ cup ground hazelnuts (about ½ cup
   shelled nuts)
12 ounces fine-quality bittersweet chocolate
   (not unsweetened)
½ stick (¼ cup) unsalted butter
¼ cup dark rum
2 large eggs
about ¼ cup confectioners' sugar for
   sprinkling cookies

In a bowl whisk together flour, baking powder, salt, and hazelnuts. In a metal bowl set over a saucepan of barely simmering water melt chocolate and butter, stirring occasionally. Stir in rum and cool. Whisk in eggs and stir in flour mixture. *Chill dough, covered, 1 hour, or until firm enough to handle.*

Halve dough and on a sheet of wax paper form each half into a 10-inch log, using paper as a guide. *Chill logs, wrapped in wax paper, 4 hours, or until firm. Dough keeps, chilled, 1 week, or frozen, 1 month. Thaw frozen dough in refrigerator until sliceable, about 4 hours.*

Preheat oven to 350° F. Lightly butter 2 baking sheets.

Cut logs into ½-inch-thick rounds and arrange about 1 inch apart on baking sheets. Bake cookies in batches in middle of oven 8 minutes and transfer to racks. Cool cookies completely and sprinkle with confectioners' sugar. *Cookies keep in airtight containers at room temperature 4 days.* Makes about 36 cookies.

Pecan Thins

½ stick (¼ cup) unsalted butter,
   softened
6 tablespoons sugar
⅛ teaspoon salt
2 large egg whites
½ teaspoon vanilla
4 tablespoons all-purpose flour
1 cup pecans, chopped fine, lightly toasted,
   and cooled completely

Preheat oven to 425° F. and generously butter 2 large baking sheets.

In a bowl beat together butter, sugar, and salt until light and fluffy and beat in whites and vanilla until just combined. Sift flour over batter and fold in. Fold in pecans.

Drop batter by rounded teaspoons about 3 inches apart onto well-buttered baking sheets and with back of a fork pat into 2½-inch rounds. Bake cookies in batches in middle of oven until golden around edges, about 5 minutes. Working quickly, with a metal spatula carefully loosen cookies immediately and transfer to racks to cool completely. (If cookies become too firm to remove from baking sheets, return to oven for a few seconds to soften.) *Cookies keep, layers separated by wax paper, in an airtight container 1 day.* Makes about 32 cookies.

Peanut Butter and Jelly Cookies

¾ cup all-purpose flour
¾ teaspoon salt
½ teaspoon baking soda
⅓ cup creamy peanut butter
½ stick (¼ cup) unsalted butter, softened
⅓ cup firmly packed brown sugar
1 large egg
½ teaspoon vanilla
⅓ cup granulated sugar
3 tablespoons grape jelly

Preheat oven to 375° F.

In a bowl whisk together flour, salt, and baking soda. In another bowl whisk together peanut butter, butter, and brown sugar until smooth and whisk in egg and vanilla. Add flour mixture to peanut butter mixture, stirring until combined well.

Roll pieces of dough into 1-inch balls and roll in granulated sugar. Arrange balls about 2 inches apart on a large baking sheet and bake in middle of oven 10 minutes. Working quickly, with the back of a ¼-teaspoon measuring spoon make an indentation about ½ inch in diameter in center of each cookie. Fill each indentation with a slightly heaping ¼ teaspoon jelly and bake cookies 10 minutes more, or until golden. Transfer cookies to racks to cool. Makes about 30 cookies.

Crystallized-Ginger Spice Bars

3 cups all-purpose flour
1 teaspoon baking soda
½ teaspoon salt
2 teaspoons ground ginger
½ teaspoon ground cloves
¼ teaspoon ground cinnamon
2 sticks (1 cup) unsalted butter, softened
1 cup sugar
½ cup unsulfured molasses
1 large egg
3 ounces crystallized ginger, chopped
   coarse (about ½ cup)
1½ tablespoons freshly grated orange zest

In a bowl whisk together flour, baking soda, salt, and ground spices. In another bowl with an electric mixer beat together butter and sugar until light and fluffy. Add molasses, egg, flour mixture, crystallized ginger, and zest and beat until a dough forms.

On a sheet of wax paper pat dough into an 8- by 5-inch rectangle, about 1 inch thick. *Chill dough, wrapped in wax paper, 4 hours, or until firm. Dough keeps, chilled, 1 week, or frozen, 1 month. Thaw frozen dough in refrigerator until sliceable, about 4 hours.*

Preheat oven to 350° F. Lightly butter 2 baking sheets.

Cut dough crosswise into slices about ⅙ inch thick and arrange about 2 inches apart on baking sheets. Bake bars in batches in middle of oven until deep golden brown, 8 to 10 minutes, and transfer to racks to cool. *Bars keep in airtight containers at room temperature 4 days.* Makes about 46 bars.

Cinnamon Pecan Shortbread

⅓ cup pecans, chopped fine
½ stick (¼ cup) unsalted butter, softened
2 tablespoons confectioners' sugar
½ cup all-purpose flour
¼ teaspoon salt
¼ teaspoon cinnamon
⅛ teaspoon baking powder

Preheat oven to 350° F. and butter a small baking sheet.

In a small skillet cook pecans in 1 tablespoon butter with salt to taste over moderate heat, stirring, until golden and let cool.

In a bowl with an electric mixer beat together remaining 3 tablespoons butter and confectioners' sugar until light and fluffy. Into another bowl sift together flour, salt, cinnamon, and baking powder and beat into butter mixture with pecans until just combined.

On a lightly floured surface knead dough about 8 times, or until it just comes together. With floured hands form dough into a ball and on baking sheet flatten into a 5-inch disk (about ½ inch thick). With floured tines of a fork score disk into 8 wedges and with flat sides of tines press edge decoratively.

Bake shortbread in middle of oven 20 minutes, or until pale golden, and cool on baking sheet on a rack 10 minutes. While shortbread is still warm, carefully cut through score marks with a knife to separate wedges. Makes 8 wedges.

Chewy Coconut Macadamia Bars

For shortbread layer
2 cups all-purpose flour
2 sticks (1 cup) cold unsalted butter, cut
   into bits
⅔ cup confectioners' sugar
½ teaspoon salt
For topping
½ stick (¼ cup) unsalted butter
½ cup firmly packed brown sugar
¾ cup canned coconut cream such as Coco Lopez
¼ cup heavy cream
2 tablespoons fresh lemon juice
a 7-ounce package sweetened flaked coconut
   (about 2⅔ cups)
a 7-ounce jar macadamia nuts (about 1⅓ cups),
   large pieces halved

Preheat oven to 350° F. and butter a 13- by 9-inch baking pan.
Make shortbread layer:
In a food processor pulse shortbread ingredients just until a dough forms. Pat dough evenly onto bottom of pan and bake 20 minutes, or until pale golden.

Make topping while shortbread is baking:

In a large saucepan melt butter over low heat and remove pan from heat. Whisk in brown sugar until dissolved and whisk in coconut cream, heavy cream, and lemon juice until combined well. Stir in flaked coconut and nuts.

Pour topping over shortbread. Reduce temperature to 325° F. and bake confection until top is golden and center is bubbling, 45 to 50 minutes. Cool confection completely in pan on a rack and cut into bars. *Bars keep, wrapped well and chilled, 4 days, or frozen, 3 weeks.* Serve bars chilled or at room temperature. Makes about forty 3- by 1-inch bars.

PHOTO ON PAGE 59

Strawberry and Apricot Linzertorte Hearts

1½ cups blanched almonds, toasted and cooled
3 tablespoons granulated sugar
1 cup confectioners' sugar
2¼ cups all-purpose flour
½ cup cornstarch
½ teaspoon cinnamon
¾ teaspoon freshly grated lemon zest
¾ teaspoon salt
2¼ sticks (1 cup plus 2 tablespoons) cold
    unsalted butter, cut into pieces

1 large whole egg
1 large egg yolk
⅔ cup apricot jam, heated, strained,
    and cooled
⅔ cup strawberry jam, heated, strained,
    and cooled

In a food processor pulse almonds with granulated sugar until chopped fine. Add confectioners' sugar, flour, cornstarch, cinnamon, zest, and salt and pulse until combined well. Add butter and pulse until combined. Add whole egg and egg yolk and pulse until dough just holds together. Divide dough into fourths and form into disks (dough will be sticky). *Chill disks, wrapped in plastic wrap, at least 2 hours and up to 3 days.*

Preheat oven to 325° F.

Keeping remaining disks chilled, roll out 1 dough disk between sheets of wax paper into a ¼-inch-thick round (10 to 11 inches in diameter) and freeze between wax paper on a tray until very firm, about 10 minutes. Roll out and freeze remaining 3 dough disks in same manner.

Remove top sheet of paper from 1 round and with a 3½-inch heart-shaped cutter cut out hearts, chilling scraps. If dough becomes too soft to work with at any time, freeze on wax paper until very firm. With a 1-inch heart-shaped cutter cut and lift out centers (making 2 additional decorative heart cutouts in some cookies) from half of large hearts, reserving centers for scraps.

Arrange whole hearts and cut-out hearts about ½ inch apart on baking sheets and bake in batches in middle of oven 12 to 15 minutes, or until edges are pale golden. Cool cookies on baking sheets 5 minutes. (Cookies will continue to firm up as they cool.) With a spatula carefully transfer cookies to racks to cool completely. Make more cookies with remaining 3 dough rounds and dough scraps in same manner.

On a work surface arrange whole hearts, bottoms down. Drop 1 teaspoon of either jam on each cookie, spreading almost to edges, and top with cut-out hearts. Spoon some remaining jam into centers. *Cookies keep, chilled between layers of wax paper, in an airtight container, 4 days. Bring cookies to room temperature before serving.* Makes about 24 cookies.

Tutti-Frutti Cookies

1¾ cups all-purpose flour
2 teaspoons baking powder
½ teaspoon salt
1 stick (½ cup) unsalted butter, softened
1 cup sugar
¼ cup sour cream
1 large egg
2 cups sweetened flaked coconut, toasted
    until golden and cooled
1 cup packed dried apricots (about 7 ounces),
    quartered
1 cup dried cranberries (about 5 ounces)

In a bowl whisk together flour, baking powder, and salt. In another bowl with an electric mixer beat together butter and sugar until light and fluffy. Add flour mixture, sour cream, and egg and beat until a dough forms. Stir in flaked coconut, apricots, and cranberries.

Halve dough and on a sheet of wax paper form each half into a 10-inch log, using paper as a guide. *Chill logs, wrapped in wax paper, 4 hours, or until firm. Dough keeps, chilled, 1 week, or frozen, 1 month. Thaw frozen dough in refrigerator until sliceable, about 4 hours.*

Preheat oven to 350° F. Lightly butter 3 baking sheets.

Cut logs into ⅓-inch-thick rounds with a serrated knife and arrange about 2 inches apart on baking sheets. Bake cookies in batches in middle of oven until pale golden, about 12 minutes, and transfer to racks to cool. *Cookies keep in airtight containers at room temperature 4 days.* Makes about 56 cookies.

PIES, TARTS, AND PASTRIES

Apple Pie with Walnut Streusel

For pastry dough
1½ cups all-purpose flour
2 tablespoons granulated sugar
¾ teaspoon salt
1 stick (½ cup) plus 2 tablespoons cold
    unsalted butter

4 to 6 tablespoons ice water
For topping
2 tablespoons unsalted butter, softened
2 tablespoons firmly packed brown sugar
2 tablespoons all-purpose flour
¼ cup chopped walnuts
For filling
3 pounds Golden Delicious or Jonagold apples
    (about 6 medium)
½ cup firmly packed brown sugar
¼ cup granulated sugar
2 tablespoons all-purpose flour
1 tablespoon fresh lemon juice
¾ teaspoon cinnamon

2 tablespoons milk
1 tablespoon granulated sugar

Accompaniment: sour cream ice cream (page 224)

Make pastry dough:
In a large bowl with a pastry blender or in a food processor blend or pulse together flour, sugar, salt, and butter until mixture resembles coarse meal. Add 2 tablespoons ice water and toss with a fork or pulse until incorporated. Add enough remaining ice water, 1 tablespoon at a time, tossing or pulsing to incorporate, until mixture begins to form a dough. On a work surface smear dough in 3 or 4 forward motions with heel of hand to slightly develop gluten and make dough easier to work with. Form dough into a ball and flatten to form a 1-inch-thick disk. Chill dough, wrapped in plastic wrap, 30 minutes.

Make topping while dough is chilling:
In a small bowl with your fingertips blend butter, brown sugar, and flour until smooth and blend in nuts. Chill topping, covered.

Make filling:
Peel and core apples. Cut apples into ½-inch wedges and in a bowl toss with remaining filling ingredients to coat.

Preheat oven to 350° F.

On a lightly floured surface roll out dough into a 15-inch round (about ⅛ inch thick) and fold loosely into quarters for ease of handling. Unfold dough in a well-seasoned 10-inch cast-iron skillet or 10-inch deep-dish (1½-quart) pie plate, easing to fit and letting dough overhang rim of skillet or pie plate.

Spoon filling into shell and fold pastry overhang over filling, leaving center uncovered. Bake pie in middle of oven 1 hour (pie will not be completely cooked) and remove from oven.

Crumble topping over center of pie, breaking up any large chunks. Brush crust with milk and sprinkle with sugar. Bake pie in middle of oven 30 minutes more, or until crust is golden and filling is bubbling. Cool pie on a rack.

Serve pie warm or at room temperature with ice cream.

Lime Curd and Toasted Almond Tart with Fruit Compote

For crust
⅔ cup sliced almonds, toasted until golden
    and cooled completely
¼ cup sugar
¼ teaspoon salt
1 cup vanilla wafer crumbs (from about
    twenty 1½-inch cookies)
½ stick (¼ cup) unsalted butter, softened

For filling
1 cup plus 1 tablespoon sugar
1 stick (½ cup) plus 1 tablespoon cold unsalted
    butter, cut into pieces
4 large eggs, beaten lightly
½ cup fresh lime juice (from about 4 limes)
1 tablespoon freshly grated lime zest (from
    about 2 limes)

For compote
3 cups fresh Bing cherries, cut into ¼-inch dice
⅔ cup ¼-inch dice fresh pineapple
½ mango, cut into ¼-inch dice
2 firm-ripe apricots, peeled and cut into
    ¼-inch dice
⅔ cup raspberries, picked over and quartered
1 teaspoon sugar

Make crust:
Preheat oven to 350° F. and butter a 9-inch tart pan with a removable fluted rim.

In a food processor pulse almonds, sugar, and salt until almonds are ground fine. In a bowl toss nut mixture with cookie crumbs and butter until combined well.

Sprinkle half of crumb mixture onto bottom of pan near rim, pressing evenly up side. Sprinkle remaining crumb mixture onto bottom and press evenly over bottom, joining edge. Bake crust in lower third of oven 10 minutes, or until a deeper shade of golden, and cool on a rack.

Make filling:

In a heavy saucepan cook sugar, butter, eggs, and lime juice over moderately low heat, whisking frequently, until thick enough to hold marks of whisk and first bubble appears on surface, 12 to 15 minutes. Immediately pour curd through a sieve into a bowl. Stir in zest and cool. *Filling may be made 1 week ahead and chilled, its surface covered with plastic wrap.*

Spoon filling evenly into crust and cover surface with a buttered round of wax paper. *Chill tart, covered, at least 1 hour and up to 24.*

Make compote:

In a bowl gently toss compote ingredients together and let stand 15 minutes.

Remove side of tart pan and transfer tart to a plate. Serve tart, cut into wedges, with fruit compote on the side.

PHOTO ON PAGE 33

Pear and Sour Cherry Mincemeat Pie

For mincemeat
2½ pounds firm-ripe Bartlett or Anjou pears
  (about 5)
2 tablespoons fresh lemon juice
⅔ cup sugar
1 cup water
½ cup dried sour cherries (about 3 ounces)
⅓ cup golden raisins
½ teaspoon cinnamon
½ teaspoon ground allspice
¼ teaspoon freshly grated nutmeg
⅛ teaspoon salt
¾ cup walnuts, lightly toasted and
  chopped fine
2 tablespoons brandy

2 recipes pastry dough (recipe follows)
an egg wash made by beating 1 large
  egg yolk with 1 teaspoon water
For assembly
one 9-inch cardboard round*

* available at specialty cookware shops and by
  mail order from N.Y. Cake & Baking
  Distributors, 56 West 22nd Street,
  New York, NY 10010, tel. (212) 675-CAKE

Make mincemeat:
Peel, quarter, and core pears. Chop pears coarse
and in a bowl toss with lemon juice.

In a dry 3½- to 4-quart heavy saucepan cook ⅓ cup
sugar over moderate heat, stirring with a fork, until melted and cook, without stirring, swirling pan,
until a golden caramel. Remove pan from heat and
carefully add water down side of pan (caramel will
steam and harden). Return pan to heat and simmer
mixture, stirring, until caramel is dissolved. Add
pears, remaining ⅓ cup sugar, cherries, raisins,
spices, and salt and simmer, stirring occasionally at
beginning of cooking and frequently toward end to
prevent sticking, until thickened, about 50 minutes.

Stir in walnuts and brandy and cook, stirring, 1
minute. Cool mincemeat. *Mincemeat may be used
immediately but will improve in flavor if kept,
covered and chilled, at least 1 day and up to 1 week.*

On a lightly floured surface with a floured rolling

pin roll out half of dough ⅛ inch thick (about a 12-
inch round). Fit dough into a 9-inch (1-quart
capacity) pie plate and trim edge, leaving a ¾-inch
overhang. Chill shell 30 minutes.

On lightly floured surface roll out remaining
dough ⅛ inch thick (about a 10-inch round) and with
a sharp large knife or pastry wheel cut into ½-inch-
wide strips. Put 9-inch cardboard round on a baking
sheet and arrange 4 pastry strips ¾ inch apart in
middle of round. Working with 1 pastry strip at a
time, weave remaining strips over and under pastry
strips on round, beginning in middle and working
out to sides and letting excess hang off round. Freeze
lattice top, covered loosely, on round on baking
sheet until firm, about 30 minutes.

Preheat oven to 425° F.

Spoon mincemeat into shell, smoothing top. Lift
lattice top together with round off baking sheet and
slide pastry carefully onto pie. (If pastry sticks to
baking sheet or round, pry loose carefully with a
small knife.) Let lattice top soften until pliable and
trim flush with rim of pie plate. Roll shell overhang up over edge of lattice top, crimping edge
decoratively. Brush lattice top with egg wash and
bake pie in middle of oven until pastry is golden and
filling just begins to bubble around edge, about 25
minutes. Transfer pie to a rack and cool. Serve pie
warm or at room temperature.

PHOTO ON PAGE 74

Pastry Dough

1¼ cups all-purpose flour
¾ stick (6 tablespoons) cold unsalted butter,
  cut into bits
2 tablespoons cold vegetable shortening
¼ teaspoon salt
2 to 4 tablespoons ice water

In a bowl with a pastry blender or in a food
processor blend or pulse together flour, butter,
shortening, and salt until mixture resembles coarse
meal. Add 2 tablespoons ice water and toss or pulse
until incorporated. Add remaining ice water, 1
tablespoon at a time, tossing with a fork or pulsing to
incorporate, until mixture begins to form a dough.
On a work surface smear dough in 3 or 4 forward

motions with heel of hand to slightly develop gluten in flour and make dough easier to work with. Form dough into a ball and flatten to form a disk. Wrap dough in plastic wrap and chill 1 hour. Makes enough dough for a single-crust 9- to 10-inch pie.

Maple Pumpkin Pie

2 recipes pastry dough (recipe precedes)
an egg wash made by beating 1 large
   egg yolk with 1 teaspoon water
1 cup Grade B maple syrup*
2 cups canned solid-pack pumpkin
1 teaspoon cinnamon
1 teaspoon ground ginger
½ teaspoon salt
1 cup heavy cream
⅔ cup milk
2 large eggs

*available at some specialty foods shops and by
   mail order from Highland Sugarworks,
   Waitsfield, VT, tel. (802) 496-4012

On a lightly floured surface with a floured rolling pin roll out two thirds dough ⅛ inch thick (about a 14-inch round). Fit dough into a 10-inch (1½-quart capacity) pie plate and trim edge, leaving a ½-inch overhang. Crimp edge decoratively and chill shell 30 minutes. *Shell may be made 1 day ahead and chilled, covered loosely with plastic wrap.*

Preheat oven to 375° F.

On lightly floured surface roll out remaining dough ⅛ inch thick (about a 10-inch round). With a 2-inch leaf-shaped cutter cut out 16 leaves and transfer to a baking sheet. Chill pastry leaves until firm, about 15 minutes.

Brush leaves with some egg wash (being careful not to drip onto edges) and bake in middle of oven until golden, about 12 minutes. Transfer leaves to a rack and cool. *Pastry leaves may be made 1 day ahead and kept in an airtight container at room temperature.*

In a 3- to 3½-quart heavy saucepan gently boil maple syrup until a small amount dropped into a bowl of cold water forms a soft ball, about 210° F. on a candy thermometer, and cool slightly. In a bowl whisk together pumpkin, cinnamon, ginger, salt, cream, milk, and eggs and whisk in maple syrup.

Pour filling into shell and brush edge of shell with some egg wash. Bake pie in middle of oven 1 hour, or until filling is set but center still trembles slightly. (Filling will continue to set as pie cools.) Transfer pie to a rack to cool completely.

Garnish pie with pastry leaves just before serving.

PHOTO ON PAGE 74

ZOE MAVRIDIS

Lemon Cajun Sweet Dough Pies

For sweet dough
5 cups all-purpose flour
2 teaspoons baking powder
½ teaspoon salt
1 stick (½ cup) unsalted butter, softened
¼ cup vegetable shortening
1½ cups sugar
2 large eggs
⅔ cup milk
1 teaspoon vanilla
For filling
½ cup sugar
2 tablespoons cornstarch
⅛ teaspoon salt
½ cup water
¼ cup milk
2 large egg yolks
2 teaspoons unsalted butter
¼ cup fresh lemon juice
1 teaspoon freshly grated lemon zest

Make sweet dough:
Into a bowl sift together flour, baking powder, and salt. In bowl of a standing electric mixer beat together butter, shortening, and sugar until light and fluffy. Beat in eggs, 1 at at time, beating well after each addition, and beat in milk and vanilla (batter will appear curdled). With mixer on low speed beat in flour mixture, a little at a time, until it forms a dough. Halve dough and form each piece into a disk. *Chill dough, wrapped in plastic wrap, until firm, about 3 hours.*

Cut twenty-four 6-inch squares of wax paper. Roll out 1 piece of dough between 2 sheets of plastic wrap into a 12-inch round (about ⅛ inch thick). Cut out 6 rounds with a 5-inch round cutter, sandwiching each round between 2 squares of wax paper, and stack on a baking sheet. If dough becomes too soft to work with, transfer it to a baking sheet and chill until firm. Roll out and cut remaining piece of dough in same manner, sandwiching rounds between remaining squares of wax paper, and stack on baking sheet. Chill rounds until firm and wrap each stack carefully with plastic wrap to prevent drying. *Dough may be made 1 day ahead and chilled.*

Make filling:
In a heavy saucepan whisk together sugar, cornstarch, and salt and gradually whisk in water and milk until cornstarch is dissolved. In a bowl whisk together yolks. Cook milk mixture over moderate heat, whisking, until it comes to a boil. Gradually whisk about ½ cup hot milk mixture into yolks and whisk yolk mixture into remaining hot milk mixture. Bring custard to a slow boil over moderate heat, whisking, and boil, whisking, 1 minute. Remove pan from heat and whisk in butter, lemon juice, and zest until butter is melted. Cover surface of filling with plastic wrap. *Filling may be made 1 day ahead and chilled. Do not stir filling or it will break down.*

Preheat oven to 375° F. Butter 2 baking sheets.

Discard top square of wax paper from 1 dough round and spoon 1 tablespoon filling onto center of round. Using wax paper fold dough over to form a half circle, enclosing lemon filling, and press edges together lightly. Transfer pie to baking sheet, discarding paper, and crimp edge with a fork. Prick pie once with fork. Make 11 more pies with remaining dough rounds and filling in same manner.

Bake pies in 2 batches in middle of oven 15 minutes, or until golden brown around edges (dough will crack open slightly), and transfer to racks to cool. *Pies may be made 4 hours ahead and chilled, covered.* Serve pies chilled or at room temperature (do not let pies stand more than 30 minutes at room temperature). Makes 12 individual sweet dough pies.

PHOTO ON PAGE 48

Chocolate Ganache Tartlets with Sweet Cherries

¾ cup plus ⅔ cup well-chilled heavy cream
6 ounces fine-quality bittersweet chocolate
   (not unsweetened), chopped
6 cocoa tartlet shells (recipe
   follows)

Accompaniment: 24 to 30 dark sweet cherries, pitted, halved, and tossed with 2 teaspoons sugar

In a small saucepan bring ¾ cup cream just to a boil. Reduce heat to low and add chocolate, stirring until smooth. Transfer ¾ cup mixture to a bowl, reserving remainder in pan for glazing tartlets. Add ⅓ cup cream to mixture in bowl, stirring until *ganache* is combined well. *Chill ganache until thick and cold, about 1 hour.*

In a small bowl whisk remaining ⅓ cup cream until it just holds stiff peaks. With an electric mixer beat chilled *ganache* until light and fluffy, about 30 seconds (do not overbeat or it will become grainy). Remove tartlet shells from tartlet pans (use a thin, flexible knife to help remove shells if necessary). Fold whipped cream into *ganache* until combined well and spread in tartlet shells, smoothing tops.

Heat reserved chocolate mixture over low heat, stirring, until melted and just warm. Working quickly, with 1 tartlet at a time, spoon about 1 tablespoon chocolate glaze onto top, tilting tartlet to allow glaze to completely cover filling. Chill tartlets until glaze is set, about 30 minutes. *Tartlets may be made 2 days ahead and chilled, wrapped in plastic wrap.*
Serve tartlets with cherries. Makes 6 tartlets.

PHOTO ON PAGE 47

Cocoa Tartlet Shells

¾ cup all-purpose flour
6 tablespoons confectioners' sugar
¼ cup unsweetened cocoa powder
¼ teaspoon salt
⅛ teaspoon baking powder
¾ stick (6 tablespoons) cold unsalted butter,
   cut into bits
1 to 2 tablespoons ice water

Into a bowl sift together flour, confectioners' sugar, cocoa powder, salt, and baking soda and with a pastry blender or your fingertips blend in butter until mixture resembles coarse meal. Add 1 tablespoon ice water, tossing mixture with a fork until water is incorporated, and add enough remaining ice water, ½ tablespoon at a time, tossing to incorporate, until a dough begins to form. Form dough into a ball and divide into 6 pieces. Form each piece into a ball and flatten to form a disk. Wrap each disk in plastic wrap and chill 30 minutes.

Preheat oven to 375° F.

Roll out 1 piece of dough between 2 sheets of plastic wrap into a 5-inch round (about ⅛ inch thick). Discard top sheet of plastic wrap and invert dough onto a 3½-inch tartlet pan (1 inch deep), discarding remaining sheet of plastic wrap. Fit dough into pan and trim flush with edge of pan, pressing dough gently against side of pan. Prick bottom of shell with a fork and chill while preparing remaining shells. Make and chill 5 more shells with remaining dough in same manner.

Line shells with foil and bake on a baking sheet in middle of oven 10 minutes. Remove foil and bake shells until cooked through, about 5 minutes more (pastry will no longer be shiny). Cool shells in pans on a rack. *Tartlet shells may be made 3 days ahead and kept in pans in airtight containers.* Makes 6 cocoa tartlet shells.

Blood-Orange Crostata

1 recipe rich sweet pastry dough (recipe follows)
raw rice or dried beans for weighting shell
For pastry cream
1½ cups milk
4 large egg yolks
½ cup sugar
¼ cup all-purpose flour
1½ teaspoons freshly grated orange zest
2 tablespoons grappa, or to taste

4 blood oranges*
4 small navel oranges
⅓ cup orange marmalade

*available seasonally at specialty produce markets
  and by mail order from Chefs' Produce Team,
  tel. (213) 624-8909

Preheat oven to 425° F.

On a lightly floured surface roll out dough into a 15-inch round (about ⅛ inch thick) and fit it into an 11-inch tart pan with a removable fluted rim. Trim dough flush with rim and lightly prick bottom all over with a fork. Chill shell until firm, about 30 minutes.

Line shell with foil and fill with rice or beans. Bake shell in middle of oven 15 minutes. Remove rice or beans and foil carefully and bake shell until golden, about 8 minutes more. Cool shell in tart pan on a rack. *Shell may be made 1 day ahead and kept in an airtight container at room temperature.*

Make pastry cream:

In a 1½-quart heavy saucepan bring milk just to a simmer over moderate heat. In a metal bowl whisk together yolks, sugar, flour, and zest and add hot milk in a stream, whisking. Transfer mixture to pan and bring to a boil over moderate heat, whisking constantly. Simmer pastry cream, whisking constantly, 1 minute and transfer to a bowl. Whisk in grappa and cool, stirring occasionally. *Chill pastry cream, its surface covered with plastic wrap, until cold at least 4 hours and up to 2 days.*

With a sharp knife cut a slice from top and bottom of each orange to expose flesh and arrange, a cut side down, on a cutting board. Cutting from top to bottom, remove peel and pith. Cut oranges crosswise into thin slices and drain slices in one layer on several thicknesses of paper towel 15 minutes.

In a small saucepan bring marmalade to a simmer, stirring, and force through a fine sieve into a bowl, pressing hard on solids. Discard solids.

Spread pastry cream evenly in tart shell. Arrange orange slices decoratively over pastry cream, overlapping them slightly to cover cream, and brush with marmalade. *Crostata may be made 2 hours ahead and chilled, covered. Bring crostata to room temperature before serving.*

PHOTO ON PAGE 79

Rich Sweet Pastry Dough

2 cups all-purpose flour
⅓ cup sugar
½ teaspoon salt
1½ sticks (¾ cup) cold
   unsalted butter, cut into bits
6 large egg yolks

In a bowl with a pastry blender or in a food processor blend or pulse together flour, sugar, and salt. Add butter and blend or pulse until mixture resembles coarse meal. Add yolks and, if blending by hand, stir until mixture forms a dough. If using a food processor pulse until mixture forms large clumps and with hands form mixture into a dough.

On a work surface smear dough in 3 or 4 forward motions with heel of hand to slightly develop gluten in flour and make dough easier to work with. Form dough into a ball and flatten to form a disk. *Chill dough, wrapped in plastic wrap, at least 1 hour and up to 1 day.* Makes enough dough for an 11- to 12-inch tart.

Frozen Chocolate Bourbon Parfaits

8 ounces fine-quality bittersweet chocolate
(not unsweetened), chopped
½ cup plus 2 tablespoons water
2 tablespoons bourbon
4 large eggs
¾ cup granulated sugar
1 teaspoon unflavored gelatin
3½ cups well-chilled heavy cream
⅓ cup confectioners' sugar

Garnish: 8 praline pieces*

*available by mail order from The Praline
Connection, tel. (800) 392-0362 or
(504) 943-3934

In a double boiler or a metal bowl set over a
saucepan of barely simmering water melt chocolate
in ½ cup water, stirring until smooth, and stir in
bourbon until combined well. Remove top pan of
double boiler or bowl from heat.

In a large metal bowl with a handheld electric
mixer beat eggs and granulated sugar until combined.
Set bowl over a large saucepan of simmering water
and beat mixture until light and thickened, about
6 minutes.

In a very small saucepan sprinkle gelatin over
remaining 2 tablespoons water and let stand 1 minute to soften. Heat gelatin mixture over moderate
heat, stirring, until gelatin is dissolved. Beat chocolate and gelatin mixtures into egg mixture and cool
to room temperature.

In a bowl beat 1½ cups heavy cream until it just
holds stiff peaks. Fold cream into chocolate mixture
thoroughly and divide among eight 1½- to 2-cup
stemmed glasses. *Freeze parfaits, covered with
plastic wrap, until set, about 1 hour.*

In a bowl beat remaining 2 cups heavy cream until it holds soft peaks. Sift confectioners' sugar over
cream and beat until cream just holds stiff peaks.

Transfer whipped cream to a pastry bag fitted
with a decorative tip and pipe onto parfaits. Garnish
parfaits with praline pieces. *Freeze parfaits until*

*solid, about 4 hours. Parfaits may be made 2 days
ahead and frozen, covered.*

Let parfaits stand at room temperature 15 minutes
before serving. Serves 8.

Banana Coconut Ice Cream

2 firm-ripe medium bananas
½ cup well-stirred canned cream of coconut
such as Coco Lopez
⅓ cup heavy cream
1 teaspoon vanilla
1 teaspoon fresh lemon juice

Cut bananas into ½-inch-thick slices and arrange
slices in one layer in a shallow baking pan. Freeze
bananas 15 minutes, or until firm. In a blender or
food processor purée frozen bananas with remaining
ingredients until smooth. Freeze mixture in an ice-
cream maker. Makes about 2½ cups.

Peanut Butter Chocolate Ripple Ice Cream

1⅔ cups whole milk
1 cup creamy peanut butter
½ cup plus 3 tablespoons sugar
2 teaspoons vanilla
3 tablespoons water
1½ ounces fine-quality bittersweet
chocolate (not unsweetened),
chopped

In a saucepan simmer milk, peanut butter, and ½
cup sugar over moderate heat, stirring until smooth,
about 1 minute. Stir in vanilla and cool mixture to
room temperature. Freeze mixture in an ice-cream
maker.

While ice cream is freezing, in a small saucepan
simmer water and remaining 3 tablespoons sugar,
stirring until sugar dissolves. Add chocolate, stirring
until smooth, and cool sauce to room temperature.

Spread one fourth ice cream in a 2-quart container
and top with one third sauce. Layer remaining ice
cream and sauce in same manner and with a spatula
swirl sauce and ice cream together. Freeze ice cream,
covered with plastic wrap, until hard. Makes about
1 quart.

Honey Porter Prune Ice Cream

1 cup pitted prunes, chopped
½ cup porter such as Samuel Adams Honey Porter
　(not a bitter porter such as Sierra Nevada)
3 tablespoons honey
1 tablespoon cornstarch
3 large egg yolks
2 cups milk
1 cup sugar
1 teaspoon vanilla
1 cup well-chilled heavy cream

In a small heavy saucepan combine prunes, porter, and honey and cook over moderate heat, stirring occasionally, until most liquid is evaporated, 10 to 15 minutes. Cool prune mixture.

In a bowl whisk together cornstarch, yolks, and a pinch salt. In a heavy saucepan stir together milk and sugar and bring to a bare simmer. Add hot milk mixture to yolk mixture in a stream, whisking, and transfer custard to pan. Bring custard to a boil over moderate heat, whisking constantly, and boil, whisking constantly, 2 minutes.

Pour custard into a metal bowl set in a larger bowl of ice and cold water and cool, stirring. Stir in vanilla, cream, and prune mixture and freeze in an ice-cream maker. Makes about 1 quart.

PHOTO ON PAGE 21

Ice-Cream Bombes with Brandied Dried Cranberries and Cherries

six 7-ounce disposable translucent soft plastic
　cups*
6 ounces fine-quality bittersweet chocolate
　(not unsweetened), chopped
about 2¼ cups super-premium vanilla ice cream,
　softened
about ½ cup creamy caramel sauce (recipe
　follows)
6 tablespoons ground pecan praline
　(page 223)

Accompaniment: brandied dried cranberries
　and cherries (page 223)
Garnish: 12 pecan praline shards (reserved from
　praline recipe, page 223)

*available at supermarkets under store brand
　name

With scissors carefully cut through rims of cups and cut evenly around each cup to create a 2¾-inch-deep cup.

In a double boiler or a metal bowl set over a saucepan of barely simmering water melt chocolate, stirring until smooth, and remove double boiler or pan from heat. With a small pastry brush, lightly coat insides of cups with chocolate just to cover and on a tray freeze cups, right side up, until chocolate is firm, about 3 minutes. Add more coats of chocolate in same manner until an ⅛-inch-thick chocolate coating is formed inside each cup.

Spoon about 2 heaping tablespoons ice cream into bottom of each cup, smoothing surface with the back of a long-handled small metal spoon. Freeze cups until firm, about 30 minutes. Top ice cream in each cup evenly with 1 heaping tablespoon caramel sauce and sprinkle evenly with 1 tablespoon ground praline. Freeze cups 15 minutes. Top praline in each cup with a scant ¼ cup ice cream, filling just to rim and smoothing with a spatula. *Freeze cups until ice cream is frozen hard, about 1 hour. Ice-cream bombes may be prepared up to this point 5 days ahead and kept frozen, covered, in plastic cups.*

To unmold *bombes,* carefully tear rim of each cup and continue tearing to remove all of cup. *Ice-cream bombes may be unmolded 4 hours ahead and kept frozen, wrapped in plastic wrap.*

Arrange *bombes*, ice-cream sides down, on 6 plates. Spoon brandied fruit over and around *bombes* and garnish with praline shards. Serves 6.

PHOTO ON PAGE 83

Creamy Caramel Sauce

½ cup sugar
¼ cup water
¼ cup light corn syrup
6 tablespoons heavy cream

In a heavy saucepan stir together sugar, water, corn syrup, and a pinch salt and boil over moderate heat, stirring, until sugar is dissolved. Boil mixture, without stirring, until a golden caramel. Remove pan from heat and stir in cream. Cool sauce. *Sauce may be made 2 days ahead and chilled, covered. Bring sauce to room temperature before using.* Makes about ¾ cup.

Pecan Praline

2 cups sugar
¾ cup pecans, chopped coarse
¼ teaspoon salt

Lightly oil a baking sheet.

In a dry heavy saucepan cook sugar over moderate heat, stirring with a fork, until melted and cook sugar, without stirring, swirling pan, until a golden caramel. Stir in pecans with salt until coated well. Immediately pour mixture onto oiled baking sheet, tilting baking sheet to make a thin layer, and cool completely, about 20 minutes. Carefully remove praline in shards from baking sheet. Break about one eighth shards into smaller pieces and in a food processor pulse until ground coarse (you will need 6 tablespoons for *bombes*). Break remaining praline into 12 shards for garnishing desserts. *Praline may be made 2 days ahead, ground praline kept in an airtight container at cool room temperature (if it clumps, regrind in food processor before using), and shards kept between sheets of wax paper in another airtight container at room temperature.*

Brandied Dried Cranberries and Cherries

¼ cup sugar
½ cup water
½ cup dried cranberries (about 2½ ounces)
½ cup dried sour cherries (about 2½ ounces)
2 tablespoons brandy such as Cognac

In a small saucepan simmer all ingredients except brandy, stirring, 5 minutes and remove pan from heat. Stir in brandy and cool. *Brandied fruits may be made 2 days ahead and chilled, covered. Bring brandied fruits to room temperature before serving.* Makes about 1¼ cups.

Chocolate Malted Ice Cream with Malted Milk Balls

3 large egg yolks
⅔ cup plus 1 tablespoon malted milk powder
1 tablespoon cornstarch
4½ ounces fine-quality bittersweet chocolate (not unsweetened), chopped
¾ cup sugar
2½ cups milk
2 cups heavy cream
2 teaspoons vanilla
1½ cups malted milk balls such as Whoppers, halved

In a heatproof bowl whisk together yolks, malted milk powder, cornstarch, and a pinch salt until smooth and stir in chocolate.

In a dry heavy saucepan cook sugar over moderate heat, stirring with a fork, until melted, about 4 minutes, and cook, without stirring, swirling pan, until a golden caramel, about 30 seconds.

Remove pan from heat and into side of pan add milk carefully (mixture will steam and caramel will harden). Add cream and cook over moderate heat, stirring, until caramel is dissolved.

Gradually add caramel mixture to yolk mixture in a stream, whisking until smooth. Transfer mixture to pan and cook over moderately low heat, stirring, until a candy thermometer registers 170° F. (do not boil).

Pour custard through a fine sieve into a bowl and cool completely. Stir in vanilla and freeze custard in an ice-cream maker, adding malted milk balls during last few minutes of freezing. Makes about 1½ quarts.

Butternut and Hickory Nut Ice Cream

2 tablespoons unsalted butter
¾ cup butternuts* (about 3 ounces), chopped
¾ cup hickory nuts* (about 3 ounces), chopped
¼ teaspoon plus ⅛ teaspoon salt
1 cup sugar
1 tablespoon cornstarch
4 large egg yolks
2½ cups milk
1 teaspoon vanilla
2 cups well-chilled heavy cream

*available seasonally by mail order from American Spoon Foods, tel. (800) 222-5886 or (616) 347-9030

Preheat oven to 350° F.

In a small saucepan melt butter and stir in nuts and ¼ teaspoon salt. Transfer nuts to a baking sheet and bake in middle of oven until fragrant and one shade darker, about 6 minutes. Cool nuts completely.

In a 2½- to 3-quart heavy saucepan whisk together sugar and cornstarch and whisk in yolks, milk, and remaining ⅛ teaspoon salt until combined well. Cook custard over moderate heat, whisking, until it just comes to a boil and simmer, whisking, 1 minute. Transfer custard to a bowl and cool. Chill custard, covered, until cold. Stir in vanilla and cream until custard is combined well and freeze in an ice-cream maker. Transfer ice cream to a metal bowl and stir in nuts. Harden ice cream in freezer until firm. *Ice cream may be made 1 week ahead and kept frozen, covered.* Makes about 1½ quarts.

Sour Cream Ice Cream

2 cups half-and-half
1 cup sugar
1 vanilla bean, split lengthwise
8 large egg yolks
2 cups (1 pint) sour cream

In a heavy saucepan combine half-and-half, ¾ cup sugar, and vanilla bean and bring just to a boil. Remove saucepan from heat. In a bowl whisk together yolks and remaining ¼ cup sugar and add

hot half-and-half mixture in a stream, whisking. Transfer custard to pan and cook over moderately low heat, stirring, until it registers 170° F. on a candy thermometer.

Remove pan from heat. Scrape seeds from vanilla bean into custard and discard pod. Stir sour cream into custard until combined well and pour through a fine sieve into a bowl. Chill custard until cold and freeze in an ice-cream maker. Makes about 1 quart.

Cucumber Anise Granita

¾ cup sugar
¾ cup water
3 seedless cucumbers, peeled and seeded
1 teaspoon Ricard or other anise-flavored liqueur

In a saucepan bring sugar and water to a boil, stirring until sugar is dissolved, and cool syrup.

Coarsely chop enough of cucumbers to measure 6 cups and in a blender purée with syrup in 2 batches until smooth. Transfer purée to a shallow metal baking pan and stir in anise liqueur. Freeze mixture, covered, stirring and crushing lumps with a fork about every 30 minutes, until mixture is firm but not frozen hard, 2 to 3 hours. *Granita may be made 2 days ahead and kept frozen, covered. Just before serving, scrape granita with a fork to lighten texture.* Makes about 4 cups.

Tropical Fruit Champagne Granita

½ cup sugar
½ cup water
3 cups ½-inch chunks fresh pineapple (preferably from 6 baby pineapples, reserving hollowed shells for serving)
4 cups chilled passion-fruit nectar* or juice
¾ cup chilled Champagne

*available by mail order from Balducci's, tel. (800) BALDUCCI

In a saucepan bring sugar and water to a boil, stirring until sugar is dissolved, and cool syrup.

In a blender or food processor purée pineapple

with ¼ cup plus 2 tablespoons syrup (reserving remaining syrup for another use). Stir in nectar or juice and Champagne. *Pineapple mixture may be made 1 day ahead and chilled, covered.*

Transfer pineapple mixture to a shallow metal baking pan and freeze, stirring and crushing lumps with a fork every hour, until mixture is firm but not frozen hard, about 3 to 4 hours. *Granita may be made 2 days ahead and frozen, covered. Just before serving, scrape granita with a fork to lighten texture.*

Scoop *granita* into reserved baby pineapple shells or bowls. Makes about 9 cups, serving 6.

☙ Each serving about 181 calories,
0 grams fat

Watermelon and Raspberry Sorbet

1 cup water
⅔ cup sugar
a 2¾-pound piece of watermelon, rind and seeds discarded, flesh cut into chunks (4½ cups)
4 teaspoons fresh lemon juice
1 cup fresh raspberries

In a saucepan simmer water with sugar, stirring, until sugar dissolves. In a blender purée watermelon, sugar syrup, lemon juice, and ½ cup raspberries and strain through a fine sieve into a bowl, pressing hard on solids. *Chill mixture, covered, until cold, about 2 hours.* Freeze mixture in an ice-cream maker. Serve scoops garnished with remaining ½ cup raspberries. *Sorbet may be made 1 week ahead.* Makes about 5 cups.

☙ Each ½-cup serving with berries
about 76 calories, 0 grams fat

PHOTO ON PAGE 84

Lemon Blueberry Cobbler

2 cups picked-over blueberries
1 teaspoon freshly grated lemon zest
⅓ cup sugar
1 tablespoon fresh lemon juice
1 teaspoon cornstarch
⅔ cup all-purpose flour
1 teaspoon baking powder
⅛ teaspoon ground cardamom
½ cup heavy cream

Preheat oven to 400° F. and butter an 8-inch (1½ quart) glass pie plate.

In a bowl toss together blueberries, zest, sugar, lemon juice, and cornstarch until combined well and transfer to pie plate.

Into another bowl sift together flour, baking powder, cardamom, and a pinch salt. Add cream and stir until mixture just forms a dough. Drop dough in 5 mounds on blueberry mixture and bake in middle of oven until biscuits are golden and cooked through, about 25 minutes. Serves 2.

Cinnamon-Sugar Apple Rings

2 McIntosh apples
1 tablespoon unsalted butter, melted
1½ tablespoons sugar combined with ½ teaspoon cinnamon

Accompaniment: vanilla ice cream

Set broiler rack about 4 inches from heat and preheat broiler.

Core apples and cut crosswise into ¼-inch-thick rings, discarding ends. Brush both sides of rings with butter and arrange in one layer in a shallow baking pan. Broil apple rings until edges just begin to turn golden, about 5 minutes. Sprinkle rings evenly with cinnamon sugar and broil until glazed and golden, about 2 minutes more.

Serve apples with ice cream. Serves 2.

Melon Compote

1½ cups sugar
½ cup water
¼ cup fresh lime juice
a 1-inch piece gingerroot, peeled and grated
1½ teaspoons ground cumin
freshly ground black pepper to taste
2 cups ¾-inch watermelon balls (from about
   a 3-pound piece, seeded)
2 cups ¾-inch honeydew melon balls (from
   about a 3-pound piece, seeded)
2 cups ¾-inch cantaloupe balls (from about
   a 3-pound piece, seeded)

In a 1-quart saucepan bring sugar and water to a boil, stirring until sugar is dissolved, and simmer 2 minutes. Cool syrup and stir in lime juice, gingerroot, cumin, pepper, and salt to taste. In a bowl toss together melon balls and syrup. *Chill compote, covered, until cold, at least 2 hours and up to 3 days.* Serves 6.

PHOTO ON PAGE 2

Strawberry Phyllo Shortcakes

1½ tablespoons unsalted butter, melted
two 17- by 12-inch sheets *phyllo,* thawed
   if frozen
1½ cups strawberries, sliced thin
2 tablespoons honey
1 tablespoon currant- or citrus-flavored vodka
   if desired

Accompaniment: lightly sweetened
   whipped cream

Preheat oven to 350° F. and brush a baking sheet with some butter.

On a work surface arrange 1 sheet *phyllo* with a long side facing you and brush evenly with some butter. On this, layer and brush remaining sheet *phyllo* in same manner. Cut layered *phyllo* crosswise into 4 rectangles. Top 2 rectangles with other 2 rectangles and cut each stack into three 4-inch squares (for a total of 6 squares). On baking sheet bake *phyllo* squares in middle of oven until golden and crisp, about 12 minutes, and cool on a rack.

While squares are baking, in a bowl toss together strawberries, honey, and vodka until combined well.

Assemble shortcakes:
Arrange 1 *phyllo* square on each of 2 plates and top with one third strawberry mixture. Make 2 more layers with remaining 4 squares and strawberry mixture in same manner and top with whipped cream. Serves 2.

Honeydew in Cardamom Lime Syrup
with Vanilla Cream

For syrup
⅔ cup sugar
⅓ cup fresh lime juice
⅓ cup water
zest of 2 limes, removed in strips with
   a vegetable peeler
½ teaspoon ground cardamom, or to taste
For cream
⅔ cup no-salt low-fat cottage cheese
3 tablespoons sour cream
1 tablespoon sugar
½ teaspoon vanilla
1 to 2 teaspoons fresh lime juice

8 cups ¾- to 1-inch honeydew melon balls
   (from about two 5-pound melons, seeded)

Garnish: freshly grated lime zest

Make syrup:
In a small saucepan simmer syrup ingredients, stirring, until sugar is dissolved, about 1 minute. Remove pan from heat and cool syrup completely. Discard zest. *Syrup may be made 1 day ahead and chilled, covered.*

Make cream:
In a small food processor blend cream ingredients and a pinch salt until very smooth, about 1 minute. *Chill cream, covered, at least 3 hours and up to 24.*

Just before serving, in a large bowl toss together melon balls and syrup and divide among 6 stemmed glasses. Top each serving with a generous dollop of cream and garnish with zest. Serves 6.

✐ Each serving about 213 calories, 2 grams fat
(9% of calories from fat)

PUDDINGS AND SOUFFLÉS

Gingered Brioche Summer Pudding with Sour Cream Mascarpone

1 cup sugar
¾ cup water
5 teaspoons finely grated peeled fresh gingerroot, or to taste
4 firm-ripe nectarines (about 1¾ pounds), pitted and cut into ½-inch wedges
4 firm-ripe plums (about 1½ pounds), pitted and cut into ½-inch wedges
3 cups picked-over blueberries, rinsed
2 teaspoons fresh lemon juice
four to eight ½-inch-thick slices brioche or challah (about ½ pound)

Accompaniment: sour cream *mascarpone* (recipe follows)

In a large saucepan bring sugar, water, and gingerroot to a boil, stirring until sugar is dissolved. Stir in fruit and simmer gently, covered, carefully stirring occasionally, until blueberries just begin to burst, about 5 minutes. Remove saucepan from heat and stir in lemon juice. Transfer fruit mixture to a shallow baking dish to cool as quickly as possible. Transfer 1½ cups cooled fruit mixture to a bowl and reserve, covered and chilled.

Preheat oven to 400° F.

On a baking sheet arrange bread slices in one layer and toast in middle of oven, turning them if necessary, until golden brown on both sides. Transfer bread to a rack to cool.

In an 8-inch square glass baking dish set inside a larger shallow baking dish arrange half of bread slices, overlapping slightly if necessary and trimming to fit, and top with half of unchilled fruit mixture. Layer remaining bread slices and unchilled fruit mixture in same manner. Cover surface of pudding with plastic wrap. Put another 8-inch square glass or metal baking dish on top of plastic wrap and weight pudding evenly with about 6 pounds of weight (such as cans of food). *Chill pudding at least 8 hours and up to 1 day.*

Just before serving, remove weights, baking dish, and plastic wrap from pudding, reserving juice that has spilled over into larger baking dish, and cut pudding into 6 portions. Transfer 4 portions with a spatula to plates and spoon reserved juices and chilled fruit mixture around them.

Serve pudding with sour cream *mascarpone*. Serves 4 generously.

Sour Cream Mascarpone

½ cup sour cream
½ cup *mascarpone**
2 tablespoons confectioners' sugar, or to taste

*available at specialty foods shops and some supermarkets

In a small bowl whisk together sour cream, *mascarpone*, and confectioners' sugar. *Mixture may be made 1 day ahead and chilled, covered.* Makes about 1 cup.

Pumpkin Bread Pudding with Cranberry Caramel Sauce

1 loaf pumpkin cranberry bread
  (page 112)
For ginger custard
⅓ cup minced peeled fresh gingerroot
¾ cup sugar
2 tablespoons water
2 cups milk
1 cup heavy cream
3 large whole eggs
3 large egg yolks

Accompaniment: cranberry caramel sauce
  (recipe follows)

Preheat oven to 350° F. and butter a 9- by 2-inch round cake pan. Line cake pan with a round of wax paper and butter wax paper.

Cut enough ¼-inch-thick slices from loaf to line side of cake pan, trimming slices so that tops are flush with rim of pan. Gently press slices against side of cake pan to make them adhere.

Cut enough of remaining loaf, including scraps, into ½-inch pieces to measure 5 cups and put in bottom of cake pan.

Make custard:
In a heavy saucepan bring gingerroot, sugar, and water to a boil, stirring until sugar is dissolved, and simmer 5 minutes. Add milk and cream and bring just to a simmer. Remove pan from heat.

In a heatproof bowl whisk together whole eggs and yolks and add hot milk mixture in a stream, whisking. Pour custard through a fine sieve onto bread pieces in bottom of cake pan, pressing hard on gingerroot, and coat pieces well (bread pieces will float to surface of custard).

Put cake pan in a larger pan and add enough water to larger pan to reach halfway up side of cake pan. Bake pudding in middle of oven 45 to 50 minutes, or until custard is set and a skewer inserted in center comes out clean. Remove cake pan from larger pan and cool pudding on a rack. *Chill pudding, covered, until cold, at least 4 hours and up to 1 day.*

To unmold pudding, run a thin knife around edge of cake pan and dip pan into a bowl of hot water 15 seconds. Invert a large plate over cake pan and invert pudding onto plate. Peel off wax paper and invert pudding right side up onto another large plate. Bring pudding to room temperature and cut into wedges. (If serving pudding warm, transfer wedges to a baking sheet and reheat in a 325° F. oven.)

Serve pudding at room temperature or warm with caramel sauce. Serves 6 generously.

PHOTO ON PAGE 71

Cranberry Caramel Sauce

1 cup picked-over fresh or frozen cranberries
1½ cups sugar
½ cup water

In a food processor purée cranberries and transfer to a small bowl.

In a dry heavy saucepan cook sugar over moderate heat, stirring with a fork, until melted and cook, without stirring, swirling pan, until a golden caramel. Remove pan from heat and carefully add water and cranberry purée (caramel will steam and harden). Return pan to heat and simmer sauce, stirring, 10 minutes, or until caramel is dissolved. Pour sauce through a fine sieve into a heatproof bowl, pressing hard on solids, and cool completely.

Sauce may be made 4 days ahead and chilled, covered. Bring sauce to room temperature before serving. Makes about 1½ cups.

Apricot Soufflés with Vanilla Rum Crème Anglaise

6 ounces dried apricots
   (about 1½ cups)
1½ cups water
¾ cups sugar plus additional for coating
   ramekins
1 tablespoon fresh lemon juice
1 tablespoon dark rum if desired
½ teaspoon vanilla
5 large egg whites
¼ teaspoon cream of tartar

Accompaniment: vanilla rum *crème anglaise*
   (recipe follows)

In a heavy saucepan simmer apricots, water, and ½ cup sugar, covered, 20 minutes. Transfer hot mixture to a food processor and purée until very smooth. Force purée through a fine sieve into a bowl and stir in lemon juice, rum, vanilla, and a pinch salt. Cool purée completely. *Purée may be made 2 days ahead and chilled, covered. Bring purée to room temperature before proceeding.* Transfer purée to a large bowl.

Preheat oven to 350° F. Generously butter six 7-ounce (3½- by 1¾-inch) ramekins and coat with additional sugar, knocking out excess.

In another large bowl with an electric mixer beat whites with a pinch salt until foamy. Beat in cream of tartar and beat whites until they hold soft peaks. Beat in remaining ¼ cup sugar, a little at a time, and beat meringue until it just holds stiff peaks. Whisk about one fourth meringue into purée to lighten and fold in remaining meringue gently but thoroughly. Ladle batter into ramekins and bake soufflés on a baking sheet in middle of oven 20 to 25 minutes, or until puffed, golden brown, and just set in center.

Remove ramekins from oven. With 2 forks pull open center of each soufflé and pour some *crème anglaise* into each opening. Serve soufflés immediately. Serves 6.

PHOTO ON PAGE 29

Vanilla Rum Crème Anglaise

2 cups half-and-half
½ vanilla bean, split lengthwise
5 large egg yolks
¼ cup sugar
1 tablespoon dark rum, or to taste

In a small heavy saucepan bring half-and-half just to a boil with vanilla bean and remove pan from heat. With a knife scrape seeds from bean into half-and-half, discarding pod.

In a bowl whisk together yolks, sugar, and a pinch salt and whisk in hot half-and-half in a stream. Transfer custard to pan and cook over moderately low heat, stirring constantly with a wooden spoon, until thickened (170° F. on a candy thermometer), but do not boil. Pour sauce through a fine sieve into a bowl and cool, stirring occasionally. Stir in rum. *Chill sauce, covered, until very cold, at least 2 hours and up to 2 days.* Makes about 2¼ cups.

Regular and sweet basmati rice have the same flavor and texture. For a whiter pudding use the sweet variey, available at East Indian markets and by mail order from Kalustyan's, 123 Lexington Avenue, New York, NY 10016, tel. (212) 685-3451.

Chilled Banana and Pistachio Rice Pudding

1 cup long-grain *hasmati* rice (preferably sweet)
½ cup shelled natural pistachios
1 tablespoon unsalted butter
1 teaspoon ground cardamom
¼ teaspoon cinnamon
¼ teaspoon freshly grated nutmeg
¾ cup sugar
3 cups whole milk
2 cups heavy cream
2 bananas, cut into ¼-inch dice

Garnish: about ¼ cup shelled natural pistachios

Accompaniment: melon compote (page 226)

In a bowl soak rice in cold water to cover 30 minutes and drain in a sieve. Rinse rice under cold water and drain.

In a small saucepan blanch pistachios in boiling water 3 minutes and drain in a sieve. Rinse pistachios under cold water and pat dry. Rub off skins and chop nuts coarse.

In a heavy 3-quart saucepan melt butter over low heat and cook cardamom, cinnamon, nutmeg, and sugar, stirring, 1 minute. Add rice, milk, and cream and simmer gently, uncovered, stirring occasionally, until rice is tender, about 18 to 20 minutes.

Cool rice pudding and transfer to a serving dish. Stir in chopped pistachios and bananas. *Chill rice pudding, covered, until cold, at least 4 hours and up to 2 days.*

Garnish pudding with whole pistachios and serve with compote. Serves 6.

PHOTO ON PAGE 2

BEVERAGES

White Sangría

⅓ cup fresh lemon juice
⅓ cup fresh lime juice
1 cup fresh orange juice
1 cup seltzer or club soda
1½ cups ginger ale
a 750-ml. bottle dry white wine, chilled
½ cup Pimm's Cup
1 navel orange, cut into wedges
1 lemon, cut into wedges

In a large pitcher stir together citrus juices, seltzer or club soda, ginger ale, wine, Pimm's, and half of orange and lemon wedges.

Add ice cubes and serve white sangría with remaining orange and lemon wedges. Makes about 8 cups, serving 6.

🍃 Each serving about 192 calories,
0 grams fat

PHOTO ON PAGE 41

Cider and Tequila Hot Toddies

4 cups apple cider
1 cup cranberry juice cocktail
½ cup Tequila
¼ cup triple sec or other orange-flavored liqueur

Garnish: lime slices

In a saucepan heat cider and cranberry juice cocktail just until hot (do not boil) and remove from heat. Stir in Tequila and liqueur. Serve toddies in mugs, garnished with lime slices. Makes about 6 cups, serving 6.

PHOTO ON PAGE 17

Amaretto Mimosas

3 cups fresh orange juice, strained
¼ cup almond-flavored liqueur such as
    Amaretto di Saronno, or to taste
a 750-ml. bottle chilled sparkling wine
    such as Freixenet

In a pitcher stir together orange juice and liqueur. Fill each of 6 Champagne flutes halfway with some juice mixture and top off with sparkling wine. Makes about 12 drinks.

Lemon Shandies

1 cup sugar
3 cups water
four 3-inch strips lemon zest, removed
    with a vegetable peeler
1 cup fresh lemon juice
2 fresh mint sprigs
chilled beer, such as pale ale

In a small saucepan bring sugar and 1 cup water to a boil, stirring until sugar is dissolved, and stir in zest. Cool sugar syrup to room temperature.

Transfer syrup to a pitcher and stir in remaining 2 cups water, lemon juice, and mint. Chill lemonade until cold. (Makes about 4½ cups lemonade.)

Pour ¼ cup lemonade, or to taste, into each of 4 chilled beer glasses and top off with beer. Serves 4.

PHOTO ON PAGE 53

Mojito with Basil
(Rum, Lime, Mint, and Basil Cocktail)

2 fresh mint sprigs, chopped
2 fresh basil sprigs, chopped
1 tablespoon sugar
3 tablespoons fresh lime juice
1½ ounces (3 tablespoons) light rum
chilled club soda or seltzer

Garnishes: fresh mint and basil sprigs and
   lime slices

In a tall glass with back of a spoon crush mint and basil with sugar and lime juice until sugar is dissolved and stir in rum. Add ice cubes and top off drink with club soda or seltzer.

Stir drink well and garnish with mint, basil, and lime. Makes 1 drink.

🍃 Each serving about 155 calories,
0 grams fat

PHOTO ON PAGE 6

Bloody Mary

1 ounce (2 tablespoons) vodka
⅔ cup tomato juice
drained bottled horseradish to taste
Worcestershire sauce to taste
Tabasco sauce to taste
celery salt to taste
freshly ground black pepper to taste

Garnishes: lemon wedge, celery rib and/or
   cucumber stick

In a tall glass filled with ice cubes combine vodka and tomato juice and stir in seasonings. Garnish Bloody Mary with lemon wedge and celery rib and/or cucumber stick. Makes 1 drink.

PHOTO ON PAGE 24

Frozen Cappuccinos

1 cup freshly brewed espresso, cooled to room
   temperature
2 cups ice cubes

¼ cup half-and-half or whole milk
3 tablespoons superfine sugar, or to taste
¼ teaspoon cinnamon
¼ cup Kahlúa or other coffee-flavored liqueur
   if desired

Garnish: cinnamon

In a blender blend all ingredients until smooth but still thick. Divide mixture between 2 tall glasses and sprinkle with cinnamon. Makes 2 drinks.

Pineapple Mint Frozen Daiquiris

⅓ cup light or amber rum, or to taste
1½ cups 1-inch pineapple chunks
2 tablespoons superfine sugar, or to taste
2 teaspoons fresh lime juice, or to taste
3 fresh mint leaves
2 cups ice cubes

Garnish: mint sprigs and/or pineapple chunks
   skewered with wooden picks

In a blender blend all ingredients until smooth but still thick. Divide mixture between 2 large stemmed glasses and garnish with mint and/or pineapple. Makes 2 drinks.

Spiced Red Zinger Rum Punch

a 2-inch piece fresh gingerroot
5½ cups water
½ cup sugar
1 cinnamon stick
4 whole cloves
10 Celestial Seasonings Red Zinger
   tea bags
¾ cup amber rum, or to taste
1 navel orange, sliced

Peel gingerroot and cut crosswise into thin slices. In a medium saucepan boil water, gingerroot, sugar, cinnamon stick, and cloves, stirring, until sugar is dissolved. Add tea bags and remove pan from heat. Steep tea until cool.

Discard tea bags and cinnamon stick and transfer tea to a pitcher. *Chill tea, covered, at least 12 hours and up to 1 day.* Remove gingerroot and cloves with a slotted spoon and discard. Stir in amber rum and orange slices.

Serve punch over ice in stemmed glasses. Makes about 6½ cups.

NON-ALCOHOLIC

Frosted Double Chocolate Malted

5 tablespoons malted milk powder
1 tablespoon easy dark chocolate sauce
   (page 201)
⅔ cup cold milk
about 1 pint good-quality-premium chocolate
   ice cream (not super-premium)

In a milk-shake mixer or blender blend malted milk powder, chocolate sauce, and milk at low speed until smooth. Add ice cream and blend 10 to 15 seconds, or until thick and slushy. Pour mixture into 2 tall glasses. Serves 2.

Black Cows

2 tablespoons chocolate syrup
4 to 6 scoops super-premium vanilla ice cream
8 to 12 ounces root beer

Accompaniment if desired: whipped cream

In each of 2 tall glasses stir together 1 tablespoon chocolate syrup and 1 scoop ice cream until mixture is just combined but still frozen. Pour about ¼ cup root beer down side of each glass. To each glass add 1 or 2 more scoops ice cream and enough root beer to just top glass with foam. Serves 2.

Sparkling Mango Limeade

3 ripe mangoes (about 2½ pounds total)
1½ cups fresh lime juice
1½ cups water
1 cup superfine sugar plus additional to taste
seltzer or club soda

Garnish: lime wedges

Peel mangoes and cut flesh from pits. In a blender purée mango flesh with lime juice, water, and 1 cup sugar until smooth.

Force purée through a sieve into a pitcher or bowl, pressing on any solids. Chill purée, covered, until cold and stir in additional sugar. (Purée will be slightly thick. Makes about 5½ cups limeade purée.) *Limeade purée keeps, covered and chilled, 2 days.*

Fill tall glasses with ice and add enough limeade purée to fill each glass by three quarters. Top off drinks with seltzer or club soda, stirring well, and garnish with lime wedges.

Orange Berry Coolers

2 cups strawberries, hulled
2 cups raspberries, picked over
2½ cups fresh orange juice
½ cup superfine sugar plus additional
   to taste
1 tablespoon fresh lime juice, or to taste
seltzer or club soda

In a blender blend berries, orange juice, ½ cup superfine sugar, and lime juice until smooth. Force purée through a fine sieve into a large measuring cup or bowl, pressing hard on solids. Chill purée, covered, until cold and stir in additional sugar. (Makes about 5 cups berry purée.) *Purée keeps, covered and chilled, 2 days.*

Fill tall glasses with ice and add enough berry purée to fill each glass by three quarters. Top off drinks with seltzer or club soda and stir well.

233

Iced Lemon Ginger "Tea"

a 4-inch piece fresh gingerroot
6 cups water
½ cup honey
½ cup sugar
zest of 2 lemons, removed with a
     vegetable peeler
1 cup fresh lemon juice

Garnish: lemon slices

Peel gingerroot and cut crosswise into thin slices. In a medium saucepan boil water, gingerroot, honey, sugar, and zest, stirring, until sugar is dissolved. Remove pan from heat and steep "tea," covered, 45 minutes. Uncover tea and cool completely.

Remove gingerroot and zest with a slotted spoon and discard. Transfer tea to a pitcher and stir in lemon juice. *Chill tea, covered, until cold and up to 2 days.*

Serve tea over ice in tall glasses and garnish with lemon slices. Makes about 7 cups.

Coconut and Mint Lassi
(Savory Yogurt Cooler)

4 cups well-stirred canned unsweetened coconut
     milk*
4 cups well-chilled plain yogurt
½ cup packed fresh mint leaves, washed well,
     spun dry, and sliced thin
1 cup unsweetened dessicated coconut*, lightly
     toasted

*available at Asian markets, natural foods stores,
     and some supermarkets

In a bowl whisk together coconut milk, yogurt, and salt and pepper to taste and stir in mint and ¾ cup coconut. Pour *lassi* into chilled glasses and sprinkle with remaining ¼ cup coconut. Makes about 9 cups.

PHOTO ON PAGE 60

Coriander, Ginger, and Chili Lassi
(Spicy Yogurt Cooler)

4 cups well-chilled plain yogurt
1 cup fresh coriander sprigs, washed well,
     spun dry, and chopped coarse
1 tablespoon chopped peeled fresh gingerroot
1 fresh *serrano* chili, seeded and chopped
     (wear rubber gloves)
1 teaspoon ground cumin

In a blender blend together *lassi* ingredients until smooth and pale green, about 1 minute. Serve *lassi* in chilled glasses. Makes about 5 cups.

PHOTO ON PAGE 60

CUISINES OF
THE WORLD

THE FLAVORS OF
GREECE

Azure water as far as the eye can see; plaintive melodies of a bouzouki at a Volos wedding; elderly shepherds fingering their worry beads outside the kafeneia in Metsovo; wrinkled old village women gossiping over their embroidery; chic Athenians lunching alfresco at a trendy ouzeri; time-worn stone fortresses on the Peloponnese; endless sweet-scented lemon groves on Crete — Greece is a land of striking impressions. Beyond the magnificence of such a beautiful and vital land and the resonance of its history, there is the feeling of a place where the pleasures of everyday life are appreciated, particularly when it comes to eating.

In fact, food has always been at the center of Greek life. A distinct Greek cuisine began to develop with the advent of the Minoan civilization on Crete and Santorini. Trade with North Africa brought onions and dates to the islands, and land was cleared for grapevines and olive groves. In classical times, culinary culture thrived and the art of dining and dinner party conversation became a part of civilized society. When the Roman Empire supplanted Athens in importance on the world stage, Greeks were employed as teachers and chefs. Later, with the expansion of the Byzantine Empire, centered in Constantinople, Greek culinary influence spread north and east throughout the Balkans and the area that is now Turkey. Naturally, in turn, Greek cuisine absorbed foreign flavors.

During Greece's "dark years," a succession of invasions by Franks, Venetians, Vlachs, Slavs, and Ottomans caused great turbulence, and the cuisine further evolved with the introduction of various new crops and spices. When the Byzantine Empire fell to the Ottomans in the 15th Century, Eastern influence was strictly imposed, as evinced by Turkish names used for foods and preparations. During the 400 years of Ottoman rule, however, traditional Greek culture and culinary practices were preserved in the monasteries, and, after the fall of the Ottoman empire, many dishes were renamed once again. Over the centuries — due to occupation, war, and trade — lemons, potatoes, eggplants, tomatoes, spinach, and okra were assimilated into the cuisine.

In the late 1920s an influential Greek chef, Nicholas Tselementes, attempted to refine Greek peasant cooking by eliminating the spices associated with the Ottomans. The result, many believe, did more harm to traditional Greek cooking

The Acropolis

than good. In recent years, mechanization, export demands, and inexpensive European imports have reduced the number of "ancient" (traditional) crops. Western influences also have taken a toll: The American hamburger has replaced *souvlaki* as the favorite "fast food." Luckily, there is renewed interest, especially among chefs and cooking enthusiasts, in preserving the authentic culinary treasures of Greece. For now, though, *tavernas* (family-style restaurants) and Greek homes are still the best places to find such fare.

Today, enjoying aromatic, colorful dishes and lively conversation with family and friends is an essential part of everyday life in Greece. Meals are true social events, and many dishes are prepared in advance so that everyone can enjoy each other as well as the food. In the villages, where life is more relaxed, the main meal of the day begins in the afternoon and lasts for hours. A table is usually set up in a shaded courtyard, and *mezedes* (appetizers) are put out to nibble on with a glass of *ouzo* (the anise-flavored liquor) or wine. After an hour or so, bread, salad, and a main course are added. Family and guests alike are expected to serve themselves a succession of small helpings and to pass, as needed, their empty wine glasses to the host for refilling. Fresh fruit and cheese are served at the end of the meal; later still, pastries, syruped fruits, or candies are savored away from the dinner table with coffee.

Authentic Greek cooking is not fussy. The cuisine is based on freshness — the purity of domestically grown produce is of utmost importance — and sauces and seasonings never overpower a dish. Since the climate is temperate, there are two harvests a year — in the spring and fall — that allow for bountiful crops. Greeks love their fruit (figs, grapes, plums, cherries, peaches, apricots), vegetables (zucchini, onions, carrots, beets, artichokes, peas), greens (dandelions, mustard greens, chicory, chard, arugula, romaine), and herbs (oregano, thyme, mint). Various regions also are exceptionally well-suited for vineyards, and olive and lemon groves cover many areas. As there are literally thousands of miles of coastlines and hundreds of islands, it is no wonder that seafood (octopus, squid, red mullet, shrimp, swordfish) is a staple. And, although meat is limited in the daily diet, the shepherding of sheep and goats keeps the passion for lamb dishes and cheese satisfied.

Since freshness is key, Greeks mainly eat seasonal foods, but certain items are dried (fish, herbs, legumes, and tomatoes) or preserved (fruits, honey, olives, vegetables) for year-round use. These long-lasting foodstuffs are indispensable on remote islands. Although harvests determine the ingredients featured in a season, it is the Greek Orthodox Church that sets the patterns of fasting and feasting throughout the year. Lent and Advent are times of privation, followed by the explosion of festive rich dishes during Easter and Christmas. Breads for holy days, in particular, take on many different forms during the year.

On the following pages we discuss the basics of Greek cooking, including herbs, spices, and other essential flavors; cheeses and dairy foods; and the ubiquitous tissue-thin pastry sheets, phyllo. Three menus offer a variety of dining experiences — the Easter and Santorini menus are typical of those found in Greek homes today, while the *mezedes* cocktail party, although it contains many traditional dishes, is a bit more improvisational.

To celebrate Easter, the highlight of the religious and culinary year, we present a feast of favorite Greek dishes to enjoy all afternoon and well into the evening. The holiday table boasts the family's best linen and china as well as a bowl of red-dyed eggs, the traditional Greek Easter symbol of new life. To start, there are three *mezedes* — a zucchini and onion pie, carp-roe spread, and stuffed grape leaves. Then, a luscious lamb fricassee (using lamb shoulder) with *horta* (greens) and *avgolemono* (egg and lemon sauce) substitutes for the more common spit-grilled spring lamb. (Fricassee was once the Easter dish of the Cycladic islands before spit-grilled lamb, the preferred entrée of the area around Athens, became the norm.) Side dishes include classic roasted potatoes with olive oil, lemon, garlic, and oregano; an artichoke, pea, and carrot mixture drizzled with *avgolemono*; and a romaine, arugula, and watercress salad dressed with a bit of lemon juice, extra-virgin olive oil, and dill seed. We conclude with the quintessential Greek dessert, *baklava*, as well as *kaltsounakia* (sweet cheese pies), individual pastries filled with farmer cheese and feta.

Few settings are as spectacular as the island of Santorini, the inspiration for our summer dinner, where meals are ideally served on a terrace overlooking the sea. Since this small isle has limited natural food supplies, dishes are simple and straightforward. Tomatoes are left out in the sun to dry, and our *domatokeftedes* (tomato patties) are brimming with their intense flavor. Dried yellow split peas are combined with scallions, capers, and oregano to make a luscious fava spread that is typical of the island. (Note that in Greece "fava" refers to a dish of creamy puréed yellow or green split peas, not fava (broad) beans.) Locally caught *barbounia* (red mullet), grilled and sauced, is also a specialty here; we offer this fish as the centerpiece of our meal (red snapper may be substituted). Two salads — a beet and greens salad and a country tomato salad with feta — as well as stuffed baby eggplant offer make-ahead accompaniments that can be served at room temperature. Hours later, the evening concludes with grilled fresh figs and soft Manouri cheese drizzled with thyme honey.

Finally, we turn to our cocktail party featuring *mezedes*. Although *mezedes* appear on tables throughout Greece as tasty tidbits before a meal, in recent years, Athenian *ouzeris* (cafés) have become popular spots where a collection of these little dishes are often ordered for dinner. Our buffet is a feast featuring many of these favorites, some with new twists. We've included seafood dishes: salt cod fritters with *skordalia* (our garlic sauce has the consistency of a spread) and grilled octopus with plenty of oregano (octopus can be purchased frozen from many fishmongers); lamb and beef meatballs; stewed large lima beans with tomatoes; roasted pearl onions with honey and vinegar glaze; familiar phyllo triangles filled with greens and two cheeses; and three essentials — olives and feta in herbed lemon olive oil; eggplant spread; and cucumber yogurt dip. Should you wish to indulge, there is even a heavenly creamy orange cinnamon rice pudding finale. Although we've included a number of different *mezedes*, most can be prepared ahead of time (like many Greek dishes, the flavor actually improves). For maximum flexibility, all recipes can be doubled, so you may want to eliminate a dish or two and double-up on others.

Let the Flavors of Greece take you to a sunny land where a handful of pure ingredients are combined without fuss in healthful, delicious ways. Often simple things are the best; certainly this is true of the foods of Greece.

HERBS, SPICES, AND OTHER ESSENTIALS

When Greek cooking is reduced to its basic elements, the ingredients that stand out above all are olive oil, lemon juice, garlic, and oregano. Mixed together to marinate fish or dress a country salad, they capture the essence of Greek cuisine. Other seasonings such as cinnamon, cloves, mint, and dill frequently punctuate sweet and savory dishes, adding liveliness. Typically, however, herbs and spices are used with restraint; rarely do more than two or three appear in a dish. Complex, layered spice mixtures that characterize other Eastern Mediterranean cuisines aren't employed here. Instead, the best cooks rely on freshness and the pure, simple goodness of their ingredients — briny fish and seafood, mountain-raised lamb, and vegetables or greens picked straight from the garden or in the wild.

Traditionally, aromatic herbs are gathered from the hillsides and dried for use throughout the year.

Herbs grown amid arid rock and limestone under the searing summer sun become fragrant and pungent, and drying them further concentrates their flavor. While many Mediterranean cuisines rely on fresh herbs, in Greece dried herbs are preferred (with the exception of parsley, dill, and sometimes mint). Oregano and thyme, for instance, always are dried.

Other herbs are used in unexpected ways. Although white-washed pots of basil decorate the courtyards of nearly every Greek home, the herb rarely makes an appearance in the kitchen. Instead, it is reputed to be an effective bug repellent. Dried herbs often are brewed for healthful beverages or home remedies: mint is favored at breakfast, chamomile makes a calming evening drink, and sage, although sometimes used to season meats, more commonly aids digestion. In rural areas, cooks still heat their domed ovens with fragrant brushwood,

243

vine cuttings, and herb branches for baking bread. Likewise, outdoor roasts for celebrations require little preparation of the meat: The lambs or kids have fed on scrub scented with wild herbs and they are spit-roasted over flames fueled with equally aromatic herbs, vines, and olive wood.

Greek dishes benefit from one intangible ingredient: resting time. With the exception of grilled meats and fish, many taste better the next day after their flavors have had a chance to blend and intensify. In particular, Greek "salads" (a term used to describe a variety of dips, spreads, as well as vegetable combinations) improve with time. Likewise, the flavors of our *melitzanosalata* (eggplant spread, page 273), *gigantes* (stewed large lima beans with tomatoes, page 275), and *arni fricassee* (lamb stew with greens, page 256), are enhanced when made ahead. Many dishes also are at their best when served at room temperature. Throughout Greece, cooks prepare foods in advance (often before the heat of midday), allow them to rest, then serve them later at room temperature. The dishes are seasoned as they are prepared and salted and peppered again, as needed, just before they are put on the table.

For authentic flavor, you'll need to seek out a good Greek, Mediterranean, or Middle Eastern market for some special ingredients: bottles of green to golden olive oil, authentic cheeses (page 247), fresh-baked pita bread, flavorful herbs and spices (Greek dried herbs are much more potent than those found in supermarkets), a wide assortment of olives, and especially *tarama* (salted fish roe) and spoon sweets (fruit preserves in very sweet syrup) which aren't available elsewhere. To find a Greek market near you, try contacting a Greek Orthodox church in your area. There also are several good mail-order sources listed on page 249.

Herbs and spices:

Cinnamon (kanella) flavors both sweet and savory dishes. The ground meat mixtures of *keftedakia* (lamb and beef meatballs, page 274) and *moussaka*, as well as desserts such as *rizogalo* (rice pudding, page 277), are always seasoned with a bit of ground cinnamon or a cinnamon stick.

Cloves (moskokarfi) decorate and flavor desserts. Diamond-shaped pieces of *baklava* (page 258) are often studded with a whole clove. A pinch of ground cloves or nutmeg is sometimes added to greens, stuffings, and ground meat mixtures.

Dill (anitho) sprigs and dried dill seed enliven salads, fish, greens, vegetables, and pickles.

Garlic (skordo), pounded in a mortar with olive oil and lemon juice, is the base of many Greek dishes. Garlic is employed as a seasoning in marinades and sauces, and even as a cure-all remedy. Since garlic is frequently uncooked, choose only fresh, young, firm garlic without any green sprouts.

Mint (diosmos) is milder fresh than dried. Either way, it is used generously in salads, such as *tzatziki* (page 272), and in fillings for stuffed vegetables. Dried leaves are brewed for morning tea.

Oregano (rigani), the most pervasive Greek seasoning, is always dried, since fresh oregano can be bitter. Greek or Mediterranean dried oregano found in Greek markets is fresher, sweeter, and more fragrant than the usual supermarket variety. It is sold dried in bunches; crumble the leaves from the branches as needed.

Thyme (thymari), a peppery herb similar to oregano but more subtly flavored, is usually dried to season grilled or roasted meats and fish. It can be used interchangeably with oregano.

OTHER ESSENTIALS:

Capers *(kapari)* are the buds of a shrub that grows wild along stone walls or rocks in the Mediterranean region. Small capers preserved in vinegar make a flavorful garnish for dishes such as *fava Santorinis* (yellow split pea spread, page 264).

Grape Leaves *(ambelofila)* not only are tasty wrappers for *dolmades* (stuffed grape leaves, page 255), but also protect foods during grilling. Small poultry and fish benefit from a grape leaf wrapping, which keeps them from charring and imparts delicate flavor. Grape leaves packed in brine are available in most supermarkets.

Honey *(meli).* Greece's most famous honey is from Mount Hymettus, near Athens. Although it can vary, Greek honey tastes predominantly of wild herbs and thyme. Substitute any fragrant amber or clover honey. We flavor honey with fresh thyme in *manouri me meli ke fistikia* (manouri cheese with thyme honey and pistachios, page 267).

Olives *(elies).* The quintessential Greek table olive is the purple-black, almond-shaped Kalamata. Cured in brine and wine vinegar, then soaked in olive oil, Kalamatas are firm and succulent. Other varieties include the giant fleshy *Atalandis*; round and sweet *Amfissas*; and meaty oily salt-cured *Thasos*. Cracked green olives are often flavored with lemon or herbs.

Olive Oil *(ladi).* In Greece, the best quality olive oil is cold-pressed from olives grown in the vicinity of the city of Kalamata, in the Peloponesse, or near the town of Hania, in Crete. Greek extra-virgin oil is mellow, green-golden, clean-flavored, and peppery-tasting. Unfortunately, the finest oils are rarely exported. There are, however, about fifteen Greek brands of quality extra-virgin oil imported to America in small quantities. We recommend the *Horia* brand.

Spoon Sweets *(gliko)* are fruit preserves in very sweet syrup. Sour cherry spoon sweets can be bought at Greek markets (try the *Kronos* brand). Home cooks, however, make their own from several different fruits: Muscat grapes, quinces, and green walnuts are popular. Spoon sweets traditionally are served on a saucer accompanied by a glass of cold spring water to welcome guests. We mix spoon sweets with soda water for *vissinada* (sour cherry drink, page 264).

Tarama, the pale pink roe of carp or grey mullet preserved in salt, was originally eaten only during Lent or on fast days. With the addition of olive oil and a few other ingredients, it becomes *taramosalata* (carp-roe spread, page 254).

Vinegar *(xsithi).* The homemade or artisanally produced red-wine vinegars of Greece are less acidic and somewhat sweeter than commercially produced vinegars. Since Greek vinegars aren't available in the U.S., we suggest trying Italian balsamic vinegar mixed with a little red-wine vinegar or lemon juice.

Wild Greens *(horta)* are picked on the hillsides or in the fields before the plants flower. Bitter greens —mustard greens, chicory, dandelion greens, escarole, Swiss chard, or a mix of pungent greens— are cooked to make them milder. They are baked in phyllo, such as our *hortopitakia* (phyllo triangles filled with mustard greens, page 276); cooked in stews, such as our *arni fricassee* (lamb fricassee with dandelion greens, page 256); or are simply boiled and dressed with lemon juice and olive oil. Purslane, watercress, arugula, and other young, tender field greens are usually eaten raw in salads. Many greens, naturally full of vitamins and minerals, are thought to have medicinal properties.

CHEESES AND DAIRY FOODS

Shepherds have always been a part of Greek life. Myths of the gods as revealed by the constellations were woven by these solitary men, and only twice yearly, in the spring and fall, did their labor come to fruition at the time of cheese-making. Today, the best traditional Greek cheeses are still made from sheep's or goat's milk in the seasonal cycle, employing the same methods used for thousands of years. Although national brands and imported cheeses are increasingly available in Greece, artisanally produced cheeses continue to be made in villages. Unfortunately, few of these delicious cheeses are exported widely, although you may find them in areas that have strong Greek communities.

Cheese is an integral part of the Greek diet. It is enjoyed at breakfast and lunch with a bit of bread; in the evenings, the most basic *mezedes* (appetizer) combination is feta with plump black olives to accompany a glass of *ouzo* or wine. Dessert usually consists of cheese and fruit. Fresh white farmer or pot cheeses are eaten within days of being made, and there is also a tradition of aged cheeses. Creamy, thick Greek yogurt is a passion here, an altogether different experience from the American version. It is eaten plain, or with fruit, honey, or a spoonful of sweet preserves, or in salads like *tzatziki* (page 272). Cheeses are used in various dishes as well, from toppings for stuffed vegetables to fillings for savory and sweet phyllo pies. Easter specialties, such as *kaltsounakia* (sweet cheese pies, page 259), are traditionally made with several cheeses, many of which are freshly produced in the spring.

The widest selection of Greek cheeses can be found in Greek markets. Specialty cheese stores and some supermarkets normally stock feta and some firm varieties like *kasseri*. Middle Eastern stores carry yogurt made in the Greek style, feta, and perhaps *haloumi*. When buying any imported cheese, it is best to find a shop with frequent turnover for maximum freshness, and where you can taste before you buy.

Yogurt (giaourti). Greek yogurt, made from sheep's milk, is much thicker, creamier, and richer-tasting than American yogurt, which is made from cow's milk. *To use American yogurt in Greek recipes it must be drained*: put it in a sieve or colander lined with cheesecloth set over a bowl and chill, covered, at least 8 hours and up to 24. Use plain or low-fat yogurt (not nonfat), without thickeners or stabilizers. In Greece, yogurt is made in large clay pots, which adds a distinctive taste, and has a thick crust from the cream that rises to the top. Greek style yogurt made in America (usually from cow's milk) also has a creamy crust and is delicious, as are sheep's and goat's milk yogurts, available from regional dairies (mail order sources, page 249). However, they may not drain as well as American-style brands.

Manouri, a soft, fresh whey cheese, has fresh cream or milk added to make it creamy and rich. Very lightly salted, *manouri* is eaten with honey and fruit for an incredibly delicious dessert; or sprinkle it with salt and thyme, drizzle with olive oil, and serve with olives. In some Greek stores it may be labelled *mizithra*. However, since *mizithra* may be aged, make sure you're buying a fresh cheese. The best substitute is *ricotta salata*.

Feta, the best known Greek cheese, is a soft, creamy, tangy white cheese traditionally made from sheep's milk and preserved in brine, which imparts its characteristic salty taste. Served at most meals, feta provides the essential salty component to complement the mild seasoning of most Greek dishes. In Greece, farmhouse versions made from goat's milk are firm and sharp. Feta is widely available and most Greek or Middle Eastern markets offer choices from several different countries: Bulgarian is often the best; French and Israeli are quite good. Much of the feta labelled Greek is

actually made in Sardinia, or elsewhere in Italy, and is generally of good quality. The feta in most supermarkets is made from cow's milk and can be bland and chalky or, alternately, quite pungent.

Haloumi, a white salty chewy sheep cheese usually seasoned with mint, is especially popular in Cyprus but is enjoyed throughout Greece and in the Balkans. It is often grilled or sautéed for serving on grilled bread or shaved with a vegetable peeler to top salads. Although delicious, it has an unusual texture and squeaks as you chew it.

Kasseri, a semi-hard spun-curd cheese made from sheep's milk, is soft, pale yellow, and oily. The most popular cheese in Greece (outselling even feta), it is eaten as a table cheese with fruit, tossed in salads, sprinkled on casseroles, and used to top pizza.

Kefalograviera, a hard oily cheese, is made in several regions of Greece. The best ones are from Crete or from Naxos, where they are made from sheep's milk or from a combination of sheep's milk and cow's milk. It is served as a table cheese.

Kefalotyri, which literally means head cheese, is a large hard yellow sheep's milk cheese similar to *kasseri*. However, since it is aged longer, it is nuttier, saltier, and more flavorful. *Pecorino* from Sardinia or Tuscany (not *Pecorino Romano*) can be used as a substitute.

L. MAESTRO

PHYLLO

Many of Greece's favorite dishes, *mezedes,* main courses, and desserts included — are made with phyllo (meaning "leaf") dough. Homemade phyllo is rolled or stretched out very thin, buttered or oiled, and stacked. As it bakes, the layers puff up and separate into a crisp, buttery pastry crust or shell.

Arguably the best phyllo today is still made in Metsovo, in northern Greece, where the women have perfected the art of making paper-thin sheets of dough with flour, water, and a bit of olive oil, usually to enclose local wild greens in spiral-shaped pies. Tools of the trade include their nimble fingers, special round boards, and extra-long rolling pins. In other parts of Greece, particularly in the villages, people gather to make phyllo. On Icaria, a remote Aegean island, at least two people stretch the dough by swinging it around and around on their fists to see how thin it can be pulled without tearing.

Fortunately, commercial phyllo is an excellent substitute. Although phyllo is readily available in the freezer case at specialty foods stores and most supermarkets, for easiest handling it is best to buy it fresh in Greek markets where the turnover is high. Phyllo dough comes in one-pound packages, and an unopened box keeps in the refrigerator for several weeks and in the freezer for months. We recommend the Apollo brand (available in most supermarkets) for most recipes and the Athens Foods brand (available in Greek and Middle Eastern markets), a slightly thicker pastry, for recipes that require more handling.

Phyllo requires special care: If frozen, it should be thawed in its unopened box in the refrigerator for eight hours or overnight and then brought to room temperature (still in the box) for about 2 hours. (If the phyllo is stored in the refrigerator, bring it to room temperature before using.) Carefully unroll the sheets onto a dry surface and immediately cover them with a piece of plastic wrap and a kitchen towel to keep them from drying out and cracking. Use a pastry brush or feather to butter each sheet separately on a work surface, brushing the edge first to avoid cracking. Then, working from the center out, brush any wrinkles toward the edge. Work as quickly as possible with each exposed sheet.

Perhaps one of the most popular ways to use this dough is in phyllo triangles (see our version, *hortopitakia*, page 276). These delicate *mezedes* require quite a bit of handling, however, so we recommend using the thicker Athens Foods brand phyllo. And, since you will be working with two buttered phyllo strips at a time, you must work quickly to keep the dough pliable. Once the triangles are formed, they can be frozen on baking sheets before being stored in freezer bags. As with many foods made with phyllo, our triangles freeze beautifully — the pastry remains light and crisp.

Often, phyllo is used simply as a crust. Our Easter Dinner begins with a *kolokithopita* (zucchini and onion pie, page 254) that features a double phyllo crust. Several sheets of phyllo are brushed with oil and layered into a metal pie plate, piece by piece, as the pan is turned to create an even overhang. After the filling is added, more sheets of phyllo are layered in the same manner to top the pie. The excess dough is cut off with scissors before rolling up the edge into a pretty border.

And, of course, an entire category of Greek sweets is made with phyllo. The most popular one, *baklava* (honey and nut filled pastries, page 258), is baked, then drenched with a warm honey syrup. It is a favorite of all eastern Mediterranean countries, and, although quite sweet, a wonderful indulgence. To be good, *baklava* requires some work — the walnuts must be chopped fine by hand (not in a food processor) to keep them light and fluffy, and the nut mixture should be sprinkled evenly onto each layer of phyllo. Also, contrary to the belief of many restaurateurs, *baklava* does not keep indefinitely; it should be enjoyed within five days. Making our *baklava* is an excellent way to get accustomed to handling phyllo, as the sheets are pre-cut to pan size and simply need to be buttered and layered.

MAIL ORDER SOURCES

C & K Importing
2771 West Pico Boulevard, Los Angeles, CA 90006
tel. (213) 737-2970
for olive oils, spoon sweets, dried herbs and spices, cheeses, phyllo, and many other specialty ingredients

9th Avenue Cheese Market
615 9th Avenue, New York, NY 10036
tel. (212) 397-0399; fax (212) 757-8265
for cheeses, olive oils, and some other ingredients

Ninth Avenue International
543 Ninth Avenue, New York, NY 10036
tel. (212) 279-1000
for olive oils, tarama, spoon sweets, dried herbs and spices, some cheeses, and other ingredients

Dean & Deluca
560 Broadway, New York, NY 10012
tel. (800) 221-7714 or (212) 431-1691, ext. 268
for olive oils, tarama, spoon sweets, dried herbs and spices, cheeses, phyllo, and many other specialty ingredients

Old Chatham Sheepherding Co.
(formerly Hollow Road Farms)
Shaker Museum Road, Old Chatham, NY 12136
tel. (518) 794-9774
for sheep's milk yogurt, and several fresh sheep's milk cheeses, which, while not traditionally Greek, are similar to Greek farmer cheeses

Red-Dyed Easter Eggs

GREEK EASTER FEAST

Kolokithopita
(Zucchini and Onion Pie)

Dolmades
(Stuffed Grape Leaves)

Taramosalata
(Carp-Roe Spread)

•

Arni Fricassee me Horta
(Lamb Fricassee with Greens)

Avgolemono
(Egg and Lemon Sauce)

Aginares, Pizelia, ke Karotta
(Artichokes, Peas, and Carrots)

Patates sto Fournio
(Lemon, Garlic, and Oregano Roasted Potatoes)

Maroulosalata
(Romaine, Arugula, and Watercress Salad with Dill Dressing)

Domaine Carras Limnio, Red Wine of Khalkidiki, 1994

•

Baklava
(Nut-Filled Phyllo Pastries)

Kaltsounakia
(Sweet Cheese Pies)

•

Serves 8

Lamb Fricassee with Greens;
Artichokes, Peas, and Carrots;
Lemon, Garlic, and Oregano
Roasted Potatoes

Zucchini and Onion Pie

Sweet Cheese Pies

NOTE: *Many of the ingredients used in this menu are available at Greek markets and by mail order (sources on page 249).*

Kolokithopita
(Zucchini and Onion Pie)

2 tablespoons olive oil plus about ⅓ cup for
 brushing *phyllo*
1 large onion, chopped
1 pound zucchini, shredded
¾ cup crumbled feta (preferably Greek,
 about 4 ounces)
1 large egg, beaten lightly
2 tablespoons fine semolina
2 tablespoons chopped fresh mint leaves
nine 17- by 12-inch *phyllo* sheets, thawed if
 frozen, stacked between 2 sheets plastic
 wrap, and covered with a kitchen towel

In a large skillet heat 2 tablespoons oil over moderate heat until hot but not smoking and cook onion, stirring occasionally, until softened but not browned. Add zucchini and salt to taste and cook, stirring occasionally, until zucchini is tender and any liquid is evaporated, about 10 minutes. Transfer zucchini mixture to a bowl and cool slightly. Stir in feta, egg, semolina, mint, and salt and pepper to taste until combined.

Arrange 1 *phyllo* sheet on a work surface and brush with some oil. Transfer oiled sheet to a 9-inch metal pie plate, pressing gently into bottom and allowing *phyllo* to overhang rim evenly. Top with 4 more sheets brushed with oil in same manner, overhanging corners in different directions so that overhang is even all around edge.

Preheat oven to 375° F.

Spoon filling into *phyllo* shell and smooth top. Arrange 1 *phyllo* sheet on work surface and brush with some oil. Arrange oiled sheet over filling, allowing edges to overhang rim, and layer remaining 3 *phyllo* sheets, brushed with oil, in same manner as for shell.

With scissors trim *phyllo* overhang to 1 inch beyond rim and roll it toward center of pie to form an edge just inside rim. *Pie may be prepared up to this point 1 day ahead and chilled, covered.*

Bake pie in middle of oven 45 minutes, or until golden. Cool pie in pie plate on a rack.

Serve *kolokithopita,* cut into wedges, at room temperature. Serves 8 as an hors d'oeuvre.

Taramosalata
(Carp-Roe Spread)

12 slices firm white sandwich bread, crusts
 removed
a 10-ounce jar *tarama* (carp roe, sources
 on page 249)
⅓ cup fresh lemon juice
1¼ cups extra-virgin olive oil (preferably Greek)
½ cup packed fresh flat-leafed parsley leaves,
 washed well, spun dry, and chopped fine
2 scallions, chopped fine

Accompaniment: country bread slices

Into a bowl of water dip bread slices, 1 at a time, and squeeze gently to remove excess water. In bowl of a standing electric mixer beat bread and *tarama* at high speed until smooth. With motor running add lemon juice alternately with oil, a little at a time, beating well after each addition. Add parsley and scallions and beat until combined well. (Alternatively, carp-roe spread may be made in a food processor, although it will not be as fluffy.) Transfer spread to a bowl. *Spread may be made 2 days ahead and chilled, covered.*

Serve *taramosalata* at room temperature with bread. Serves 8 as an hors d'oeuvre.

Dolmades
(Stuffed Grape Leaves)

half a 1 pound jar brine-packed grape leaves
 (about 30 leaves, sources on page 249)
1½ cups water
½ teaspoon salt
¾ cup long-grain rice
1 onion, chopped fine
3 tablespoons olive oil
¾ cup diced fennel bulb (sometimes called anise)
½ cup pine nuts, toasted until golden
½ cup fresh dill, chopped
⅓ cup dried currants
3 tablespoons fresh lemon juice
about 1½ cups chicken broth

Accompaniment: drained yogurt (procedure on
 page 247)

Bring a large saucepan of water to a boil for grape leaves.

In a bowl rinse grape leaves in several changes of cold water and blanch in batches in boiling water 3 minutes. Transfer leaves with a slotted spoon to a colander to drain and refresh under cold water. Drain leaves well.

In a saucepan bring 1½ cups water and salt to a boil and stir in rice. Cook rice, covered, over moderately low heat until water is absorbed, 17 to 20 minutes, and transfer to a bowl. In a heavy skillet cook onion in 1½ tablespoons oil over moderate heat, stirring, until tender and golden and stir into rice with fennel, pine nuts, dill, currants, 2 tablespoons lemon juice, and salt and pepper to taste until combined well.

Arrange 1 grape leaf, smooth side down, on a kitchen towel. Trim stem flush with leaf (if leaf is large trim to 5½ inches across), reserving stem and any trimmings. Spoon about 1 tablespoon filling onto leaf near stem end and roll up filling tightly in leaf, folding in sides and squeezing roll to pack filling. (Roll should be about 3½ inches long.) Make more rolls with remaining leaves and filling in same manner.

In a small saucepan heat broth just to a simmer and keep warm, covered. Line bottom of a 3-quart heavy saucepan with reserved stems and trimmings and any remaining grape leaves. Arrange rolls, seam sides down and close together, in layers over leaves, seasoning each layer with salt. Pour remaining 1½ tablespoons oil and remaining tablespoon lemon juice over rolls and cover with an inverted heatproof plate slightly smaller than pan, pressing down lightly, to keep leaves from unrolling. Add just enough broth to pan to come up to rim of plate and bring to a boil. Reduce heat to low and cook rolls, covered with plate and lid, 45 minutes, or until leaves are tender and most of liquid is absorbed.

Remove pan from heat and cool rolls, covered. Using plate to hold back rolls, pour off remaining liquid. Transfer rolls to a platter, discarding remaining stems, trimmings, and grape leaves. *Stuffed grape leaves may be made 1 week ahead and chilled, covered.*

Serve stuffed grape leaves chilled or at room temperature with yogurt. Makes about 25 *dolmades*, serving 8 as an hors d'oeuvre.

Arni Fricassee me Horta
(Lamb Fricassee with Greens)

4 pounds boneless lamb shoulder, cut into
  2-inch chunks
3 tablespoons olive oil
2 large onions, chopped
½ cup dry white wine
about 4 cups water
2 pounds leeks (white and pale green parts only),
  cut into 5- by ½-inch strips and washed well
2 pounds dandelion greens or arugula, washed
  well and drained

Accompaniment: avgolemono (recipe follows)

Season lamb with salt and pepper. In an 8-quart
heavy kettle heat oil over moderately high heat until hot but not smoking and brown lamb all over in
batches, transferring pieces to a large plate. In
drippings remaining in kettle cook onions with salt
to taste, stirring occasionally, until softened, about
5 minutes, and stir in wine.

Return lamb with any juices that have accumulated on plate to kettle and add enough water to
almost cover meat. Simmer lamb, covered, 1½
hours, or until very tender. *Fricassee may be pre-*
pared up to this point 2 days ahead and cooled,
uncovered, before chilling, covered. Bring fricassee
to a simmer before proceeding.

Stir leeks and greens into *fricassee* and simmer
10 minutes, or until tender. Transfer lamb and vegetables with a slotted spoon to a deep platter,
reserving cooking liquid for making *avgolemono*,
and keep warm.

Serve *arni fricassee* with *avgolemono*. Serves 8.

Avgolemono
(Egg and Lemon Sauce)

4 cups strained lamb cooking liquid from
  arni fricassee (recipe precedes) or
  3 cups chicken broth
3 large eggs
1 large egg white
¼ cup fresh lemon juice

In a large saucepan bring lamb cooking liquid
or chicken broth to a boil. If using lamb broth boil
until reduced to about 3 cups. In bowl of a standing electric mixer beat eggs, white, and lemon juice
on high speed until frothy, about 5 minutes. With
motor running, add 2 cups hot broth in a stream.
Transfer egg mixture and remaining cup broth to
top of a double boiler or to a metal bowl set over a
pan of simmering water and cook, whisking, until
sauce is just thickened and foamy (do not boil), 5 to
10 minutes. Transfer *avgolemono* to a sauceboat and
serve immediately. Makes about 3 cups.

Aginares, Pizelia, ke Karotta
(Artichokes, Peas, and Carrots)

5 lemon halves
10 medium to large artichokes (5 to
    6 pounds total, preferably with
    long stems)
1 pound carrots, cut into 2-inch-long pieces
    and thicker pieces halved
    lengthwise
1¼ pounds fresh peas in their pods, shelled,
    or a 10-ounce package frozen peas
2 tablespoons chopped fresh dill

Accompaniment: *avgolemono* (recipe precedes)

Into a bowl of cold water squeeze juice from 2 lemons, dropping squeezed halves into water.

Keeping artichoke stem intact, bend back outer leaves of one artichoke until they snap off close to base and discard several more layers of leaves until exposed leaves are pale green at top and pale yellow at base.

With a sharp stainless-steel knife, cut off top inch of artichoke. Trim fibrous parts from base of artichoke, being careful not to break off stem. Cut a thin slice from base of stem to expose a fresh cross section. Trim outer green fibrous part from stem, leaving pale core intact.

Pull leaves open and with a small spoon scrape out choke and any spiky purple-tipped leaves. Cut artichoke into eight wedges and rub wedges all over with cut side of remaining lemon half. Put artichoke in bowl of lemon water and repeat procedure with remaining artichokes. *Artichokes may be prepared up to this point 1 day ahead and chilled in lemon water, covered.*

With a slotted spoon transfer artichokes to a saucepan and pour lemon water through a fine sieve into a large measuring cup. To saucepan add carrots, 1½ cups strained lemon water, enough water to cover vegetables, and salt to taste and simmer until vegetables are tender, about 15 minutes, stirring in peas during last 5 minutes of cooking time. With a slotted spoon transfer vegetables to a bowl and toss with dill and salt and pepper to taste.

Serve artichokes, peas, and carrots with *avgolemono*. Serves 8.

Patates sto Fournio
(Lemon, Garlic, and Oregano Roasted Potatoes)

3½ pounds russet (baking) potatoes
¼ cup olive oil
4 garlic cloves, chopped
1½ teaspoons dried oregano (preferably Greek)
¼ cup fresh lemon juice
¼ cup water

Preheat oven to 425° F.

Peel potatoes and cut into quarters. In a large nonreactive roasting pan toss potatoes with oil, garlic, oregano, and salt and pepper to taste and arrange potatoes in one layer. Add lemon juice and water and roast in middle of oven, stirring occasionally, until tender, about 45 minutes. Serves 8.

L. MAESTRO

Maroulosalata
(Romaine, Arugula, and Watercress Salad with
Dill Dressing)

1 small head romaine, washed well, spun dry, and
    torn into bite-size pieces (about 8 cups)
1 bunch arugula, washed well, spun dry, tough
    stems discarded, and large leaves torn into
    bite-size pieces (about 4 cups)
1 bunch watercress, washed well, spun dry, and
    tough stems discarded (about 4 cups)
3 scallions, sliced thin
3 tablespoons fresh lemon juice
⅓ cup extra-virgin olive oil (preferably Greek)
1 teaspoon dill seeds

In a large bowl combine greens and scallions. In a small bowl beat together lemon juice, oil, and dill seeds with a fork and pour over salad. Season salad with salt and pepper and toss to coat. Serves 8.

257

Baklava
(Nut-Filled Phyllo Pastries)

1 pound walnuts (about 4 cups), chopped fine
    with a knife
⅓ cup sugar
1 teaspoon cinnamon
thirteen 17- by 12-inch *phyllo* sheets (about
    ¾ pound), thawed if frozen, halved crosswise
    with scissors, and halves stacked between
    2 sheets plastic wrap and covered with a
    kitchen towel
2 sticks (1 cup) unsalted butter, melted and cooled
about 1 tablespoon whole cloves
For syrup
½ cup water
1 cup honey
½ cup sugar
1 tablespoon fresh lemon juice

Preheat oven to 375° F.

In a bowl stir together chopped walnuts, sugar, and cinnamon.

Arrange 1 *phyllo* sheet on a work surface, keeping remaining sheets covered, and brush with some butter. Put buttered *phyllo* in bottom of a 13- by 9-inch metal baking pan and top with 5 more buttered sheets.

Sprinkle ½ cup nut mixture over *phyllo* in pan and top with 2 *phyllo* sheets, buttering them and arranging them so that nut mixture is completely covered. Repeat layering in same manner, topping each ½ cup nut mixture with 2 *phyllo* sheets, until all nut mixture is used.

Top *baklava* with remaining *phyllo* sheets, buttering them in same manner as bottom layer and covering top evenly.

Using a sharp knife with a ruler as a guide, make 4 lengthwise cuts, 1¾ inches apart, to divide *baklava* into 5 strips. Make diagonal cuts, 1½ inches apart, to divide *baklava* into about 25 diamonds (there will be irregular pieces around edge). Leaving white milky liquid in pan, pour remaining butter evenly over top and press a clove into center of each diamond.

Reduce oven temperature to 325° F. and bake *baklava* 1 hour, or until golden.

Make syrup while baklava is baking:

In a saucepan bring syrup ingredients to a boil, stirring until sugar is dissolved, and simmer syrup 5 minutes, or until reduced to about 1½ cups.

Pour warm syrup over hot *baklava* and cool in pan on a rack. *Let baklava stand, covered, at room temperature at least 12 hours for flavors to develop and up to 5 days.*

Serve *baklava* in paper cupcake liners if desired. Makes about 25 pieces *baklava*.

Kaltsounakia
(Sweet Cheese Pies)

For filling
1 cup full-fat farmer or cottage cheese
4 ounces feta (preferably Greek), crumbled
   (about ¾ cup)
⅓ cup granulated sugar
1 large egg
1 teaspoon freshly grated orange zest
2 teaspoons brandy

For pastry dough
1½ cups all-purpose flour
2 tablespoons granulated sugar
¾ teaspoon baking powder
¾ teaspoon salt
¾ stick (6 tablespoons) cold unsalted butter,
   cut into bits
1 large egg
1 teaspoon vanilla
about 2 tablespoons cold water

1 large egg yolk
2 tablespoons milk
1 tablespoon confectioners' sugar

Make filling:
In a food processor or blender pulse filling ingredients until almost smooth. Transfer mixture to a bowl and chill while making pastry.

Make pastry dough:
In a bowl with a pastry blender or in a food processor blend or pulse together flour, sugar, baking powder, and salt until combined well and add butter, blending or pulsing until mixture resembles coarse meal. In a small bowl whisk together egg and vanilla and add to flour mixture, tossing with a fork or pulsing until incorporated. Add cold water, ½ tablespoon at a time, tossing with fork or pulsing to incorporate, until mixture just forms a dough. Gather dough into a ball and knead gently 3 or 4 times.

Preheat oven to 375° F. and grease a large baking sheet.

Divide dough into 12 pieces and roll each piece into a ball. On a lightly floured surface with a floured rolling pin roll out 1 ball into a 5½-inch round and spoon 1½ tablespoons filling onto center. Fold an edge of pastry round toward middle not quite to center of filling and fold opposite edge toward center in same manner, leaving about ½ inch of filling exposed. Fold remaining edges toward middle in same manner to form a square packet and transfer to baking sheet. Make more pastries with remaining dough and filling in same manner.

In a small bowl whisk together yolk and milk and brush onto pastry dough. Bake pastries in middle of oven 25 minutes, or until golden. Loosen pastries with a metal spatula and cool on baking sheet on a rack. Spoon confectioners' sugar into a fine sieve and dust over pastries. Makes 12 *kaltsounakia*.

Manouri Cheese, Grilled Fresh Figs, and Fresh Fruit

SUMMER DINNER ON SANTORINI

Vissinada
(Sour Cherry Drink)

Fava Santorinis
(Yellow Split Pea Spread with
Scallion and Capers)

Domatokeftedes
(Tomato Patties)

•

Barbounia Skordata
(Grilled Red Mullet with Lemon Garlic Dill Sauce)

Patzaria Salata
(Beet and Greens Salad with
Balsamic Vinegar)

Melitzanes Yemistes
(Baked Baby Eggplant Stuffed with
Raisins and Pine Nuts)

Horiatiki Salata
(Country Tomato Salad)

Santorini, White Wine of the Island, Boutari 1995

•

Manouri me Meli ke Fistikia
(Manouri Cheese with Thyme Honey and Pistachios)

Syka me Moschato Krassi
(Grilled Fresh Figs with Samos Wine)

Fresh Fruit

•

Serves 6

Grilled Red Mullet with Lemon Garlic Dill Sauce;
Beet and Greens Salad with Balsamic Vinegar;
Country Bread; Baked Baby Eggplant Stuffed with
Raisins and Pine Nuts; Country Tomato Salad

NOTE: *Many of the ingredients used in this menu are available at Greek markets and by mail order (sources on page 249).*

Vissinada
(Sour Cherry Drink)

6 cups fresh chilled seltzer or club soda
about 2 cups sour cherry spoon sweets
  (sources on page 249)

Fill 6 tall glasses with ice and fill each three-fourths full with fresh seltzer or club soda. Add 5 tablespoons spoon sweets, or to taste, to each drink and stir to combine. Makes 6 drinks.

Fava Santorinis
(Yellow Split Pea Spread with Scallion and Capers)

½ pound dried yellow split peas (preferably Greek, about 1 cup), picked over, rinsed, and drained well
2¾ cups water
1 small onion, chopped
1 garlic clove, chopped fine
1 bay leaf
½ teaspoon dried oregano (preferably Greek), crumbled
3 tablespoons extra-virgin olive oil (preferably Greek) plus additional for drizzling *fava*
2 teaspoons chopped drained capers
1 tablespoon chopped scallion
1 tablespoon fresh lemon juice, or to taste
coarse salt to taste

Garnish: chopped drained capers and scallion
Accompaniment: thinly sliced French bread, lightly toasted

In a saucepan bring peas, water, onion, garlic, bay leaf, oregano, and 1 tablespoon oil to a boil. Simmer mixture, uncovered, stirring occasionally at beginning of cooking and frequently toward end to avoid sticking, about 30 minutes, or until most of liquid is absorbed and peas form a paste. Transfer paste to a bowl, discarding bay leaf, and cool.

Stir in capers, scallion, 2 tablespoons oil, and lemon juice and season with coarse salt. *Fava may be made 2 days ahead and chilled, covered. Bring fava to room temperature before serving.*

Garnish *fava* with capers and scallion and drizzle with additional oil. Serve *fava* with toasts. Makes about 2 cups, serving 6 as an hors d'oeuvre.

Domatokeftedes
(Tomato Patties)

¾ cup all-purpose flour
2 teaspoons baking powder
1 teaspoon coarse salt, or to taste
1 tablespoon olive oil plus additional for frying
1 small onion, chopped fine (about ¾ cup)
1 garlic clove, minced
1¼ pounds plum tomatoes, seeded and cut into ¼-inch dice (about 1¼ cups)
½ cup sun-dried tomatoes packed in oil, drained and chopped fine
¼ cup packed fresh mint leaves, washed well, spun dry, and chopped fine (about 2 tablespoons)
¼ cup packed fresh parsley sprigs, washed well, spun dry, and chopped fine (about 2 tablespoons)

Garnish: fresh mint sprigs and leaves
Accompaniment if desired: tzatziki (page 272)

In a bowl whisk together flour, baking powder, and coarse salt.
In a deep 12-inch heavy skillet heat 1 tablespoon oil over moderate heat until hot but not smoking and cook onion, stirring, until softened. Add garlic and

cook, stirring, 1 minute. Transfer onion mixture to a large bowl and cool.

Add plum tomatoes, sun-dried tomatoes, mint, and parsley. Stir in flour mixture until a thick batter is formed. With wet hands form batter into about eighteen 2½- by 1-inch oval patties, transferring to a platter.

Line a baking sheet with paper towels.

In a skillet heat ¼ inch oil over moderate heat until hot but not smoking and fry patties, 6 at a time, until golden brown on both sides, about 3 minutes total, transferring with a slotted spoon to baking sheet to drain. Sprinkle patties with salt and pepper to taste. (Tomato patties may be kept warm in a 250° F. oven 30 minutes.)

Garnish patties with mint and serve with *tzatziki* for dipping. Makes about 18 *domatokeftedes*, serving 6 as an hors d'oeuvre.

Barbounia Skordata
(Grilled Red Mullet with Lemon Garlic Dill Sauce)

2¼ pounds whole red mullet (about 8) or
    2 pounds whole small red snapper (about 4),
    cleaned
about 8 fresh dill sprigs plus 2 tablespoons
    chopped fresh dill
coarse salt to taste
freshly ground black pepper to taste
¼ cup fresh lemon juice
3 large garlic cloves, minced
½ cup extra-virgin olive oil (preferably Greek)

Garnish: fresh dill sprigs and lemon halves

Rinse fish and pat dry. Arrange fish in a baking dish just large enough to hold them in one layer. Divide dill sprigs among cavities of fish and season fish inside and out with coarse salt and pepper.

In a bowl whisk together lemon juice, garlic, oil, and coarse salt and pepper to taste. Pour ⅓ cup sauce over fish, reserving remainder for serving, and turn fish to coat. Marinate fish, covered, at cool room temperature, turning occasionally, 30 minutes.

Prepare grill.

Remove fish from marinade and discard marinade. Pat fish dry and season with coarse salt and pepper. Grill fish on an oiled rack set 5 to 6 inches over glowing coals, turning once, 4 minutes for mullet and 7 for snapper, or until just cooked through. (Alternatively, fish may be grilled in a hot well-seasoned ridged grill pan over moderate heat.)

With a metal spatula carefully transfer fish to a platter. Stir chopped dill into reserved lemon sauce and pour sauce over fish. Garnish fish with dill and lemon. Serves 6.

Patzaria Salata
(Beet and Greens Salad with Balsamic Vinegar)

2½ pounds beets with greens, beets scrubbed and
    trimmed, leaving about 1 inch of stems
    attached, and greens reserved
2 large bunches dandelion greens, coarse stems
    discarded (about 2½ cups packed greens)
2 tablespoons extra-virgin olive oil (preferably
    Greek)
2½ tablespoons balsamic vinegar
coarse salt to taste
freshly ground black pepper to taste

In a kettle cover beets by 1 inch with salted water. Simmer beets, covered, 35 minutes, or until tender, and drain. When beets are cool enough to handle, slip off and discard skins and stems. Cut beets lengthwise into wedges. *Beets may be prepared up to this point 1 day ahead and chilled, covered. Bring beets to room temperature before serving.*

In a 6-quart kettle bring 5 quarts salted water to a boil for greens.

Remove and discard stems from beet greens. Wash beet and dandelion greens well and drain. Stir greens into boiling water and cook 8 minutes, or until tender. Drain greens in a colander, pressing with a large spoon to remove excess water. Coarsely chop greens and transfer to a bowl. While still warm toss greens with 1 tablespoon each of oil and vinegar and season with coarse salt and pepper.

Arrange greens on a platter and top with beet wedges. Drizzle beets and greens with remaining tablespoon oil and remaining 1½ tablespoons vinegar and sprinkle with coarse salt and pepper. *Salad may be made 3 hours ahead and kept, covered loosely, at room temperature.* Serves 6.

Melitzanes Yemistes
(Baked Baby Eggplant Stuffed with Raisins and Pine Nuts)

4 baby eggplants or 2 small eggplants
    (about 1 pound total)
2 teaspoons coarse salt
¼ cup olive oil
1 small onion, chopped fine (about 1 cup)
1 small red bell pepper, chopped fine
    (about 1 cup)
2 garlic cloves, minced
¼ cup pine nuts, lightly toasted and cooled
⅓ cup fresh bread crumbs
3 tablespoons raisins
¾ cup freshly grated *kefalotyri* cheese or
    Pecorino (about 2½ ounces)
¼ cup fresh parsley leaves, washed well,
    spun dry, and chopped

Garnish: chopped fresh parsley leaves

Preheat oven to 375° F.

Halve eggplants lengthwise and sprinkle cut sides with coarse salt. Stand halves in a colander and drain 30 minutes. Pat eggplant dry.

In a large heavy skillet heat oil over moderate heat until hot but not smoking and brown eggplant in batches, cut sides down, until flesh is golden brown and just tender, about 4 minutes. Turn eggplant over and cook 1 minute more. Transfer eggplant to a plate to cool.

Pour off all but about 1 tablespoon oil from skillet. Add onion and sauté over moderately high heat, stirring, until golden brown, about 10 minutes. Add bell pepper and sauté, stirring, until tender. Add garlic and sauté, stirring, 1 minute. Transfer onion mixture to a large bowl to cool.

When eggplant is cool enough to handle, scoop out flesh, leaving a ¼-inch shell (do not puncture skin). Coarsely chop flesh and stir into onion mixture with pine nuts, bread crumbs, raisins, ½ cup cheese, parsley, and salt and pepper to taste.

Preheat oven to 375° F.

Arrange eggplant shells in a shallow baking dish (preferably terra-cotta) just large enough to hold them in one layer. Spoon filling into shells, mounding it, and sprinkle tops with remaining ¼ cup cheese. *Stuffed eggplant may be prepared 4 to 6*

hours ahead and chilled, covered. Bake eggplant in middle of oven 20 minutes, or until golden brown.

Garnish eggplant with parsley and serve warm or at room temperature. Serves 6.

Horiatiki Salata
(Country Tomato Salad)

5 vine-ripened tomatoes (about 2 pounds),
    quartered
1 small green bell pepper, cut into thin strips
1 small cucumber, halved lengthwise and cut
    crosswise into ¼-inch-thick slices
1 small red onion, sliced thin
½ cup Kalamata olives, pitted
2 teaspoons dried oregano (preferably Greek),
    crumbled
coarse salt to taste
freshly ground black pepper to taste
¼ pound feta (preferably Greek), broken into
    chunks
¼ cup extra-virgin olive oil (preferably Greek)

Garnish: fresh oregano sprigs

In a large bowl gently toss together tomatoes, bell pepper, cucumber, onion, olives, oregano, and coarse salt and black pepper. Add feta and drizzle salad with oil. Sprinkle salad with black pepper.

Garnish salad with oregano sprigs. Serves 6.

Manouri me Meli ke Fistikia
(Manouri Cheese with Thyme Honey and Pistachios)

½ cup honey (preferably Greek)
2 tablespoons fresh thyme leaves
¾ pound *manouri* cheese or *ricotta salata*
    at room temperature
⅓ cup shelled natural pistachios,
    lightly toasted

Accompaniments
grilled fresh figs with Samos wine
    (recipe follows)
fresh fruit

In a small saucepan heat honey over low heat just until warm (do not boil). Remove pan from heat and stir in thyme. Cool honey 15 minutes.

Cut cheese into wedges and arrange on a platter. Drizzle thyme honey over cheese and sprinkle with pistachios. Serve cheese with grilled figs and fresh fruit. Serves 6.

Syka me Moschato Krassi
(Grilled Fresh Figs with Samos Wine)

18 fresh figs
3 cups Samos (sweet Greek wine) or
    California Muscat
2 cinnamon sticks, halved
three 2-inch strips fresh lemon zest

Prepare grill or keep grill used for grilling fish warm.

Put figs in a heatproof bowl. In a saucepan bring remaining ingredients to a boil and pour over figs. Macerate figs 30 minutes at room temperature.

With a slotted spoon transfer figs to a clean rack (or a sheet of foil set on a rack) set 5 to 6 inches over warm coals. Transfer wine mixture to a saucepan and heat to warm over low heat. Heat figs, covered, turning once, 4 minutes, or until heated through (do not char). Transfer figs to a large shallow bowl and pour wine mixture over them.

Serve figs warm. Serves 6.

Olives and Feta in Herbed Lemon Olive Oil

A COCKTAIL PARTY FEATURING MEZEDES

Bacaliaros Skordalia
(Salt Cod Fritters with Garlic Sauce)

Tzatziki
(Cucumber Yogurt Dip)

Elies Marinates me Feta
(Olives and Feta in Herbed Lemon Olive Oil)

Melitzanosalata
(Eggplant Spread)

Keftedakia
(Lamb and Beef Meatballs)

Gigantes
(Stewed Large Lima Beans with Tomatoes)

Kremydakia Glykoxina
(Roasted Pearl Onions with Honey and Vinegar Glaze)

Oktapodi sta Karvouna
(Grilled Octopus with Oregano)

Hortopitakia
(Phyllo Triangles Filled with Mustard Greens and Cheese)

Grilled Pita Bread

Metaxa ouzo

Retsina of Attica, Markou Brothers *Kretikos, White Wine of Crete, Boutari 1995*

•

Rizogalo
(Creamy Orange Cinnamon Rice Pudding)

•

Serves 12

Opposite: Eggplant Spread, Grilled Pita, Lamb and Beef Meatballs; Salt Cod Fritters with Garlic Sauce; Stewed Large Lima Beans with Tomatoes; and Phyllo Triangles Filled with Mustard Greens and Cheese

Above: Grilled Octopus with Oregano; Lamb and Beef Meatballs; Cucumber Yogurt Dip; Olives and Feta in Herbed Lemon Olive Oil; Roasted Pearl Onions with Honey and Vinegar Glaze

NOTE: *Many of the ingredients used in this menu are available at Greek markets and by mail order (sources on page 249).*

Bacaliaros Skordalia
(Salt Cod Fritters with Garlic Sauce)

1½ pounds center-cut salt cod, cut into 1-inch
 pieces
For garlic sauce
a ½-pound russet (baking) potato
2 cups torn crustless firm white sandwich bread
 (about 4 slices)
½ cup walnuts
4 large garlic cloves, minced
3 tablespoons fresh lemon juice
1 tablespoon balsamic vinegar
1 cup extra-virgin olive oil (preferably Greek)

2 cups all-purpose flour
1 teaspoon baking powder
1½ cups milk
vegetable oil for deep-frying

In a large bowl cover salt cod with cold water by 1 inch. *Soak cod, covered and chilled, changing water 3 times daily, 2 days.*

Make garlic sauce:

In a large saucepan cover potato with cold salted water by 1 inch and boil gently until tender, about 35 minutes. When potato is cool enough to handle but still warm, peel it and force through a ricer or food mill into a bowl. Keep potato warm, covered.

In a food processor pulse bread and walnuts until chopped fine. Add garlic, lemon juice, and vinegar and blend until combined well. With motor running add oil in a slow stream and blend until smooth. Whisk bread mixture into warm potato and season with salt and pepper. *Skordalia may be made 1 day ahead and chilled, covered. Bring skordalia to room temperature before serving.*

Drain cod and pat dry with paper towels. In a bowl whisk together flour, baking powder, and salt and pepper to taste and stir in milk just until a thick batter is formed.

Stir about 16 pieces of cod into batter to coat. In a heavy kettle heat 2 inches oil to 375° F. on a deep-fat thermometer. Working quickly but carefully, remove cod from batter, 1 piece at a time, scraping excess batter off on edge of bowl, and add to oil. Fry cod pieces until golden, about 3 minutes, and transfer with a slotted spoon to paper towels to drain. Coat and fry remaining cod in batches in same manner, returning oil to 375° F. before frying each batch.

Serve *bacaliaros* warm or at room temperature with *skordalia*. Makes about 72 fritters and 2½ cups sauce.

Tzatziki
(Cucumber Yogurt Dip)

3 pounds plain low-fat yogurt
2 seedless cucumbers, peeled, seeded, and
 chopped fine (about 3 cups)
5 garlic cloves, minced
2 tablespoons extra-virgin olive oil (preferably
 Greek)
1½ tablespoons chopped fresh dill
1 tablespoon finely chopped fresh mint leaves
1 tablespoon white-wine vinegar

Put yogurt in a large sieve or colander lined with a double thickness of cheesecloth and set over a large bowl. *Drain yogurt, covered and chilled, 24 hours.* Discard whey in bowl and transfer yogurt to cleaned and dried bowl. Stir in remaining ingredients and salt and pepper to taste. *Chill tzatziki, covered, at least 4 hours and up to 3 days.* Makes about 4½ cups.

Elies Marinates me Feta
(Olives and Feta in Herbed Lemon Olive Oil)

3 tablespoons fresh rosemary leaves
6 fresh lemon thyme or thyme sprigs
¾ pound drained Kalamata olives (about 2 cups)
¾ pound drained Greek green olives (about 2 cups)
¾ pound firm feta (preferably Greek), broken into bite-size pieces
six 3-inch strips fresh lemon zest
2 tablespoons fresh lemon juice
2 cups extra-virgin olive oil (preferably Greek)

With a mortar and pestle or with flat side of a heavy knife bruise rosemary and thyme until fragrant and in a large bowl gently combine with all remaining ingredients (avoid further breaking up feta). *Marinate olive and feta mixture, covered and chilled, gently stirring occasionally, at least 2 days and up to 5.*

In a large sieve set over a bowl drain olives and feta and transfer to another bowl. Flavored oil keeps, covered and chilled, 1 week and can be used in salad dressings. Makes about 6 cups olives and feta.

Melitzanosalata
(Eggplant Spread)

6 pounds eggplant (about 6 medium)
½ cup minced red onion
4 garlic cloves, minced
⅓ cup packed fresh flat-leafed parsley leaves, washed well, spun dry, and minced
½ cup extra-virgin olive oil (preferably Greek)
¼ cup red-wine vinegar
2 tablespoons drained capers, chopped fine
¼ cup mayonnaise or drained plain low-fat yogurt (procedure on page 247)

Garnish: finely chopped seeded vine-ripened tomato
Accompaniment: grilled pita loaves (preferably Mediterranean-style, without pocket)

Prepare grill.
Pierce eggplants in several places with a fork and grill on a rack set 5 to 6 inches over glowing coals, turning occasionally, until very soft, 30 to 40 minutes. (Alternatively, eggplants may be broiled under a preheated broiler about 6 inches from heat. Broiled eggplant will not have a smoky flavor.) In a shallow baking pan cool eggplants until they can be handled. Halve eggplants lengthwise and discard as many seeds as possible. Scrape flesh from skins into a large sieve set over a bowl. *Drain eggplant, covered and chilled, 1 day.* Discard bitter juices.

In a food processor in two batches pulse eggplant with remaining ingredients until a coarse purée forms. Transfer spread to a bowl and season with salt and pepper. *Chill spread, covered, at least 3 hours and up to 3 days.*

Garnish *melitzanosalata* with tomato and serve chilled or at room temperature with grilled pita. Makes about 6 cups.

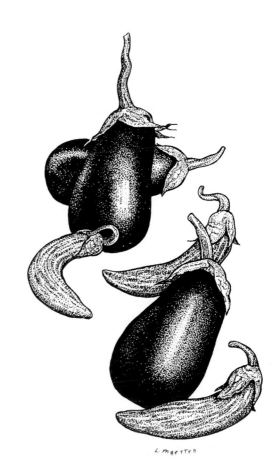

L. Maertten

273

Keftedakia
(Lamb and Beef Meatballs)

For meatballs

4 slices firm white sandwich bread, crusts
   discarded and bread torn into large pieces
   (about 2 cups)
½ cup dry red wine
¾ pound ground lamb
½ pound ground chuck
1 onion, chopped fine
2 garlic cloves, minced
1 large egg, beaten lightly
½ cup freshly grated *kefalotyri* cheese or
   Pecorino (about 1½ ounces)
¼ cup fresh mint leaves, washed well, spun
   dry, and minced
¼ teaspoon cinnamon
¼ teaspoon freshly grated nutmeg

3 tablespoons olive oil
¼ cup dry red wine
¼ cup water

Make meatballs:

In a large bowl soak bread in wine until soft. Add remaining meatball ingredients and salt and pepper to taste and knead with hands until combined well. Chill meatball mixture, covered, 1 hour. In a large heavy skillet test meatball mixture for seasoning by sautéing a walnut-sized ball in a small amount of oil and season remaining meatball mixture with salt and pepper if necessary. Form remaining meatball mixture into walnut-sized balls, transferring them to a large baking sheet.

Preheat oven to 350° F.

In skillet heat remaining oil over moderately high heat until hot but not smoking and brown meatballs in batches, without crowding, shaking skillet gently so that meatballs maintain their shape. Transfer meatballs as browned with a slotted spatula to a roasting pan and between batches loosen brown bits in skillet with spatula to prevent sticking. Deglaze skillet with wine over high heat, scraping up brown bits, and stir in water. Pour wine mixture over meatballs.

Bake meatballs in middle of oven, uncovered, until just cooked through, about 15 minutes. *Meatballs may be made 1 day ahead and cooled completely before chilling, covered. Reheat meatballs in a preheated 350° F. oven until heated through.* Makes about 72 *keftedakia*.

Gigantes
(Stewed Large Lima Beans with Tomatoes)

2 cups picked-over dried large lima beans
  (from about a 1-pound bag)
2 small onions, chopped fine
2 carrots, chopped fine
½ cup extra-virgin olive oil
  (preferably Greek)
2 small garlic cloves, minced
¾ pound vine-ripened tomatoes, peeled,
  seeded, and chopped fine
hot red pepper flakes to taste
½ cup packed fresh flat-leafed parsley leaves,
  washed well, spun dry, and minced

In a 3-quart heavy saucepan cover beans with cold water by 2 inches and bring to a boil, skimming froth. Simmer beans, partially covered, until tender, about 30 minutes, and drain in a colander.

In pan cook onions and carrots in oil over moderately low heat, stirring occasionally, until carrots are tender. Stir in garlic and tomatoes and cook, stirring occasionally, until garlic is fragrant. Stir in beans and season with salt and pepper flakes. Remove pan from heat and cool beans. *Stewed beans may be made 3 days ahead and chilled, covered. Bring beans to room temperature before proceeding.* Stir in parsley. Makes about 6 cups *gigantes*.

Kremydakia Glykoxina
(Roasted Pearl Onions with Honey and Vinegar Glaze)

1½ pounds red and white pearl onions (about
  6 cups), unpeeled
1 cup balsamic vinegar
2 tablespoons honey (preferably
  Greek)

In a large saucepan of boiling water blanch onions 3 minutes and drain. Cool onions until they can be handled and peel, trimming root ends.

Preheat oven to 350° F.

In a 9-inch square baking pan stir together vinegar, honey, and salt and pepper to taste and stir in onions. Roast onions until tender, about 1 hour and 45 minutes. *Onions may be prepared up to this point 3 days ahead and chilled, covered. In a saucepan* simmer onion mixture until heated through before proceeding.

Transfer onions with a slotted spoon to a large shallow bowl and in a saucepan simmer liquid until thickened and reduced to about ½ cup.

Spoon glaze over onions and serve onions warm or at room temperature. Serves 12.

Frozen octopus comes in varying sizes. Adjust the simmering time accordingly for knife-tender octopus.

Oktapodi sta Karvouna
(Grilled Octopus with Oregano)

three 2-pound octopuses, thawed if frozen and
  rinsed
1 lemon, cut into ¼-inch-thick slices
2 teaspoons salt
1 teaspoon whole black peppercorns
1½ cups extra-virgin olive oil (preferably Greek)
¼ cup red-wine vinegar
2½ tablespoons dried oregano (preferably Greek)

Cut octopus pouches (heads) from tentacles, leaving enough pouch to keep tentacles attached in 1 piece (for small octopuses discard pouches). In an 8-quart kettle combine octopus pouches and tentacles, lemon, salt, peppercorns, and water to cover by 1 inch and simmer gently, covered, until octopus is knife-tender, 20 to 30 minutes. In a colander drain octopus and cool until it can be handled. With hands rub off purplish skin from pouches and tentacles (skin around suction cups may not come off completely). In a large bowl whisk together remaining ingredients and salt and pepper to taste and add octopus, turning to coat. *Marinate octopus, covered and chilled, 1 day.*

Prepare grill.

Transfer octopus to paper towels to drain and reserve marinade. Grill octopus on an oiled rack set 5 to 6 inches over glowing coals, turning occasionally, until browned, about 6 minutes. Cut octopus into bite-size pieces (leave small octopus whole) and toss with reserved marinade. *Octopus may be made 1 day ahead and chilled, covered.* Serve octopus at room temperature. Serves 12.

Hortopitakia
(Phyllo Triangles Filled with Mustard Greens and Cheese)

1½ pounds mustard greens, washed well and
    drained
¼ cup water
2 small onions, minced
1 tablespoon olive oil
¼ pound firm feta (preferably Greek),
    crumbled fine
2 ounces grated *kefalotyri* cheese or Pecorino
½ teaspoon dried oregano (preferably Greek),
    crumbled
1½ teaspoons minced fresh mint leaves
a pinch freshly grated nutmeg
about 2 sticks (1 cup) unsalted butter
about thirty 18- by 14-inch sheets Athens Foods
    phyllo (sources on page 249), thawed if frozen,
    stacked between 2 sheets plastic wrap and
    covered with a kitchen towel

Tear mustard greens leaves from stems and discard stems. In an 8-quart kettle cook greens in water clinging to leaves and ¼ cup water, covered, over moderately low heat, stirring occasionally, until tender. In a colander drain greens until cool enough to handle and squeeze very dry by handfuls. Chop greens coarse and transfer to a bowl.

In a small heavy skillet cook onions in oil over moderately low heat, stirring occasionally, until softened. Into greens stir onions, cheeses, oregano, mint, nutmeg, and salt and pepper to taste until combined well.

In a small heavy saucepan melt butter and cool slightly. Working quickly to keep *phyllo* from drying out, put 1 *phyllo* sheet on a work surface, keeping remaining *phyllo* covered, and brush it lightly with some butter. Cut sheet in half lengthwise and fold each half in half lengthwise. Brush each strip with some butter. Working with 1 strip at a time, mound 2 level teaspoons filling in one corner of each strip and fold *phyllo* over filling, enclosing it and forming a triangle. Continue to fold up strip, maintaining triangle shape, and brush top of triangle lightly with some butter. Make more triangles with remaining *phyllo* and filling in same manner. *Triangles may be kept frozen 3 weeks: Arrange triangles in one layer on unbuttered baking sheets*

and freeze, uncovered, before storing in sealable plastic bags.

Preheat oven to 375° F.

Transfer frozen or freshly made triangles to buttered baking sheets and bake in batches in middle of oven until puffed and golden, about 20 minutes. Serve triangles warm or at room temperature. Makes about 50 *hortopitakia*.

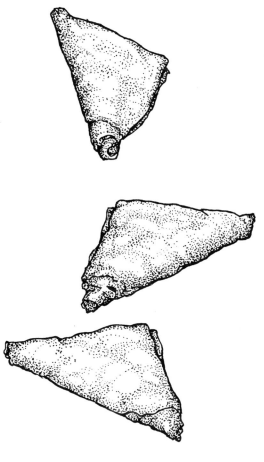

L. maestro

Rizogalo
(Creamy Orange Cinnamon Rice Pudding)

1 cup short-grain white rice or
    Arborio rice
4 cups milk
1 cup water
¾ cup sugar
1 tablespoon unsalted butter
a 3-inch cinnamon stick
1 large egg
1½ cups well-chilled heavy cream
2 teaspoons freshly grated orange zest
ground cinnamon to taste

In a 4-quart heavy saucepan stir together rice, milk, water, ½ cup sugar, butter, cinnamon stick, and a pinch salt. Cook mixture at a bare simmer, stirring frequently to prevent sticking, 1 hour, or until very thick and creamy and rice is very tender. Discard cinnamon stick.

In a bowl whisk together remaining ¼ cup sugar, egg, ½ cup cream, and zest. Slowly whisk about 1 cup rice mixture into egg mixture and whisk egg mixture into remaining rice mixture. Cook pudding over low heat, stirring, 3½ minutes (do not boil) and transfer to a large bowl. Cool pudding completely. *Pudding may be made up to this point 2 days ahead and chilled, covered.*

In a bowl with an electric mixer beat remaining cup cream until it holds soft peaks and fold into pudding. Divide *rizogalo* among twelve 1-cup glasses and sprinkle with cinnamon. Serves 12.

FRESH FROM THE FARMERS MARKET

On a brisk sunny morning, New York City's Union Square Greenmarket is abuzz with the news that fava beans and dandelion greens have finally arrived, a sure sign of spring. The same morning at Pike's Place Market in downtown Seattle, fishermen heave a new run of king salmon onto iced tables next to shimmering tuna and mahimahi. And in Dallas farmers and early customers alike savor crisp-fried *sopaipillas* dunked in steaming cups of coffee. All across the country, farmers, fishermen, bakers, and cheesemakers are bringing their goods directly to market and selling them with the help of relatives or a few employees. These traditional "farmers markets," brimming with fresh, seasonal food, have become one of the best resources for home cooks and professional chefs alike. At the same time, these venues support the efforts of local growers and food artisans and help to preserve small farms.

Traditional farmers markets range from open-air summertime gatherings in parking lots or plazas to permanent structures that house year-round marketplaces. Some markets sell only produce, but most have a few stands of homemade prepared foods and baked goods. Larger markets display seemingly endless bounties of produce, cheese, grains, fish, poultry, meat, and preserves and condiments. Shopping at your local farmers market allows you to interact with the community that grows your food. If you're concerned about additives and spraying (and who isn't these days?), here's an opportunity to find out about organic farming—that is, cultivating crops without using synthetic pesticides or fertilizers. Just remember, produce grown without spraying or with limited pesticides isn't always as beautiful as supermarket specimens. Apples won't be quite as shiny as you expect—they're unwaxed—but their skins are tender. Organically raised poultry and meats, and eggs from organically fed chickens, can also be found for sale. Since farmers market foods are at their peak of perfection, enjoy them as soon as you can for maximum freshness and flavor.

Some farmers grow specialty items for chefs, such as ethnic produce or baby vegetables, and sell their entire or the public. Now you can support growers who take risks and try unusual items such as chayote (a pearlike squash), lovage (a strong celery-flavored herb), and exotic mushrooms (such as *cremini* and *chanterelle*). Also look for "heirloom" fruits and vegetables which are grown from seeds that have been handed down, in some cases, for hundreds of years. Once you've tasted Luther Hill sweet corn or Yellow Perfection tomatoes, your impression of these everyday foods is sure to change. While valued for their superior taste, heirloom varieties aren't viable for supermarket sale because they can't be packed and shipped long distances. At a farmers market, where such commercial considerations are irrelevant, the sheer variety and freshness of produce is remarkable.

Buying at a farmers market is different from grocery shopping at your supermarket, so it takes a bit of practice at first. Early shoppers generally have the pick of the market, while late afternoon buyers find plenty of bargains on produce that won't last another day. In any event, a quick walk through the market allows you to compare quality and prices before buying. To keep foods fresh, select hardy vegetables and baked goods first, then more delicate produce, and finally poultry, meat, fish, and dairy products. Toting along an ice cooler ensures that perishables remain cool. For ease of carrying other items bring along sturdy canvas bags or string mesh bags. And, because you'll be paying for items separately, it's best to have change and small bills on hand, ideally kept in a money belt to leave your hands free.

The following recipes, organized by season, are based on the foods that you'll find when you frequent a farmers market throughout the year. We've included recipes for familiar crops that appear in profusion as well as for more unusual ones. Many of these recipes are intentionally open-ended to encourage you to try different varieties: If you come across a squash that you've never seen before, give it a try in the Buttercup Squash and Cheddar Gratin; or vary the greens in the Pasta with Exotic Mushrooms and Collard Greens. Here's a chance to savor *all* the possibilities.

Lovage

Chives

Chervil

M. Shields

SPRING

Sugar snap peas (sometimes called sugar peas) have tender pods, so there is no need to shell them. Lovage adds a potent celery and herbal note to the soup. If you prefer, celery leaves are less assertive.

Chilled Sugar Snap Pea Soup with Lovage

white and pale green parts of 2 leeks (about ½ pound), chopped, washed well, and drained
2 tablespoons unsalted butter
1 cup ½-inch dice peeled boiling potato
2 cups low-salt chicken broth
1 cup water
1 pound sugar snap peas, trimmed
2 tablespoons chopped fresh lovage or celery leaves
2 cups well-shaken buttermilk

Garnish: whole fresh lovage or celery leaves

In a large saucepan cook leeks in butter over moderate heat, stirring, until softened. Add potato, broth, and water and bring to a boil. Add sugar snaps and simmer, partially covered, 5 minutes, or until sugar snaps are crisp-tender. With a slotted spoon transfer about 20 sugar snaps to a bowl and cool. Stir in chopped lovage or celery leaves and simmer soup 5 minutes more, or until sugar snaps and potatoes are tender. Remove pan from heat to cool slightly.

In a blender purée soup in batches with buttermilk and pour through a sieve into a bowl. Chop reserved sugar snaps and stir into soup with salt and pepper to taste. Chill soup, covered, until cold, about 2 hours.

Serve soup garnished with lovage or celery leaves. Makes about 6 cups, serving 4 to 6.

Goat cheese, available in many farmers markets from early spring to early fall, is creamy and mild-flavored when a few weeks old; it becomes crumbly and sharper tasting as it matures. Try making these toasts with a younger cheese and sprinkle them with your choice of fresh herbs and edible flowers.

Goat Cheese Toasts with Fresh Herbs

a 1-pound country-style round bread loaf, sliced ¾ inch thick
1 large garlic clove
6 ounces soft mild goat cheese
2 tablespoons extra-virgin olive oil
⅓ cup chopped mixed fresh herbs and edible flowers such as chives, basil, thyme, chervil, scented geranium, and marigold, washed well and spun dry if necessary
freshly ground black pepper

Preheat broiler.
In a shallow baking pan broil bread slices about 3 inches from heat 1 minute, or until tops are golden. Turn over slices and broil 1 minute, or until golden. Rub 1 side of each toast with garlic and spread with goat cheese. Cut toasts into thirds and arrange on a platter. Drizzle toasts with oil and sprinkle with herbs and flowers. Season toasts with pepper. Serves 6 to 8.

Radish varieties, both round and cylindrical, have varying degrees of heat; choose smaller ones, less than 1 inch in diameter, for the best taste and texture. Mâche, also known as lamb's lettuce, is a delicate narrow-leaved salad green with mild, nutty flavor. Its threadlike roots should be cut off before the greens are washed and spun dry.

Radish and Mâche Salad with Warm Ginger Vinaigrette

2 cups trimmed radishes (about 2 bunches)
4 cups *mâche* (lamb's lettuce) or baby spinach, washed well and spun dry
1 tablespoon unsalted butter
½ teaspoon minced peeled fresh gingerroot
2 tablespoons rice vinegar
1 tablespoon vegetable oil
coarse kosher salt
freshly ground black pepper

Using a mandoline or other manual slicer, slice radishes thin. In a bowl toss together radishes and greens.

In a small saucepan heat butter and gingerroot just until butter is melted. Remove pan from heat and whisk in vinegar and oil until slightly thickened.

Immediately pour vinaigrette over salad and toss gently until leaves are coated and slightly wilted. Season salad with salt and pepper and serve immediately. Serves 4.

When buying fresh favas, also known as broad beans, look for large, full, light green pods. Asparagus, another harbinger of spring, has earthy flavor. The earliest stalks are the most tender—look for round apple-green stalks with tightly closed purple-tinged tips.

Salmon with Fava Beans and Asparagus

1½ cups fresh fava beans (from about 1½ pounds fresh fava bean pods)
½ pound asparagus, cut diagonally into 1-inch pieces
three 2-inch-long strips fresh lemon zest, removed with a vegetable peeler and cut into thin julienne strips

¼ cup fresh lemon juice
¼ cup plus 1 tablespoon extra-virgin olive oil
1 tablespoon minced fresh chives
1½ pounds skinless center-cut salmon fillet, cut into 4 pieces
1 teaspoon coarse salt

Bring a large saucepan of salted water to a boil for blanching vegetables.

Blanch fava beans in boiling water 2 minutes and transfer with a slotted spoon to a bowl. Blanch asparagus in boiling water 3 minutes, or until crisp-tender. In a sieve drain asparagus and refresh under cold water. Transfer asparagus to another bowl. Working over bowl split each fava bean skin with a fingernail and gently squeeze out bean.

In a small bowl whisk together zest, lemon juice, ¼ cup oil, and chives and season with table salt and pepper to taste.

In a medium skillet heat remaining tablespoon oil over moderately low heat. Add salmon and sprinkle with coarse salt. Cook salmon, covered, 7 minutes. Turn salmon and cook, uncovered, 3 minutes, or until just cooked through. Add vegetables and dressing and cook, covered, until heated through, about 1 minute. Serves 4.

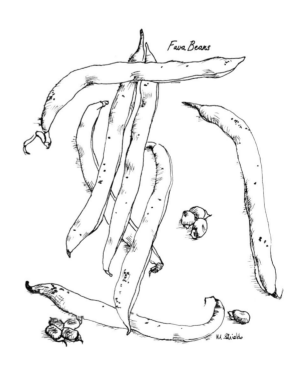

Fava Beans

Beet Greens

Organically raised poultry, sold at many farmers markets, is fed a natural diet free from chemicals and hormones. In this recipe the full flavor and firmer texture of an organic chicken is paired with your choice of bitter greens—dandelion or beet greens are milder, while mustard or collard greens have a more assertive taste.

Orange Tarragon Chicken with Greens

a 3½-pound chicken, cut into serving pieces
all-purpose flour for dredging
3 tablespoons vegetable oil
2 onions, chopped coarse
2 garlic cloves, chopped
1 cup dry white wine
½ cup fresh orange juice
½ teaspoon freshly grated orange zest
1 tablespoon chopped fresh tarragon leaves or
   1 teaspoon dried tarragon, crumbled
4 cups coarsely chopped greens such as mustard,
   dandelion, collard, and/or beet, washed well
   and drained

Season chicken with salt and pepper and dredge in flour, knocking off excess.

In a large heavy skillet heat 2 tablespoons oil over moderately high heat until hot but not smoking and brown chicken in batches, transferring to a plate. Wipe skillet clean. Add remaining tablespoon oil to skillet and cook onions and garlic over moderate heat, stirring, until softened. Add wine, orange juice, zest, and dried tarragon (if using) and boil 3 minutes. Return chicken and any juices that have accumulated on plate to skillet and simmer, covered, 30 minutes, or until chicken is just cooked through. Transfer chicken with tongs to a plate. Add greens and fresh tarragon (if using) to skillet and simmer, partially covered, 15 to 25 minutes, or until greens are just tender. Season greens with salt and pepper. Return chicken to skillet and simmer until heated through. Serves 4.

Although Bing is the quintessential sweet cherry, you may find many sweet colorful varieties—Angela, Black Tartarian, Van, Royal Ann, Rainier, and Stella—all equally delicious, in your area. Look for firm, glossy, plump fruit with green stems.

Sweet Cherry Almond Clafouti

3 cups pitted sweet cherries
⅓ cup almond paste (about 3½ ounces)
2 tablespoons unsalted butter, softened
⅓ cup sugar plus 1 tablespoon for sprinkling
   clafouti
3 large eggs
1 cup milk
1 teaspoon vanilla
¼ teaspoon salt
¼ cup all-purpose flour

Accompaniment: whipped cream

Preheat oven to 350° F. and butter a shallow 1½-quart baking dish.

Spread cherries in one layer in baking dish. In a bowl with an electric mixer beat together almond paste, butter, and ⅓ cup sugar and add eggs, 1 at a time, beating until smooth. Beat in milk, vanilla, and salt until combined well and beat in flour just until smooth. Pour batter over cherries and sprinkle top with remaining tablespoon sugar. Bake *clafouti* in middle of oven 50 minutes, or until golden, and cool slightly on a rack.

Serve *clafouti* warm with whipped cream. Serves 4 to 6.

Although rhubarb is a vegetable, we treat it like a fruit, sweetening it with lots of sugar to tame its extreme acidity. Look for crisp, ruby-red stalks, and if the leaves are still attached, discard them as they can be toxic.

Glazed Rhubarb Galette

a ½-pound frozen puff pastry sheet, thawed
1 pound rhubarb, trimmed and cut diagonally into
⅓ cup sugar
1 teaspoon cornstarch
1 teaspoon freshly grated orange zest
¼ cup strawberry preserves, forced through a sieve

Accompaniment: whipped cream or vanilla
ice cream

Preheat oven to 375° F.

On a lightly floured surface roll out pastry into a 12-inch square and arrange on a baking sheet. Trim off corners with scissors to form a 12-inch round.

In a bowl toss together rhubarb, sugar, cornstarch, and zest. Leaving a 1-inch border, arrange rhubarb slices in concentric circles on top of dough and sprinkle any remaining sugar mixture on top. Fold in border of dough, pinching to form an edge around rhubarb.

Bake *galette* in middle of oven 35 minutes, or until pastry is golden brown. While still hot, brush *galette* with preserves and cool on a rack.

Serve *galette* at room temperature with whipped cream or ice cream. Serves 4.

SUMMER

Tart little currants are most often made into jelly. Usually a clear bright red (there are also black and white varieties), currants should be purchased in clusters and washed just before using. Either Gorgonzola or Roquefort is delicious in this salad, but give local blue cheeses a try—on the East coast, look for Westfield Farms Hubbardston Blue; in the Midwest, sample Maytag Blue.

Chicken Salad with Fresh Currants and Blue Cheese

2 whole skinless boneless chicken breasts
   (about 1 pound total), halved
½ cup chopped celery
¼ cup mayonnaise
¼ cup plain yogurt
2 tablespoons chopped fresh basil or
   parsley leaves
1 cup fresh currants
¼ cup crumbled blue cheese
2 tablespoons lightly toasted almonds,
   chopped coarse

In a deep 12-inch skillet arrange chicken in one layer and cover with salted water. Bring water to a boil and poach chicken at a bare simmer 12 minutes. Remove skillet from heat and cool chicken in poaching liquid 30 minutes.

Drain chicken and cut into bite-size pieces. In a large bowl toss chicken with celery, mayonnaise, yogurt, and basil or parsley. Gently fold in currants, blue cheese, and salt and pepper to taste until just combined.

Serve salad sprinkled with almonds. Serves 4.

Fully ripe fresh apricots are readily available in California and can also be found in farmers markets in areas that are free from late-spring frosts. Look for plump firm fruit that is deep yellow or orange; avoid green-tinged fruit as it will not ripen further.

Tomato, Apricot, and Mozzarella Salad

2 medium vine-ripened tomatoes, cored and
    each cut into 12 wedges
3 fresh ripe apricots (about ¾ pound), pitted
    and each cut into 8 wedges
¼ pound fresh mozzarella, cut into 1-inch pieces
1½ teaspoons chopped fresh thyme leaves
2 teaspoons white-wine vinegar
¾ teaspoon honey (not dark)
1 tablespoon vegetable oil
coarse salt
cracked black pepper

On a large plate combine tomatoes, apricots, and mozzarella and sprinkle with thyme. In a small bowl whisk together vinegar and honey until honey is dissolved and whisk in oil in a stream until emulsified. Drizzle dressing over salad and season with salt and pepper. Serves 4.

Long green chilies offer mild to medium heat and are a spicy counterpoint to garlicky grilled steak. Although chilies grown in New Mexico and California are the most potent, several similar varieties (such as the Hungarian yellow wax pepper) are grown in other states and make fine alternatives.

Grilled Steak with Marinated Roasted Chilies

½ pound fresh mild to medium-hot long green
    chilies, such as New Mexico or Anaheim
    (about 6)
2 tablespoons extra-virgin olive oil
1 tablespoon fresh lemon juice
2 tablespoons chopped fresh coriander sprigs
¼ teaspoon salt
⅛ teaspoon sugar
a 1-inch-thick shell or sirloin steak (1½ to 2
    pounds)
½ teaspoon garlic salt
¼ teaspoon coarsely ground black pepper

Prepare grill.

Grill chilies on an oiled rack set as close to glowing coals as possible, turning occasionally, until charred on all sides. Transfer chilies to a bowl and let steam, covered, until cool enough to handle, about 10 minutes. Wearing rubber gloves, peel chilies and cut off tops, discarding seeds and ribs. Chop chilies coarse and in a bowl toss with oil, lemon juice, coriander, salt, and sugar.

Rub steak with garlic salt and black pepper and grill on oiled clean rack set 5 to 6 inches over glowing coals about 6 minutes on each side for medium-rare. Transfer steak to a cutting board and let stand 10 minutes.

Cut steak diagonally across grain into thin slices and serve with chilies. Serves 4.

Chayote, also known as mirliton, is a pale green, pear-shaped squash that adds mild flavor and crunch to our salsa. Look for small chayotes, about six inches long, with smooth skin, and avoid those with brown spots. If you are unable to find chayote, use zucchini or any other summer squash. For extra heat, include some chopped chili seeds. Our salsa is delicious scooped up with tortilla chips, or spooned over chicken or fish.

Chayote, Corn, and Tomato Salsa

a ½-pound chayote, halved, center seed discarded,
    and chayote cut into ¼-inch dice
1 cup fresh corn (cut from about 2 ears)
2 tablespoons olive oil
1 cup chopped sweet onion such as Vidalia or
    Walla Walla
1 pound vine-ripened tomatoes, seeded and
    chopped
1 large garlic clove, minced
2 fresh *jalapeño* chilies, seeded and chopped
    (wear rubber gloves)
3 tablespoons fresh lime juice
2 tablespoons chopped fresh coriander sprigs
1 teaspoon salt, or to taste

In a skillet cook chayote and corn in oil over moderate heat, stirring, 7 minutes, or until vegetables are just tender. Remove skillet from heat and stir in remaining ingredients. Transfer salsa to a bowl and let stand 30 minutes. *Salsa may be made 2 days ahead and chilled, covered. Bring salsa to room temperature before serving.* Makes about 6 cups.

This pretty, refreshing finale combines three common melons, but feel free to substitute other ripe varieties. Shiny green lemon verbena leaves are added for strong lemon flavor and a powerful lemon-lime aroma. Keep this herb in mind to flavor chicken and fish dishes.

Macerated Melon with Lemon Verbena

½ cantaloupe, seeded and cut into bite-size pieces or scooped into balls (about 2 cups)
½ small honeydew melon, seeded and cut into bite-size pieces or scooped into balls (about 2 cups)
a 3-pound piece watermelon, seeded and cut into bite-size pieces or scooped into balls (about 2 cups)
1 tablespoon finely chopped fresh lemon verbena leaves or mint leaves
2 tablespoons dry vermouth
1 tablespoon raspberry vinegar

In a large bowl toss together ingredients. *Chill melon at least 1 hour and up to 8.* Serves 4 to 6.

When bushels and bushels of peaches appear at the farmers market, they are at their best. You'll need very ripe juicy peaches for our wine; or use over-ripe ones—just cut out any bruised spots first.

Peach Wine

4 very ripe peaches, peeled, pitted, and sliced
2 tablespoons sugar
2 tablespoons peach schnapps or orange-flavored liqueur
a 750-ml. bottle Chablis or white Zinfandel

In a pitcher stir together peaches, sugar, and schnapps or liqueur until sugar is dissolved and stir in wine. *Chill mixture, covered, 8 hours to let flavors develop.* Makes about 4 cups.

FALL

Quinces resemble large Golden Delicious apples in shape and color, but they have a flowery fragrance and are inedible when raw. Even when fully ripe, quinces are very hard.

Pork Braised with Quince and Fennel

a 3-pound boneless pork loin, shoulder, or butt, rolled and tied
2 tablespoons all-purpose flour
2 tablespoons vegetable oil
2 quinces, cut into 1-inch pieces, including skins and cores
1 medium fennel bulb (sometimes called anise), trimmed, leaving 4 inches of stalks, and cut into ½-inch-thick slices
1½ cups beef broth
2 tablespoons molasses
1 teaspoon fennel seeds

Preheat oven to 350° F.
Season pork with salt and pepper and coat with flour. In a heavy ovenproof kettle heat oil over moderately high heat until hot but not smoking and brown pork on all sides. Add remaining ingredients and bring to a boil. Braise pork, tightly covered, in middle of oven 1½ to 2 hours, or until tender when tested with a fork.

Transfer pork to a cutting board. Pour quince mixture through a sieve into a saucepan, pressing hard on solids and scraping purée from bottom of sieve into pan. Bring sauce to a boil and season with salt and pepper.

Cut pork into ¼-inch-thick slices and serve with sauce. Serves 6 to 8.

Our gratin can be made with virtually any winter squash, and we hope you'll experiment with the different varieties found in fall and winter markets.

Buttercup Squash and Cheddar Gratin

1½ pounds buttercup, butternut, or other winter
    squash, peeled, seeded, and cut into 1-inch
    pieces (about 4 cups)
¾ cup apple cider
1 large garlic clove, minced
1 tablespoon unsalted butter
¾ cup coarsely grated sharp Cheddar

In a large heavy saucepan simmer squash, cider, garlic, butter, and salt and pepper to taste, covered, stirring occasionally, 20 minutes, or until squash is tender but not falling apart. Transfer squash with a slotted spoon to a shallow flameproof baking dish or 4 individual gratin dishes. Boil cider mixture until reduced to about 2 tablespoons and spoon evenly over squash.

Preheat broiler.

Sprinkle squash with Cheddar and broil about 4 inches from heat until cheese is bubbling, about 3 minutes. Serves 4.

Parsnips—long, beige-colored roots—are sweet and richly flavored. Buy crisp small or medium parsnips after the first frost or they will be bitter. Jerusalem artichokes are knobby and difficult to peel; if you'd like, simply scrub them thoroughly.

Roasted Root Vegetable Hash

2 tablespoons unsalted butter
1 tablespoon vegetable oil
3 parsnips, peeled and cut into ½-inch cubes
    (about 2 cups)
3 carrots, peeled and cut into ½-inch cubes
    (about 2 cups)
½ pound Jerusalem artichokes (also called
    sunchokes), peeled and cut into ½-inch
    cubes (about 2 cups)
½ pound boiling or baking potatoes, peeled and
    cut into ½-inch cubes (about 2 cups)
4 medium shallots, peeled and quartered
¼ cup chicken broth

Preheat oven to 500° F.

In a jellyroll pan (15½ by 10½ by 1 inch) heat butter and oil in middle of oven until butter is melted. Add remaining ingredients and salt and pepper to taste and toss well. Spread vegetables evenly in pan and roast, turning with a spatula every 10 minutes, 25 minutes, or until tender. Serves 4 as a side dish.

Any firm apple, such as Macoun, Jonathan, or Empire, will be delicious here. However, with some 7,000 different apple varieties grown in the United States, be sure to give lesser-known or heirloom varieties, such as Egremont Russet and Newtown Pippin, a try.

Cornmeal Pancakes with Sautéed Apples

½ stick (¼ cup) unsalted butter
⅔ cup yellow cornmeal
⅔ cup all-purpose flour
2 teaspoons baking powder
1 tablespoon sugar
½ teaspoon salt
1 large egg
1¼ cups milk
2 crisp apples, peeled, cored, and cut
    into 1-inch chunks
½ cup maple syrup
vegetable oil for brushing griddle

In a small saucepan melt 3 tablespoons butter over low heat. In a bowl stir together cornmeal, flour, baking powder, sugar, and salt and stir in melted butter, egg, and milk until just smooth (batter will be thin). Let batter stand at room temperature while sautéing apples.

In a large non-stick skillet heat remaining tablespoon butter over moderately high heat until foam subsides. Add apples and sauté, stirring, 5 minutes. Add maple syrup and boil 2 minutes, or until slightly thickened. Transfer mixture to a bowl and keep warm, covered.

Preheat oven to 200° F.

Heat a griddle over moderate heat until hot enough to make drops of water scatter over its surface and brush lightly with oil. Working in batches, drop batter onto griddle to form 3-inch pancakes and cook 1 minute on each side, or until golden and cooked through. Transfer pancakes as cooked to a heatproof platter and keep warm, uncovered, in oven.

Serve pancakes with apples and syrup spooned on top. Makes about twenty-four 3-inch pancakes, serving 4 to 6.

M. Shields

Fresh green or blue-purple figs should be plump and, when they are very ripe, soft to the touch and a bit shriveled near the pointed stem.

Fresh Figs with Brandy Caramel Cream

½ cup sugar
1 cup heavy cream
2 tablespoons sour cream
2 to 4 teaspoons brandy
½ teaspoon vanilla
⅛ teaspoon salt
⅛ teaspoon freshly grated nutmeg
12 fresh figs

In a dry heavy saucepan cook sugar over moderate heat until it begins to melt and continue to cook, stirring and swirling pan, until a golden caramel.

Remove pan from heat and carefully pour ⅓ cup heavy cream down side of pan (mixture will steam and caramel will harden). Return pan to heat and cook, stirring, until caramel is dissolved. Transfer mixture to a metal bowl and stir in sour cream, 2 teaspoons brandy, vanilla, salt, and grated nutmeg. Chill caramel mixture, covered, until cold, about 30

minutes. (Alternatively, set bowl in a larger bowl of ice and cold water and chill caramel mixture, stirring frequently, until cold and thickened.)

In a bowl with an electric mixer beat remaining ⅔ cup heavy cream until it just holds stiff peaks. Add caramel mixture and beat until combined well, adding additional brandy to taste if desired.

Quarter figs, cutting through pointed ends but leaving rounded ends intact, and open each to form a "flower". Arrange 2 figs on each of 6 plates and spoon a dollop of caramel cream into center of each fig. Serves 6.

Crisp, firm-ripe pears, such as Bartlett, Anjou, and Bosc, are great for baking, but many lesser known or heirloom varieties, such as Kieffer, Winter Nelis, Clapp's Favorite, and Packham's Triumph, are equally delicious.

Pear and Cranberry Crisp

1 cup old-fashioned or instant rolled oats
⅓ cup firmly packed brown sugar
3 tablespoons all-purpose flour
½ teaspoon cinnamon
¼ teaspoon salt
3 tablespoons unsalted butter, softened
5 firm-ripe pears (about 2½ pounds)
1 cup picked-over cranberries
3 tablespoons granulated sugar
1 tablespoon fresh lemon juice

Accompaniment: whipped cream or vanilla
    ice cream

Preheat oven to 350° F.

In a bowl stir together oats, brown sugar, flour, cinnamon, and salt. Add butter and blend with fingers until crumbly. Peel and core pears. Cut pears into eighths and in a 9-inch square baking dish toss with cranberries, granulated sugar, and lemon juice. Sprinkle oat mixture onto fruit mixture and bake in middle of oven 1 hour and 10 minutes, or until top is golden and juices are bubbling around edges. Cool crisp slightly on a rack.

Serve crisp warm with whipped cream or ice cream. Serves 6.

WINTER

Naturally, the eggs for our spread needn't come from organically raised hens, but we encourage you to experience the flavor of these fresh eggs that are readily available at many farmers markets.

Green Peppercorn Egg Salad Spread

6 hard-cooked large eggs
¼ cup finely chopped onion
¼ cup finely chopped celery
½ cup packed fresh parsley leaves, washed well and spun dry
1½ teaspoons drained bottled green peppercorns
2 bottled or canned flat anchovy fillets
1 teaspoon Dijon mustard
¼ cup olive oil
2 teaspoons fresh lemon juice, or to taste
2 tablespoons freshly grated Parmesan

Accompaniment: crackers or toast points

In a bowl coarsely mash eggs with a fork and stir in onion and celery. In a blender blend remaining ingredients until almost smooth and stir into egg mixture with salt to taste until combined well.

Serve spread with crackers or toasts points. Serves 6 as an hors d'oeuvre.

Blood oranges, harvested primarily in California, Arizona, and Florida, appear in regional markets from mid-December until spring. They are worth seeking out for their intense crimson color and luscious flavor.

Blood Orange and Avocado Salad with Curried Lime Dressing

2 tablespoons fresh lime juice
1 teaspoon honey
½ teaspoon curry powder
¼ teaspoon salt
3 tablespoons vegetable oil
4 blood oranges
2 small firm-ripe avocados

spinach leaves or lettuce, washed well and spun dry, for lining plates

In a small bowl whisk together lime juice, honey, curry powder, and salt until honey is dissolved and whisk in oil in a stream until emulsified.

With a sharp knife cut peel and pith from oranges. Working over a bowl, cut orange sections free from membranes, letting them drop into bowl. Halve avocados and discard pits. Peel halves and cut into ½-inch-thick slices.

Line 4 plates with spinach or lettuce and arrange orange sections and avocado slices decoratively on greens. Whisk dressing and drizzle over salads. Serves 4.

If you are on the East coast look for bay scallops, the preferred tiny mollusks, with sweet, succulent meat. In other areas, use large sea scallops and halve them.

Bay Scallops with Beet Greens and Bacon

4 slices bacon
1 small onion, sliced thin
¼ cup dry white wine
2 tablespoons water
4 cups beet greens (from about 2 bunches), coarse stems discarded and leaves washed well, drained, and chopped coarse
1 pound whole bay scallops or halved sea scallops

Accompaniment: country-style bread

In a heavy skillet cook bacon over moderate heat until crisp and transfer to paper towels to drain. Pour off all but about 1 tablespoon drippings and in drippings remaining in skillet cook onion, stirring, until softened and slightly browned. Add wine, water, and greens and simmer, covered, stirring occasionally, 10 minutes, or until greens are crisp-tender. Add scallops and simmer, uncovered, stirring, 2 minutes, or until scallops are just cooked through. Crumble bacon and stir into scallop mixture with salt and pepper to taste.

Divide scallop mixture among 4 plates and serve with bread. Serves 4 as a first course.

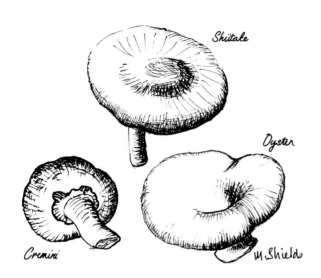

Shiitake

Oyster

Cremini

M. Shields

Exotic mushrooms give meaty flavor to pasta dishes, and here we suggest a mix of several varieties for added depth and complexity. Look for moist, firm mushrooms that smell woodsy and avoid washing them—simply wipe them with damp paper towels.

Pasta with Exotic Mushrooms and Collard Greens

½ pound *bucatini* or *linguine*
1 pound mixed exotic mushrooms such as *cremini,
    shiitake,* and oyster, cleaned and trimmed
½ cup sliced shallots
2 large garlic cloves, minced
2 tablespoons olive oil
¾ pound collard greens, stems discarded and
    leaves washed well, drained, and sliced thin
2 tablespoons unsalted butter
1 cup beef broth
½ cup dry white wine
¼ teaspoon dried hot red pepper flakes, or to taste
⅓ cup freshly grated Parmesan

Bring a kettle of salted water to a boil for pasta.

If using *cremini* mushrooms, keep whole or halve if desired; if using *shiitake* mushrooms, discard stems and slice caps; and if using oyster mushrooms, keep stems attached and halve.

In a large skillet cook shallots and garlic in oil over moderate heat, stirring, until softened and beginning to brown. Add mushrooms, greens, and butter and cook, stirring occasionally, 10 minutes. Add broth, wine, red pepper flakes, and salt to taste and simmer 2 minutes. Cover skillet and simmer mixture 3 minutes, or until greens are tender.

Cook pasta in boiling water until *al dente*. Drain pasta well in a colander and add to mushroom mixture with Parmesan and salt and pepper to taste, tossing to combine. Serves 4 as a first course, or 2 as a main course.

Female pheasants are smaller in size and tend to be a bit more plump and tender than male birds. Farm-raised pheasants will be less gamy tasting than those hunted in the wild due to their controlled diet

Roasted Pheasant and Sweet Potatoes with Balsamic Vinegar

2 tablespoons unsalted butter, softened
1 garlic clove, minced
1 tablespoon minced fresh rosemary leaves or 1
    teaspoon dried rosemary, crumbled
½ teaspoon salt
½ teaspoon freshly ground black pepper
a 2½-pound female pheasant, rinsed and patted dry
1 pound sweet potatoes (about 2 medium), peeled,
    halved lengthwise, and cut into ½-inch-thick
    slices
½ cup balsamic vinegar
⅓ cup chicken broth

Preheat oven to 375° F.

In a small bowl blend together butter, garlic, rosemary, salt, and pepper. In a shallow baking dish arrange pheasant, breast side up, and put 2 teaspoons garlic butter in cavity. Loosen skin near breastbone and rub 2 teaspoons garlic butter under skin. Rub remaining garlic butter on skin. Arrange sweet potatoes around pheasant and pour vinegar and broth on top of each.

Roast pheasant in middle of oven, basting occasionally, 45 minutes, or until juices run clear when fleshy part of a thigh is pierced. Transfer pheasant to a platter and roast potatoes until tender, about 5 minutes more. Spoon potatoes and pan juices around pheasant. Serves 2.

GUIDES TO THE TEXT

GENERAL INDEX

Page numbers in *italics* indicate color photographs
☺ indicates recipes that can be prepared in 45 minutes or less
☺+ indicates recipes that can be prepared in 45 minutes but require additional unattended time
🍃 indicates recipes that are leaner/lighter

INDEX OF RECIPE TITLES

Page numbers in *italics* indicate color photographs

311

TABLE SETTING ACKNOWLEDGMENTS

To avoid duplication below of table setting information within the same menu, the editors have listed all such credits for silverware, plates, linen, and the like in its most complete form under "Table Setting."

Any items in the photograph not credited are privately owned.
All addresses are in New York City unless otherwise indicated.

Back Jacket

Cherry Tomato, Ricotta, and Olive Galette: See Picnic Setting credits for Ballooning Picnic.

Frontispiece

Chilled Banana and Pistachio Rice Pudding; Melon Compote (page 2): Silver porcelain bowls and "Pearl" ceramic plates—Takashimaya, 693 Fifth Avenue.

Table of Contents

Table Setting (page 6): See Table Setting credits for Easter Luncheon.
Mojitos with Basil (page 6): Highball glasses designed by Ward Bennett for Sasaki—Barneys New York, Madison Avenue at 61st Street.

The Menu Collection

Table Setting (page 10): See Table Setting credits for An Italian Christmas Eve.

New Year's Tapas Party

Buffet Setting (page 13): "Guerland" ceramic dinner plates; four-panel screen—ABC Carpet & Home, 888 Broadway. "Century" flatware—Crate & Barrel. For stores call (800) 323-5461. "Tabellini" glass-and-pewter wineglasses—Zona, 97 Greene Street. "Savoir Vivre" Sherry glasses; "Tutti-Frutti" napkins by Primrose

Bordier for Jacquard Français—Ad Hoc Softwares, 410 West Broadway. Ceramic dish (olives) and tureen (romaine)—Dean & DeLuca, 560 Broadway. Leaf plate (carrot salad)—Wolfman•Gold & Good Company, 117 Mercer Street. Candles—E.A.T. Gifts, 1062 Madison Avenue. English seventeenth-century oak table—Newel Art Galleries, Inc., 425 East 53rd Street. Painted leather side chair by Keller-Williams (available through decorator)—John Rosselli & Assoc., 979 Third Avenue.
Citrus-and-Clove Marinated Shrimp; Potato Saffron Omelet; Meatballs in Tomato Garlic Sauce (page 14): Stoneware charger (omelet)—Dean & DeLuca, 560 Broadway. "Teema" ceramic dinner plate by Arabia (meatballs)—Moss, 146 Greene Street.
Manchego Cheese with Quince Paste; Hazelnut Cookies (page 15): "Merletto" glass dessert plate—ABC Carpet & Home, 888 Broadway. Steel fruit stand by Dover—Wolfman•Gold & Good Company, 117 Mercer Street.

Après-Ski Dinner

Table Setting (page 16): Handmade ceramic dinner plates by Paul Nelson; wire basket—William-Wayne & Co., 850 Lexington Avenue. Inlaid flatware—Aris Mixon, 381 Amsterdam Avenue. Hand-blown wineglasses—

Dean & DeLuca, 560 Broadway. Handmade wood flower basket—Canyon Road, 250 Greenwich Avenue, Greenwich, Connecticut 06830. *Photographed at Saddle Ridge at Beaver Creek, Colorado. For information call (800) 859-8242.*

A Beer Tasting Party

Table Setting (page 18): "Plough" Armetale metal dinner plates—for information call Wilton Armetale Consumer Information Center, (800) 553-2048. Italian pewter and stainless-steel flatware—Frank McIntosh Home Collection at Henri Bendel, 712 Fifth Avenue. Glass beakers—Simon Pearce, 500 Park Avenue at 59th Street. Linen napkins—The Guess Home Collection, 465 West Broadway. Jute place mats—Wolfman • Gold & Good Company, 117 Mercer Street. Bronze deer candlesticks; tole tray—William-Wayne & Co., 850 Lexington Avenue. Nineteenth-century Swedish pine table and chairs—Evergreen Antiques, 1249 Third Avenue. Nineteenth-century painted dresser—Pamela Scurry's Wicker Garden, 1318 Madison Avenue. Tin measures (from a set of six); English heraldic tin shields; horn and wood sconces (all nineteenth-century)—Bob Pryor Antiques, 1023 Lexington Avenue.

Beer-Braised Sausages and Sauerkraut; Caraway Parsley Potatoes; Arugula, Endive, and Radicchio Salad with Mustard Vinaigrette (page 19): "Queen Anne" Armetale metal platter—for stores call Wilton Armetale Consumer Information Center, (800) 553-2048.

Celebrating Mardi Gras

Crawfish Tomato Etouffée in Puff Pastry Shells; Panéed Veal with Fried Lemon Slices; Sautéed Spinach and Garlic; Confetti Vegetable Slaw (pages 22 and 23) : "Mayfair" porcelain dinner and salad plates—Sasaki, for stores call (212) 686-5080. Acrylic-handled flatware—Takashimaya, 693 Fifth Avenue. "Neoclassical Vase" cotton fabric—F. Schumacher & Co., 939 Third Avenue.

Brunch in the Kitchen

Bloody Marys (page 24): Wineglasses; carafe; tray—William-Wayne & Co., 850 Lexington Avenue. Glass dishes; celery glass; pepper mill—Bridge Kitchenware Corp., 214 East 52nd Street.
Table Setting (page 25): "Dot" earthenware plates and mugs by Barbara Eigen—(special order) Anthropology, 1365 Post Road, Westport, Connecticut 06880, (203) 259-0043. "Recamier" wood-handled flatware by Scof—Wolfman•Gold & Good Company, 117 Mercer Street. Linen napkins—Tabletoppings by Frank McIntosh at Henri Bendel, 712 Fifth Avenue. Woven palm placemats by Dransfield & Ross—Barneys New York, Madison Avenue at 61st Street. French rattan armchairs, circa 1920—Newel Art Galleries, 425 East 53rd Street. Flowers—Zezé, 398 East 52nd Street.
Photographed in the kitchen of Mr. and Mrs. John Thomas.

Dinner in the Kitchen

Table Setting (page 26): "Masquerade" faience plates by Cassis & Co.—Kitchen Classics, Main Street, Bridgehampton, New York, 11932,

(800) 251-2421. "Folio" stainless-steel flatware—Pavillon Christofle, 680 Madison Avenue. Wineglasses by Laure Japy—Hoagland's, 175 Greenwich Avenue, Greenwich, Connecticut 06830. Chateau X hand-painted straw placemats by Jane Krolik; linen napkins—Tabletoppings by Frank McIntosh at Henri Bendel, 712 Fifth Avenue. Carafe—Pottery Barn. For stores call (800) 922-5507. Candles—Wolfman•Gold & Good Company, 117 Mercer Street. Steel armchairs—William-Wayne & Co., 850 Lexington Avenue. Sub-Zero refrigerator—for stores call (800) 444-7820. GE Profile convection oven and microwave—for stores call GE Answer Center, (800) 626-2000. Thermador "Professional" cooktop—for stores call (800) 735-4328. ASKO dishwasher (model ASEA 1502)—for stores call (800) 367-2444. Artists Editions Kohler porcelain sink—for stores call (414) 457-4441.
Brandied Chicken Liver Pâté; Artichoke Olive Dip with Fennel Crudités (page 27): Fioriware platter; vintage earthenware mold; horn-handled spreader—Wolfman•Gold & Good Company, 117 Mercer Street. "Brummel" crystal wineglasses—Baccarat, 625 Madison Avenue.
Photographed in the kitchen of Mr. and Mrs. John Evans.

Easter Luncheon

Table Setting (page 30): Fioriware ceramic plates and soup bowls—for stores call Fioriware, (614) 454-7400. "Tahiti" bamboo and sterling flatware—Buccellati, 46 East 57th Street. Wineglasses by Thomas; water glasses—ABC Carpet & Home, 888 Broadway. Linen napkins and place mats by Glenn Thomas Progressive—Barneys New York, Madison Avenue at 61st Street. French iron café chairs—Newel Art Galleries, 425 East 53rd Street. Flowers—Zezé, 398 East 52nd Street.
Rosemary, Lemon, and Garlic Leg of

Lamb with Roasted Potatoes (page 32): Ivory-handled carving set, circa 1870—James II Galleries, Ltd., 11 East 57th Street.
Lime Curd and Toasted Almond Tart (page 33): Sterling and ivory trowel (as lime curd tart server), circa 1920—James II Galleries, Ltd., 11 East 57th Street.
Photographed in a conservatory designed and built by Oak Leaf Conservatories, (800) 360-6283.

Ballooning Picnic

Picnic Setting (page 34): Plastic glasses (soup)—Gracious Home, 1220 Third Avenue. Wood-handled flatware—Williams Sonoma. For stores call (800) 541-2233. Gmundner Keramik ceramic pitcher and dinner plates—for stores call Landhaus, (914) 763-3802. Patrick Frey cotton throw—for stores call Roseline Crowley, Inc., (203) 785-9376. Wineglasses—Pier One Imports. For stores call (800) 245-4595.

Saturday Picnic Lunch

Apricot Ginger Biscotti (page 36): Glasses—Pottery Barn. For stores call (800) 922-5507. Cotton napkins—ABC Carpet & Home, 888 Broadway.
Picnic Setting (page 37): Wicker bottle cover—Wolfman•Gold & Good Company, 117 Mercer Street. Rattan-wrapped vacuum jug (near seats)—Barneys New York, Madison Avenue at 61st Street.

Grilled Steak Dinner

Table Setting (page 38): "Twist" iron flatware; "Vintage" wineglasses; iron cage hurricane lamps—Pottery Barn. For stores call (800) 922-5507. Cotton napkins; enamel jug, circa 1900; wooden table and console—Wolfman•Gold & Good Company, 117 Mercer Street. Wooden salad serving bowl—Pier One Imports. For stores call (800) 245-4595. Wooden bowls—Williams-Sonoma. For stores call (800) 541-2233.

Sunday Brunch

Buffet Setting (page 40): "Classico" plates by Cyclamen Studio—for stores call (510) 843-4691. Kappa shell plates—Bergdorf Goodman, 754 Fifth Avenue. "Madeline" flatware—Pottery Barn. For stores call (800) 922-5507. Linen and raffia napkins—for stores call Archipelago, (212) 334-9460. Flowers—Arrangement, Miami Art & Design Centre, 3841 N.E. Second Avenue, Suite 403, Miami, Florida, (305) 576-9922.

White Sangría (page 41): "Lyra" crystal wineglasses—Baccarat, 625 Madison Avenue. "Symphony" crystal pitcher by Orrefors—Galleri Orrefors Kosta Boda, 58 East 57th Street.

Poolside Dinner

Grilled Citrus Salmon and Grilled Mango; Bibb Lettuce with Sherry Vinaigrette (page 43): Porcelain chargers and dinner plates—for stores call Archipelago, (212) 334-9460. "Century" sterling flatware—Tiffany & Co., 727 Fifth Avenue. "Kentia" crystal wine-glasses—for stores call Lalique, (800) 993-2580. Linen napkins—Frank McIntosh Home Collection at Henri Bendel, 712 Fifth Avenue. Iron and glass dinner table—Details at Home, 1031 Lincoln Road, Miami Beach, Florida, (305) 531-1325. "Voiles de Lumière" silk scarf—Hermès, 11 East 57th Street.

An Elegant Dinner Party

Table Setting (pages 44 and 45): Puiforcat "Variations Green" porcelain presentation plates—for stores call (800) 993-2580. "Feather Edge" sterling flatware—James Robinson, 480 Park Avenue. Beaded placemats and napkins by Dransfield and Ross—for stores call (212) 741-7278. Arcadia Collection silver-plate vase and bowls designed by Larry Laslo for Creative Gifts International—Brambles, 50 Main Street, Southampton, New York 11968, (516) 283-5171. "Ribbon" candlesticks—The

L.S Collection, 469 West Broadway.

Louisiana Seafood Boil

Picnic Setting (page 49): Lemonade glasses and bottles—Crate & Barrel. For stores call (800) 323-5461. Sauce glasses—Pan American Phoenix, 857 Lexington Avenue. Cotton dish towels—Williams Sonoma. For stores call (800) 541-2233. Citronella candle—Pottery Barn. For stores call (800) 922-5507.

Dinner on the Fourth

Bacon and Basil-Wrapped Chicken Breasts; Summer Vegetable Ragout (page 50): "Star" ceramic service and bread-and-butter plates; ceramic salad plates; blue water glasses—Fishs Eddy, 889 Broadway. "Paris" stainless-steel flatware by David Mellor; "Round" wineglasses—Simon Pearce, 500 Park Avenue at 59th Street. "Spinnaker Stripe" cotton placemat fabric (available through decorator)—Waverly, (800) 423-5881. "Sussex Petit Cord" placemat trim from Schumacher (available through decorator)—Design Information, (800) 332-3384. "Railroad" lanterns—Pottery Barn. For stores call (800) 922-5507.

Lunch on the Deck

Grilled Pizzas; Romaine, Arugula, and Avocado Salad (page 52): Sutherland teak tray by John Hutton—Treillage, Ltd., 418 East 75th Street. Wooden salad bowl—Pottery Barn. For stores call (800) 922-5507.

Lemon Shandies; Steamed Mussels with Orange, Fennel, and Garlic (page 53): Italian handmade wooden buffet plates—for stores call Vietri, (800) 277-5933. Stoneware pie plate (mussels)—Broadway Panhandler, 477 Broome Street. Yellow and blue Japanese ceramic bowls by Hakusan—Ad Hoc Softwares, 410 West Broadway. "Chelsea" acrylic-handled flatware by Scof—for stores call Mariposa, (800) 788-1304. "Patrick" glasses—Crate & Barrel. For stores call (800) 323-5461. Linen towels—

Bragard, 215 Park Avenue South, Suite 1801. "Hamaca Verde," "Hamaca Rojo," and "Hamaca Azul" cotton pillow fabric (available through decorator)—Donghia Designs, 979 Third Avenue. Folding teak chairs—R&R Pool & Patio, 600 East Putnam Avenue, Cos Cob, Connecticut 06830. Acid-washed pail—Wolfman • Gold & Good Company, 117 Mercer Street.

Shrimp Gazpacho with Basil Croutons (page 54): Boda Nova glass plates and bowls—Ad Hoc Softwares, 410 West Broadway.

Grilled Pizza with Yellow Squash, Mozzarella, and Lemon Thyme (page 55): Weber 22½-inch enameled steel kettle grill—Weber-Stephen Products, (800) 446-1071.

Photographed on Fripp Island, South Carolina. For information call Fripp Island Resort (800) 845-4100.

Picnic Afloat

Picnic Setting (page 56): Blue glass dinner plates and salad plates by Izabel Lam—The L•S Collection, 469 West Broadway. "Clipper" porcelain dinner plates (flag border) by Richard Ginori—Hoagland's, 175 Greenwich Avenue, Greenwich, Connecticut, (203) 869-2127. "Orvieto" flatware—Williams-Sonoma. For stores call (800) 541-2233. Yellow-rimmed tumblers; white, blue, and yellow napkins—Wolfman•Gold & Good Company, 117 Mercer Street. Wire basket—Crate & Barrel. For stores call (800) 323-5461. Ian Mankin pillow fabrics—Coconut Company, 131 Greene Street.

Tomato Eggplant Spread and Parmesan Toasts (page 57): Yellow bowl and white plates—Wolfman•Gold & Good Company, 117 Mercer Street. "Good Luck" highball glasses by Handle With Care—The L•S Collection, 469 West Broadway. Red-checked napkin—Crate & Barrel. For stores call (800) 323-5461.

Striped Bass Escabeche with Bell Peppers and Green Beans; Goat

Cheese and Thyme Potato Cake (page 58): Blue glass platter by Izabel Lam—The L•S Collection, 469 West Broadway.
Chewy Coconut Macadamia Bars (page 59): "Splash" platter by Annieglass—Annieglass, (800) 347-6133.

A Taste of India

Coconut and Mint Lassi; Coriander, Ginger, and Chili Lassi (page 60): "Smyers" glasses—Bergdorf Goodman, 754 Fifth Avenue.
Fennel-Scented Spinach and Potato Samosas; Mint Chutney; Tandoori Shrimp and Mango Salad (pages 62 and 63): White ceramic dinner plates; "Mosaic" flatware—Takashimaya, 693 Fifth Avenue. Wineglasses—Wolfman•Gold & Good Company, 117 Mercer Street. Napkins by Mark Rossi—Bergdorf Goodman, 754 Fifth Avenue.
Photographed at Coconut Company, 131 Greene Street, New York City, where any items not credited above are available.

A Small Country Wedding

Zucchini Cone Filled with Lemon Mint Pea Purée; Herb-Baked Potato Chip with Crème Fraîche and Caviar (page 64): Wedgwood "Countryware" service plates and "Edmeware" dinner plates—The Waterford Wedgwood Store, 713 Madison Avenue.
Dark Chocolate Wedding Cake with Chocolate Orange Ganache and Orange Buttercream (page 65): Marseilles tablecloth, circa 1870—Françoise Nunnallé, (212) 246-4281 (by appointment only). Flower garlands—Zezé, 398 East 52nd Street.
Fresh Fig, Mascarpone, and Pesto Torte (page 66): Sterling pitcher—F. Gorevic & Son, Inc., 635 Madison Avenue.
Table Setting (page 67): Limoges "Blanc de Blanc" and "Promenade" plates by Philippe Deshoulieres—for stores call (800) 993-2580. Sterling forks and spoons by H. Meyen &

Co.; eighteenth-century Champagne flutes—Bardith, 901 Madison Avenue. Bone-handled fish servers; sterling ladle—F. Gorevic & Son, Inc., 635 Madison Avenue. "Birgitta" wineglasses—Crate & Barrel. For stores call (800) 323-5461.

Feasting on Game

Table Setting (page 69): Large ceramic service plates by Molin—Wolfman• Gold & Good Company, 117 Mercer St. Wineglasses by Calvin Klein—Bloomingdale's, 1000 Third Avenue. "Hampton" stainless-steel flatware—Pottery Barn. For stores call (800) 922-5507. Silk-screened linen napkins—Simon Pearce, 500 Park Avenue at 59th St. Nineteenth-century mahogany and mother-of-pearl screen and carved wood panel—Tucker Robbins, (212) 366-4427 (by appointment only). Chicken eggs—Windfall Farms, Union Square Greenmarket. Duck and goose eggs—Fifth Floor Farm Kitchen, Union Square Greenmarket. Quail eggs—Balducci's, 424 Sixth Avenue.

Thanksgiving Dinner

Roast Turkey with Sage and Sherried Cider Giblet Gravy (page 72): Chamberlain Worcester Imari porcelain platter, circa 1840—Bardith, 901 Madison Avenue.
Table Setting (page 73): Eighteenth- and nineteenth-century English earthenware and porcelain plates; engraved wineglasses, circa 1820—Bardith, 901 Madison Avenue. "Faneuil" sterling flatware—Tiffany & Co., 727 Fifth Avenue. "Monticello" etched wineglasses (water)—Metropolitan Museum of Art Shop, 1000 Fifth Avenue. "Brummel" wineglasses—Baccarat, 625 Madison Avenue. Linen place mats—Ad Hoc Softwares, 410 West Broadway. Cobalt wine rinsers, circa 1830, hyacinth vases, circa 1860—S. Wyler, 941 Lexington Avenue. Silver-plate julep cups—William-Wayne & Co., 850 Lexington Avenue.

Chestnut and Bacon Dressing; Mashed Potatoes and Leeks with Thyme (page 75): Victorian silver-plate basket, circa 1875—S. Wyler, 941 Lexington Avenue. "Cortina" silver-plate baking dish—Pavillion Christofle, 680 Madison Avenue.

An Italian Christmas Eve

Table Setting (page 76): Marble plates—Gordon Foster, 1322 Third Avenue. "Butterfly Garden" plates and tureen; "Les Trésors de la Mer" plates; and crystal and gold wineglasses by Gianni Versace for Rosenthal—Gianni Versace, 647 Fifth Avenue. "Trifid" hand-forged sterling flatware; ebony handled dinner knives—James Robinson, Inc., 480 Park Avenue. Victorian silver-plate goblets; English glass epergnes, circa 1840—James II Galleries, Ltd., 11 East 57th St. Cotton and linen napkins—for stores call Anichini, (800) 553-5309. Vintage crystal and gilt salt cellars; English enamel and sterling seafood fork—S. Wyler, 941 Lexington Avenue. "Vienne Gold" crystal pitcher—Baccarat, 625 Madison Avenue. "Syntesy" footed crystal bowl—Rogaska, 685 Madison Avenue.
Tuna and Roasted Pepper Crostini; Baked Clams Oreganate (page 77): "Medusa D'Or" plate by Gianni Versace for Rosenthal—Gianni Versace, 647 Fifth Avenue. Heatproof silver-plate pan—S. Wyler, 941 Lexington Avenue.
Salt Cod, Fennel, and Potato Cannelloni; Spaghetti with Lobster and Mussels (page 78): Copper gratin pan—Bridge Kitchenware Corp., 214 East 52nd St. "Les Trésors de la Mer" platter by Gianni Versace for Rosenthal—Gianni Versace, 647 Fifth Avenue.
Blood-Orange Crostata (page 79): "Les Trésors de la Mer" bread plates by Gianni Versace for Rosenthal—Gianni Versace, 647 Fifth Avenue.

Christmas Dinner

Table Setting (page 81): "Platinum"

plates (white with platinum rim)—Calvin Klein, 654 Madison Avenue. "Roman Antique Platinum" plates—Annieglass, (800) 347-6133. English silver-plate flatware, circa 1880—S. Wyler, 941 Lexington Avenue. Wineglasses—Crate & Barrel. For stores call (800) 323-5461. Angel Zimick napkins— Barneys New York, Madison Avenue at 61st St. Marseilles tablecloth, circa 1880—Françoise Nunnalle, (212) 246-4281. Metal "bamboo" chairs, circa 1930—Newel Art Galleries, 425 East 53rd St. Hand-painted silver finish on chairs—Richard Pellicci, (914) 271-6710.

Dining on the Light Side

Marinated Shrimp with Pickled Watermelon Rind; Black-Eyed Pea Salad with Watercress and Peach; Sliced Tomatoes and Cucumbers (page 85): "Celery" and "Oyster" dinner plates, "Baguette" silver-plate flatware,

"Raggedy" armchair with slipcover — Wolfman•Gold & Good Company, 117 Mercer Street. Hemp napkins—Ad Hoc Softwares, 410 West Broadway. Bunching tables—Crate & Barrel Furniture. For stores call (800) 323-5461. Sony Trinitron Color Video TV—for stores call (800) 222-7669.

Dining on the Light Side

Broiled Portobello Mushrooms with Zucchini-Scallion Topping; Turkey, Potato, and Roasted Garlic Ravioli with Sun-Dried Tomato Sauce (page 87): All items in these photographs are privately owned.

A Recipe Compendium

Grilled Marinated London Broil; Grilled Red Onions with Balsamic Vinegar and Rosemary; Yellow Pepper Orzo Gratin; Sliced Tomatoes; Grilled Zucchini (page 88): See credits for Grilled Steak Dinner.

Greek Easter Feast

Table Setting; Zucchini and Onion Pie; Sweet Cheese Pies (pages 252 and 253): All items in these photographs are privately owned.

Summer Dinner on Santorini

Table Setting (pages 262 and 263): "Rhodes" serving bowl (beets); salad plates (back)—Pottery Barn. For stores call (800) 922-5507. "Country Fair" dinner plates; "Picardie" juice glasses—Williams Sonoma. For stores call (800) 541-2233.

A Cocktail Party Featuring Mezedes

Buffet Spread (page 271): Glazed "Olive Branch" bowl (olives); glasses (ouzo)—Crate & Barrel. For stores call (800) 323-5461. "Rhodes" pitcher (flowers)—Pottery Barn. For stores call (800) 922-5507.

CREDITS

Grateful acknowledgment is made to the following for permission to reprint recipes previously published in *Gourmet* Magazine:

Michele Scicolone: Baked Zucchini with Parmesan and Prosciutto (page 185); Parmesan Foccacia (page 112); Potato Casserole with Prosciutto (page 182). Copyright © 1996 by Michele Scicolone. Reprinted by permission of the author.

Zanne Early Stewart: Oyster Loaf with Guacamole (page 134); Frosted Double Chocolate Malted; Easy Dark Chocolate Sauce (page 201); Chocolate Malted Ice Cream with Malted Milk Balls (page 223). Copyright © 1996 by Zanne Early Stewart. Reprinted by permission of the author.

The following photographers have generously given permission to reprint their photographs. Some of these photographs have previously appeared in *Gourmet* Magazine.

Cotten Alston: "Chania Harbor, Crete" (page 268). Copyright © 1992.

Conan Owen: "Pensioner in Archway, Naxos" (page 250). Copyright © 1996.

Helen Wisdom: Vase on Wall (pages 236 and 237); "The Acropolis" (page 238); "Santorini" (page 260). Copyright © 1996.

Greek National Tourist Organization: "Ladies Stringing Tomatoes" (page 7). Copyright © 1996.

If you are not already a subscriber to *Gourmet* Magazine and would be interested in subscribing, please call *Gourmet's* toll-free number, 1-800-365-2454.

If you are interested in purchasing additional copies of this book or other *Gourmet* cookbooks, please call 1-800-438-9944.